Sixth Workshop on NLP for Similar Languages, Varieties and Dialects (VarDial 2019)

Minneapolis, Minnesota, USA
7 June 2019

ISBN: 978-1-5108-8768-8

NAACL HLT 2019

**The Workshop
on NLP for Similar Languages, Varieties and Dialects**

Proceedings of the Sixth Workshop

July 7, 2019
Minneapolis, USA

Preface

This volume includes the 25 papers presented in the Sixth Workshop on NLP for Similar Languages, Varieties and Dialects (VarDial), which was co-located with the Annual Conference of the North American Chapter of the Association for Computational Linguistics (NAACL) and was held on June 7, 2019 in Minneapolis, USA.

This is the first time that VarDial is co-located with NAACL and the second time that the workshop is organized in North America. The previous five editions of the workshop were co-located with COLING (in 2014 in Dublin, Ireland; in 2016 in Osaka, Japan; and in 2018 in Santa Fe, USA), with RANLP (in 2015 in Hissar, Bulgaria), and with EACL (in 2017 in Valencia, Spain).

VarDial continues to be the main venue dedicated to the research on similar languages, varieties, and dialects within the CL/NLP community. We are happy to see that VarDial keeps growing, building on the success of the previous editions. This year we received 17 regular workshop submissions, and we accepted 10 papers, which were presented at the workshop. The accepted papers deal with various topics related to language variation such as cross-lingual annotation projection in part-of-speech tagging, machine translation between similar languages and dialects, and the processing of code-switched (or mixed) data, to name a few.

Together with the sixth edition of the workshop, we organized the third edition of the VarDial Evaluation Campaign, which featured five shared tasks. One shared task was a re-run from previous editions, the third German Dialect Identification (GDI), and we had four new tasks: Cross-lingual Morphological Analysis (CMA), Discriminating between Mainland and Taiwan variation of Mandarin Chinese (DMT), Moldavian vs. Romanian Cross-dialect Topic identification (MRC), and Cuneiform Language Identification (CLI). A total of 22 teams submitted official runs to one or more of the five shared tasks, and 14 system description papers appear in this volume along with a shared task report by the evaluation campaign and the task organizers.

Shared tasks have been organized since the workshop's first edition. Most of these tasks were on language and dialect identification, while a few others dealt with NLP tasks such as morphosyntactic tagging and cross-lingual dependency parsing. The focus of the language and dialect identification competitions at VarDial has always been on diatopic variation using synchronic contemporary data. This year, the CLI shared task included historical languages for the first time at VarDial, and it was the most popular shared task of the campaign, which demonstrates the interest of the community in this topic. To further respond to this interest, we included topics related to the diachronic/diatopic variation interplay in the call for papers as topics of interest for VarDial, e.g., philogenetic methods, and historical dialects.

We take this opportunity to thank the VarDial program committee for their thorough reviews. We further thank the VarDial Evaluation Campaign shared task organizers and the participants. Finally, we thank the workshop participants who presented regular research papers, for the valuable feedback and discussions.

The VarDial workshop organizers:

Marcos Zampieri, Preslav Nakov, Shervin Malmasi, Nikola Ljubešić, Jörg Tiedemann, and Ahmed Ali

Organizers:

Marcos Zampieri, University of Wolverhampton (UK)
Preslav Nakov, Qatar Computing Research Institute, HBKU (Qatar)
Shervin Malmasi, Amazon (United States)
Nikola Ljubešić, Jožef Stefan Institute (Slovenia)
Jörg Tiedemann, University of Helsinki (Finland)
Ahmed Ali, Qatar Computing Research Institute, HBKU (Qatar)

Program Committee:

Željko Agić, IT University of Copenhagen (Denmark)
Cesar Aguilar, Pontifical Catholic University of Chile (Chile)
Laura Alonso y Alemany, University of Cordoba (Argentina)
Eric Atwell, University of Leeds (UK)
Jorge Baptista, University of Algarve and INESC-ID (Portugal)
Eckhard Bick, University of Southern Denmark (Denmark)
Johannes Bjerva, University of Copenhagen (Denmark)
Francis Bond, Nanyang Technological University (Singapore)
Aoife Cahill, Educational Testing Service (USA)
David Chiang, University of Notre Dame (USA)
Paul Cook, University of New Brunswick (Canada)
Marta Costa-Jussà, Universitat Politècnica de Catalunya (Spain)
Jon Dehdari, Think Big Analytics (USA)
Liviu Dinu, University of Bucharest (Romania)
Stefanie Dipper, Ruhr University Bochum (Germany)
Sascha Diwersy, University of Montpellier (France)
Mark Dras, Macquarie University (Australia)
Tomaž Erjavec, Jožef Stefan Institute (Slovenia)
Pablo Gamallo, University of Santiago de Compostela (Spain)
Binyam Gebrekidan Gebre, Phillips Research (The Netherlands)
Cyril Goutte, National Research Council (Canada)
Nizar Habash, New York University Abu Dhabi (UAE)
Chu-Ren Huang, Hong Kong Polytechnic University (Hong Kong)
Radu Ionescu, University of Bucharest (Romania)
Jeremy Jancsary, Nuance Communications (Austria)
Tommi Jauhiainen, University of Helsinki (Finland)
Surafel Melaku Lakew, FBK (Italy)
Lung-Hao Lee, National Taiwan Normal University (Taiwan)
John Nerbonne, University of Groningen (Netherlands) and University of Freiburg (Germany)
Kemal Oflazer, Carnegie-Mellon University in Qatar (Qatar)
Maciej Ogrodniczuk, IPAN, Polish Academy of Sciences (Poland)
Petya Osenova, Bulgarian Academy of Sciences (Bulgaria)
Santanu Pal, Saarland University (Germany)
Barbara Plank, IT University of Copenhagen (Denmark)
Francisco Rangel, Autoritas Consulting (Spain)
Taraka Rama, University of Oslo (Norway)
Reinhard Rapp, University of Mainz (Germany) and University of Aix-Marsaille (France)

Paolo Rosso, Technical University of Valencia (Spain)
Fatiha Sadat, Université du Québec à Montréal, UQAM (Canada)
Tanja Samardžić, University of Zurich (Switzerland)
Felipe Sánchez Martínez, Universitat d'Alacant (Spain)
Kevin Scannell, Saint Louis University (USA)
Yves Scherrer, University of Helsinki (Finland)
Serge Sharoff, University of Leeds (UK)
Kiril Simov, Bulgarian Academy of Sciences (Bulgaria)
Milena Slavcheva, Bulgarian Academy of Sciences (Bulgaria)
Marko Tadić, University of Zagreb (Croatia)
Liling Tan, Rakuten Institute of Technology (Singapore)
Joel Tetreault, Grammarly (USA)
Francis Tyers, Indiana University (USA)
Taro Watanabe, Google Inc. (Japan)
Pidong Wang, Machine Zone Inc. (USA)

VarDial Evaluation Campaign and Shared Task Organizers:

Marcos Zampieri, University of Wolverhampton (UK) - VarDial Evaluation Campaign
Shervin Malmasi, Amazon (USA) - VarDial Evaluation Campaign
Yves Scherrer, University of Helsinki (Finland) - GDI Shared Task
Tanja Samardžić (University of Zurich, Switzerland) - GDI Shared Task
Francis Tyers Indiana University (USA) - CMA Shared Task
Miikka Silfverberg, University of Helsinki (Finland) - CMA Shared Task
Natalia Klyueva, The Hong Kong Polytechnic University (Hong Kong) - DMT Shared Task
Tung-Le Pan, The Hong Kong Polytechnic University (Hong Kong) - DMT Shared Task
Chu-Ren Huang, The Hong Kong Polytechnic University (Hong Kong) - DMT Shared Task
Radu Ionescu, University of Bucharest (Romania) - MRC Shared Task
Andrei Butnaru, University of Bucharest (Romania) - MRC Shared Task
Tommi Jauhiainen, University of Helsinki (Finland) - CLI Shared Task

Invited Speaker:

David Yarowsky, Johns Hopkins University

Table of Contents

Conference Program

Friday, June 7, 2019

9:15–9:30	***Opening***

9:30–10:00   *A Report on the Third VarDial Evaluation Campaign*
Marcos Zampieri, Shervin Malmasi, Yves Scherrer, Tanja Samardzic, Francis Tyers, Miikka Silfverberg, Natalia Klyueva, Tung-Le Pan, Chu-Ren Huang, Radu Tudor Ionescu, Andrei M. Butnaru and Tommi Jauhiainen

10:00–10:30   *Improving Cuneiform Language Identification with BERT*
Gabriel Bernier-Colborne, Cyril Goutte and Serge Leger

10:30–11:00   ***Coffee break***

11:00–11:30   *Joint Approach to Deromanization of Code-mixed Texts*
Rashed Rubby Riyadh and Grzegorz Kondrak

11:30–12:00   *Char-RNN for Word Stress Detection in East Slavic Languages*
Ekaterina Chernyak, Maria Ponomareva and Kirill Milintsevich

12:00–12:30   *Modeling Global Syntactic Variation in English Using Dialect Classification*
Jonathan Dunn

12:30–14:00   ***Lunch***

14:00–15:00   ***Invited talk — David Yarowsky (Johns Hopkins University): Massively Multilingual Translingual Knowledge Transfer***

15:00–15:30   *Language Discrimination and Transfer Learning for Similar Languages: Experiments with Feature Combinations and Adaptation*
Nianheng Wu, Eric DeMattos, Kwok Him So, Pin-zhen Chen and Çağrı Çöltekin

15:30–16:00   ***Coffee break***

16:00–17:00   ***Poster Session***

A Report on the Third VarDial Evaluation Campaign

Marcos Zampieri[1], Shervin Malmasi[2], Yves Scherrer[3], Tanja Samardžić[4]
Francis Tyers[5], Miikka Silfverberg[3], Natalia Klyueva[6], Tung-Le Pan[6]
Chu-Ren Huang[6], Radu Tudor Ionescu[7], Andrei Butnaru[7], Tommi Jauhiainen[3]

[1]University of Wolverhampton, [2]Harvard Medical School, [3]University of Helsinki
[4]University of Zurich, [5]Indiana University, [6]The Hong Kong Polytechnic University
[7]University of Bucharest

`m.zampieri@wlv.ac.uk`

Abstract

In this paper, we present the findings of the Third VarDial Evaluation Campaign organized as part of the sixth edition of the workshop on Natural Language Processing (NLP) for Similar Languages, Varieties and Dialects (VarDial), co-located with NAACL 2019. This year, the campaign included five shared tasks, including one task re-run – German Dialect Identification (GDI) – and four new tasks – Cross-lingual Morphological Analysis (CMA), Discriminating between Mainland and Taiwan variation of Mandarin Chinese (DMT), Moldavian vs. Romanian Cross-dialect Topic identification (MRC), and Cuneiform Language Identification (CLI). A total of 22 teams submitted runs across the five shared tasks. After the end of the competition, we received 14 system description papers, which are published in the VarDial workshop proceedings and referred to in this report.

1 Introduction

The series of workshops on Natural Language Processing (NLP) for Similar Languages, Varieties and Dialects (VarDial) has reached its sixth edition in 2019, evidencing the interest of the CL/NLP community in this topic. The third VarDial Evaluation Campaign[1] featuring five shared tasks, described in detail in this report, has been organized as part of VarDial 2019 co-located with the 2019 Annual Conference of the North American Chapter of the Association for Computational Linguistics (NAACL). It follows two editions of the campaign organized in 2017 with four tasks (Zampieri et al., 2017) and in 2018 with five tasks (Zampieri et al., 2018).

Since its first edition, shared tasks have been organized as part of the VarDial, most notably the

Discriminating between Similar Languages organized from 2014 to 2017 (Zampieri et al., 2014, 2015; Malmasi et al., 2016). The shared tasks organized at VarDial helped providing evaluation benchmarks and public datasets (e.g. (Tan et al., 2014)) for different tasks such as dialect identification, morphosyntactic tagging, and cross-lingual dependency parsing. Similar languages such as Bulgarian and Macedonian, and Czech and Slovak, along with varieties and dialects of Arabic, German, Hindi, Portuguese, and Spanish have been included in the competitions organized within the scope of VarDial.

In this paper, we present the results and main findings of the third VarDial Evaluation Campaign. The five tasks organized this year were: German Dialect Identification (GDI) presented in Section 4, Cross-lingual Morphological Analysis (CMA) presented in Section 5, Discriminating between Mainland and Taiwan variation of Mandarin Chinese (DMT) presented in Section 6, Moldavian vs. Romanian Cross-dialect Topic identification (MRC) presented in Section 7, and finally, Cuneiform Language Identification (CLI) presented in Section 8. In Table 1, we include references to the 14 system description papers written by the participants of the campaign and published in the VarDial workshop proceedings.

2 Shared Tasks at VarDial 2019

The five shared tasks organized as part of the VarDial Evaluation Campaign 2019 are listed next:

Third German Dialect Identification (GDI):
After two successful editions of the (Swiss) German Dialect Identification task, we organized a third iteration of this task at VarDial 2019. We focused again on four Swiss German dialect

---

[1]`https://sites.google.com/view/`
`vardial2019/campaign`

1

areas (Basel, Bern, Lucerne, and Zurich). We provided updated speech transcripts for all dialect areas, but also released two complementary data sources: acoustic data in the form of iVectors, and (predicted) word-level normalisation. In particular, the Arabic Dialect Identification (ADI) task organized in previous VarDial evaluation campaigns showed that acoustic features may substantially improve dialect identification. We wanted to investigate whether this also holds in the slightly different GDI setting.

Cross-lingual Morphological Analysis (CMA): At VarDial 2019, we introduce the task of cross-lingual morphological analysis. Given a word in an unknown related language, for example "navifraghju" ("shipwreck" in Corsican), a human speaker of several related languages is able to deduce that it is a noun in the singular by making deductions from similar words, for example: "naufrag" (Catalan), "naufragio" (Spanish, Italian), "naufrágio" (Portuguese), "naufrage" (French) and "naufragiu" (Romanian). At CMA, we invited participants to create computational models able to do the same. Two language families were represented in the dataset, Romance (fusional morphology) and Turkic (agglutinative morphology). In the "Closed" track, participants were given a set of word forms with all valid morphological analyses in six languages and asked to predict the valid morphological analyses for a seventh, unseen language. In the "Semi-Closed" track, the process was the same, only participants were provided with additional raw data by the organisers. This was in the form of raw text Wikipedia dumps, bilingual dictionaries from the Apertium project and any treebanks available in the known languages from the Universal Dependencies project.

Discriminating between Mainland and Taiwan variation of Mandarin Chinese (DMT): Like English, Mandarin has several varieties among the speaking communities and two dominant standard varieties (Lin et al., 2018). This task aims to discriminate between these two standard varieties of Mandarin Chinese: Putonghua (Mainland China) and Guoyu (Taiwan). We provide a corpus of approximately 10,000 sentences from newspapers for each Mandarin variety. The main task is to determine if a sentence is written in the Mandarin

variety of Mainland China or from Taiwan. It is important to note that since a direct consequence and the most salient feature of the variations is the use of different orthographic systems in China (simplified) and Taiwan (traditional), so the task is designed to focus on the linguistic rather than orthographic differences. Each sentence in the corpus is tokenized and punctuations are removed from the texts, as well as converted from original traditional orthography to simplified, and vice versa. Hence both the traditional and the simplified versions of the same corpus are available so that participant can choose either version and won't be able to use orthographic cues. The results are evaluated in two separate tracks (Simplified and Traditional).

Moldavian vs. Romanian Cross-dialect Topic identification (MRC): In the Moldavian vs. Romanian Cross-topic Identification shared task, we provided participants with the MOROCO data set (Butnaru and Ionescu, 2019) which contains Moldavian and Romanian samples of text collected from the news domain. The samples belong to one of the following six topics: culture, finance, politics, science, sports, and tech. The samples are pre-processed in order to eliminate named entities. For each sample, the data set provides corresponding dialectal and category labels. To this end, we proposed three subtasks for the 2019 VarDial Evaluation Campaign. The first sub-task was a binary classification by dialect task, in which a classification model is required to discriminate between the Moldavian and the Romanian dialects. The second subtask was a Moldavian to Romanian cross-dialect multi-class classification by topic task, in which a model is required to classify the samples written in the Romanian dialect into six topics, using samples written in the Moldavian dialect for training. Finally, the third subtask was a Romanian to Moldavian cross-dialect multi-class classification by topic task, in which a model is required to classify the samples written in the Moldavian dialect into six topics, using samples written in the Romanian dialect for training.

Cuneiform Language Identification (CLI): This shared task focused on discriminating between languages and dialects originally written using the cuneiform script. The task included 2 dif-

Team	GDI	CMA	DMT	MRC	CLI	System Description Papers
Adaptcenter			✓			
BAM	✓					(Butnaru, 2019)
dkosmajac	✓					
DTeam				✓		(Tudoreanu, 2019)
SharifCL					✓	(Doostmohammadi and Nassajian, 2019)
ghpaetzold	✓		✓		✓	
gretelliz92			✓			
ekh					✓	
IUCL			✓			(Hu et al., 2019)
HSE		✓				(Mikhailov et al., 2019)
itsalexyang			✓			(Yang and Xiang, 2019)
lonewolf				✓		
MineriaUNAM		✓				
NRC-CNRC					✓	(Bernier-Colborne et al., 2019)
R2I_LIS				✓		(Chifu, 2019)
PZ					✓	(Paetzold and Zampieri, 2019)
SC-UPB				✓		(Onose and Cercel, 2019)
situx					✓	
SUKI	✓		✓			(Jauhiainen et al., 2019b)
tearsofjoy	✓		✓	✓	✓	(Wu et al., 2019)
TübingenOslo		✓				(Çöltekin and Barnes, 2019)
Twist Bytes	✓				✓	(Benites et al., 2019)
Total	**6**	**3**	**7**	**5**	**8**	**14**

Table 1: The teams that participated in the Third VarDial Evaluation Campaign.

ferent languages: Sumerian and Akkadian. Furthermore, the Akkadian language was divided into six dialects: Old Babylonian, Middle Babylonian peripheral, Standard Babylonian, Neo Babylonian, Late Babylonian, and Neo Assyrian. These languages and dialects were used in ancient Mesopotamia and span a time period of 3,000 years. For training and development, we provided the participants with varying amounts of text encoded in Unicode cuneiform signs for each language or dialect.

3 Participating Teams

The Third VarDial Evaluation Campaign received a positive response from the NLP community. A total of 51 teams enrolled to participate in the five shared tasks of the campaign and 22 of them submitted runs to one or more tasks. This is a similar participation rate to VarDial 2018 when 54 teams signed up and 24 teams submitted runs to five shared tasks, a record for the workshop.

In VarDial 2019, the participants could choose to participate in one or more shared tasks. Table 1 lists the participating teams, the shared tasks they took part in, and a reference to each of the 14 system description papers published in the VarDial workshop proceedings.

4 Third German Dialect Identification GDI

The third edition of the (Swiss) German Dialect Identification task was based on the same data source and split as in 2018, but offered the participants the possibility to make use of word-level normalizations and/or acoustic features. The GDI task again covered four Swiss German dialect areas, namely Basel, Bern, Lucerne, and Zurich.

4.1 Dataset

As in 2017 and 2018, we extracted the training and the test datasets from the ArchiMob corpus of Spoken Swiss German (Samardžić et al., 2016; Scherrer et al., in press). This corpus currently contains 43 oral history interviews with informants speaking different Swiss German dialects. Each interview was transcribed by one of four transcribers, using transcription guidelines based on the writing system "Schwyzertütschi

Dialäktschrift" (Dieth, 1986). The transcriptions exclusively used lower case.

We provided the same data splits as in 2018, but with slightly reduced sizes due to additional filtering. The training set contained utterances from at least three interviews per dialect. The development and test sets each contained utterances from at least one other interview per dialect. Participants were encouraged to include the development data as additional training material in their final systems. This year, we also provided word-level normalizations and acoustic features.

The normalizations have been produced automatically using character-level statistical machine translation at utterance level and re-aligning the normalizations with their source words (see Scherrer and Ljubešić (2016) for details on the approach). We estimated that this word-level normalization format would allow participants to experiment with various feature representations such as character alignments. The normalization language resembles Standard German, but deviates from it in many respects.

The acoustic features, in the form of 400-dimensional i-vectors, were extracted from the source audio data, aligned with the text at the level of segments whose length is between 4s and 10s. Our extraction procedure follows closely the steps proposed in the previous work on Arabic dialects (Ali et al., 2016; Dehak et al., 2011). As in the previous work, we use the Kaldi collection of tools[2] to perform different calculations needed for the extraction of i-vectors. While i-vectors are expected to model the difference between individual speakers and the general background model, the question is open whether they offer some reliable dialect-level information, which can be exploited by the classification algorithms. Given that there is no speaker overlap between training and test data in our current GDI setup, dialect-level information is necessary for improving over the baseline.

4.2 Participants and Approaches

Six participants submitted their systems to the GDI task this year. In the following paragraphs, we shortly describe the best system submitted by each participant. Many participants also provided alternative systems.

tearsofjoy: This submission is based on a linear SVM classifier using character 1–5-grams, word 1–2-grams as well as the iVector features. The character and word features are weighted by BM25. Semi-supervised adaptation to the test data was also used.

SUKI: This submission uses the HeLI method, which is based on relative frequencies of character 4-gram features with smoothing. One of its key characteristics is the semi-supervised adaptation to the test data, as proposed in 2018.

Twist Bytes: This submission relies on a SVM meta-classifier that uses multiple tf-idf-weighted character and word features. Acoustic features are used in a base SVM classifier, whose predictions serve as input for the meta-classifier. Semi-supervised adaptation to the test data was also used.

BAM: This system is an ensemble of three models, a character-level convolutional neural network, a character-level LSTM, and a string kernel model.

dkosmajac: This submission relies on a quadratic discriminant analysis classifier for the iVectors and on a random forest classifier for the text. The output of both classifiers is fed into a random forest meta-classifier to produce the final predictions.

ghpaetzold: This system consists of a recurrent neural network that learns representations of sentences based on their words, and of words based on their characters.

The baseline consists of a linear SVM classifier using only word unigrams as features.

4.3 Results

Table 2 shows the performance of different methods on the GDI data in terms of macro-averaged F1 scores. The three best models all include semi-supervised adaptation to the test data. The impact of the iVectors is hard to assess: on the one hand, it was expected to be low due to the lack of speaker overlap between training and test data, but on the other hand semi-supervised adaptation should be able to generalize test speaker properties from the acoustic signal. The results do not bear out this second hypothesis. None of the participants used

[2]https://github.com/
kaldi-asr/kaldi/blob/
08869e31da51d688ee582dc924193b19530a2d32/
egs/lre07/v1/lid/extract_ivectors.sh

Rank	Team	Transcripts	iVectors	Normalization	Adaptation	F1 (macro)
1	tearsofjoy	✓	✓		✓	0.7593
2	SUKI	✓			✓	0.7541
3	Twist Bytes	✓	✓		✓	0.7455
4	BAM	✓				0.6255
	Baseline	✓				*0.6078*
5	dkosmajac	✓	✓			0.5616
6	ghpaetzold	✓				0.5575

Table 2: Results and rankings of GDI participants. The table also specifies the data formats and techniques used by the participants.

the normalized data. As in previous years, systems based on neural networks did not reach competitive scores, possibly also due to the absence of adaptation.

4.4 Summary

In this third iteration of the GDI task, we provided additional data formats such as acoustic data and word-level normalizations. Six teams participated in the GDI task. Three of them used the acoustic data, but results do not seem to indicate large gains. In contrast, semi-supervised adaptation to the test set seems to be crucial to attain state-of-the-art results.

5 Cross-lingual Morphological Analysis (CMA)

Morphological analysis is one of the cornerstones of natural language processing for morphologically complex languages. Currently, rule-based finite-state morphological analyzers represent the state-of-the-art for this task, however, developing rule-based analyzers is a substantial task. It entails creation of extensive word lists and grammatical descriptions. This requires both linguistic expertise and technical expertise in the rule formalism which is used. Hence, there exists a demand for less labor intensive approaches especially for low-resource languages.

Classically, rule-based analyzers have been augmented with statistical guessers which provide analyses for out-of-lexicon word forms (Lindén, 2009). Recently, purely data-driven morphological analysis has received increasing attention (Nicolai and Kondrak, 2017; Silfverberg and Hulden, 2018; Moeller et al., 2018; Silfverberg and Tyers, 2019). Purely data-driven systems learn an analysis model from a data set of morphologically analyzed word forms and can then be applied to unseen word forms.

The shared task on cross-lingual morphological analysis (CMA) investigates a new dimension of the morphological analysis task. The task was to leverage data for related languages in building a purely data-driven analyzer for a target language. No annotated target language data was provided to the competitors.

The CMA task investigated related-language analysis for the Romance and Turkic language families. Competitors were provided morphologically analyzed training data in six Romance languages (Asturian, Catalan, French, Italian, Portuguese and Spanish) and six Turkic languages (Bashkir, Crimean Tatar, Kazakh, Kyrgyz, Tatar and Turkish). Using these datasets, they built morphological analyzers for two surprise languages: the Romance language Sardinian and the Turkic language Karachay-Balkar. The competitors had access to the input word forms in the Sardinian and Karachay-Balkar test sets but, as stated above, they did not receive any morphologically analyzed data in either of the target languages.

5.1 Dataset

The dataset was compiled specifically for the shared task. We used the Wikipedias in all the languages to create a frequency list of surface tokens for each language. We then analysed these lists using the morphological analysers from the Apertium (Forcada et al., 2011) project. The lists of analyses were trimmed to include only open-class parts of speech (nouns, adjectives, adverbs and verbs). We then removed any form which did not include at least one analysis in an open class. After this we took the top 10,000 wordforms for each language.

The tagsets were converted from Apertium-style to Universal Dependencies (Nivre et al.,

Team	Turkic			Romance		
	Analysis	Lemma	Tag	Analysis	Lemma	Tag
HSE	35.61	**56.99**	38.75	*23.28*	*38.82*	*46.42*
MineriaUNAM	0.00	0.56	0.00	0.33	0.44	37.76
TübingenOslo	31.53	52.74	38.93	23.67	31.36	**61.33**
BASELINE-I	**39.46**	54.94	44.18	22.94	31.56	51.88
BASELINE-II	39.44	53.82	**44.29**	**26.51**	**34.65**	58.54

Table 3: Results for the CMA task. Bold indicates the best scoring system, while *italics* indicates an 'unofficial' result that was submitted after the deadline. These scores are F-scores. For the Analysis column every part of the analysis had to be correct, for the Lemma column the lemma had to be correct and for the Tag column just the part-of-speech tag had to be correct. BASELINE-I refers to the neural system and BASELINE-II to the neural ensemble described in Section 5.3.

2016) using a longest-match set overlap method running on tag-lookup tables, for example, the Apertium tag `<n>` was converted to the Universal Dependencies tag `NOUN`, while Apertium's `<p1>` was translated into Universal Dependencies `Number=Plur|Person=1`.

Finally, each of the word forms was labelled with the language it came from and the lists were merged into language family specific lists.

5.2 Participants and Approaches

HSE This team constructed a POS specific cross-lingual morpheme inventory using the annotated training data. They then predicted target language POS tags using a bidirectional LSTM encoder-decoder model with attention. Finally, they used the POS specific morpheme inventory to predict morphological features using a greedy algorithm. Lemmatization was accomplished by suffix stripping. To deal with language specific orthographic conventions, the team first automatically transcribed all the training data into a joint orthographic representation: For Romance languages, diacritics were removed and for Turkic languages, all data sets were transcribed into Cyrillic script. To build the morpheme inventories, word forms were morphologically segmented using Morfessor (Smit et al., 2014).

MinerialUNAM No system description paper was submitted by this team.

TübingenOslo This team divided the morphological analysis task into two sub-tasks: lemmatization and morphological tag prediction. First, a bidirectional GRU encoder was used to encode the input word form into a representation vector. This vector was fed into a GRU decoder network which generated a lemma. A number of feed forward networks were then used to predict morphological features and POS tag using the representation vector as input. Each morphological feature type, for example number and case, was predicted by a separate feed forward network. Additionally, this team reports results for a linear baseline system which delivers competitive performance for the Turkic language family.

5.3 Baseline System

The first baseline system BASELINE-I (Silfverberg and Tyers, 2019) formulates the morphological analysis task as a character-level string transduction task. It uses an LSTM encoder-decoder model with attention (Bahdanau et al., 2014) for performing the string transduction. To this end, the system is trained to translate input word forms like *andaluza* (feminine singular for the noun or adjective *andaluz* 'Andalusian' in Spanish) into a set of output analyses: `andaluz+A+Num=Sg|Gend=Fem` and `andaluz+N+Number=Sg|Gend=Fem`.

Since a word form may have multiple valid morphological analyses with different lemmas, POS tags and MSDs (for example, *andaluza* has two), the baseline model needs to be able to generate multiple output analyses given an input word form. This is accomplished by extracting several output candidates from the model using beam search and selecting the most probable candidates as model outputs. The number of outputs is controlled by a probability threshold hyperparameter p. The system extracts the least number of top scoring candidates whose combined probability mass is greater than p. Additionally, the number of output candidates is restricted using a single hyperparameter N which is a firm upper bound for the number of analyses a word may receive. The hyperparameters p and N are tuned by treating the training set for one of the languages as held-out data (Asturian for Romance languages and Crimean Tatar for Turkic languages). After tuning the hyperparameters, the model was trained on the complete annotated training data.

The second baseline system BASELINE-II is an ensemble of five instances of the neural baseline systems BASELINE-I described above. Each instance was trained identically apart from random initialization of model parameters. We compute the probability for an output analysis as the arithmetic mean of the probabilities assigned by each of the five component models. Output analyses are generated in the same manner as for the BASELINE-I model.

5.4 Results

Given an input word form, systems return a set of analyses each of which consists of a lemma and a morphological tag. Systems are evaluated for F1-score with regard to the gold standard set of complete analyses, lemmas and tags for each input word form. Table 3 shows results for the CMA task.

5.5 Summary

Three teams participated in this first iteration of the cross-lingual analysis task. Two of the teams employed variations of neural encoder-decoder systems. Apart from lemmatization performance, it proved to be difficult to attain consistent improvements over the neural baseline systems. However, the suffix stripping approach used by the HSE team did deliver clear improvements in lemmatization for both Turkic and Romance languages.

6 Discriminating between Mainland and Taiwan variation of Mandarin Chinese (DMT)

Mandarin, with over 900 million native speakers, is one of the ten main dialect groups of Chinese, along with Yue, Min, Wu, and others (often also referred to as Sinitic languages). Inside Mandarin, there is also a variety of divergence within. Mandarin (i.e. the language of the mandarins (the officers)) has been the official language of the government by convention for over a thousand years

but has also become the common language both in spoken language and written text by constitution in the modern era, first by the Nationalists (ROC) after 1911, and then by the Communists PRC in 1949. In daily non-technical usage, both Chinese or Mandarin refers to either or both of these standard forms of Mandarin as the lingua franca of the Chinese people, including both their spoken and written forms (Huang and Shi, 2016). Although the later version (called Putonghua (普通话, common language) superseded the older version (called Guoyu (國語, national language) in Mainland China, and the latter version persists in Taiwan and can be viewed to be related, important variations arose since 1949 for several reasons (Lin et al., 2018).

First, and most of all, the two varieties developed in relative isolation from each other and under different political systems for over 50 years during the Cold War era. Second, each has its own regulating bodies as well as different contextual influences. Third, Guoyu has more southern influences than Putonghua, even though both are based on Beijing Mandarin. Note that Putonghua in China is written with simplified Chinese characters with Pinyin romanization for pedagogy; while Guoyu in Taiwan is written in traditional characters and uses the Zhuyin system (sometimes called bopomofo) for pedagogy. With recent more frequent exchanges at different levels of China and Taiwan, some of the differences have begun to get absorbed.

6.1 Dataset

Texts to distinguish between the two variations were compiled from the two existing corpora of news: Sinica Corpus for Taiwan Mandarin (Chen et al., 1996) and LCMC (The Lancaster Corpus of Mandarin Chinese, (McEnery and Xiao, 2003)) for Mainland Mandarin. Both corpora are segmented and tokenized. We remove the punctuation and unify the orthography used to eliminate orthographic cues. Since both corpora are balanced corpora, our initial thought was to provide genre-aware classification. However, inspection of both corpora suggested the genres were not defined in the same way and are not distributed homogeneously. In the next edition this idea may be exploited by using some additional resources as genre vs. regional variations which is an important and yet under-explored issue in similar languages

(Hou and Huang, 2019).

Thus, as input data, we got 21492 lines/sentences of LCMC corpus and 46158 lines/sentences from Sinica Corpus. The clean-up included removing lines containing Latin characters in Named Entities (as potential contextual cues) and lines shorter than 4 tokens. The LCMC portion is reduced to 12072 sentences after clean-up, and Sinica Corpus data is reduced correspondingly for balance.

The data were converted into utf-8 encoding, and split into training, development and test sets in the following proportions respectively for each variety: 9385/1000/1000 lines. Each of the sets was mixed pairwise: Taiwanese with Mainland train/dev/test sets, and shuffled. The test set was formed from the last 1000 lines of each of the corpus to make sure there is no intersection between training and test data.

The sets prepared as described above were then run through a character converter to form two tracks: Traditional and Simplified. As it was stated in the introduction of this Section, Mainland uses simplified characters while in Taiwan traditional characters are used. The conversion ensures that the DMT task is not orthography dependent and will allow us to compare results of teams working on both sets of data. Conversion from simplified to traditional and from traditional to simplified characters were made by opencc converter [3] (in effect, coding sets with some lexical conversion as well). However, conversion cannot be 100% accurate in both directions, it will have some information lost.

6.2 Participants and Approaches

A total of seven systems participated in the shared task, and as a result, 17 runs each were performed for both the simplified and the traditional set. Five of the teams performed three runs each for both sets of data and the other two only performed once for each. The results were given out in confusion matrices, which calculate the number of sentences that were identified as being labeled correctly and incorrectly. Four of the teams that participated in the shared task used the training and development data exclusively in order to obtain the final result.

Here is a more detailed explanation of the approaches conducted by the teams based on the descriptions provided by the participants:

Adaptcenter: A dictionary was built which contain the 5,000 high frequency words which were assigned values. Then the convolutional neural network (CNN) method was employed to the training and test test, which results in the CNN model. At the end, the two methods were combined, improving from either of the methods.

ghpaetzold: This system is a 2-layer compositional recurrent neural network that learns numerical representations of sentences based on their words, which were in turn based on their characters. The system receives, as input, the text from the instance being classified only, with no other additional features or resources. The model was trained exclusively on the training data provided, and was validated on the development set provided. The model was implemented in Pytorch.

gretelliz92: A simple preprocessing was carried out to preserve all the characteristics that can be discriminative between the two types of texts that are analyzed, with the combination of a linguistic feature based on tf-idf. Therefore, in this step only the texts with fasttext word embedding for Chinese were represented. The vectors obtained in the preprocessing are used as input of the model which consists of a Bidirectional long short-term memory (Bi-LSTM) layer, whose output is inputted to a fully connected neural network of 4 dense layers with the relu activation function, along with one output layer with the softmax function.

IUCL (submitted as 'hezhou'): An ensemble model was used containing the five following classifiers: 1) a pre-trained BERT model for Chinese, 2) a long short-term memory model with word-embeddings which was trained on People Daily's News, one of China's leading newspapers, 3) support vector machine (SVM) and Naive Bayes classifiers with word n-gram and context-free grammar features, 4) a sequential model with a global average pooling layer, 5) a word-based bi-LSTM model. They were, in turn, ensembled in three different methods: 1) assigning the class which has the highest probability (confidence) from any classifier, 2) assigning the class with the highest average probability, 3) using an SVM to predict the class from the probabilities given by all of the classifiers.

itsalexyang: A multinomial Naive Bayes and BiLSTM ensemble model was used to train the model. For multinomial Naive Bayes, it is trained using presence vs. absence (0 vs. 1) vectors based on feature combinations of character-level

---

bigrams and trigrams as input. For BiLSTM, the Word2vec method was trained on the dataset to obtain word embedding matrices, then the word embedding sequences can be used as input sentence representations. A forward and a backward LSTM is used to process the sequence and produce hidden states, which contain information from contexts in two opposite directions. After obtaining the hidden state sequence, max-over-time pooling operation is applied to form a fix-size vector as sentence representations, which will be fed into a hidden dense layer with 256 units and a final dense layer to predict. After training with these base classifiers, an average of output probabilities from all the models is then taken and used to make the final prediction.

SUKI: A custom coded language identifier was made using the product of relative frequencies of character n-grams. It is a Naive Bayes classifier that uses relative frequencies as probabilities. The lengths of the character n-grams used ranged from 1 to 14 for the Traditional track and from 1 to 15 for the Simplified Track. Instead of multiplying the relative frequencies, their negative logarithms were summed up. As a smoothing value, the negative logarithm of an n-gram appearing only once multiplied by a penalty modifier was used. In this case, the penalty modifier was 1.3. For the Simplified track, similar language model (LM) adaptation was used as in GDI 2018 (Jauhiainen et al., 2018a). In addition, a separate confidence threshold was used. For the Traditional track, the LM adaptation was also used, but the results were split in 4 parts and all the information from one part was added to the language models at once. The n-gram models used, penalty modifier, the confidence threshold, and the number of splits in adaptation was optimized using the development data.

tearsofjoy: This is a linear SVM classifier (one-vs-rest multi-class classifier) with character n-grams ranging from the order 1 to 4 combined with word unigrams (as the effect of word n-grams on the development set is negligible). All n-gram features are combined into a single feature matrix and weighted by BM25. The model is tuned for optimum 'C' parameter (5.8 for this approach) and maximum n-gram order on the training/development set. The data was modified by adding the test instances that are classified with a classifier trained on the training set with high confidence to the training set, and re-training the classifier with the additional 'silver' data from the test set.

6.3 Results

In the Table 4 we present the results of the teams in terms of F1-scores alongside with the summary of the methods that they have employed in order to train a model. One of the teams (IUCL, marked in italics in the table) used additional resources (pretrained word embeddings) while training.

6.4 Summary

From the obtained results we can see that sophisticated approaches involving Deep Learning models do not necessarily outperform the traditional methods like Naive Bayes or SVM. We have manually analysed the sentences that got wrong prediction for most systems. Majority of those sentences were of the generic themes, which suggests the key factor for identifying the variation was topical rather than grammatical.

Another observation coming from the confusion matrices: for some systems the percentage of cases when Mainland label was predicted while Taiwanese was the True label, sometimes was half as much than for the other way round.

Finally, comparing results from both tracks by the same team, it is shown that differences in F1 are general quite small and performance ranking is relatively stable and independent of the track (i.e. orthography). This reassures robustness of the set. It is interesting to observe though that the better performing teams tend to have bigger deviation than the teams with lower performance. For instance, the smallest delta (0.001249321) came from gretelliz92; while the higher delta (0.035017912) came from SUKI. While SUKI's performance is more than 15% higher (Delta F1 roughly 0.15).

While the default hypothesis was that the more robust system should be the one least affected by choice of orthographic representation, the DMT task results suggest that it would be the other way around. That is, the system that performs better in differentiating varieties of similar languages should be 'biased' to pick up the differences hence could be affected by representational variations. The least biased system (i.e. seemingly 'robust') in fact has the less discriminating power.

DMT - Traditional

Rank	Team	Method	Features used	F1
1	SUKI	Naive Bayes	ch. n-grams	0.9084
2	*IUCL*	*ens:BERT, LSTM, SVM etc.*	*word emb.*	*0.9008*
3	tearsofjoy	linear SVM	ch. and word n-grams	0.8843
4	itsalexyang	ens: Naive Bayes,BiLSTM	word2vec	0.8687
5	Adaptcenter	CNN	freq-based value assign.	0.8317
6	ghpaetzold	RNN	ch. numeral representations	0.7959
7	gretelliz92	bi-LSTM , Relu	tf-idf	0.7483

DMT - Simplified

Rank	Team	Method	Features used	F1
1	*IUCL*	*ens:BERT, LSTM, SVM etc.*	*word emb.*	*0.8929*
2	tearsofjoy	linear SVM	ch. and word n-grams	0.8737
3	SUKI	Naive Bayes	ch. n-grams	0.8734
4	itsalexyang	ens:Naive Bayes, BiLSTM	word2vec	0.8530
5	Adaptcenter	CNN	freq-based value assign.	0.8124
6	ghpaetzold	RNN	ch. numeral representations	0.7934
7	gretelliz92	bi-LSTM, Relu	FastText word embeddings	0.7496

Table 4: The macro F1-scores for DMT-Traditional and DMT-Simplified shared task alongside with the summary of methods and features used by the teams.

7 Moldavian vs. Romanian Cross-dialect Topic identification (MRC)

Romanian (RO) is the language currently spoken in Romania, which is part of the Balkan-Romance group of languages. Besides Romanian, the group contains three other dialects: Aromanian, Istro-Romanian, and Megleno-Romanian. In order to distinguish Romanian within the Balkan-Romance group in comparative linguistics, it is referred to as *Daco-Romanian*. Moldavian (MD) is a subdialect of Daco-Romanian, that is spoken in the Republic of Moldova and in northeastern Romania. The delimitation of the Moldavian (sub)dialect, as with all other Romanian (sub)dialects, is mainly based on phonetic features and only marginally by morphological, syntactical, and lexical characteristics. Although the spoken dialects in Romania and the Republic of Moldova are different, the two countries share the same literary standard (Minahan, 2013). Some linguists (Pavel, 2008) consider that the border between Romania and the Republic of Moldova does not correspond to any significant isoglosses to justify a dialectal division. Therefore, separating between Romanian and Moldavian is a challenging task. The aim of the MRC shared task is (i) to determine to what the extent

Set	#samples	#tokens
Training	21,719	6,705,334
Development	11,845	3,677,795
Private Test	5,923	1,836,705
Total	**39,487**	**12,219,834**

Table 5: The number of samples (#samples) and the number of tokens (#tokens) contained in the training, development (public validation plus test sets) and private test sets included in the MOROCO dataset.

the two (sub)dialects can be automatically distinguished and (ii) to assess the performance of applying machine learning models trained on one dialect, e.g. Moldavian, directly (without fine-tuning) to the other, e.g. Romanian.

7.1 Dataset

The dataset used in the MRC shared task was recently introduced in (Butnaru and Ionescu, 2019). The publicly available corpus[4], released before the MRC shared task, contains 33,564 samples collected from the news domains in Romania and Re-

---

[4]`https://github.com/butnaruandrei/MOROCO`

public of Moldova. The samples belong to one of the following six topics: culture, finance, politics, science, sports, and tech. For the competition, we provided a distinct and private test set of 5,923 samples. The public validation and test sets we unified into a single development set for the competition. Table 5 provides the number of samples and the number of tokens in each subset (training, development and private test). The whole corpus is formed of 39,487 samples with over 12 million tokens. Since we provide both dialectal and category labels for each sample, we proposed three subtasks for the competition:

- Binary classification by dialect (subtask 1) – the task is to discriminate between the Moldavian and the Romanian dialects.

- MD→RO cross-dialect multi-class categorization by topic (subtask 2) – the task is to classify the samples written in the Romanian dialect into six topics, using a model trained on samples written in the Moldavian dialect.

- RO→MD cross-dialect multi-class categorization by topic (subtask 3) – the task is to classify the samples written in the Moldavian dialect into six topics, using a model trained on samples written in the Romanian dialect.

7.2 Participants and Approaches

DTeam. The approach of DTeam is based on an ensemble model that combines two character-level convolutional neural networks (CNN) using Support Vector Machines (SVM). The first CNN is based on a skip-gram model that is trained using softmax loss. The second CNN is trained using triplet loss (Schroff et al., 2015). DTeam submitted a single run to each of the three MRC subtasks.

lonewolf. The lonewolf team submitted three runs for subtask 1. The first run is based on a character-level bigram classification model to discriminate between Moldavian and Romanian examples using Add-One Smoothing for out-of-vocabulary items. The second and the third runs are based on word-level bigram classification models. The second run uses Add-One Smoothing for out-of-vocabulary items, while the third run uses Good-Turing Smoothing.

R2I_LIS. The R2I_LIS team submitted three runs for subtask 1. All their runs are based on a set of 40 features that include: the average length of a token, the average number of tokens per sentence, the number of tokens inside each text document, the number of occurrences of selected single characters, the number of occurrences of selected punctuation characters, the number of occurrences of the letter 'î' inside a word (not as the first character), the number of occurrences of selected words and the number of occurrences of the token \$NE\$ which replaces named entities. The third run uses a normalized version of these features. All runs are based on a majority voting scheme applied on five classification models: k-Nearest Neighbors, Logistic Regression, Support Vector Machines, Neural Networks and Random Forests. For the first and the third runs, the models are trained on both training and development sets. For the second run, the model is trained only on the training set.

SC-UPB. The SC-UPB team first cleaned the dataset by removing stopwords as well as special characters. The first run submitted to each of the three subtasks is based on a model that represents text as the mean of word vectors given by a pre-trained FastText model (Grave et al., 2018). The representation is provided as input to a Recurrent Neural Network with gated recurrent units, which is trained using the Adam optimizer with a batch size of 64 for 20 epochs and early stopping. The second run submitted to each of the three subtasks is based on a hierarchical attention network introduced by Yang et al. (2016). The model is trained using the Adam optimizer with a batch size of 64 for 20 epochs and early stopping.

tearsofjoy. The tearsofjoy team used a linear SVM classifier with a combination of character and word n-gram features, which are weighted with the BM25 weighting scheme. Their model's parameters are tuned independently for each subtask, using random search and 5-fold cross-validation. The tearsofjoy team also tried a transductive learning approach which is based on retraining the model by adding confident predictions from the test set to the training set, an idea previously studied in (Ionescu and Butnaru, 2018).

7.3 Results

After the submission deadline, we noticed that two teams (tearsofjoy and SC-UPB) submitted runs containing less than the expected number of labels (5,923) for the test examples. Hence, their original (unmodified) submissions could not be eval-

Rank	Team	Run	F1 (macro)
1	DTeam	1	0.8950
2	R2I_LIS	3	0.7964
3	tearsofjoy	1	0.7573
4	lonewolf	2	0.7354
5	SC-UPB	1	0.7088

Table 6: Results on MRC subtask 1 (binary classification by dialect).

Rank	Team	Run	F1 (macro)
1	tearsofjoy	1	0.6115
2	SC-UPB	1	0.4813
3	DTeam	1	0.3856

Table 7: Results on MRC subtask 2 (multi-class categorization by topic of Romanian text samples using Moldavian text samples for training).

Rank	Team	Run	F1 (macro)
1	tearsofjoy	1	0.5533
2	SC-UPB	1	0.4808
3	DTeam	1	0.4472

Table 8: Results on MRC subtask 2 (multi-class categorization by topic of Moldavian text samples using Romanian text samples for training).

uated. In order to evaluate their runs, we tried to fix the problem by adding random labels using the following options: (i) at random locations in the submission files or (ii) at the end of the submission files. In the evaluation, we considered the option that provided better performance for the runs submitted by tearsofjoy and SC-UPB.

The best run of each participant in MRC subtask 1 is presented in Table 6. We notice that DTeam uses an approach based on deep learning, which surpasses the shallow approaches of R2I_LIS and tearsofjoy teams.

Table 7 contains the F1 (macro) score of the best run of each participant in MRC subtask 2. This time, we notice that the winning approach is shallow. It surpasses the other approaches based on deep neural networks. The ranking for subtask 2 is identical to the ranking for subtask 3, as shown in Table 8.

7.4 Summary

We proposed three MRC subtasks for VarDial 2019. Three participants submitted runs for all three subtasks, and another two participants submitted runs only for subtask 1. Two teams (DTeam and SC-UPB) proposed systems based on deep neural networks, while the other teams proposed shallow approaches based on handcrafted features. For subtask 1, the winning solution is a deep learning system. For subtasks 2 and 3, the winning solution is a shallow learning system. Hence, it remains unclear which of the two learning approaches, deep or shallow, provides better results in Moldavian vs. Romanian Cross-dialect Topic identification.

8 Cuneiform Language Identification (CLI)

The first edition of the CLI shared task was a language identification task concentrating on distinguishing between languages and dialects which were originally written with cuneiform signs. It included two completely separate languages: Akkadian and Sumerian. We had only one variety for Sumerian, but for Akkadian, we included six separate dialects: Old Babylonian, Middle Babylonian peripheral, Standard Babylonian, Neo-Babylonian, Late Babylonian, and Neo-Assyrian.

8.1 Dataset

The dataset used in the CLI shared task, as well as its creation, is described in detail by Jauhiainen et al. (2019a). The dataset was created using openly available transliterations originating from the Open Richly Annotated Cuneiform Corpus (Oracc). [5] In Oracc, the texts, originally written using the cuneiform script, are mostly stored in transliterated form. A special conversion program was used to transform these transliterated texts to Unicode cuneiform encoding. The data consists of texts originally appearing in one line of cuneiform writing. Word boundaries were not marked in the original script, but in the transliterations the word boundaries were marked. In order to produce more realistic cuneiform writing, the word boundaries were again removed in the conversion to Unicode cuneiform. Each line, thus, may consist of one or more words.

The sizes of the training sets for each language varied, and the exact number of lines in each can be seen in Table 9. In addition to the training set, the participants were provided with 668 lines of development data for each language. The test set had 985 lines for each language.

Language or Dialect	Training
Sumerian	53,673
Old Babylonian	3,803
Middle Babylonian peripheral	5,508
Standard Babylonian	17,817
Neo-Babylonian	9,707
Late Babylonian	15,947
Neo-Assyrian	32,966

Table 9: Number of lines for each language or dialect in the CLI training set.

8.2 Participants and Approaches

In addition to the best performing system from each team, we have collected information about some of their other submissions if the systems used were clearly different. This information can be seen together with the test results in Table 10. The baseline methods and their results included in the table are described by Jauhiainen et al. (2019a).

The **NRC-CNRC** team submitted three runs. Their first submission was based on SVMs using character n-grams with different weighting schemes. Their second submission used a voting ensemble comprised of the previous SVMs and probabilistic classifiers. Their third and winning submission was based on a deep neural network (modified version of the BERT model) taking characters as input. With the deep neural network they had a second pre-training phase in which an unsupervised method was used to learn information from, and in a way adapt, to the test set. For more detailed information see the description by Bernier-Colborne et al. (2019).

The **tearsofjoy** team submitted two runs using SVMs. The better of their runs had two stages. After the first stage, those lines claimed by only one of the one-vs-all classifiers were added to the training data. This functions as one iteration of language model (LM) adaptation similar to the one used by Jauhiainen et al. (2018b) in the 2018 Indo-Aryan language identification (ILI) shared task. However, using language model adaptation improved their F1-score only by 1.6%. Their system is better described by Wu et al. (2019).

The **TwistBytes** team submitted two runs using SVMs. The better of their runs used tf-idf features with binary tf values and smoothed idf for character n-grams 1–3. Benites et al. (2019) describe the

two systems in more detail.

The **PZ** team used a SVM metaclassifier ensemble of several linear SVM classifiers trained using character n-gram and character skip-gram features. Paetzold and Zampieri (2019) give further details.

The **SharifCL** team submitted three runs and their best performing system was an ensemble of a SVM and a NB classifier (Doostmohammadi and Nassajian, 2019).

The **ghpaetzold** team submitted only one run using 2-layer compositional recurrent neural network that learns numerical representations of sentences based on their words, and of words based on their characters. Their system is described in more detail by Paetzold and Zampieri (2019).

The **ekh** team used a sum of relative frequencies of character bigrams together with a penalty value for those bigrams or unigrams that were not found from a language.

The **situx** team used a Random Forest classifier. Their results are below a random baseline and we suspect there might have been some processing problems when generating the results from test set.

8.3 Results

Table 10 shows the performance of different methods on the CLI dataset. The ranked results are bolded in the table. To the best of our knowledge, this is the first time a language identification shared task has been won using neural networks in addition to the first MRC subtask.

8.4 Summary

We were happy to see such a widespread interest in the CLI shared task. The NRC-CNRC team did not participate in the other shared tasks, so we cannot directly compare the performance of their deep neural network between different writing systems. The only other team using neural networks was the ghpaetzold and the performance of their RNN is more in line what we have used to expect from neural networks when compared with the SVMs.

The second ranking team, tearsofjoy, used LM adaptation on the test set. They did the same with the GDI and the DMT tasks and were ranked very high in them as well. The difference in F1 score between their adaptive and non-adaptive systems is surprisingly small in CLI, as the test data in CLI was supposed to be out-of-domain when compared with the training and the development sets (Jauhiainen et al., 2019a).

Rank	Team	Method	Features used	F1
1.	**NRC-CNRC**	**Deep Neural Network + adapt.**	**characters**	**0.7695**
2.	**tearsofjoy**	**Lin. SVM with LM adapt.**	**ch. n-grams 1–5**	**0.7632**
	tearsofjoy	Lin. SVM	ch. n-grams 1–4	0.7511
	NRC-CNRC	SVM + NB ensemble	ch. n-grams 1–5	0.7449
3.	**Twist Bytes**	**Lin. SVM**	**ch. n-grams 1–3**	**0.7433**
	NRC-CNRC	SVM	ch. n-grams 1–4	0.7414
4.	**PZ**	**SVM ensemble**	**ch. n-grams 1–5, skip-grams**	**0.7347**
5.	**SharifCL**	**SVM + NB ensemble**	**ch. n-grams 1–4**	**0.7210**
	Baseline-3	Prod. of rel. freq.	ch. n-grams 1–4	0.7206
	SharifCL	SVM	ch. n-grams 1–4	0.7171
	Baseline-4	Voting ensemble	ch. n-grams 1–15	0.7163
	Baseline-5	HeLI	ch. n-grams 1–3 + lines	0.7061
	Twist Bytes	Lin. SVM	ch. n-grams 1–7, words	0.6669
	Baseline-1	Simple scoring	ch. n-grams 1–10	0.6554
	Baseline-2	Sum of rel. freq.	ch. n-grams 3–15	0.6016
6.	**ghpaetzold**	**RNN**	**characters, words**	**0.5562**
7.	**ekh**	**Sum of rel. freq. + spec. penalt.**	**ch. 2-grams**	**0.5501**
8.	**situx**	**Random Forest**	**ch. n-grams 2–4, spec.**	**0.1276**

Table 10: The macro F1-scores attained by the participating teams and the baseline methods with the CLI dataset. The official ranked results are bolded.

9 Conclusion

In this paper, we presented the results and the main findings for the five shared tasks organized as part of the Third VarDial Evaluation Campaign. One task was a re-run from previous years (GDI), and four new tasks were organized: CMA, DMT, MRC, and CLI.

A total of 22 teams submitted runs across the five shared tasks. We included short descriptions for each participant's systems in this report. A complete description is available in the system description papers, which were presented in the VarDial workshop and published in the workshop proceedings. We included references to all system description papers in this report in Table 1.

Acknowledgments

We would like to thank the participants of the Third VarDial Evaluation Campaign for their participation, support, and feedback. We further thank the VarDial workshop program committee members for thoroughly reviewing the shared task system description papers and this report.

The GDI organizers would like to thank Thayabaran Kathiresan and Lei He (University of Zurich) for their valuable help with the preparation of the iVectors.

The CLI organizer is grateful to his colleagues at the Centre of Excellence in Ancient Near Eastern Empires (ANEE) of the University of Helsinki for their invaluable assistance.

References

Ahmed Ali, Najim Dehak, Patrick Cardinal, Sameer Khurana, Sree Harsha Yella, James Glass, Peter Bell, and Steve Renals. 2016. Automatic Dialect Detection in Arabic Broadcast Speech. In *Proceedings of INTERSPEECH*.

Dzmitry Bahdanau, Kyunghyun Cho, and Yoshua Bengio. 2014. Neural machine translation by jointly learning to align and translate. *arXiv preprint arXiv:1409.0473*.

Fernando Benites, Pius von Däniken, and Mark Cieliebak. 2019. TwistBytes - Identification of Cuneiform Languages and German Dialects at VarDial 2019. In *Proceedings of VarDial*.

Gabriel Bernier-Colborne, Cyril Goutte, and Serge Léger. 2019. Improving Cuneiform Language Identification with BERT. In *Proceedings of VarDial*.

Andrei Butnaru and Radu Tudor Ionescu. 2019. MOROCO: The Moldavian and Romanian Dialectal Corpus. *arXiv preprint arXiv:1901.06543*.

Andrei M. Butnaru. 2019. BAM: A combination of deep and shallow models for German Dialect Identification. In *Proceedings of VarDial*.

Çağrı Çöltekin and Jeremy Barnes. 2019. Neural and Linear Pipeline Approaches to Cross-lingual Morphological Analysis. In *Proceedings of VarDial*.

Keh-Jiann Chen, Chu-Ren Huang, Li-Ping Chang, and Hui-Li Hsu. 1996. Sinica Corpus : Design Methodology for Balanced Corpora. In *Proceedings of PACLIC*.

Adrian-Gabriel Chifu. 2019. The R2I_LIS Team Proposes Majority Vote for VarDial's MRC Task. In *Proceedings of VarDial*.

Najim Dehak, Pedro A. Torres-Carrasquillo, Douglas Reynolds, and Reda Dehak. 2011. Language recognition via i-vectors and dimensionality reduction. In *Proceedings of INTERSPEECH*.

Eugen Dieth. 1986. *Schwyzertütschi Dialäktschrift*, 2 edition. Sauerländer.

Ehsan Doostmohammadi and Minoo Nassajian. 2019. Investigating Machine Learning Methods for Language and Dialect Identification of Cuneiform Texts . In *Proceedings of VarDial*.

Mikel Forcada, Mireia Ginestí-Rosell, Jacob Nordfalk, Jim O'Regan, Sergio Ortiz-Rojas, Juan Antonio Pérez-Ortiz, Felipe Sánchez-Martínez, Gema Ramírez-Sánchez, and Francis M. Tyers. 2011. Apertium: a free/open-source platform for rule-based machine translation. *Machine Translation*, 25:127–144.

Edouard Grave, Piotr Bojanowski, Prakhar Gupta, Armand Joulin, and Tomas Mikolov. 2018. Learning Word Vectors for 157 Languages. In *Proceedings of LREC*.

Renkui Hou and Chu-Ren Huang. 2019. (to appear) Classification of Regional and Genre Varieties of Chinese: A correspondence analysis approach based on comparable balanced corpora. *Journal of Natural Language Engineering*.

Hai Hu, Wen Li, He Zhou, Zuoyu Tian, Yiwen Zhang, and Liang Zou. 2019. Ensemble Methods to Distinguish Mainland and Taiwan Chinese. In *Proceedings of VarDial*.

Chu-Ren Huang and Dingxu Shi. 2016. *A Reference Grammar of Chinese*. Cambridge University Press.

Radu Tudor Ionescu and Andrei M. Butnaru. 2018. Improving the results of string kernels in sentiment analysis and Arabic dialect identification by adapting them to your test set. In *Proceedings of EMNLP*.

Tommi Jauhiainen, Heidi Jauhiainen, Tero Alstola, and Krister Lindén. 2019a. Language and Dialect Identification of Cuneiform Texts. In *Proceedings of VarDial*.

Tommi Jauhiainen, Heidi Jauhiainen, and Krister Lindén. 2018a. HeLI-based experiments in Swiss German dialect identification. In *Proceedings of VarDial*.

Tommi Jauhiainen, Heidi Jauhiainen, and Krister Lindén. 2018b. Iterative language model adaptation for Indo-Aryan language identification. In *Proceedings of VarDial*.

Tommi Jauhiainen, Heidi Jauhiainen, and Krister Lindén. 2019b. Discriminating between Mandarin Chinese and Swiss-German varieties using adaptive language models . In *Proceedings of VarDial*.

Jingxia Lin, Dingxu Shi, Menghan Jiang, and Chu-Ren Huang. 2018. Variations in World Chineses. *The Routledge Handbook of Applied Chinese Linguistics*.

Krister Lindén. 2009. Guessers for finite-state transducer lexicons. In *Proceedings of CICLing*.

Shervin Malmasi, Marcos Zampieri, Nikola Ljubešić, Preslav Nakov, Ahmed Ali, and Jörg Tiedemann. 2016. Discriminating between Similar Languages and Arabic Dialect Identification: A Report on the Third DSL Shared Task. In *Proceedings of VarDial*.

A. M. McEnery and R. Z. Xiao. 2003. The Lancaster Corpus of Mandarin Chinese.

Vladislav Mikhailov, Lorenzo Tosi, Anastasia Khorosheva, and Oleg Serikov. 2019. Initial Experiments In Cross-Lingual Morphological Analysis Using Morpheme Segmentation. In *Proceedings of VarDial*.

James Minahan. 2013. *Miniature Empires: A Historical Dictionary of the Newly Independent States*. Routledge.

Sarah Moeller, Ghazaleh Kazeminejad, Andrew Cowell, and Mans Hulden. 2018. A neural morphological analyzer for Arapaho verbs learned from a finite state transducer. In *Proceedings of the Workshop on Computational Modeling of Polysynthetic Languages*.

Garrett Nicolai and Grzegorz Kondrak. 2017. Morphological analysis without expert annotation. In *Proceedings of EACL*.

Joakim Nivre, Marie-Catherine de Marneffe, Filip Ginter, Yoav Goldberg, Jan Hajič, Chris Manning, Ryan McDonald, Slav Petrov, Sampo Pyysalo, Natalia Silveira, Reut Tsarfaty, and Dan Zeman. 2016. Universal Dependencies v1: A Multilingual Treebank Collection. In *Proceedings of LREC*.

Cristian Onose and Dumitru-Clementin Cercel. 2019. SC-UPB Team at the VarDial 2019 Evaluation Campaign: Moldavian vs. Romanian Cross-Dialect Topic Identification. In *Proceedings of VarDial*.

Gustavo H. Paetzold and Marcos Zampieri. 2019. Experiments in Cuneiform Language Identification. In *Proceedings of VarDial*.

Vasile Pavel. 2008. Limba română – unitate în diversitate (Romanian language – there is unity in diversity). *Romanian Laguage Journal*, XVIII(9–10).

Tanja Samardžić, Yves Scherrer, and Elvira Glaser. 2016. ArchiMob – a corpus of spoken Swiss German. In *Proceedings of LREC*.

Yves Scherrer and Nikola Ljubešić. 2016. Automatic Normalisation of the Swiss German ArchiMob Corpus Using Character-level Machine Translation. In *Proceedings of KONVENS*.

Yves Scherrer, Tanja Samardžić, and Elvira Glaser. in press. Digitising Swiss German – how to process and study a polycentric spoken language. *Language Resources and Evaluation*.

Florian Schroff, Dmitry Kalenichenko, and James Philbin. 2015. FaceNet: A unified embedding for face recognition and clustering. In *Proceedings of CVPR*.

Miikka Silfverberg and Mans Hulden. 2018. Initial experiments in data-driven morphological analysis for Finnish. In *Proceedings of the Fourth International Workshop on Computatinal Linguistics of Uralic Languages*.

Miikka Silfverberg and Francis Tyers. 2019. Data-Driven Morphological Analysis for Uralic Languages. In *Proceedings of the Fifth International Workshop on Computational Linguistics for Uralic Languages*.

Peter Smit, Sami Virpioja, Stig-Arne Grönroos, Mikko Kurimo, et al. 2014. Morfessor 2.0: Toolkit for statistical morphological segmentation. In *Proceedings of EACL*.

Liling Tan, Marcos Zampieri, Nikola Ljubešic, and Jörg Tiedemann. 2014. Merging Comparable Data Sources for the Discrimination of Similar Languages: The DSL Corpus Collection. In *Proceedings of BUCC*.

Diana-Elena Tudoreanu. 2019. DTeam @ VarDial 2019: Ensemble based on skip-gram and triplet loss neural networks for Moldavian vs. Romanian cross-dialect topic identification. In *Proceedings of VarDial*.

Nianheng Wu, Eric DeMattos, Kwok Him So, Pin-zhen Chen, and Çağrı Çöltekin. 2019. Language Discrimination and Transfer Learning for Similar Languages: Experiments with Feature Combinations and Adaptation. In *Proceedings of VarDial*.

Li Yang and Yang Xiang. 2019. Naive Bayes and BiLSTM Ensemble for Discriminating between Mainland and Taiwan Variation of Mandarin Chinese. In *Proceedings of VarDial*.

Zichao Yang, Diyi Yang, Chris Dyer, Xiaodong He, Alex Smola, and Eduard Hovy. 2016. Hierarchical attention networks for document classification. In *Proceedings of NAACL*.

Marcos Zampieri, Shervin Malmasi, Nikola Ljubešić, Preslav Nakov, Ahmed Ali, Jörg Tiedemann, Yves Scherrer, and Noëmi Aepli. 2017. Findings of the VarDial Evaluation Campaign 2017. In *Proceedings of VarDial*.

Marcos Zampieri, Shervin Malmasi, Preslav Nakov, Ahmed Ali, Suwon Shon, James Glass, Yves Scherrer, Tanja Samardžić, Nikola Ljubešić, Jörg Tiedemann, Chris van der Lee, Stefan Grondelaers, Nelleke Oostdijk, Dirk Speelman, Antal van den Bosch, Ritesh Kumar, Bornini Lahiri, and Mayank Jain. 2018. Language identification and morphosyntactic tagging: The second VarDial evaluation campaign. In *Proceedings of VarDial*.

Marcos Zampieri, Liling Tan, Nikola Ljubešić, and Jörg Tiedemann. 2014. A Report on the DSL Shared Task 2014. In *Proceedings of VarDial*.

Marcos Zampieri, Liling Tan, Nikola Ljubešić, Jörg Tiedemann, and Preslav Nakov. 2015. Overview of the DSL Shared Task 2015. In *Proceedings of LT4VarDial*.

Improving Cuneiform Language Identification with BERT

Gabriel Bernier-Colborne, Cyril Goutte, Serge Léger
National Research Council Canada
{Gabriel.Bernier-Colborne, Cyril.Goutte, Serge.Leger}@nrc-cnrc.gc.ca

Abstract

We describe the systems developed by the National Research Council Canada for the Cuneiform Language Identification (CLI) shared task at the 2019 VarDial evaluation campaign. We compare a state-of-the-art baseline relying on character n-grams and a traditional statistical classifier, a voting ensemble of classifiers, and a deep learning approach using a Transformer network. We describe how these systems were trained, and analyze the impact of some preprocessing and model estimation decisions. The deep neural network achieved 77% accuracy on the test data, which turned out to be the best performance at the CLI evaluation, establishing a new state-of-the-art for cuneiform language identification.

1 Introduction

The goal of the Cuneiform Language Identification (CLI) shared task (Zampieri et al., 2019) was to predict the language or language variety of a short segment of text written using cuneiform symbols. These language varieties include Sumerian (SUX) and 6 different dialects of Akkadian: Old Babylonian (OLB), Middle Babylonian peripheral (MPB), Standard Babylonian (STB), Neo Babylonian (NEB), Late Babylonian (LTB), and Neo Assyrian (NEA). The dataset for the shared task was built from the Open Richly Annotated Cuneiform Corpus,[1] as described by Jauhiainen et al. (2019).

The NRC-CNRC team submitted 3 systems to the CLI shared task. The first one is a standard approach using Support Vector Machines (SVM) trained on character n-grams. The second one is an ensemble using plurality voting among several classifiers trained on different feature sets. This is essentially the approach that reached state-of-the-art on previous discriminating similar languages

[1][http://oracc.museum.upenn.edu]

(DSL) shared tasks (Goutte et al., 2014, 2016). Our last submission is a deep learning approach based on character embeddings and a Transformer network, similar to BERT (Devlin et al., 2018).

The following section quickly reviews related work. We then describe the dataset and data processing (Section 3) and the systems we built for the shared task (Section 4), before presenting the experimental results in Section 5.

2 Related Work

Jauhiainen et al. (2018c) provide a thorough survey of research on language identification. Regarding the state-of-the-art, they point out that "generally speaking, linear-kernel SVMs have been widely used for [language identification], with great success across a range of shared tasks" (Jauhiainen et al., 2018c). These SVMs usually exploit character n-grams as features.

Given that text segments in the CLI dataset (see Section 3) are often very short, it is worth noting that the character-level language model-based system of Jauhiainen et al. (2016) achieved state-of-the-art results on texts longer than 25 characters, according to an empirical comparison of 7 methods on 285 different language varieties (Jauhiainen et al., 2017). On shorter texts containing less than 20 characters, the method of Vatanen et al. (2010), using a naive Bayes classifier based on smoothed character n-gram probabilities, performed better.

Jauhiainen et al. (2018c) point out that the use of neural networks for language identification has increased since 2016, with varying success. Medvedeva et al. (2017) compared SVMs to a feed-forward neural network that takes as input the average embedding of the character n-grams in the text, trained using multi-task learning, and found that "traditional models, such as SVMs, per-

17

Proceedings of VarDial, pages 17–25
Minneapolis, MN, June 7, 2019 ©2019 Association for Computational Linguistics

form better on this task than deep learning techniques" (Medvedeva et al., 2017, p. 161). On the other hand, Ali (2018) used character-level CNNs and RNNs and obtained strong results at VarDial 2018 (Zampieri et al., 2018), including second place on 2 dialect identification tasks (for Arabic and German). To our knowledge, we are the first to apply the recently proposed BERT method (Devlin et al., 2018) to the language identification problem.

3 Data

As this was a closed task, the only data we used is the Cuneiform Language Identification dataset created for this task (Jauhiainen et al., 2019). The training set provided is unbalanced, the number of cases per class ranging from 3803 (OLB) to 53,673 (SUX). On the contrary, the development set is balanced, containing 668 cases for each class. See Table 1 for full statistics.

One challenging aspect of the data is that most of the text segments are very short. The segments in the training set contain only 7 characters on average. More than half of the segments contain 5 characters or less, and more than 10% contain a single character. On the tail end of the distribution, a dozen segments contain more than 64 characters, and only one contains more than 128 characters. Again, the dev set is significantly different, as all segments with less than 3 characters were filtered out.

Another challenging aspect of this data is the low frequency of many of the cuneiform symbols. The training data contains 550 unique characters. 39 of these only appear once, and 128 appear 10 times or less. If we look at the development set, we find that it contains 365 unique characters, and 3 of these are not found in the training data.

One other important property of the training data is that it contains many duplicates, both within classes and between classes. The training set contains 139,421 segments, but only 86,454 are unique. The most frequent segment appears 3223 times, in 6 of the 7 classes. The second most frequent appears 1460 times, always in the same class (LTB).[2]

We processed the training and development sets provided to create our own cross-validation folds. Before creating the folds, we applied a dedupli-

---

[2]Note that this means that almost 10% of the examples in the LTB class are the same text.

Class	# segments	
	raw	dedup
SUX	54,341	22,240
OLB	4,471	3,901
MPB	6,176	5,578
STB	18,485	16,327
NEB	10,375	8,595
LTB	16,615	8,665
NEA	33,634	26,614
Total	144,097	91,920

Table 1: Number of segments per class (train+dev), before (raw) and after (dedup) deduplication.

cation step to the combined training and development data using the following strategy: we kept only one instance of every (segment, label) pair; for segments belonging to all 7 classes, however, we only kept one labeled instance, where the label is the most frequent label for that segment. The resulting per-class statistics are provided in Table 1.

We then folded the deduplicated data (containing both the training and dev sets). Since the official development set was balanced, and we suspected the test set would be likewise, we created our folds such that the test set (and dev set) of each fold were balanced, containing $\frac{m}{k}$ (rounded to the nearest whole number) examples in each class, where m is the minimum class frequency in the combined training and development data, and k is the number of folds. With $k = 5$ and $m = 3901$, we obtained dev and test sets containing either 780 or 781 examples for each class. This is larger than the official development set, and thus the training sets are smaller than the official training set.

Note that during development of our deep learning approach, we decided to fully deduplicate the training data, keeping only the most frequent label for each segment.

The cross-validation folds were used as follows to train the models: parameters were estimated on the training part of each fold, the dev part was used for setting extra parameters, e.g. for classifier calibration (see Section 4), and the test part was used to provide an unbiased estimate of the resulting performance. Note that, as specifically encouraged by the shared task organizers, the final systems were retrained on the combined training and development sets.

4 Methods

In this section, we describe the systems that we developed for the CLI task.

4.1 SVM-based models

Our SVM-based models exploit a straightforward pipeline that provides a strong baseline for language identification. This pipeline has three stages:

1. n-gram extraction and counting

2. feature weighting

3. estimation of calibrated statistical classifiers

Extracting and counting character n-grams from cuneiform text is straightforward as there is no whitespace or punctuation requiring special pre-processing, e.g., tokenization. This is done for unigrams, bigrams, trigrams, 4-grams and 5-grams. Note that for segments smaller than the n-gram size, the full segment is retained regardless of its size: the trigram corresponding to a segment of length 3 will therefore appear in the 4-gram and 5-gram feature spaces. We apply a feature weighting scheme combining log term frequency, inverse document frequency and cosine normalization, a.k.a. `ltc` in the SMART weighting scheme.[3]

One binary SVM classifier is trained for each of the seven classes in one-vs-all manner, weighting the minority class examples according to the ratio of class sizes. We then calibrate each classifier in order to produce proper probabilities. This is done using isotonic regression (Zadrozny and Elkan, 2002), estimated on a left-out dev set. This allows the output of the 7 classifiers to be well-behaved probabilities that we can compare in order to predict the most probable class, or use in further post-processing in combination with other classifier's outputs. The best model, as estimated by cross-validation, used n-grams of length 1 to 4, which we denote later by `char[1-4]`.

Note that we also tried a two-stage approach similar to that of Goutte et al. (2014) using various class groupings (eg. Sumerian vs. Akkadian dialects), but this did not prove particularly helpful.

---

[3][https://en.wikipedia.org/wiki/SMART_Information_Retrieval_System]

4.1.1 Voting ensemble

Ensemble methods have proven quite successful on language identification (Malmasi and Dras, 2018) and other language classification tasks (Goutte and Léger, 2017). We therefore submitted a system that performs plurality voting among several classifiers. The base classifiers are obtained by training calibrated SVM classifiers, as described above, on various feature spaces combining n-grams of various lengths. We also trained probabilistic classifiers (similar to Naive Bayes) on the same feature spaces. Although the overall performance of the probabilistic classifiers was consistently lower than that of the SVMs, they provide a valuable addition to the ensemble because their prediction patterns are different from those of the SVMs.

The ensemble was built by adding base classifiers to the ensemble, in decreasing order of overall performance, as long as the estimated voting performance, using a cross-validation estimator, increases. For our submission, the resulting voting ensemble contains 15 base classifiers, among which 10 are SVM-based and 5 are probabilistic classifiers. That submission is referred to below as 'voting ensemble' or simply 'Ensemble' in tables.

4.2 BERT approach

Our second approach is a slightly modified version of the BERT model (Devlin et al., 2018).

We train a deep neural network which takes sequences of characters as input, using (partially) unsupervised pre-training, followed by supervised fine-tuning on the CLI training data. The network is composed of a stack of bidirectional Transformer modules (Vaswani et al., 2017) which encode the input sequence. The output of the encoder is fed to an output layer, which varies from one stage of training to the next.

First, we pre-train the model on unlabeled text using 2 pre-training tasks: a masked language model (MLM) and sentence pair classification (SPC).

The MLM pre-training task is exactly as described by Devlin et al. (2018). The goal of this task is to predict symbols chosen at random based on all the other symbols in the segment. Note that for this language identification task, the MLM pre-training task might be viewed as learning a *multi-language model*, that is a single model that can

"

predict characters based on context for all 7 of the cuneiform language varieties, and must therefore learn the specific markers of each variety.

As for the SPC pre-training task proposed by Devlin et al. (2018), we adapted it to account for the fact that the segments in the training data are not in sequential order and are not divided into documents. We therefore split the training data into 7 pseudo-documents corresponding to the 7 classes (different cuneiform language varieties), and the task is to predict whether 2 segments belong to the same class. This is a very simple adaptation, but it introduces a supervised signal into the pre-training task, as we use the CLI labels to split the data into pseudo-documents. Learning to predict whether 2 segments belong to the same language should be helpful to predict the language variety used in a specific text, when we fine-tune the model on this task later on.

Thus, the first phase of pre-training uses an output layer (or *head*) for both the MLM and SPC tasks. The first is a softmax over characters, which takes as input the encoding of a segment, where the characters to predict have been masked. The second is a binary softmax, which takes as input the joint encoding of 2 sentences, which we join together using a special symbol that indicates the boundary between 2 sentences.

This is followed by a second phase of pre-training where we include the unlabeled test data in the training data. Since we don't know the labels of the test data, it would not make sense to use the (modified) SPC task for pre-training, so we only use MLM, which is fully unsupervised with respect to the CLI task. We re-train the weights of the feature extractor (i.e. encoder) using a single head for MLM.

Once the model is fully pre-trained, we fine-tune it on the target task, i.e. to predict the language variety of each text, using the labeled training and dev data. For this, we use the feature extractor learned during the 2 phases of pre-training, and add a new head for language identification, which is simply a softmax over the 7 language varieties.

The vocabulary (or alphabet) is composed of every character in the Unicode range for cuneiform characters. Note that characters in the test data which were not in the training data can still be modeled to some extent because of the inclusion of the unlabeled test data during the second phase of pre-training.

Our hyperparameter settings largely resemble those used by Devlin et al. (2018) (for their smaller model):

- Nb Transformer layers: 12

- Nb attention heads: 12

- Hidden layer size: 768

- Feed forward/filter size: 3072

- Hidden activation: gelu

- Dropout probability: 0.1

- Max sequence length: 128

- Optimizer: Adam

- Learning rate for pre-training: 1e-4

- Batch size for pre-training: 64

- Training steps: 500K and 100K for pre-training (phases 1 and 2 respectively), and 20K for fine-tuning

- Warmup steps: 10K for both pre-training (phase 1 only) and fine-tuning

As for the fine-tuning stage, we do a small grid search, over the following hyperparameter settings:

- Batch size: {16, 32}

- Learning rate: {1e-5, 2e-5, 3e-5, 5e-5}

We did a few *ad hoc* tests on our own development set (using one of the folds we created for cross-validation) to assess the impact of deduplication and the various pre-training strategies (using SPC or not, doing a second phase where we include the test data), which is how we arrived at our final model. We also tuned the number of training steps for fine-tuning on this dev set. We will not present the results of these tests here, but will show the results of ablation tests we conducted on the official dev set in Section 5.3.

Note that our final model was fine-tuned on the combined training and dev set, which we fully deduplicated, by keeping only one instance of each text, along with its most frequent label. The unlabeled test set examples were also used during the second phase of pre-training.

Our code is available at `https://github.com/gbcolborne/lang_id`.

5 Results

We discuss the results of our official submissions in the following section. We also analyze the impact of various high-level modelling decisions, look at potential sources of errors, and conduct some ablation tests.

5.1 Test results

The scores of our 3 official submissions on the test set are shown in Table 2. Our best scores were achieved by the deep learning approach. This run was ranked first overall. Our voting ensemble would have been ranked 2nd, and our single SVM would have been ranked 3rd.

System	F1 (macro)	Accuracy
Jauhiainen (2019)	0.7206	-
char[1-4]	0.7414	0.7453
Ensemble	0.7449	0.7494
BERT	**0.7695**	**0.7711**

Table 2: Results of our 3 official runs on the CLI test set. For comparison, best F-score from (Jauhiainen et al., 2019)

The BERT model achieves an absolute gain of almost 2.5 F-score points over the voting ensemble. As for the voting ensemble, it produced an absolute gain of 0.35 F-score points over the best single SVM.

A detailed breakdown of our results on each of the 7 classes (languages) is presented in Table 3. These results show that the deep learning approach produces the best results on all but one of the classes, sometimes by quite a margin (e.g. OLB).

The 3 classes on which our scores are lowest are Standard Babylonian (STB), Neo Babylonian (NEB), and Neo Assyrian (NEA). As we can see in the confusion matrix for our best run, illustrated in Figure 1, the BERT model often confuses both NEB and STB texts as NEA, which may be partly due to the fact that NEA is the most frequent class in the deduplicated training data.

5.2 SVM performance anaysis

We relied on a cross-validation estimate described in Section 3 in order to guide several high-level decisions, as described in Section 4. Official shared task results (see Table 2), however, turned out to be significantly lower than the cross-validation estimate we based our decisions on. This raises the

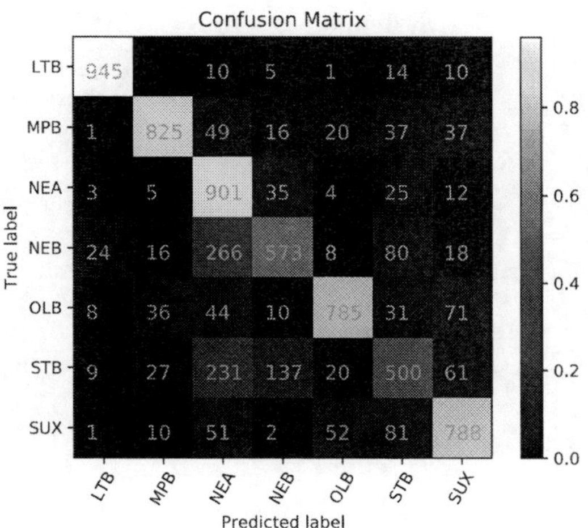

Figure 1: Confusion matrix for our best run (BERT) on the CLI test set.

question of how different the estimate would have been had we relied on the official dev set instead of full cross-validation, and whether this may have changed our decisions, for example with respect to which model to submit.

Another issue is the segment duplication mentioned in Section 3 as well as by Jauhiainen et al. (2019). Removing duplicated segments makes the training data more similar to the dev and test sets, however, it also greatly reduces the amount of segments available for training our models. We investigate this trade-off by re-training a few key models on the original training data, without performing any deduplication. For these comparisons, we use our best single model, char[1-4], the next best single model, char[1-3], and the voting ensemble.

Table 4 shows the results of these experiments. It turns out that the performance estimated by cross-validation is consistently 12–13 points higher than the performance estimated on the dev set. Note also that contrary to Jauhiainen et al. (2019), who report marginally better F-scores on the dev than on the test set, we obtained 3–4 points higher F-score on the final test set than on the dev set.

Comparing the results obtained on raw vs. deduplicated training data, we see that the cross-validation estimate is about 1 point higher when models are trained on the deduplicated data, but the difference on the dev is much smaller (0.06–0.22 points). For the voting ensemble, it turns out that dev performance is actually slightly better

System	LTB	MPB	NEA	NEB	OLB	STB	SUX
char[1-4]	0.9317	0.8296	**0.7402**	0.6317	0.7681	0.5345	0.7539
Ensemble	0.9339	0.8339	0.7336	0.6316	0.7774	0.5344	0.7692
BERT	**0.9565**	**0.8666**	0.7103	**0.6500**	**0.8373**	**0.5705**	**0.7952**

Table 3: Class-wise F-score of our 3 official runs on the CLI test set.

	CV		Dev	
System	raw	dedup	raw	dedup
Ensemble	0.8345	**0.8431**	**0.7114**	0.7092
char[1-3]	0.8226	0.8337	0.7055	0.7061
char[1-4]	0.8241	0.8347	0.7006	0.7026

Table 4: Impact of estimating model performance (macro F1) on the cross-validation (CV) estimator vs. dev set, and impact of deduplicating the training data on the resulting performance. char[1-N] are single SVM models trained on n-grams of length 1 to N.

when duplicates are not removed from the training data.

Finally, one concern is whether these differences would have an impact on model selection or high-level modelling choices. It turns out that according to dev set performance, the char[1-3] model is better than the char[1-4] model we submitted, by about half a point. It will be interesting to check whether this difference is matched on test performance, once reference labels are available.

5.3 BERT ablation tests

We carried out a few simple ablation tests on the BERT model, using the official development set for validation and testing. We split this dev set into two random subsets of equal size, which we will call *dev-A* and *dev-B*. One half was used to optimize the number of training epochs (i.e. to do early stopping), and the other half was used as a held out test set, to get an unbiased estimate of the accuracy of the model.

These tests were meant to assess the impact of:

- Using both MLM and SPC for pre-training (phase 1)

- Doing a second phase of pre-training (MLM only) on both the training and dev data

- Deduplicating the training data

We pre-trained 4 models on the official training set, one in the same manner as our official run, one

without SPC, one without deduplication, and one without SPC nor deduplication.

We then re-trained these 4 models on the combined training and dev sets (both halves). Only MLM was used (as we are using the dev set for evaluation, so we assume we don't have the dev labels). Deduplication was applied only for the models that were initially pre-trained on deduplicated data.

We then fine-tuned the 8 resulting models (4 with re-training, 4 without) on the labeled training set. Again, we use deduplicated training data for the models that were pre-trained on deduplicated data.

For each of the 8 fine-tuning configurations, we did 5 replications of the fine-tuning phase using different seeds for the random number generators, to assess the impact of random initialization (note that the random initialization only affects the output head since the models were pre-trained). This is estimated by computing the 95% confidence interval on the scores obtained on the 5 runs.

We did these 5 replications twice, first with dev-A as dev set and dev-B as test set, then the other way around. This would allow us to evaluate the stability of the evaluation metrics over different sets of validation and test instances, as well as the stability of the optimal number of training epochs. This procedure is sometimes referred to as estimating "split-half reliability". Note that our results on either half of the dev set are not exactly comparable to results on the full dev set.

For these ablation tests, we reduced the batch size for pre-training from 64 to 48, due to time constraints and limited access to GPUs. For fine-tuning, we used a learning rate of 1e-5 and a batch size of 32.

The results are shown in Table 5. These results show that the biggest gains were obtained by doing a second phase of pre-training (with MLM only) on both the training and test data. If we only do the first pre-training phase, we lose about 5 points of F-score (absolute). If we drop SPC for pre-training (and use only MLM for both pre-training

Dedup?	Pretraining	Retrain?	Score (dev-A)	Score (dev-B)
Yes	Complete	Yes	**0.789** $\pm$ 0.003	**0.794** $\pm$ 0.005
		No	0.738 $\pm$ 0.006	0.745 $\pm$ 0.005
	MLM only	Yes	0.751 $\pm$ 0.005	0.746 $\pm$ 0.005
		No	0.733 $\pm$ 0.006	0.727 $\pm$ 0.007
No	Complete	Yes	0.755 $\pm$ 0.005	0.772 $\pm$ 0.007
		No	0.732 $\pm$ 0.007	0.744 $\pm$ 0.008
	MLM only	Yes	0.727 $\pm$ 0.002	0.740 $\pm$ 0.003
		No	0.725 $\pm$ 0.004	0.730 $\pm$ 0.005

Table 5: BERT ablation test results: mean F1 (macro) with 95% confidence interval. *Retrain* means the 2nd phase of pre-training (MLM only), which includes the unlabeled dev and test data.

phases), we lose 4-5 points as well. And if we don't deduplicate the training data (and use both MLM and SPC for the initial pre-training), we lose 2-3 points.

It is important to note that if we optimized the other hyperparameters (notably the learning rate), the results we would achieve with these various training strategies would be different.

As for the number of training epochs, under the optimal training conditions (with dedup and full pre-training), the dev score peaked after only 1 or 2 epochs,[4] and this result was stable across both test sets (i.e. dev-A and dev-B), the optimal number of epochs being 1.2 ± 0.555 in one case and exactly 1.0 ± 0.0 in the other.

It would be interesting to see if the SVM-based model can reach the same accuracy as BERT if we adapt it to the test data, e.g. using self-training. The team ranked second on this CLI task used a form of self-training to adapt an SVM to the test data, and their F-score on the test set (0.7632) was not very far behind the score we achieved with BERT (0.7695). Furthermore, results of the German Dialect Identification and Indo-Aryan Language Identification tasks at Var-Dial 2018 (Zampieri et al., 2018) showed that the best results were obtained by systems that were adapted to the test data (Jauhiainen et al., 2018a,b).

5.4 Error analysis

Using the predictions of the BERT model on dev-A,[5] we analyzed the impact of text length on the error rate, as we suspected that the short length of the texts would be a major source of errors. This analysis showed that the error rate is around 32%

for the shortest texts in dev-A (length 3), and falls to 12% for texts containing 10 characters. 83% of all errors were made on texts containing 9 characters or less, 9.1 characters being the average length of the texts in dev-A.

We also looked at the impact of OOV characters, but this is not a significant source of errors, as only 3 texts in the official dev set contain a character that was not seen during training.

Finally, we checked if any of the texts in the official dev set were seen during training, and this was the case for 574 of 4676 texts. Of these 574 cases, we find 49 cases where the label in the dev set was not seen during training, and 6 additional cases where the training labels of a text contained not only the dev label, but others as well. Thus, we could say that label ambiguity (in other words, multiple class membership) was a source of errors for a little over 1% of texts in the dev set.

6 Conclusion

In this paper, we described the systems built by the NRC-CNRC team for the Cuneiform Language Identification shared task at the 2019 VarDial evaluation campaign. We adapted the BERT model to the language identification task, and compared this deep learning approach to statistical classifiers trained on character n-grams, which have long provided a strong baseline for language identification tasks. Our results using the BERT model surpass those obtained with an ensemble of classifiers trained on different feature sets comprising n-grams of varying lengths, achieving an absolute gain of about 2.5 F-score points on the test set, and establishing the state-of-the-art for cuneiform language identification. This is largely due to the ability to conduct unsupervised learning on the test set before making predictions, as well as the mod-

---

[4]This suggests we should try an even smaller learning rate.

[5]Results on dev-B are similar.

ified sentence pair classification task we use for pre-training.

For future work, it would be interesting to model the shape of cuneiform symbols, or their transliterations, in order to better capture similarities between symbols. We also plan on testing BERT on other language identification datasets. Finally, we plan on casting this problem as a multi-label classification problem, as we believe this could be a better approach for the CLI task, and related tasks on discriminating similar languages.

References

Mohamed Ali. 2018. Character level convolutional neural network for arabic dialect identification. In *Proceedings of the Fifth Workshop on NLP for Similar Languages, Varieties and Dialects (VarDial 2018)*, pages 122–127.

Jacob Devlin, Ming-Wei Chang, Kenton Lee, and Kristina Toutanova. 2018. BERT: pre-training of deep bidirectional transformers for language understanding. *CoRR*, abs/1810.04805.

Cyril Goutte and Serge Léger. 2017. Exploring optimal voting in native language identification. In *Proceedings of the 12th Workshop on Innovative Use of NLP for Building Educational Applications*, pages 367–373, Copenhagen, Denmark. Association for Computational Linguistics.

Cyril Goutte, Serge Léger, and Marine Carpuat. 2014. The NRC system for discriminating similar languages. In *Proceedings of the First Workshop on Applying NLP Tools to Similar Languages, Varieties and Dialects (VarDial)*, pages 139–145, Dublin, Ireland.

Cyril Goutte, Serge Léger, Shervin Malmasi, and Marcos Zampieri. 2016. Discriminating Similar Languages: Evaluations and Explorations. In *Proceedings of the Language Resources and Evaluation (LREC)*, Portoroz, Slovenia.

Tommi Jauhiainen, Heidi Jauhiainen, Tero Alstola, and Krister Lindén. 2019. Language and Dialect Identification of Cuneiform Texts. In *Proceedings of the Sixth Workshop on NLP for Similar Languages, Varieties and Dialects (VarDial)*.

Tommi Jauhiainen, Heidi Jauhiainen, and Krister Lindén. 2018a. HeLI-based experiments in Swiss German dialect identification. In *Proceedings of the Fifth Workshop on NLP for Similar Languages, Varieties and Dialects (VarDial 2018)*, pages 254–262.

Tommi Jauhiainen, Heidi Jauhiainen, and Krister Lindén. 2018b. Iterative language model adaptation for indo-aryan language identification. In *Proceedings of the Fifth Workshop on NLP for Similar Languages, Varieties and Dialects (VarDial 2018)*, pages 66–75.

Tommi Jauhiainen, Krister Lindén, and Heidi Jauhiainen. 2016. HeLI, a Word-Based Backoff Method for Language Identification. In *Proceedings of the Third Workshop on NLP for Similar Languages, Varieties and Dialects (VarDial3)*, pages 153–162, Osaka, Japan.

Tommi Jauhiainen, Krister Lindén, and Heidi Jauhiainen. 2017. Evaluation of language identification methods using 285 languages. In *Proceedings of the 21st Nordic Conference on Computational Linguistics*, pages 183–191. Association for Computational Linguistics.

Tommi Jauhiainen, Marco Lui, Marcos Zampieri, Timothy Baldwin, and Krister Lindén. 2018c. Automatic language identification in texts: A survey. *arXiv preprint arXiv:1804.08186*.

Shervin Malmasi and Mark Dras. 2018. Native language identification with classifier stacking and ensembles. *Computational Linguistics*, 44(3):403–446.

Maria Medvedeva, Martin Kroon, and Barbara Plank. 2017. When sparse traditional models outperform dense neural networks: the curious case of discriminating between similar languages. In *Proceedings of the Fourth Workshop on NLP for Similar Languages, Varieties and Dialects (VarDial)*, pages 156–163.

Ashish Vaswani, Noam Shazeer, Niki Parmar, Jakob Uszkoreit, Llion Jones, Aidan N Gomez, Łukasz Kaiser, and Illia Polosukhin. 2017. Attention is all you need. In *Advances in Neural Information Processing Systems*, pages 5998–6008.

Tommi Vatanen, Jaakko J Väyrynen, and Sami Virpioja. 2010. Language identification of short text segments with n-gram models. In *Proceedings of LREC*.

B. Zadrozny and C. Elkan. 2002. Transforming classifier scores into accurate multiclass probability estimates. In *Proceedings of the Eighth International Conference on Knowledge Discovery and Data Mining (KDD'02)*.

Marcos Zampieri, Shervin Malmasi, Preslav Nakov, Ahmed Ali, Suwon Shuon, James Glass, Yves Scherrer, Tanja Samardžić, Nikola Ljubešić, Jörg Tiedemann, Chris van der Lee, Stefan Grondelaers, Nelleke Oostdijk, Antal van den Bosch, Ritesh Kumar, Bornini Lahiri, and Mayank Jain. 2018. Language Identification and Morphosyntactic Tagging: The Second VarDial Evaluation Campaign. In *Proceedings of the Fifth Workshop on NLP for Similar Languages, Varieties and Dialects (VarDial)*, Santa Fe, USA.

Marcos Zampieri, Shervin Malmasi, Yves Scherrer, Tanja Samardžić, Francis Tyers, Miikka Silfverberg, Natalia Klyueva, Tung-Le Pan, Chu-Ren Huang, Radu Tudor Ionescu, Andrei Butnaru, and Tommi Jauhiainen. 2019. A Report on the Third VarDial

Evaluation Campaign. In *Proceedings of the Sixth Workshop on NLP for Similar Languages, Varieties and Dialects (VarDial)*. Association for Computational Linguistics.

Joint Approach to Deromanization of Code-mixed Texts

Rashed Rubby Riyadh and **Grzegorz Kondrak**
Department of Computing Science
University of Alberta, Edmonton, Canada
`{riyadh,gkondrak}@ualberta.ca`

Abstract

The conversion of romanized texts back to the native scripts is a challenging task because of the inconsistent romanization conventions and non-standard language use. This problem is compounded by code-mixing, i.e., using words from more than one language within the same discourse. In this paper, we propose a novel approach for handling these two problems together in a single system. Our approach combines three components: language identification, back-transliteration, and sequence prediction. The results of our experiments on Bengali and Hindi datasets establish the state of the art for the task of deromanization of code-mixed texts.

1 Introduction

Ad-hoc romanization is the practice of using the Roman script to express messages in languages that have their own native scripts (Figure 1). The phenomenon is observed in informal settings, such as social media, and is due to either unavailability of a native-script keyboard, or the writer's preference for using a Roman keyboard. Rather than following any predefined inter-script mappings, romanized texts typically constitute an idiosyncratic mixture of phonetic spelling, ad-hoc transliterations, and abbreviations. A great deal of information is lost in the romanization process due to the difficulty of representing native phonological distinctions in the Roman script. This makes *deromanization* of such messages a challenging task (Irvine et al., 2012).

Another phenomenon that further complicates the task of deromanization is *code-mixing*, which occurs when words from another language (typically English) are introduced in the messages (e.g., the word *decent* in Figure 1). Code-mixing is particularly common in multi-lingual areas such as South Asia (Bali et al., 2014). In many cases, the

(a)	tomake	to	decent	mone	hoyechilo
(b)	B	B	E	B	B
(c)	তোমাকে	তো	decent	মনে	হয়েছিল
(d)	"you"	"like"	"decent"	"in mind"	"was"
(e)			"you seemed a decent person"		

Figure 1: An example Bengali sentence that involves both romanization and code-mixing: (a) original message; (b) implied language tags; (c) target deromanization; (d) word-level translation; (e) sentence-level translation.

English words have no transliterated equivalents in the native language and script.

In this paper, we address the task of deromanization of code-mixed texts. This normalization process is necessary in order to take advantage of NLP resources and tools that are developed and trained on text corpora written in the standard form of the language, which in turn can facilitate tasks such as sentiment analysis and opinion mining in the social media. In addition, web-search queries are often expressed in a romanized form by speakers of languages that use non-Latin scripts, such as Arabic, Greek, and Hindi (Gupta et al., 2014b).

The task of deromanization of code-mixed texts is related to the study of language variation. Ad-hoc romanization represents a language variety, which resembles the usage of multiple scripts in some languages (e.g., Tajik). Code-mixing can also be considered a language variety, which exhibits similarities to dialects whose lexicons are strongly influenced by a different language (e.g., Upper Silesian).

The individual sub-tasks of deromanization of code-mixed texts have been investigated in prior work, but we are the first to incorporate them in a single system. Workshops and shared tasks have been devoted to code-mixing, including the prob-

Proceedings of VarDial, pages 26–34
Minneapolis, MN, June 7, 2019 ©2019 Association for Computational Linguistics

lem of word-level language identification (Chittaranjan et al., 2014; Choudhury et al., 2014). Transliteration and back-transliteration is a well-understood problem, which also has been the topic of several shared tasks (Duan et al., 2016; Chen et al., 2018). However, unlike romanization, transliteration is focused on names rather than dictionary words, and usually performed without considering the context of the word in a sentence. Finally, a number of papers address the deromanization of social media contents and informal texts, but propose no effective way of handling the code-mixing issue (Irvine et al., 2012; May et al., 2014). We show that this limitation leads to sub-optimal performance on deromanization.

In this paper, we propose a novel approach for tackling the problem of romanization and code-mixing together in a single system. Since sufficiently large annotated data sets for training an end-to-end approach are not available, we combine supervised models for the three main components of the complete task: (a) word-level language identification, (b) back-transliteration, and (c) word sequence prediction. These modules involve several diverse techniques, including neural networks, character-level and word-level language models, discriminative transduction, joint n-grams, and HMMs. We perform experiments on three datasets that represent two languages, including a new dataset that we have collected and annotated ourselves. The results show that our system is substantially more accurate than Google Translate, which is the only publicly available tool that can be applied to this task.

Our main contributions are: (1) a novel approach to deromanization of code-mixed texts through the combination of word-level language identification, back-transliteration, and sequence prediction; (2) a system that establishes the state of the art on the task; and (3) an annotated dataset of romanized Bengali messages. We make our code and data publicly available.[1]

2   Related Work

The tasks of deromanization and word-level language identification have been considered separately in the majority of the previous work.

---

[1] https://github.com/x3r/deromanization

2.1   Language Identification

While the identification of language of a monolingual document is a well studied problem, the task of word-level language identification has also garnered a fair amount of attention recently. A number of different approaches have been proposed for the task. Among the unsupervised approaches, dictionary-based and statistical language modeling approaches are the most common. Conditional Random Fields (CRF) and Support Vector Machines (SVMs) are among the most used supervised approaches.

The unsupervised approaches require no word-level annotation of mixed-code texts, but generally achieve low accuracy. Dictionary-based approaches make use of words and their frequencies in wordlists to determine the origin of a token (Barman et al., 2014; Das and Gambäck, 2014; Verulkar et al., 2015). However, those approaches cannot handle spelling variations and non-standard romanizations in code-mixed data. Statistical language modeling approaches employ n-gram probabilities which are derived from monolingual corpora. Both word and character n-grams have been used in the literature. The approach of Yu et al. (2013), which determines the probability of the next word being a code-switched word based on the previous n-words, achieves only 53% accuracy on the $Sinica$ (Mandarin-Taiwanese) corpus. A character n-gram based approach of Das and Gambäck (2014) achieves approximately 70% accuracy when tested on Bengali and Hindi.

The supervised approaches for language identification generally employ hand-crafted features such as capitalization information, character n-gram, and lexicon presence etc. CRFs make use of a set of features to determine the most probable language labels for a token sequence (King and Abney, 2013; Chittaranjan et al., 2014; Barman et al., 2014), and achieve accuracy in the low 90% on the evaluated languages. SVMs are also commonly employed for language classification (Barman et al., 2014) and achieve consistent performance (low 90%) on Bengali and Hindi. King and Abney (2013) employ Hidden Markov Models (HMM) trained using Expectation Maximization (EM) algorithm for the task, which can perform on par with the CRFs. Finally, supervised approaches that use contextual features generally outperform approaches that cannot utilize them.

2.2 Deromanization

Though a number of papers address the deromanization of social media contents and informal texts, they propose no effective way of handling the code-mixing issue.

Short Message Service (SMS) is a potential source of romanized texts due to the difficulty of typing in the native-script keyboard. A supervised deromanization approach of Irvine et al. (2012) uses an HMM to combine the candidates derived from a character-level transliteration model and a dictionary derived from automatically aligned words. The approach achieves 51% word-level accuracy on a self-annotated corpus of informal Urdu text messages.

Chakma and Das (2014) employ several supervised approaches for the automatic transliteration of code-mixed social media texts, which are based on joint source channel (JSC) and International Phonetic Alphabet (IPA). The experiments on Bengali-English and Hindi-English social media datasets show that the IPA-based approach outperforms the JSC-based approaches, achieving approximately 80% accuracy.

A supervised approach for converting Dialectical Arabic written in Latin script (Arabizi) to Arabic script of Al-Badrashiny et al. (2014) employs a character-level finite state transducer that generates transliteration candidates. A morphological analyzer is then used to filter the candidates and a language model to choose the output transliteration. The approach achieves 74% word-level transliteration accuracy on a Egyptian Arabizi SMS corpus.

A supervised approach of van der Wees et al. (2016) uses a character-based transliteration model which is incorporated as a component in the pipeline for an Arabizi-to-English phrase-based machine translation system. A contextual disambiguation with a character-level language model is then used for selecting between the transliteration candidates. When evaluated in the context of the NIST OpenMT evaluation campaign, the approach achieves 50% word-level accuracy on the Arabizi to Arabic deromanization.

Hellsten et al. (2017) propose a supervised approach for transliteration of romanized keyboard input to native scripts based on Weighted Finite State Transducers (WFST). The approach employs target word lists and pair language models constructed from the source and target alignments, and incorporates several weight pushing approaches for fast and memory-efficient decoding. The experiments are conducted on manually annotated Hindi and Tamil datasets and achieve 84% and 78% word-level accuracy, respectively. The approach was launched in the Google Gboard keyboard for 22 South Asian languages.

3 Methods

In this section, we present our approach for converting romanized code-mixed texts to their native scripts. It consists of three main components: language identification (Section 3.1), back-transliteration (Section 3.2), and sequence prediction (Section 3.3).

3.1 Language Identification

We approach language identification as a sequence labeling task, in which a sequence of word tokens in a code-mixed text is transformed into a sequence of the binary language tags (c.f., Figure 1b). Without loss of generality, we assume that one of the languages is English. Depending on the language label generated by this module, each input word is either fed into our back-transliteration module (Section 3.2) or copied unchanged to the final output.

Our supervised language identification module is based on the encoder-decoder model of Najafi et al. (2018).[2] On the language identification task, the encoder-decoder model achieves higher accuracy than a bi-directional Long Short Term Memory (LSTM) network with a CRF layer which is designed for sequence labeling tasks such as part-of-speech tagging (POS) and named entity recognition (NER) (Huang et al., 2015). This may be due to the nature of the language identification task, or the use of rich features in the encoder RNN.

The encoder takes character-level and word-level embedding of the input tokens as features in a bi-directional LSTM network over the input sequence. The outputs of bi-directional LSTM applied to characters of each word are concatenated and passed through a dropout layer to construct the character-level embedding. The capitalization pattern indicators (e.g. first letter is capital or all letters are capital) are then concatenated to these feature vectors. Pre-trained English word- and

---

[2]https://github.com/SaeedNajafi/ac-tagger

28

character-embeddings help the model identify English words in romanized texts. A fully-connected layer produces the final hidden vectors of the input sequence. The decoder's forward-LSTM generates output tokens incrementally from left-to-right; the output tokens are conditioned on the hidden vectors and the generated tokens from the previous steps. During the test phase, beam search is used to generate the outputs.

3.2 Back-Transliteration

Back-transliteration from romanized texts to the native scripts is difficult because there is generally only one correct way to render the romanized word to the native form (Knight and Graehl, 1998). We propose to overcome this problem by pooling the top-n predictions from three diverse transliteration systems: (a) Sequitur, a generative joint n-gram transducer; (b) DTLM, a discriminative string transducer; and (c) OpenNMT, a neural machine translation tool. In addition, we bolster the transliteration accuracy by leveraging target word lists, character language models, as well as synthetic training data, whenever possible. All of the generated candidate transliterations are then provided to the sequence prediction module, which is described in Section 3.3.

Sequitur (Bisani and Ney, 2008) is a data-driven transduction tool which derives a joint n-gram model from unaligned source-target data.[3] The model reflects the edit operations used in the conversion from source to target, and allows for the inclusion of source context in the generative model. Higher n-gram order models are trained iteratively from the lower order models. Sequitur was adopted as a baseline in the most recent NEWS shared task on transliteration (Chen et al., 2018).

DTLM is a new system that combines discriminative transduction with character and word language models (LM) derived from large unannotated corpora (Nicolai et al., 2018).[4] DTLM is an extension of DirecTL+ (Jiampojamarn et al., 2010). For target language modeling, which is particularly important in low-data scenarios, DirecTL+ uses binary n-gram features based exclusively on the forms in the parallel training data. This limitation often results in many ill-formed output candidates. DTLM avoids the error prop-

agation problem that is inherent in pipeline approaches by incorporating the LM feature sets directly into the transducer. The weights of the new features are learned jointly with the other features of DirecTL+.

In addition, the quality of transduction is bolstered by employing a novel alignment method, which is referred to as *precision alignment*.[5] The idea is to allow null substrings on the source side during the alignment of the training data, and then apply a separate aggregation algorithm to merge them with adjoining non-empty substrings. This method yields precise many-to-many alignment links that result in substantially higher transduction accuracy. DTLM was among the best-performing systems at the recent NEWS shared task on transliteration (Chen et al., 2018).

As our neural transliteration system, we adopt the PyTorch variant of the OpenNMT tool (Klein et al., 2017).[6] The system employs an encoder-decoder architecture with an attention mechanism on top of the decoder RNN. We insert word boundaries between all characters in the input and output, resulting in translation models which view characters as words and words as sentences. We apply the default translation architecture provided by OpenNMT with the exception of using a bidirectional-LSTM in the encoder model. We optionally generate additional synthetic training data for the neural system, using a simple romanization table that maps each native script character to a set of English letters.

3.3 Sequence Prediction

The transliteration systems process individual words in isolation, and thus fail to take into account the context of a word in a sentence. However, multiple native words may have the same romanized form, so the top-scoring prediction is often incorrect in the given context. To solve this problem, we propose a sequence prediction system that attempts to select the best prediction from the pooled candidate list using both the transliteration score and the word trigram language model score.

We frame the task as a Hidden Markov Model, where the romanized words are the observed states, and the words in their original scripts are the hidden states. The emission probabilities are

---

[3]https://github.com/sequitur-g2p/sequitur-g2p
[4]https://github.com/GarrettNicolai/DTLM
[5]https://github.com/GarrettNicolai/M2MP
[6]https://github.com/OpenNMT/OpenNMT-py

Task	Language	Train	Tune	Test
LI	Bengali	18660 †	2000 †	539 †
	Hindi	15980 †	1780 †	3287 †
TL	Bengali	12623 ‡	1000 ‡	363 †
	Hindi	11937 ‡	1000 ‡	2465 †

Table 1: The size of the datasets used in our experiments. The sets from the FIRE 2014 and NEWS 2018 shared tasks are marked with † and ‡, respectively.

Dataset	Bengali	English	Hindi	English
Train	48.0	52.0	46.2	53.8
Dev	87.1	12.9	-	-
Test	68.3	31.7	75.0	25.0

Table 2: The language balance in the code-mixed datasets (% of word tokens).

based on the prediction scores from the transliteration systems, which are normalized to represent valid probability distributions. The transition probabilities are based on the trigram probabilities from a word language model created with the *KenLM* language modeling tool.[7] The candidates and scores of all the systems are then concatenated together. If a transliteration candidate is generated by more than one system, the best prediction score among the systems is considered. Finally, the combined scores are normalized again.

We use a modified *Viterbi* decoder to determine the most likely transliteration sequence from the generated candidates. The scores are linearly combined to produce the score of a hidden sequence, $score(s)$. Due to the large number of n-grams and small number of transliteration candidates, the $score(s)$ is heavily skewed towards the emission scores. To mitigate this imbalance, we use exponent parameters p_t and p_e for the transition scores $T(s)$ and emission scores $E(s)$, respectively. These parameters are tuned on a development set. The scoring function is computed using the following formula:

$$score(s) = \max_k([\log T(s)]^{p_t} + [\log E(s)]^{p_e}) =$$

$$\max_k(\sum_{k=1}^{n}[\hat{T}(b_k|b_{k-1}b_{k-2})]^{p_t} + \sum_{k=1}^{n}[\hat{E}(e_k|b_k)]^{p_e})$$

where $\hat{T}$ represents the probability of transitioning from state b_{k-2} to state b_k, and $\hat{E}$ is the probability of observing e_k from state b_k.

Both generated transliteration candidates and foreign words in the code-mixed texts are sources of out-of-vocabulary (OOV) tokens. Prior to building the language model, we add a single UNK token to the corpus. During decoding, the identified English words and OOV transliterations are replaced with the UNK token. This results with OOV words being assigned very low prob-

abilities, biasing the sequence prediction module towards in-vocabulary words.

4 Data

In order to demonstrate the generality of our approach, we perform experiments on two languages: Bengali and Hindi. In addition to the datasets from the FIRE 2014 and NEWS 2018 shared tasks, we create our own annotated development set, and generate synthetic romanization data.

4.1 Code-mixed Data

The data for our language identification module is from the track on transliterated search of the FIRE 2014 shared task (Choudhury et al., 2014). The data consist of transliterated search queries, which include a substantial number of English words, as shown in Table 2. Search queries constitute a very different domain from social media messages that our system is designed for. In particular, they are rarely composed of complete sentences, which limits the ability of our sequence prediction module to take advantage of the word context.

We hold out approximately 10% of the original training data for tuning the hyper-parameters of our language identification module (Table 1). Since we have no access to the test sets of the shared task, we use the development sets as our test sets. These sets contain 100 Bengali and 500 Hindi search queries, respectively.

In order to mitigate the sparsity of annotated resources, we create our own Bengali development set. This allows us to develop and tune our system independently from the test sets. We collect romanized posts from several Facebook groups and pages, and manually deromanize them. Our development set contains 247 sentences and 1990 word tokens. The percentage of English word tokens in the development set is much smaller than in the FIRE 2014 datasets, as shown in Table 2.

---

[7]https://github.com/kpu/kenlm

System	Bengali		Hindi
	Dev	Test	Test
Majority baseline	87.1	68.3	75.0
Word-level ID	87.0	87.5	87.4
Bi-LSTM + CRF	92.4	90.9	93.2
Encoder-decoder	**95.2**	**92.2**	**95.3**

Table 3: Language identification accuracy (in %).

System	NEWS 2018 data		+ Annotated data	
	top-1	top-10	top-1	top-10
Sequitur	22.1	**58.7**	34.6	**69.3**
DTLM	29.1	43.9	40.5	61.5
NMT	**35.8**	52.1	**45.7**	63.4

Table 4: Impact of manually created transliteration data on the Bengali development set (in % word accuracy).

4.2 Transliteration Data

All back-transliteration systems are trained on the Bengali and Hindi datasets from the NEWS 2018 shared task (Chen et al., 2018). Their parameters are tuned on the corresponding development sets from the shared task. We create our back-transliteration test sets from the FIRE 2014 development sets by extracting romanized Bengali and Hindi word tokens together with their corresponding forms in the native scripts. As with the code-mixed data, the transliteration training and test sets are heterogeneous: the NEWS 2018 datasets contain mostly proper names, while the FIRE 2014 datasets contain mostly dictionary words.

We derive the character language models and target word lists for DTLM from publicly available unannotated monolingual corpora: Bengali Wikipedia[8], a Bengali news corpus[9], and a Hindi news corpus[10].

While no additional data is used for the Hindi models, we experiment with leveraging language-specific expertise to improve Bengali back-transliteration. First, since the training data contains mostly named entities, we augment it with manually-created transliterations of the most frequent 700 Bengali words from the news corpus. Second, since the performance of the neural system depends strongly on the amount of training data, we automatically generate romanizations for 50,000 Bengali words from Wikipedia.

The romanizations are generated with a context-free mapping from Bengali characters into Latin letters. As there are many ways to represent Bengali characters to Latin letters, and some Bengali characters have different representations based on their position in a word, we allow multiple mappings. For example, the Bengali character 'BO' is mapped to three English substrings: 'b', 'ba', and 'bo'. Each Bengali character is represented using on average 1.8, and maximum 3 Latin letters. (We

make our mapping publicly available.[11]) In order to estimate the quality of the mapping script, we applied it to the Bengali-English training dataset from the NEWS 2018 shared task, which yielded 21.7% word-level and 78.9% character-level accuracy.

5 Experiments

In this section, we present the results for each of the three tasks.

5.1 Setup

We tune all parameters, including the exponents p_t and p_s, of our sequence prediction module, on the Bengali development set, and apply them unchanged to both test sets. For the transliteration, we set the n-gram order of Sequitur to 6. We apply a grid-search to establish the parameters for the DTLM transducer and aligner. We set parameters of the OpenNMT system to the default settings.

For the sequence prediction, we use pre-trained Glove word-embeddings of 100 dimensions (Pennington et al., 2014), and derive the character-embedding of 32 dimensions from the training data. The training is accomplished with Adam optimizer (Kingma and Ba, 2014), dropout regularization, and batch size of 64.

5.2 Language Identification

We evaluate our encoder-decoder model against a strong general sequence tagging system (Huang et al., 2015). For this purpose, we adapt an implementation[12] of a CRF-based sequence tagging model on top of RNNs to the language identification task (Bi-LSTM + CRF). In addition, we compare to a word-level language identification system[13] based on word frequencies and character n-grams (Word-level ID). We also report the result

---

[8]https://bn.wikipedia.org/wiki/
[9]https://scdnlab.com/corpus/
[10]http://wortschatz.uni-leipzig.de/

[11]https://github.com/x3r/deromanization
[12]https://github.com/guillaumegenthial/tf_ner
[13]https://github.com/eginhard/word-level-language-id

System	Bengali		Hindi	
	top-1	top-10	top-1	top-10
Sequitur	42.0	**82.7**	**43.6**	**89.9**
DTLM	48.8	70.2	42.7	82.7
OpenNMT	**61.0**	81.7	41.1	80.4

Table 5: Back-transliteration accuracy on the test sets.

System	Bengali		Hindi
	Dev	Test	Test
Sequitur	47.6	51.0	49.2
Our system	**78.2**	**79.8**	**84.3**
w/o language ID	69.6	50.5	61.6
Google Translate	77.1	60.4	64.4

Table 6: The results on deromanization of code-mixed texts (in % word accuracy).

of a majority baseline which classifies every token as non-English.

The results are shown in Table 3. Our encoder-decoder achieves the highest accuracy on all sets, with the CRF system close behind. The lower results of the n-gram based approach highlight the issue of the ambiguity introduced through romanization. Because the gold tags for the FIRE 2014 test sets are not publicly available, we are unable to directly compare to the systems that participated in that shared task; the best reported results were 90.5% on Bengali (Banerjee et al., 2014) and 87.9% on Hindi (Gupta et al., 2014a).

5.3 Back-Transliteration

Table 4 shows the impact of enhancing the NEWS 2018 training data with manually-annotated dataset described in Section 4.2. The result is a substantial improvement in accuracy of all three back-transliteration systems. The synthetic data generated with our mapping script further boosts the top-1 accuracy of the OpenNMT system by 4.7%, but the impact on Sequitur and DTLM is negligible.

The results on the test sets are shown in Table 5. All three systems obtain similar top-1 results on Hindi. The neural system has the best top-1 accuracy on Bengali, which we attribute to the use of the synthetic data for training. However, Sequitur achieves the best accuracy among the top-10 predictions on both languages. The substantial discrepancy between the results on the Bengali development and test sets (Tables 4 and 5) are due to their different domains. The development set is curated from social media messages which contain a higher degree of spelling variation that reflects non-standard language use, while the test set consists of queries from search engine logs.

5.4 Sequence Prediction

We evaluate two variants of our system: the complete system that incorporates all three modules, and a restricted variant without language identification, which indiscriminately deromanizes ev-

ery input word. For the baseline, we concatenate the top-1 predictions of the Sequitur system. As we are unaware of another publicly-available system for deromanization of code-mixed texts, we compare to the output of Google Translate (Figure 2).[14]

The end results are presented in Table 6. Our complete system substantially outperforms Google Translate (GT) on both Bengali and Hindi test sets. Both GT and our restricted variant unconditionally deromanize all tokens regardless of their language origin. On average, 27% of errors made by GT on the test sets are due to deromanization of English words. GT outperforms our restricted variant, which we attribute to their vastly superior resources. These results highlight the importance of handling the code-mixing issue in the deromanization task.

For the reasons explained in Section 5.2, we are unable to directly compare to the systems that participated in the FIRE 2014 shared task. The best reported F-score results on the deromanization of transliterated search subtask were 7.3% for Bengali (Gupta et al., 2014a) and 30.4% for Hindi (Mukherjee et al., 2014). We attribute the superior results of our system to its ability to handle spelling variations found in romanized code-mixed texts.

5.5 Error Analysis

An example output of the proposed deromanization system is presented in Figure 3. The errors are marked in bold and red. Our system incorrectly classifies the words '1' and 'bar' as English. These errors can be attributed to the existence of words with the same spelling in English, as well as the presence of another English word 'only' in the context. Google Translate avoids making these er-

---

[14] Although Google Gboard performs word-level deromanization of a mobile keyboard input, it has no interface for automatically deromanizing large number of sentences.

Figure 2: Google Translate interface. The errors are highlighted in yellow.[15]

(a)	but	amdr	belay	only	1	bar
(b)	E	B	B	E	B	B
(c)	but	আমাদের	বেলায়	only	১	বার
(d)	"but"	"our"	"case"	"only"	"one"	"time"
(e)			"but only once in our case"			
(f)	but	আমার	বেলায়	only	1	bar

Figure 3: An example system error: (a) original message; (b) implied language tags; (c) gold output; (d) word-level translation; (e) complete translation; (f) our system output.

rors by always deromanizing all tokens; however, this indiscriminate approach also produces bewildering Bengali forms that reflect the pronunciation of English function words 'but' and 'only' (Figure 2). In addition, both systems make deromanization errors on 'amdr', which is a contracted form of the Bengali word 'amader'. This example illustrates the inherent difficulty of the task, and the importance of handling the code-mixing and deromanization together.

6 Conclusion

We have presented a joint approach for deromanization of code-mixed texts. The experiments on two languages show that our system achieves state-of-the-art results. In the future, we plan to apply our approach to other languages and scripts that involve both code-mixing and romanization.

References

Mohamed Al-Badrashiny, Ramy Eskander, Nizar Habash, and Owen Rambow. 2014. Automatic transliteration of romanized dialectal Arabic. In *Proceedings of the Eighteenth Conference on Computational Natural Language Learning*, pages 30–38.

Kalika Bali, Jatin Sharma, Monojit Choudhury, and Yogarshi Vyas. 2014. "I am borrowing ya mixing?" an analysis of English-Hindi code mixing in Facebook. In *Proceedings of the First Workshop on Computational Approaches to Code Switching*, pages 116–126.

Somnath Banerjee, Alapan Kuila, Aniruddha Roy, Sudip Kumar Naskar, Paolo Rosso, and Sivaji Bandyopadhyay. 2014. A hybrid approach for transliterated word-level language identification: Crf with post-processing heuristics. In *Proceedings of the Forum for Information Retrieval Evaluation*, pages 54–59. ACM.

Utsab Barman, Amitava Das, Joachim Wagner, and Jennifer Foster. 2014. Code mixing: A challenge for language identification in the language of social media. In *Proceedings of the first workshop on computational approaches to code switching*, pages 13–23.

Maximilian Bisani and Hermann Ney. 2008. Joint-sequence models for grapheme-to-phoneme conversion. *Speech communication*, 50(5):434–451.

Kunal Chakma and Amitava Das. 2014. Revisiting automatic transliteration problem for code-mixed romanized Indian social media text. *Social-India 2014*, 2014:42.

Nancy Chen, Xiangyu Duan, Min Zhang, Rafael E. Banchs, and Haizhou Li. 2018. News 2018 whitepaper. In *Proceedings of the Seventh Named Entities Workshop*, pages 47–54. Association for Computational Linguistics.

Gokul Chittaranjan, Yogarshi Vyas, Kalika Bali, and Monojit Choudhury. 2014. Word-level language identification using CRF: Code-switching shared task report of MSR India system. In *Proceedings of The First Workshop on Computational Approaches to Code Switching*, pages 73–79.

Monojit Choudhury, Gokul Chittaranjan, Parth Gupta, and Amitava Das. 2014. Overview of FIRE 2014 track on transliterated search. *Proceedings of FIRE*, pages 68–89.

Amitava Das and Björn Gambäck. 2014. Identifying languages at the word level in code-mixed Indian social media text. In *Proceedings of the 11th International Conference on Natural Language Processing*, pages 378–387. NLP Association of India.

---

[15]https://translate.google.com (accessed on Mar. 3, 2019)

Xiangyu Duan, Min Zhang, Haizhou Li, Rafael Banchs, and A Kumaran. 2016. Whitepaper of NEWS 2016 Shared Task on Machine Transliteration. In *Proceedings of the Sixth Named Entity Workshop*, pages 49–57.

Deepak Kumar Gupta, Shubham Kumar, and Asif Ekbal. 2014a. Machine learning approach for language identification & transliteration. In *Proceedings of the Forum for Information Retrieval Evaluation*, pages 60–64. ACM.

Parth Gupta, Kalika Bali, Rafael E Banchs, Monojit Choudhury, and Paolo Rosso. 2014b. Query expansion for mixed-script information retrieval. In *Proceedings of the 37th international ACM SIGIR conference on Research & development in information retrieval*, pages 677–686. ACM.

Lars Hellsten, Brian Roark, Prasoon Goyal, Cyril Allauzen, Françoise Beaufays, Tom Ouyang, Michael Riley, and David Rybach. 2017. Transliterated mobile keyboard input via weighted finite-state transducers. In *Proceedings of the 13th International Conference on Finite State Methods and Natural Language Processing (FSMNLP 2017)*, pages 10–19.

Zhiheng Huang, Wei Xu, and Kai Yu. 2015. Bidirectional LSTM-CRF models for sequence tagging. *arXiv preprint arXiv:1508.01991*.

Ann Irvine, Jonathan Weese, and Chris Callison-Burch. 2012. Processing informal, romanized Pakistani text messages. In *Proceedings of the Second Workshop on Language in Social Media*, pages 75–78. Association for Computational Linguistics.

Sittichai Jiampojamarn, Colin Cherry, and Grzegorz Kondrak. 2010. Integrating joint n-gram features into a discriminative training framework. In *Human Language Technologies: The 2010 Annual Conference of the North American Chapter of the Association for Computational Linguistics*, pages 697–700. Association for Computational Linguistics.

Ben King and Steven Abney. 2013. Labeling the languages of words in mixed-language documents using weakly supervised methods. In *Proceedings of the 2013 Conference of the North American Chapter of the Association for Computational Linguistics: Human Language Technologies*, pages 1110–1119.

Diederik P Kingma and Jimmy Ba. 2014. Adam: A method for stochastic optimization. *arXiv preprint arXiv:1412.6980*.

Guillaume Klein, Yoon Kim, Yuntian Deng, Jean Senellart, and Alexander Rush. 2017. OpenNMT: Open-source toolkit for neural machine translation. *Proceedings of ACL 2017, System Demonstrations*, pages 67–72.

Kevin Knight and Jonathan Graehl. 1998. Machine transliteration. *Computational linguistics*, 24(4):599–612.

Jonathan May, Yassine Benjira, and Abdessamad Echihabi. 2014. An Arabizi-English social media statistical machine translation system. In *Proceedings of the 11th Conference of the Association for Machine Translation in the Americas*, pages 329–341.

Abhinav Mukherjee, Anirudh Ravi, and Kaustav Datta. 2014. Mixed-script query labelling using supervised learning and ad hoc retrieval using sub word indexing. In *Proceedings of the Forum for Information Retrieval Evaluation*, pages 86–90. ACM.

Saeed Najafi, Colin Cherry, and Grzegorz Kondrak. 2018. Efficient sequence labeling with actor-critic training. *arXiv preprint arXiv:1810.00428*.

Garrett Nicolai, Saeed Najafi, and Grzegorz Kondrak. 2018. String transduction with target language models and insertion handling. In *Proceedings of the Fifteenth Workshop on Computational Research in Phonetics, Phonology, and Morphology*, pages 43–53.

Jeffrey Pennington, Richard Socher, and Christopher Manning. 2014. Glove: Global vectors for word representation. In *Proceedings of the 2014 conference on empirical methods in natural language processing (EMNLP)*, pages 1532–1543.

Abdul Rafae, Abdul Qayyum, Muhammad Moeenuddin, Asim Karim, Hassan Sajjad, and Faisal Kamiran. 2015. An unsupervised method for discovering lexical variations in Roman Urdu informal text. In *Proceedings of the 2015 Conference on Empirical Methods in Natural Language Processing*, pages 823–828.

Pallavi Verulkar, Rakesh Chandra Balabantray, and Rohit Arvind Chakrapani. 2015. Transliterated search of Hindi lyrics. *International Journal of Computer Applications*, 121(1).

Marlies van der Wees, Arianna Bisazza, and Christof Monz. 2016. A simple but effective approach to improve Arabizi-to-English statistical machine translation. In *Proceedings of the 2nd Workshop on Noisy User-generated Text (WNUT)*, pages 43–50.

Liang-Chih Yu, Wei-Cheng He, Wei-Nan Chien, and Yuen-Hsien Tseng. 2013. Identification of code-switched sentences and words using language modeling approaches. *Mathematical Problems in Engineering*, 2013.

Char-RNN for Word Stress Detection in East Slavic Languages

Maria Ponomareva
ABBYY
Moscow, Russia
maria.ponomareva@abbyy.com

Kirill Milintsevich
University of Tartu
Tartu, Estonia
kirill.milintsevich@ut.ee

Ekaterina Artemova
National Research University
Higher School of Economics
Moscow, Russia
echernyak@hse.ru

Abstract

We explore how well a sequence labeling approach, namely, recurrent neural network, is suited for the task of resource-poor and POS tagging free word stress detection in the Russian, Ukranian, Belarusian languages. We present new datasets, annotated with the word stress, for the three languages and compare several RNN models trained on three languages and explore possible applications of the transfer learning for the task. We show that it is possible to train a model in a cross-lingual setting and that using additional languages improves the quality of the results.

1 Introduction

It is impossible to describe Russian (and any other East Slavic) word stress with a set of hand-picked rules. While the stress can be fixed at a word base or ending along the whole paradigm, it can also change its position. The word stress detection task is important for text-to-speech solutions and word-level homonymy resolving. Moreover, stress detecting software is in demand among Russian learners.

One of the approaches to solving this problem is a dictionary-based system. It simply keeps all the wordforms and fails at OOV-words. The rule-based approach offers better results; however collecting the word stress patterns is a highly time consuming task. Also, the method cannot manage words without special morpheme markers. As shown in (Ponomareva et al., 2017), even simple deep learning methods easily outperform all the approaches described above.

In this paper we address the following research questions:

1. how well does the sequence labeling approach suit the word stress detection task?

2. among the investigated RNN-based architectures, what is the best one for the task?

3. can a word detection system be trained on one or a combination of languages and successfully used for another language?

To tackle these questions we:

1. compare the investigated RNN-based models for the word stress detection task on a standard dataset in Russian and select the best one;

2. create new data sets in Russian, Ukrainian and Belarusian and conduct a series of mono- and cross-lingual experiments to study the possibility of cross-lingual analysis.

The paper is structured as follows: we start with the description of the datasets created. Next, we present our major approach to the selection of neural network architecture. Finally, we discuss the results and related work.

2 Dataset

In this project, we approach the word stress detection problem for three East Slavic languages: Russian, Ukrainian and Belarusian, which are said to be mutually intelligible to some extent. Our preliminary experiments along with the results of (Ponomareva et al., 2017) show that using context, i.e., left and right words to the word under consideration, is of great help. Hence, such data sources as dictionaries, including Wiktionary, do not satisfy these requirements, because they provide

Proceedings of VarDial, pages 35–41
Minneapolis, MN, June 7, 2019 ©2019 Association for Computational Linguistics

only single words and do not provide context words.

To our knowledge, there are no corpora, annotated with word stress for Ukrainian and Belarusian, while there are available transcriptions from the speech subcorpus in Russian[1] of Russian National Corpus (RNC) (Grishina, 2003). Due to the lack of necessary corpora, we decided to create them manually.

The approach to data annotation is quite simple: we adopt texts from Universal Dependencies project and use provided tokenization and POS-tags, conduct simple filtering and use a crowdsourcing platform, Yandex.Toloka[2], for the actual annotation.

To be more precise, we took Russian, Ukrainian and Belarusian treebanks from Universal Dependencies project. We split each text from these treebanks in word trigrams and filtered out unnecessary trigrams, where center words correspond to NUM, PUNCT, and other non-word tokens. The next step is to create annotation tasks for the crowdsourcing platform. We formulate word stress annotation task as a multiple choice task: given a trigram, the annotator has to choose the word stress position in the central word by choosing one of the answer options. Each answer option is the central word, where one of the vowels is capitalized to highlight a possible word stress position. The example of an annotation task is provided in Fig. 1. Each task was solved by three annotators. As the task is not complicated, we decide to accept only those tasks where all three annotators would agree. Finally, we obtained three sets of trigrams for the Russian, Ukrainian and Belarusian languages of approximately the following sizes 20K, 10K, 3K correspondingly. The sizes of the resulting datasets are almost proportional to the initial corpora from the Universal Dependencies treebanks.

Due to the high quality of the Universal Dependencies treebanks and the languages being not confused, there are little intersections between the datasets, i.e., only around 50 words are shared between Ukranian and Belarusian datasets and between Russian and Ukranian and Belarusian datasets. The intersection between the Ukrainian and Russian datasets amounts around 200 words.

The structure of the dataset is straightforward: each entry consists of a word trigram and a number, which indicates the position of the word stress in the central word[3].

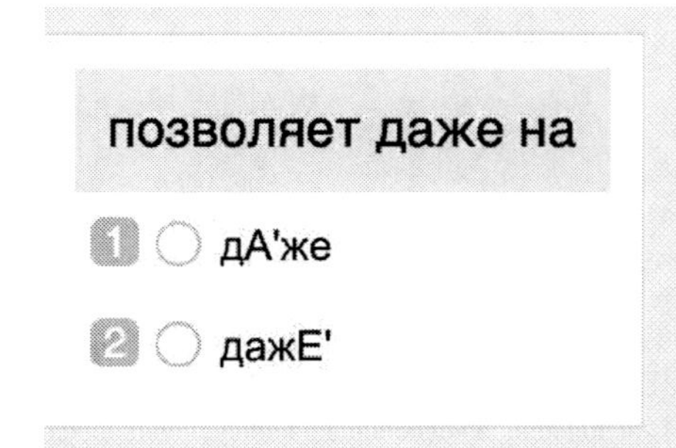

Figure 1: A screenshot of the word stress detection task from Yandex.Toloka crowdsourcing platform

3 Preprocessing

We followed a basic preprocessing strategy for all the datasets. First, we tokenize all the texts into words. Next, to take the previous and next word into account we define left and right contexts of the word as the last three characters of the previous word and last three characters of the next word. The word stresses (if any) are removed from context characters. If the previous / next word has less than three letters, we concatenate it with the current word (for example, "te_oblaká" [that-Pl.Nom cloud-Pl.Nom]). This definition of context is used since East Slavic endings are typically two-four letters long and derivational morphemes are usually located on the right periphery of the word.

Finally, each character is annotated with one of the two labels $\mathcal{L} = \{0, 1\}$: it is annotated with 0, if there is no stress, and with 1, if there should be a stress. An example of an input character string can be found in Table 1.

4 Model selection

We treat word stress detection as a sequence labeling task. Each character (or syllable) is

---

[1] Word stress in spoken texts database in Russian National Corpus [Baza dannykh aktsentologicheskoy razmetki ustnykh tekstov v sostave Natsional'nogo korpusa russkogo yazyka], http://www.ruscorpora.ru/en/search-spoken.html

[2] https://toloka.yandex.ru

[3] Datasets are avaialable at: https://github.com/MashaPo/russtressa

in	л а я	в о р о н а	т и т
out	0 0 0 0 0 0 0	1 0 0 0 0 0	0 0

Table 1: Character model input and output: each character is annotated with either 0, or 1. A trigram "белая ворона летит" ("white crow flies") is annotated. The central word remains unchanged, while its left and right contexts are reduced to the last three characters

labeled with one of the labels $\mathcal{L} = \{0, 1\}$, indicating no stress on the character (0) or a stress (1). Given a string $s = s_1, \ldots, s_n$ of characters, the task is to find the labels $Y^* = y_1^*, \ldots, y_n^*$, such that

$$Y^* = \arg \max_{Y \in \mathcal{L}^n} p(Y|s).$$

The most probable label is assigned to each character.

We compare two RNN-based models for the task of word stress detection (see Fig. 2 and Fig.3). Both models have a common input and hidden layers but differ in output layers.

The input of both models are embeddings of the characters. In both cases, we use bidirectional LSTM of 32 units as the hidden layer. Further, we describe the difference between the output layers of the two models.

4.1 Local model

The decision strategy of the local model (see Fig. 2) follows common language modeling and NER architectures (Ma and Hovy, 2016): all outputs are independent of each other. We decide, whether there should be a stress on each given symbol (or syllable) or not. To do this for each character we put an own dense layer with two units and a *softmax* activation function, applied to the corresponding hidden state of the recurrent layer, to label each input character (or syllable) with $\mathcal{L} = \{0, 1\}$.

4.2 Global model

The decision strategy of the global model (see Fig. 3) follows common encoder-decoder architectures (Sutskever et al., 2014). We use the hidden layer to encode the input sequence into a vector representation. Then, we use a dense layer of n units as a decoder to decode the representation of the input and to generate the desired sequence of $\{0, 1\}$. In comparison to the local model, in this case, we try to find the

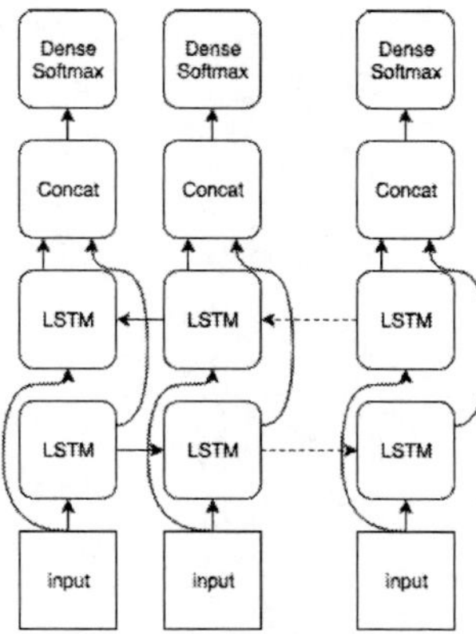

Figure 2: Local model for word stress detection

position of the stress instead of making a series of local decisions if there should be a stress on each character or not.

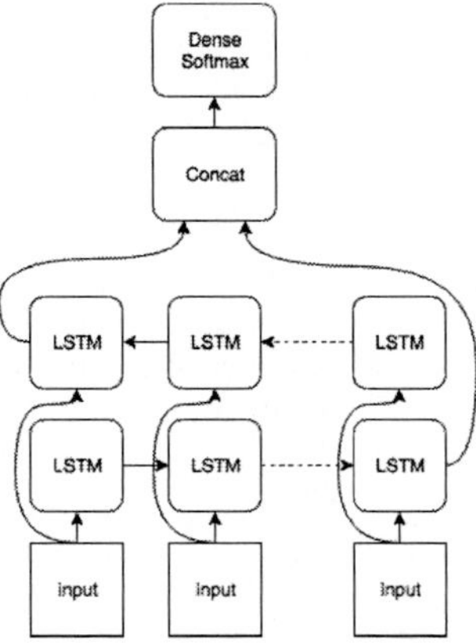

Figure 3: Global model for word stress detection

To test the approach and to compare these models, we train two models on the subcorpus of Russian National Corpus for Word stress in spoken texts, which appears to be a standard dataset for the task of word stress detection. This dataset was preprocessed according to our standard procedure, and the resulting dataset contains approximately around 1M trigrams. The results of cross-validation experiments, presented in Table 2, show that the global model outperforms significantly the local model. Hence, the global architecture is used further on in the next experiments.

We pay special attention to homographs: as one can see, in general, the quality of word stress detection is significantly lower on homographs than on regular words. However, in the majority of cases, we are still able to detect

# vowels	local	global
	all words	
2	961	983
3	940	977
4	947	976
5	960	977
6	958	973
7	924	955
8	866	923
9	809	979
avg	**952**	**979**
	homographs	
2	839	810
3	774	844
4	787	847
avg	821	819

Table 2: Accuracy scores × 1000 for two models

the word stress position for a homograph, most likely due to the understanding of the word context.

5 Experiments and results

In these series of experiments, we tried to check the following assumptions for various experiment settings:

1. monolingual setting: the presented above approach applies not only to the Russian language word stress detection but also to the other East Slavic languages

2. cross-lingual setting (1): it is possible to train a model on one language (e.g., Ukrainian) and test it on another language (e.g., Belarusian) and achieve results comparable to monolingual setting

3. cross-lingual setting (2): training on several languages (e.g., Russian and Ukrainian) will improve the results of testing on a single language (e.g., Russian) in comparison to the monolingual setting.

To conduct the experiments in these mono- and cross-lingual settings, we split the annotated datasets for Russian, Ukrainian and Belarusian randomly in the 7:3 train-test ratio and conducted 20 runs of training and testing with different random seeds. Afterward, the accuracy scores of all runs were averaged. The

Table 3 presents the results of these experiments.

	test dataset		
train dataset	Belarusian	Russian	Ukrainian
Belarusian	647	326	373
Russian	495	738	516
Ukrainian	556	553	683
Ukrainian, Belarusian	769	597	701
Russian, Belarusian	740	740	563
Russian, Ukrainian	627	756	700
Russian, Ukrainian, Belarusian	772	760	698

Table 3: Accuracy scores × 1000 for different train and test dataset combinations

The Table 3 shows, that:

1. in monolingual setting, we can get high-quality results. The scores are significantly lower than the scores of the same model on the standard dataset, due to the smaller sizes of the training datasets. Nevertheless, one can see, that our approach to word stress detection applies not only to the Russian language data, but also to the data in the Belarusian and Ukrainian languages;

2. cross-lingual setting (1): the Belarusian training dataset, being the smallest one among the three datasets, is not a good source for training word stress detection models in other languages, while the Ukrainian dataset stands out as a good source for training word stress detection systems both for the Russian and Belarusian languages;

3. cross-lingual setting (2): adding one or two datasets to the other languages improves the quality. For example, around 10% of accuracy is gained by adding the Russian training dataset to the Belarusian training dataset, while testing on Belarusian.

One possible reason for the difference of Belarusian from the other two languages can be the following. After the orthography reform in 1933, the cases of vowel reduction in the unstressed position (common phonetic feature for East Slavic languages) have been represented orthographically in the Belarusian language. However, the size of the Belarusian dataset (it is much smaller than the other two) may affect the quality as well.

6 Related Work

6.1 Char-RNN models

Several research groups have shown that character-level models are an efficient way to deal with unseen words in various NLP tasks, such as text classification (Joulin et al., 2017), named entity recognition (Ma and Hovy, 2016), POS-tagging (Santos and Zadrozny, 2014; Cotterell and Heigold, 2017), dependency parsing (Alberti et al., 2017) or machine translation (Chung et al.). The character-level model is a model which either treats the text as a sequence of characters without any tokenization or incorporates character-level information into word-level information. Character-level models can capture morphological patterns, such as prefixes and suffixes so that the model can define the POS-tag or NE class of an unknown word.

6.2 Word stress detection in East Slavic languages

Only a few authors touch upon the problem of automated word stress detection in Russian. Among them, one research project, in particular, is worth mentioning (Hall and Sproat, 2013). The authors restricted the task of stress detection to find the correct order within an array of stress assumptions where valid stress patterns were closer to the top of the list than the invalid ones. Then, the first stress assumption in the rearranged list was considered to be correct. The authors used the Maximum Entropy Ranking method to address this problem (Collins and Koo, 2005) and took character bi- and trigram, suffixes and prefixes of ranked words as features as well as suffixes and prefixes represented in an "abstract" form where most of the vowels and consonants were replaced with their phonetic class labels. The

study features the results obtained using the corpus of Russian wordforms generated based on Zaliznyak's Dictionary (approx. 2m wordforms). Testing the model on a randomly split train and test samples showed the accuracy of 0.987. According to the authors, they observed such a high accuracy because splitting the sample randomly during testing helped the algorithm benefit from the lexical information, i.e., different wordforms of the same lexical item often share the same stress position. The authors then tried to solve a more complicated problem and tested their solution on a small number of wordforms for which the paradigms were not included in the training sample. As a result, the accuracy of 0.839 was achieved. The evaluation technique that the authors propose is quite far from a real-life application which is the main disadvantage of their study. Usually, the solutions in the field of automated stress detection are applied to real texts where the frequency distribution of wordforms differs drastically from the one in a bag of words obtained from "unfolding" of all the items in a dictionary.

Also, another study (Reynolds and Tyers, 2015) describes the rule-based method of automated stress detection without the help of machine learning. The authors proposed a system of finite-state automata imitating the rules of Russian stress accentuation and formal grammar that partially solved stress ambiguity by applying syntactical restrictions. Thus, using all the above-mentioned solutions together with wordform frequency information, the authors achieved the accuracy of 0.962 on a relatively small hand-tagged Russian corpus (7689 tokens) that was not found to be generally available. We can treat the proposed method as a baseline for the automated word stress detection problem in Russian.

The global model, which is shown to be the best RNN-based architecture for this setting of the task, was first presented in (Ponomareva et al., 2017), where a simple bidirectional RNN with LSTM nodes was used to achieve the accuracy of 90% or higher. The authors experiment with two training datasets and show that using the data from an annotated corpus is much more efficient than using a dictionary since it allows to consider word frequencies and the morphological context of the word. We extend the approach of (Ponomareva et al., 2017) by training on new datasets from additional languages and conducting cross-lingual experiments.

6.3 Cross-lingual analysis

Cross-lingual analysis has received some attention in the NLP community, especially when applied in neural systems. Among a few research directions of cross-lingual analysis are multilingual word embeddings (Ammar et al., 2016; Hermann and Blunsom, 2013) and dialect identification systems (Malmasi et al., 2016; Al-Badrashiny et al., 2015). Traditional NLP tasks such as POS-tagging (Cotterell and Heigold, 2017), morphological reinflection (Kann et al., 2017) and dependency parsing (Guo et al., 2015) benefit from cross-lingual training too. Although the above-mentioned tasks are quite diverse, the undergirding philosophical motivation is similar: to approach a task on a low-resource language by using additional training data in a high-resource language or training a model on a high-resource language and fine-tune this model on a low-resource language with a probably lower learning rate.

7   Conclusion

In this project, we present a neural approach for word stress detection. We test the approach in several settings: first, we compare several neural architectures on a standard dataset for the Russian language and use the results of this experiment to select the architecture that provides the highest accuracy score. Next, we annotated the Universal Dependencies corpora for the Russian, Ukrainian and Belarusian languages with word stress using Yandex. Toloka crowdsourcing platform. The experiments conducted on these datasets consist of two parts: a) in the monolingual setting we train and test the model for word stress detection on the data sets separately; b) in the cross-lingual setting: we train the model on various combinations of the datasets and test on all three data sets. These experiments show that:

1. the proposed method for word stress detection is applicable or the Russian,

Ukrainian and Belarusian languages;

2. using an additional language for training most likely improves the quality of the results.

Future work should focus on both annotating new datasets for other languages that possess word stress phenomena and further development of cross-lingual neural models based on other sequence processing architectures, such as transformers.

References

Mohamed Al-Badrashiny, Heba Elfardy, and Mona Diab. 2015. Aida2: A hybrid approach for token and sentence level dialect identification in arabic. In Proceedings of the Nineteenth Conference on Computational Natural Language Learning, pages 42–51.

Chris Alberti, Daniel Andor, Ivan Bogatyy, Michael Collins, Dan Gillick, Lingpeng Kong, Terry Koo, Ji Ma, Mark Omernick, Slav Petrov, et al. 2017. Syntaxnet models for the conll 2017 shared task. arXiv preprint arXiv:1703.04929.

Waleed Ammar, George Mulcaire, Yulia Tsvetkov, Guillaume Lample, Chris Dyer, and Noah A Smith. 2016. Massively multilingual word embeddings. arXiv preprint arXiv:1602.01925.

Junyoung Chung, Kyunghyun Cho, and Yoshua Bengio. A character-level decoder without explicit segmentation for neural machine translation.

Michael Collins and Terry Koo. 2005. Discriminative reranking for natural language parsing. Computational Linguistics, 31:25–70.

Ryan Cotterell and Georg Heigold. 2017. Cross-lingual, character-level neural morphological tagging. arXiv preprint arXiv:1708.09157.

Elena B. Grishina. 2003. Spoken russian in russian national corpus. Russian National Corpus, 2005:94–110.

Jiang Guo, Wanxiang Che, David Yarowsky, Haifeng Wang, and Ting Liu. 2015. Cross-lingual dependency parsing based on distributed representations. In Proceedings of the 53rd Annual Meeting of the Association for Computational Linguistics and the 7th International Joint Conference on Natural Language Processing (Volume 1: Long Papers), volume 1, pages 1234–1244.

Keith Hall and Richard Sproat. 2013. Russian stress prediction using maximum entropy ranking. In Proceedings of the 2013 Conference on

Empirical Methods in Natural Language Processing, pages 879–883, Seattle, Washington, USA. Association for Computational Linguistics.

Karl Moritz Hermann and Phil Blunsom. 2013. Multilingual distributed representations without word alignment. arXiv preprint arXiv:1312.6173.

Armand Joulin, Edouard Grave, and Piotr Bojanowski Tomas Mikolov. 2017. Bag of tricks for efficient text classification. EACL 2017, page 427.

Katharina Kann, Ryan Cotterell, and Hinrich Schütze. 2017. One-shot neural cross-lingual transfer for paradigm completion. arXiv preprint arXiv:1704.00052.

Xuezhe Ma and Eduard Hovy. 2016. End-to-end sequence labeling via bi-directional lstm-cnns-crf. arXiv preprint arXiv:1603.01354.

Shervin Malmasi, Marcos Zampieri, Nikola Ljubešić, Preslav Nakov, Ahmed Ali, and Jörg Tiedemann. 2016. Discriminating between similar languages and arabic dialect identification: A report on the third dsl shared task. In Proceedings of the Third Workshop on NLP for Similar Languages, Varieties and Dialects (VarDial3), pages 1–14.

Maria Ponomareva, Kirill Milintsevich, Ekaterina Chernyak, and Anatoly Starostin. 2017. Automated word stress detection in russian. In Proceedings of the First Workshop on Subword and Character Level Models in NLP, pages 31–35.

Robert Reynolds and Francis Tyers. 2015. Automatic word stress annotation of russian unrestricted text. In Proceedings of the 20th Nordic Conference of Computational Linguistics (NODALIDA 2015), pages 173–180, Vilnius, Lithuania. Linköping University Electronic Press, Sweden.

Cicero D Santos and Bianca Zadrozny. 2014. Learning character-level representations for part-of-speech tagging. In Proceedings of the 31st International Conference on Machine Learning (ICML-14), pages 1818–1826.

Ilya Sutskever, Oriol Vinyals, and Quoc V Le. 2014. Sequence to sequence learning with neural networks. In Advances in neural information processing systems, pages 3104–3112.

Modeling Global Syntactic Variation in English
Using Dialect Classification

Jonathan Dunn
University of Canterbury
Department of Linguistics
`jonathan.dunn@canterbury.ac.nz`

Abstract

This paper evaluates global-scale dialect identification for 14 national varieties of English as a means for studying syntactic variation. The paper makes three main contributions: (i) introducing data-driven language mapping as a method for selecting the inventory of national varieties to include in the task; (ii) producing a large and dynamic set of syntactic features using grammar induction rather than focusing on a few hand-selected features such as function words; and (iii) comparing models across both web corpora and social media corpora in order to measure the robustness of syntactic variation across registers.

1 Syntactic Variation Around the World

This paper combines grammar induction (Dunn, 2018a, 2018b, 2019) and text classification (Joachims, 1998) to model syntactic variation across national varieties of English. This classification-based approach is situated within the task of dialect identification (Section 2) and evaluated against other baselines for the task (Sections 7 and 8). But the focus is modelling syntactic variation on a global-scale using corpus data. On the one hand, the problem is to use a model of syntactic preferences to predict an author's dialect membership (Dunn, 2018c). On the other hand, the problem is to take a spatially-generic grammar of English that is itself learned from raw text (c.f., Zeman, et al., 2017; Zeman, et al., 2018) and adapt that grammar using dialect identification as an optimization task: which constructions are more likely to occur in a specific regional variety?

Because we want a complete global-scale model, we first have to ask: how many national varieties of English are there? This question, considered in Sections 3 and 4, is essential for determining the inventory of regional varieties that need to be included in the dialect identification task. This

paper uses data-driven language mapping to find out where English is consistently used, given web data and Twitter data, in order to avoid the arbitrary selection of dialect areas. This is important for ensuring that each construction in the grammar receives the best regional weighting.

What syntactic features are needed to represent variation in English? As discussed in Section 6, this paper uses grammar induction on a large background corpus to provide a replicable and dynamic feature space in order to avoid arbitrary limitations (e.g., lists of function words). The other side of this problem is to optimize grammar induction for regional dialects by using an identification task to learn regional weights for each part of the grammar: how much does a single generic grammar of English vary across dialects? To what degree does it represent a single dominant dialect?

Finally, a corpus-based approach to variation is restricted to the specific domains or registers that are present in the corpus. To what degree is such a model of variation limited to a specific register? This paper uses both web-crawled corpora and social media corpora to explore the robustness of dialect models across domains (Section 8). Along these same lines, how robust is a model of syntactic variation to the presence of a few highly predictive features? This paper uses unmasking, a method from authorship verification (Koppel, et al., 2007), to evaluate the stability of dialect models over rounds of feature pruning (Section 9).

2 Previous Work

Because of its long history as a colonial language (Kachru, 1990), English is now used around the world by diverse national communities. In spite of the global character of English, dialectology and sociolinguistics continue to focus largely on sub-national dialects of En-

Proceedings of VarDial, pages 42–53
Minneapolis, MN, June 7, 2019 ©2019 Association for Computational Linguistics

glish within so-called *inner-circle* varieties (for example, Labov, et al., 2016; Strelluf, 2016; Schreier, 2016; Clark & Watson, 2016). This paper joins recent work in taking a global approach by using geo-referenced texts to represent national varieties (e.g., Dunn, 2018c; Tamaredo, 2018; Calle-Martin & Romero-Barranco, 2017; Szmrecsanyi, et al., 2016; Sanders, 2010, 2007; c.f., Davies & Fuchs, 2015). For example, this study of dialect classification contains *inner-circle* (Australia, Canada, United Kingdom, Ireland, New Zealand, United States), *outer-circle* (India, Malaysia, Nigeria, Philippines, Pakistan, South Africa), and *expanding-circle* (Switzerland, Portugual) varieties together in a single model.

The problem is that these more recent approaches, while they consider more varieties of English, have arbitrarily limited the scope of variation by focusing on a relatively small number of features (Grafmiller & Szmrecsanyi, 2018; Kruger & van Rooy, 2018; Schilk & Schaub, 2016; Collins, 2012). In practical terms, such work uses a smaller range of syntactic representations than comparable work in authorship analysis (c.f., Grieve, 2007; Hirst & Feiguina, 2007; Argamon & Koppel, 2013).

From a different perspective, we could view the modelling of dialectal variation as a classification task with the goal of predicting which dialect a sample belongs to. Previous work has draw on many representations that either directly or indirectly capture syntactic patterns (Gamallo, et al., 2016; Barbaresi, 2018; Kreutz & Daelemans, 2018; Kroon, et al., 2018). Given a search for the highest-performing approach, other work has shown that methods and features without a direct linguistic explanation can still achieve impressive accuracies (McNamee, 2016; Ionescu & Popescu, 2016; Belinkov & Glass, 2016; Ali, 2018).

On the other hand, there is a conceptual clash between potentially topic-based methods for dialect identification and other tasks that explicitly model place-specific language use. For example, text-based geo-location can use place-based topics to identify where a document is from (c.f., Wing & Baldridge, 2014; Hulden, et al., 2015; Lourentzou, et al., 2017). And, at the same time, place-based topics can be used for both characterizing the functions of a location (c.f., Adams & McKenzie, 2018; Adams, 2015) and disambiguating gazeteers (c.f., Ju, et al., 2016). This raises an

Region	CC	TW
Africa, North	123,859,000	85,552,000
Africa, Southern	59,075,000	87,348,000
Africa, Sub	424,753,000	254,200,000
America, Brazil	218,119,000	118,138,000
America, Cen.	886,610,000	383,812,000
America, North	236,590,000	350,125,000
America, South	1,163,008,000	402,150,000
Asia, Cen.	965,090,000	102,794,000
Asia, East	2,201,863,000	95,704,000
Asia, South	448,237,000	331,192,000
Asia, Southeast	2,011,067,000	245,181,000
Europe, East	4,553,101,000	322,460,000
Europe, Russia	101,444,000	105,045,000
Europe, West	2,422,855,000	823,807,000
Middle East	660,732,000	222,985,000
Oceania	164,025,000	213,064,000
TOTAL	**16.65 billion**	**4.14 billion**

Table 1: Background Corpus Size in Words by Region

important conceptual problem: when does predictive accuracy reflect *dialects* as opposed to either place-references or place-based content? While geo-referenced corpora capture both types of information, syntactic representations focus specifically on *linguistic* variation while place-references and place-based topics are part of document content rather than linguistic structure.

3   Where Is English Used?

The goal of this paper is to model syntactic variation across all major or robust varieties of English. But how do we know which varieties should be included? Rather than select some set of varieties based on convenience, we take a data-driven approach by collecting global web-crawled data and social media data to determine where English is used. This approach is biased towards developed countries with access to digital technologies. As shown in Table 1, however, enough global language data is available from both sources to determine where national varieties of English exist.

Data comes from two sources of digital texts: web pages from the Common Crawl[1] and social media from Twitter.[2] Both types of data have been used previously to study dialectal and spatial variation in language. More commonly, geo-referenced Twitter data has been taken to repre-

---

[1] http://commoncrawl.org
[2] http://twitter.com

sent language-use in specific places (e.g., Eisenstein, et al., 2010; Roller, et al., 2012; Kondor, et al., 2013; Mocanu, et al., 2013; Eisenstein, et al., 2014; Graham, et al., 2014; Donoso & Sanchez, 2017); regional variation in Twitter usage was also the subject of a shared task at PAN-17 (Rangel, et al., 2017). Web-crawled data has also been curated and prepared for the purpose of studying spatial variation (Goldhahn, et al., 2012; Davies & Fuchs, 2015), including the use of country-level domains for geo-referencing (Cook & Brinton, 2017). This paper builds on such previous work by systematically collecting geo-referenced data from both sources on a global scale. The full web corpus is available for download.[3]

For the Common Crawl data (abbreviated as CC), language samples are geo-located using country-specific top-level domains. The assumption is that a language sample from a web-site under the *.ca* domain originated from Canada (c.f., Cook & Brinton, 2017). This approach to regionalization does not assume that whoever produced that language sample was born in Canada or represents a traditional Canadian dialect group; rather, the assumption is only that the sample represents someone in Canada who is producing language data. Some countries are not available because their top-level domains are used for other purposes (i.e., *.ai, .fm, .io, .ly, .ag, .tv*). Domains that do not contain geographic information are also removed from consideration (e.g., *.com* sites). The Common Crawl dataset covers 2014 through the end of 2017, totalling 81.5 billion web pages. As shown in Table 1, after processing this produces a corpus of 16.65 billion words.

The basic procedure for processing the Common Crawl data is to look at text within paragraph tags: any document with at least 40 words within paragraph tags from a country-level domain is processed. Noise like navigational items, boilerplate text, and error messages is removed using heuristic searches and also using deduplication: any text that occurs multiple times on the same site or multiple times within the same month is removed. A second round of deduplication is used over the entire dataset to remove texts in the same language that occur in the same country. Its limited scope makes this final deduplication stage possible. For reproducibility, the code used for collecting and

processing the Common Crawl data is also made available.[4]

The use of country-level domains for geo-referencing raises two questions: First, are there many domains that are not available because they are not used or are used for non-geographic purposes? After removing irrelevant domains like *.tv*, the CC dataset covers 166 countries (30 of which are not included in the Twitter corpus) while the Twitter corpus covers 169 countries (33 of which are not included in the CC corpus). Thus, while the use of domains does remove some countries from consideration, the effect is limited. Second, does the amount of data for each country domain reflect the actual number of web pages from that country? In other words, some countries like the United States are less likely to use their top-level codes. However, the United States is still well-represented in the model. The bigger worry is that regional varieties from Africa or East Asia, both of which are under-represented in these datasets, might be missing from the model.

For the Twitter corpus, a spatial search is used to collect Tweets from within a 50km radius of 10k cities.[5] Such a search avoids biasing the selection by using language-specific keywords or hashtags. The Twitter data covers the period from May of 2017 until early 2019. This creates a corpus containing 1,066,038,000 Tweets. The language identification component, however, only provides reliable predictions for samples containing at least 50 characters. Thus, the corpus is pruned to include only those Tweets above that length threshold. As shown in Table 1, this produces a corpus containing 4.14 billion words with a global distribution. Language identification (LID) is important here because a failure to identify some regional varieties of English will ultimately bias the model. The LID system used is available for testing.[6] But given that the focus is a major language, English, the performance of LID is not a significant factor in the overall model of syntactic variation.

The datasets summarized in Table 1 include many languages other than English. The purpose is to provide background information about where robust varieties of English are found: where is

---

[3]https://labbcat.canterbury.ac.nz/download/?jonathandunn/CGLU_v3

[4]https://github.com/jonathandunn/common_crawl_corpus
[5]https://github.com/datasets/world-cities
[6]https://github.com/jonathandunn/idNet/

Country	CC	TW
South Africa	53,447,000	57,017,000
Nigeria	113,957,000	29,390,000
Canada	149,882,000	97,835,000
United States	42,890,000	220,947,000
India	71,219,000	80,038,000
Pakistan	140,190,000	34,044,000
Malaysia	198,566,000	18,296,000
Philippines	209,476,000	19,705,000
England	62,811,000	43,376,000
Ireland	43,975,000	46,045,000
Portugal	20,960,000	23,333,000
Switzerland	15,459,000	17,788,000
Australia	29,129,000	98,955,000
New Zealand	87,951,000	37,428,000
TOTAL	**1.23 billion**	**0.82 billion**

Table 2: English Varieties by Dataset in N. Words

	CC	TW
Training Samples	327,500	308,000
Testing Samples	66,500	64,000

Table 3: Samples by Function and Dataset

There are two African varieties, two south Asian varieties, two southeast Asian varieties, two native-speaker European varieties and two non-native-speaker European varieties. Taken together, these pairings provide a rich ground for experimentation. Are geographically closer varieties more linguistically similar? Is there an empirical reality to the distinction between inner-circle and outer-circle varieties (e.g., American English vs. Malaysian English)? The importance of this language-mapping approach is that it does not assume the inventory of regions.

5   Data Preparation and Division

The goal of this paper is to model syntactic variation using geo-referenced documents taken from web-crawled and social media corpora. Such geo-referenced documents represent language use *in* a particular place but, unlike traditional dialect surveys, there is no assurance that individual authors are native speakers *from* that place. We have to assume that most language samples from a given country represent the native English variety of that country. For example, many non-local residents live in Australia; we only have to assume that *most* speakers observed in Australia are locals.

In order to average out the influence of out-of-place samples, we use random aggregation to create samples of exactly 1,000 words in both corpora. For example, in the Twitter corpus this means that an average of 59 individual Tweets from a place are combined into a single sample. First, this has the effect of providing more constructions per sample, making the modeling task more approachable. Second and more importantly, individual out-of-place Tweets are reduced in importance because they are aggregated with other Tweets presumably produced by local speakers.

The datasets are formed into training, testing, and development sets as follows: First, 2k samples are used for development purposes regardless of the amount of data from a given regional variety. Depending on the size of each variety, at least 12k training and 2.5k testing samples are available. Because some varieties are represented by

English discovered when the search is not biased by looking only for English? On the one hand, some regions may be under-represented in these datasets; if national varieties are missing from a region, it could be (i) that there is no national variety of English or (ii) that there is not enough data available from that region. On the other hand, Table 1 shows that each region is relatively well-represented, providing confidence that we are not missing other important varieties.

4   How Many Varieties of English?

We take a simple threshold-based approach to the question of which regional varieties to include: any national variety that has at least 15 million words in both the Common Crawl and Twitter datasets is included in the attempt to model all global varieties of English. This threshold is chosen in order to ensure that sufficient training/testing/development samples are available for each variety. The inventory of national varieties in Table 2 is entirely data-driven and does not depend on distinctions like dialects vs. varieties, inner-circle vs. outer-circle, or native vs. non-native. Instead, the selection is empirical: any area with a large amount of observed English usage is assumed to represent a regional variety. Since the regions here are based on national boundaries, we call these national varieties. We could just as easily call them national dialects.

Nevertheless, the inventory (sorted by region) contains within it some important combinations.

much larger corpora (i.e., Tweets from American English), a maximum of 25k training samples and 5k testing samples are allowed per variety per register. This creates a corpus with 327,500 training and 66,500 testing samples (CC) and a corpus with 308,000 training and 64,000 testing samples (TW). As summarized in Table 3, these datasets contain significantly more observations than have been used in previous work (c.f., Dunn, 2018c).

6 Learning the Syntactic Feature Space

Past approaches to syntactic representation for this kind of task used part-of-speech n-grams (c.f., Hirst & Feiguina, 2007) or lists of function words (c.f., Argamon & Koppel, 2013) to indirectly represent grammatical patterns. Recent work (Dunn, 2018c), however, has introduced the use of a full-scale syntactic representations based on grammar induction (Dunn, 2017, 2018a, 2019) within the Construction Grammar paradigm (CxG: Langacker, 2008; Goldberg, 2006). The idea is that this provides a replicable syntactic representation.

A CxG, in particular, is useful for text classification tasks because it is organized around complex *constructions* that can be quantified using frequency. For example, the ditransitive construction in (1) is represented using a sequence of slot-constraints. Some of these slots have syntactic fillers (i.e., NOUN) and some have joint syntactic-semantic fillers (i.e., *V:transfer*). Any utterance, as in (2) or (3), that satisfies these slot-constraints counts as an example or instance of the construction. This provides a straight-forward quantification of a grammar as a one-hot encoding of construction frequencies.

(1) [NOUN – *V:transfer* – *N:animate* – NOUN]
(2) "He mailed Mary a letter."
(3) "She gave me a hand."

This paper compares two learned CxGs: first, the same grammar used in previous work (Dunn, 2018c); second, a new grammar learned with an added association-based transition extraction algorithm (Dunn, 2019). These are referred to as CxG-1 (the frequency-based grammar in Dunn, 2019) and CxG-2 (the association-based grammar), respectively. Both are learned from web-crawled corpora separate from the corpora used for modeling regional varieties (from Baroni, et al., 2009; Majliš & Žabokrtský, 2012; Benko,

Country	CxG-1 (CC)	CxG-2 (CC)
South Africa	+4.42%	+4.62%
Nigeria	-0.93%	-0.78%
Canada	+4.03%	+5.17%
United States	-0.98%	-1.90%
India	-3.15%	-10.38%
Pakistan	-4.76%	-17.25%
Malaysia	-3.39%	-11.51%
Philippines	-4.48%	-17.39%
England	+4.59%	+13.98%
Ireland	+4.26%	+18.62%
Portugal	-5.82%	-4.70%
Switzerland	+0.98%	+13.96%
Australia	+3.75%	+8.15%
New Zealand	+1.83%	-0.59%

Table 4: Relative Average Feature Density

2014; and the data provided for the CoNLL 2017 Shared Task: Ginter, et al., 2017). The exact datasets used are available.[7]

In both cases a large background corpus is used to represent syntactic constructions that are then quantified in samples from regional varieties. The grammar induction algorithm itself operates in folds, optimizing grammars against individual test sets and then aggregating these fold-specific grammars at the end. This creates, in effect, one large umbrella-grammar that potentially over-represents a regional dialect. From the perspective of the grammar, we can think of false positives (the umbrella-grammar contains constructions that a regional dialect does not use) and false negatives (the umbrella-grammar is missing constructions that are important to a regional dialect). For dialect identification as a task, only missing constructions will reduce prediction performance.

How well do CxG-1 and CxG-2 represent the corpora from each regional variety? While prediction accuracies are the ultimate evaluation, we can also look at the average frequency across all constructions for each national dialect. Because the samples are fixed in length, we would expect the same frequencies across all dialects. On the other hand, false positive constructions (which are contained in the umbrella-grammar but do not occur frequently in a national dialect) will reduce the overall feature density for that dialect. Because the

---

[7] https://labbcat.canterbury.ac.nz/download/?jonathandunn/CxG_Data_FixedSize

classification results do not directly evaluate false positive constructions, we investigate this in Table 4 using the average feature density: the total average frequency per sample, representing how many syntactic constructions from the umbrella-grammar are present in each regional dialect. This is adjusted to show differences from the average for each grammar (i.e., CxG-1 and CxG-2 are each calculated independently).

First, CxG-1 has a smaller range of feature densities, with the lowest variety (Portugal English) being only 10.41% different from the highest variety (UK English). This range is much higher for CxG-2, with a 36.01% difference between the lowest variety (Philippines English) and the highest variety (Irish English). One potential explanation for the difference is that CxG-2 is a better fit for the inner-circle dominated training data. This is a question for future work. For now, both grammars pattern together in a general sense: the highest feature density is found in UK English and varieties more similar to UK English (Ireland, Australia). The lowest density is found in under-represented varieties such as Portugal English or Philippines English. Any grammar-adaptation based on dialect identification will struggle to add unknown constructions from these varieties.

7 Modeling National Varieties

The main set of experiments uses a Linear Support Vector Machine (Joachims, 1998) to classify dialects using CxG features. Parameters are tuned using the development data. Given the general robust performance of SVMs in the literature relative to other similar classifiers on variation tasks (c.f., Dunn, et al., 2016), we forego a systematic evaluation of classifiers.

We start, in Table 5, with an evaluation of baselines by feature type and dataset. We have two general types of features: purely syntactic representations (CxG-1, CxG-2, Function words) and potentially topic-based features (unigrams, bigrams, trigrams). The highest performing feature on both datasets is simple lexical unigrams, at 30k dimensions. We use a hashing vectorizer to avoid a region-specific bias: the vectorizer does not need to be trained or initialized against a specific dataset so there is no chance that one of the varieties will be over-represented in determining which n-grams are included. But this has the side-effect of preventing the inspection of individual features. Vec-

Features	Prec.	Recall	F1
CxG-1 (CC)	0.80	0.80	0.80
CxG-1 (TW)	0.75	0.76	0.76
CxG-2 (CC)	0.96	0.96	0.96
CxG-2 (TW)	0.92	0.92	0.92
Funct. (CC)	0.65	0.65	0.65
Funct. (TW)	0.56	0.57	0.55
Unigrams (CC)	1.00	1.00	1.00
Unigrams (TW)	1.00	1.00	1.00
Bigrams (CC)	0.98	0.98	0.98
Bigrams (TW)	0.97	0.97	0.97
Trigrams (CC)	0.87	0.87	0.87
Trigrams (TW)	0.82	0.82	0.82

Table 5: Classification Performance By Feature Set

tors for all experiments are available, along with the trained models that depend on these vectors.[8]

As n increases, n-grams tend to represent structural rather than topical information. In this case, performance decreases as n increases. We suggest that this decrease provides an indication that the performance of unigrams is based on location-specific content (e.g., "Chicago" vs. "Singapore") rather than on purely linguistic lexical variation (e.g., "jeans" vs. "denim"). How do we differentiate between predictions based on place-names, those based on place-specific content, and those based on dialectal variation? That is a question for future work. For example, is it possible to identify and remove location-specific content terms? Here we focus instead on using syntactic representations that are not subject to such interference.

Within syntactic features, function words perform the worst on both datasets with F1s of 0.65 and 0.55. This is not surprising because function words in English do not represent syntactic structures directly; they are instead markers of the types of structures being used. CxG-1 comes next with F1s of 0.80 and 0.76, a significant improvement over the function-word baseline but not approaching unigrams. Note that the experiments using this same grammar in previous work (Dunn, 2018c) were applied to samples of 2k words each. Finally, CxG-2 performs the best, with F1s of 0.96 and 0.92, falling behind unigrams but rivaling bigrams and surpassing trigrams. Because of this, the more detailed experiments below focus only on the CxG-2 grammar.

---

[8] `https://labbcat.canterbury.ac.nz/download/?jonathandunn/VarDial_19`

Country	Prec. (CC)	Recall (CC)	F1 (CC)	Prec. (TW)	Recall (TW)	F1 (TW)
South Africa	0.94	0.96	0.95	0.92	0.94	0.93
Nigeria	0.98	0.98	0.98	0.94	0.95	0.94
Canada	0.94	0.94	0.94	0.84	0.79	0.81
United States	0.93	0.95	0.94	0.85	0.89	0.87
India	0.97	0.98	0.97	0.97	0.97	0.97
Pakistan	1.00	0.99	0.99	0.98	0.98	0.98
Malaysia	0.96	0.96	0.96	0.99	0.99	0.99
Philippines	0.98	0.97	0.98	0.98	0.98	0.98
England	0.95	0.95	0.95	0.87	0.90	0.89
Ireland	0.97	0.97	0.97	0.95	0.95	0.95
Portugual	0.99	0.98	0.98	0.93	0.90	0.92
Switzerland	0.97	0.94	0.96	0.98	0.97	0.97
Australia	0.97	0.96	0.97	0.82	0.83	0.83
New Zealand	0.91	0.92	0.91	0.92	0.90	0.91
W. AVG	**0.96**	**0.96**	**0.96**	**0.92**	**0.92**	**0.92**

Table 6: Within-Domain Classification Performance (CxG-2)

A closer look at both datasets by region for CxG-2 is given in Table 6. The two datasets (web-crawled and social media) present some interesting divergences. For example, Australian English is among the better performing varieties on the CC dataset (F1 = 0.97) but among the worst performing varieties on Twitter (F1 = 0.83). This is the case even though the variety we would assume would be most-often confused with Australian English (New Zealand English) has a stable F1 across domains (both are 0.91). An examination of the confusion matrix (not shown), reveals that errors between New Zealand and Australia are similar between datasets but that the performance of Australian English on Twitter data is reduced by confusion between Australian and Canadian English.

In Table 4 we saw that the umbrella-grammar (here, CxG-2) better represents inner-circle varieties, specifically UK English and more closely related varieties. This is probably an indication of the relative representation of the different varieties used to train the umbrella-grammar: grammar induction will implicitly model the variety it is exposed to. It is interesting, then, that less typical varieties like Pakistan English and Philippines English (which had lower feature densities) have higher F1s in the dialect identification task. On the one hand, the syntactic differences between these varieties and inner-circle varieties means that the umbrella-grammar misses some of their unique constructions. On the other hand, their greater syntactic difference makes these varieties easier to

identify: they are more distinct in syntactic terms even though they are less well represented.

Which varieties are the most similar syntactically given this model? One way to quantify similarity is using errors: which varieties are the most frequently confused? American and Canadian English have 221 misclassified samples (CC), while Canadian and UK English are only confused 36 times. This reflects an intuition that Canadian English is much more similar to American English than it is to UK English. New Zealand and Australian English have 101 misclassifications (again, on CC); but New Zealand and South African English have 266. This indicates that New Zealand English is more syntactically similar to South African English than to Australian English. However, more work on dialect similarity is needed to confirm these findings across different datasets.

8 Varieties on the Web and Social Media

How robust are models of syntactic variation across domains: in other words, does web-crawled data provide the same patterns as social media data? We conduct two types of experiments to evaluate this: First, we take dialect as a cross-domain phenomenon and train/test models on both datasets together, ignoring the difference between registers. Second, we evaluate models trained entirely on web-crawled data against testing data from social media (and vice-versa), evaluating a single model across registers. The point is to evaluate the impact of registers on syntactic variation:

Country	Prec. (CC)	Recall (CC)	F1 (CC)	Prec. (TW)	Recall (TW)	F1 (TW)
South Africa	0.88	0.06	0.10	0.68	0.31	0.43
Nigeria	0.43	0.84	0.57	0.73	0.41	0.52
Canada	0.48	0.14	0.22	0.49	0.27	0.35
United States	0.20	0.87	0.32	0.83	0.16	0.27
India	0.65	0.94	0.77	0.38	0.90	0.54
Pakistan	0.96	0.41	0.58	0.88	0.36	0.51
Malaysia	0.45	0.93	0.61	0.98	0.05	0.10
Philippines	0.73	0.61	0.66	0.87	0.22	0.35
England	0.89	0.01	0.03	0.48	0.44	0.46
Ireland	0.94	0.21	0.35	0.78	0.52	0.62
Portugal	0.02	0.00	0.00	0.22	0.17	0.19
Switzerland	0.92	0.04	0.07	0.12	0.80	0.20
Australia	0.89	0.00	0.00	0.33	0.66	0.44
New Zealand	0.27	0.53	0.36	0.64	0.40	0.49
W. AVG	**0.62**	**0.40**	**0.33**	**0.62**	**0.40**	**0.40**

Table 7: Cross-Domain Models, Trained on CC (Left) and Trained on TW (Right), CxG-2

Country	Prec.	Recall	F1
South Africa	0.91	0.92	0.92
Nigeria	0.94	0.95	0.95
Canada	0.87	0.84	0.85
United States	0.85	0.90	0.87
India	0.96	0.97	0.97
Pakistan	0.98	0.98	0.98
Malaysia	0.97	0.96	0.96
Philippines	0.97	0.97	0.97
England	0.87	0.90	0.89
Ireland	0.94	0.95	0.95
Portugal	0.94	0.90	0.92
Switzerland	0.96	0.93	0.95
Australia	0.87	0.86	0.87
New Zealand	0.89	0.87	0.88
W. AVG	**0.92**	**0.92**	**0.92**

Table 8: Single-Set Classification Performance

does Australian English have the same profile on both the web and on Twitter?

Starting with the register-agnostic experiments, Table 8 shows the classification performance if we lump all the samples into a single dataset (however, the same training and testing data division is still maintained). The overall F1 is the same as the Twitter-only results in Table 6. On the other hand, varieties like Australian English that performed poorly in Twitter perform somewhat better under these conditions. Furthermore, the observation made above that outer-circle varieties are more distinct remains true: the highest perform-ing varieties are the least proto-typical (i.e., Indian English and Philippines English).

But a single model does not perform well across the two datasets, as shown in Table 7. The model trained on Twitter data does perform somewhat better than its counterpart, but in both cases there is a significant drop in performance. On the one hand, this is not surprising given differences in the two registers: we expect some reduction in classi-fication performance across domains like this. For example, the unigram baseline suffers a similar re-duction to F1s of 0.49 (trained on CC) and 0.55 (trained on Twitter).

On the other hand, we would have more confi-dence in this model of syntactic variation if there was a smaller drop in accuracy. How can we bet-ter estimate grammars and variations in grammars across these different registers? Is it a problem of sampling different populations or is there a single population that is showing different linguistic be-haviours? These are questions for future work.

9 Unmasking Dialects

How robust are classification-based dialect models to a small number of highly predictive features? A high predictive accuracy may disguise a reliance on just a few syntactic variants. Within author-ship verification, unmasking has been used as a meta-classification technique to measure the depth of the difference between two text types (Koppel, et al., 2007). The technique uses a linear classifier to distinguish between two texts using chunks of

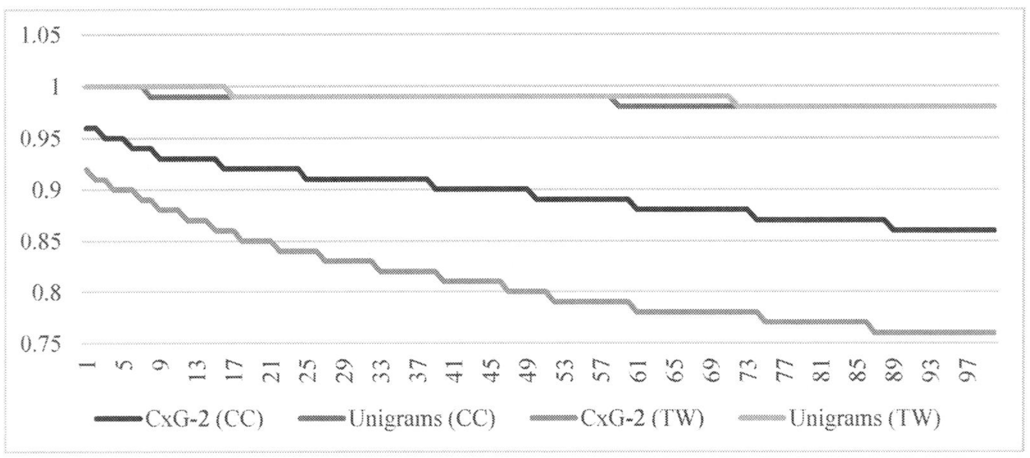

Figure 1: Performance Over 100 Rounds of Unmasking (F1)

the texts as samples. Here we distinguish between dialects with individual samples as chunks. After each round of classification, the most predictive features are removed. In this case, the highest positive and negative features for each regional dialect are removed for the next classification round. Figure 1 shows the unmasking curve over 100 rounds using the F1 score. Given that there are 14 regional dialects in the model, Figure 1 represents the removal of approximately 2,800 features.

For both datasets, the unigram baseline degrades less quickly than the syntactic model. On the one hand, it has significantly more features in total, so that there are more features to support the classification. On the other hand, given that the most predictive features are being removed, this shows that the lexical model has a deeper range of differences available to support classification than the syntactic model. Within the syntactic models, the classifier trained on web-crawled data degrades less quickly than the Twitter model and maintains a higher performance throughout.

This unmasking curve is simply a method for visualizing the robustness of a classification model. The syntactic model is less robust to unmasking than the lexical model. At the same time, we know that the syntactic model does not rely on place-names and place-based content and thus represents a more traditional linguistic approach to variation.

10   Discussion

This paper has used data-driven language mapping to select national dialects of English to be included

in a global dialect identification model. The main experiments have focused on a dynamic syntactic feature set, showing that it is possible to predict dialect membership within-domain with only a small loss of performance against lexical models. This work raises two remaining problems:

First, we know that location-specific content (i.e., place names, place references, national events) can be used for geo-location and text-based models of *place*. To what degree does a lexical approach capture linguistic variation (i.e., "pop" vs. "soda") and to what degree is it capturing non-linguistic information (i.e., "Melbourne" vs. "London")? This is an essential problem for dialect identification models. A purely syntactic model does not perform as well as a lexical model, but it does come with more guarantees.

Second, we have seen that inner-circle varieties have higher feature densities given the grammars used here. This implies that there are syntactic constructions in varieties like Philippines English that have not been modeled by the grammar induction component. While dialect identification can be used to optimize regional weights for *known* constructions, how can such *missing* constructions be adapted? This remains a challenge. While the less proto-typical dialects have higher F1s (i.e., Pakistan English), they also have lower feature densities. This indicates that some of their constructions are missing from the grammar. Nevertheless, this paper has shown that a broader syntactic feature space can be used to model the difference between many national varieties of English.

References

Adams, B. 2015. Finding Similar Places using the Observation-to-Generalization Place Model. *Journal of Geographical Systems*, 17(2): 137-156.

Adams, B. and McKenzie, G. 2018. Crowdsourcing the character of a place: Character-level convolutional networks for multilingual geographic text classification. *Transactions in GIS*, doi: 10.1111/tgis.12317.

Ali, M. 2018. Character Level Convolutional Neural Network for Arabic Dialect Identification. In *Proceedings of the Fifth Workshop on NLP for Similar Languages, Varieties and Dialects*, 122-127.

Argamon, S. and Koppel, M. 2013. A Systemic Functional Approach to Automated Authorship Analysis. *Journal of Law & Policy*, 12:299-315.

Barbaresi, A. 2018. Computationally efficient discrimination between language varieties with large feature vectors and regularized classifiers. In *Proceedings of the Fifth Workshop on NLP for Similar Languages, Varieties and Dialects*, 164-171.

Baroni, M., Bernardini, S., Ferraresi, A., and Zanchetta, E. 2009. The WaCky Wide Web: A Collection of Very Large Linguistically Processed Web-crawled Corpora. *Language Resources and Evaluation*, 43: 209-226.

Belinkov, Y. and Glass, J. 2016. A Character-level Convolutional Neural Network for Distinguishing Similar Languages and Dialects. In *Proceedings of the Third Workshop on NLP for Similar Languages, Varieties and Dialects*, 145-152.

Benko, V. 2014. Aranea: Yet Another Family of (Comparable) Web Corpora. In *Proceedings of Text, Speech and Dialogue. 17th International Conference*. 257-264.

Calle-Martin, J. and Romero-Barranco, J. 2017. Third person present tense markers in some varieties of English. *English World-Wide*, 38(1): 77-103.

Clark, L and Watson, K. 2016. Phonological leveling, diffusion, and divergence: /t/ lenition in Liverpool and its hinterland. *Language Variation and Change*, 28(1): 31-62.

Collins, P. 2012. Singular agreement in there-existentials: An intervarietal corpus-based study. *English World-Wide*, 33(1): 53-68.

Cook, P. and Brinton, J. 2017. Building and evaluating web corpora representing national varieties of English. *Language Resources and Evaluation*, 51.

Davies, M. and Fuchs, R. 2015. Expanding horizons in the study of World Englishes with the 1.9 billion word Global Web-based English Corpus (GloWbE). *English World-Wide*, 36(1): 1-28.

Donoso, G. and Sanchez, D. 2017. Dialectometric analysis of language variation in twitter. In *Proceedings of the 4th Workshop on NLP for Similar Languages, Varieties and Dialects*. 16-25.

Dunn, J. 2017. Computational Learning of Construction Grammars. *Language & Cognition*, 9(2): 254-292.

Dunn, J. 2018a. Modeling the Complexity and Descriptive Adequacy of Construction Grammars. In *Proceedings of the Society for Computation in Linguistics (SCiL 2018)*. Stroudsburg, PA: Association for Computational Linguistics. 81-90.

Dunn, J. 2018b. Multi-Unit Directional Measures of Association: Moving Beyond Pairs of Words. *International Journal of Corpus Linguistics*, 23(2): 183-215.

Dunn, J. 2018c. Finding Variants for Construction-Based Dialectometry: A Corpus-Based Approach to Regional CxGs. *Cognitive Linguistics*, 29(2): 275-311.

Dunn, J. 2019. Frequency vs. Association for Constraint Selection in Usage-Based Construction Grammar. In *Proceedings of the Workshop on Cognitive Modeling and Computational Linguistics*. Association for Computational Linguistics.

Dunn, J.; Argamon, S.; Rasooli, A.; and Kumar, G. 2016. Profile-based authorship analysis. *Literary and Linguistic Computing*, 31(4): 689-710.

Eisenstein, J.; O'Connor, B.; Smith, N.; and Xing, E. 2010. A latent variable model for geographic lexical variation. In *Proceedings of the Conference on Empirical Methods in Natural Language Processing*, 1,227-1,287.

Eisenstein, J.; O'Connor, B.; Smith, N.; and Xing, E. 2014. Diffusion of lexical change in social media. *PloSOne*, 10.1371.

Gamallo, P.; Pichel, J.; Algeria, I.; and Agirrezabal, M. 2016. Comparing two Basic Methods for Discriminating Between Similar Languages and Varieties. In *Proceedings of the Third Workshop on NLP for Similar Languages, Varieties and Dialects*, 170-177.

Ginter, F.; Hajiĉ, J.; Luotolahti, J. 2017. CoNLL 2017 Shared Task - Automatically Annotated Raw Texts and Word Embeddings, LINDAT/CLARIN digital library at the Institute of Formal and Applied Linguistics (ÃšFAL), Faculty of Mathematics and Physics, Charles University. http://hdl.handle.net/11234/1-1989.

Goldberg, A. 2006. *Constructions at Work: The Nature of Generalization in Language*. Oxford: Oxford University Press.

Goldhahn, d.; Eckart, T.; and Quasthoff, U. 2012. Building Large Monolingual Dictionaries at the

Leipzig Corpora Collection: From 100 to 200 Languages. In *Proceedings of the Conference on Language Resources and Evaluation.*

Grafmiller, J. & Szmrecsanyi, B. 2018. Mapping out particle placement in Englishes around the world: A study in comparative sociolinguistic analysis. *Language Variation and Change*, 30(3): 385-412.

Graham, S.; Hale, S.; and Gaffney, D. 2014. Where in the world are you? Geolocation and language identification on twitter. *The Professional Geographer*, 66(4).

Grieve, J. 2007. Quantitative Authorship attribution: an evaluation of techniques. *Literary and Linguistic Computing*, 22(3): 251–70.

Hirst, G. and Feiguina, O. 2007. Bigrams of syntactic labels for authorship discrimination of short texts. *Literary and Linguistic Computing*, 22(4): 405–17.

Hulden, M.; Silfverberg, M.; and Francom, J. 2015. Kernel Density Estimation for Text-Based Geolocation. In *Proceedings of the Twenty-Ninth AAAI Conference on Artificial Intelligence*, 145-150.

Ionescu, R. and Popescu, M. 2016. UnibucKernel: An Approach for Arabic Dialect Identification based on Multiple String Kernels. In *Proceedings of the Third Workshop on NLP for Similar Languages, Varieties and Dialects*, 135-144.

Joachims, T. 1998. Text categorization with support vector machines: Learning with many relevant features. In C. Nedellec (ed.), *Machine learning: ECML-98: 10th European Conference on Machine Learning*, 137-142. Berlin: Springer.

Ju, Y.; Adams, B.; Janowicz, K.; Hu, Y.; Yan, B.; and McKenzie, G. 2016. Things and Strings: Improving Place Name Disambiguation from Short Texts by Combining Entity Co-Occurrence with Topic Modeling. In *Proceedings of the 20th International Conference on Knowledge Engineering and Knowledge Management*. LNCS, vol. 10024. Springer, pp. 353-367.

Kachru, B. 1990 *The Alchemy of English: The spread, functions, and models of non-native Englishes.* Urbana-Champaign: University of Illinois Press.

Kondor, D.; Csabai, I.; Dobos, L.; Szule, J.; Barankai, N.; Hanyecz, T.; Sebok, T.; Kallus, Z.; and Vattay, G. 2013. Using robust PCA to estimate regional characteristics of language-use from geotagged twitter messages. In *Proceedings of IEEE 4th International Conference on Cognitive Infocommunications (CogInfoCom)*. 393-398.

Koppel, M., J. Schler, and E. Bonchek-Dokow. 2007. Measuring Differentiability: Unmasking Pseudonymous Authors. *Journal of Machine Learning Research*, 8: 1261-1276.

Kreutz, T. and Daelemans, W. 2018. Exploring Classifier Combinations for Language Variety Identification. In *Proceedings of the Fifth Workshop on NLP for Similar Languages, Varieties and Dialects*, 191-198.

Kroon, M.; Medvedeva, M.; and Plank, B. 2018. When Simple n-gram Models Outperform Syntactic Approaches: Discriminating between Dutch and Flemish. In *Proceedings of the Fifth Workshop on NLP for Similar Languages, Varieties and Dialects*, 244-25.

Kruger, H. and van Rooy, Bertus. 2018. Register variation in written contact varieties of English: A multidimensional analysis. *English World-Wide*, 39(2): 214-242.

Labov, W.; Fisher, S.; Gylfadottir, D.; and Henderson, A. 2016. Competing systems in Philadelphia phonology. *Language Variation and Change*, 28(3): 273-305.

Langacker, R. 2008. *Cognitive Grammar: A Basic Introduction.* Oxford: Oxford University Press.

Lourentzou, I.; Morales, A.; and Zhai, C. 2017. Text-based geolocation prediction of social media users with neural networks. In *Proceedings of 2017 IEEE International Conference on Big Data*, 696-705.

McNamee, P. 2016. Language and Dialect Discrimination Using Compression-Inspired Language Models. In *Proceedings of the Third Workshop on NLP for Similar Languages, Varieties and Dialects*, 195-203.

Mocanu, D.; Baronchelli, A.; Perra, N.; GonÃ§alves, B.; Zhang, Q. and Vespignani, A. 2013. The Twitter of Babel: Mapping world languages through microblogging platforms. *PLOSOne*, 10.1371.

Majlis, M. and Žabokrtský, Z. 2012. Language Richness of the Web. In *Proceedings of the International Conference on Language Resources and Evaluation (LREC 2012)*. https://ufal.mff.cuni.cz/w2c.

Rangel F., Rosso P., Potthast M., Stein B. 2017. Overview of the 5th Author Profiling Task at PAN 2017: Gender and Language Variety Identification in Twitter. In: Cappellato L., Ferro N., Goeuriot L, Mandl T. (eds.) *CLEF 2017 Labs and Workshops, Notebook Papers. CEUR Workshop Proceedings.* CEUR-WS.org, vol. 1866.

Roller, S.; Speriosu, M.; Rallapalli, S.; Wing, B.; and Baldridge, J. 2012. Supervised text-based geolocation using language models on an adaptive grid. In *Proceedings of the 2012 Joint Conference on Empirical Methods in Natural Language Processing and Computational Natural Language Learning*. 1,500-1,510.

Sanders, N. 2007. Measuring syntactic difference in British English. In *Proceedings of the 45th Annual Meeting of the ACL: Student Research Workshop*,1-6. Association for Computational Linguistics.

Sanders, N. 2010. *A statistical method for syntactic dialectometry.* Bloomington: Indiana. University dissertation.

Schilk, M. and Schaub, S. 2016. Noun phrase complexity across varieties of English: Focus on syntactic function and text type. *English World-Wide*, 37(1): 58-85.

Schreier, D. 2016. Super-leveling, fraying-out, internal restructuring: A century of present be concord in Tristan da Cunha English. *Language Variation and Change*, 28(2): 203-224.

Strelluf, C. 2016. Overlap among back vowels before /l/ in Kansas City. *Language Variation and Change*, 28(3): 379-407.

Szmrecsanyi, B.; Grafmiller, J.; Heller, B.; Rothlisberger, M. 2016. Around the world in three alternations: Modeling syntactic variation in varieties of English. *English World-Wide*, 37(2): 109-137.

Tamaredo, I. 2018. Pronoun omission in high-contact varieties of English: Complexity versus efficiency. *English World-Wide*, 39(1): 85-110.

Wing, B. and Baldridge, J. 2014. Hierarchical Discriminative Classification for Text-Based Geolocation. In *Proceedings of the Conference on Empirical Methods in NLP*, 336-348.

Zeman, D., et al. 2017. CoNLL 2017 Shared Task: Multilingual Parsing from Raw Text to Universal Dependencies. In *Proceedings of the Conference on Natural Language Learning*, 1-19.

Zeman, D., et al. 2018. CoNLL 2018 Shared Task: Multilingual Parsing from Raw Text to Universal Dependencies. In *Proceedings of the Conference on Natural Language Learning*, 1-21.

Language Discrimination and Transfer Learning for Similar Languages: Experiments with Feature Combinations and Adaptation

Nianheng Wu   **Eric DeMattos**   **Kwok Him So**   **Pin-zhen Chen**   **Çağrı Çöltekin**
University of Tübingen
Department of Linguistics
{nianheng.wu|eric.demattos|kwok-him.so|pinzhen.chen}@student.uni-tuebingen.de
ccoltekin@sfs.uni-tuebingen.de

Abstract

This paper describes the work done by team tearsofjoy participating in the VarDial 2019 Evaluation Campaign. We developed two systems based on Support Vector Machines: SVM with a flat combination of features and SVM ensembles. We participated in all language/dialect identification tasks, as well as the Moldavian vs. Romanian cross-dialect topic identification (MRC) task. Our team achieved first place in German Dialect identification (GDI) and MRC subtasks 2 and 3, second place in the simplified variant of Discriminating between Mainland and Taiwan variation of Mandarin Chinese (DMT) as well as Cuneiform Language Identification (CLI), and third and fifth place in DMT traditional and MRC subtask 1 respectively. In most cases, the SVM with a flat combination of features performed better than SVM ensembles. Besides describing the systems and the results obtained by them, we provide a tentative comparison between the feature combination methods, and present additional experiments with a method of adaptation to the test set, which may indicate potential pitfalls with some of the data sets.

1 Introduction

Language identification is a text classification task that has been studied extensively in the field of Natural Language Processing. The general concept and common implementations are described in the recent survey by Jauhiainen et al. (2018c). A more challenging task is discerning closely related languages or dialects of the same language. In recent years, the VarDial Evaluation Campaign has organized a multitude of shared tasks on classifying these with textual and spoken data (Malmasi et al., 2016; Zampieri et al., 2017, 2018). This year's VarDial evaluation campaign (Zampieri et al., 2019) featured one rerun (Swiss German di-

alect identification) and three new closely-related language identification tasks (Mainland vs. Taiwan varieties of Mandarin, Romanian vs. Moldavian, and cuneiform language identification, with the latter covering seven related languages within a wide historical time frame). Our focus has been German dialect identification (GDI) and discriminating between mainland and Taiwan varieties of Mandarin (DMT). However, we submitted predictions for all language identification tasks.

While closely-related languages (or dialects) pose a challenge for language identification, they also provide opportunities for cross-lingual transfer where available resource and tools in one language is adapted to another, similar language variety. This year's evaluation campaign also features two cross-lingual transfer tasks. Namely, cross-lingual morphological analysis (CMA), and cross-lingual topic identification between Romanian and Moldavian (MRC). The CMA is a substantially different task than language identification. However, the MRC subtasks on cross-lingual topic identification can be solved by the very same text classification models used for language identification. Hence, we also participated in the cross-lingual classification subtasks of the MRC.

Our base model is a linear support vector machine (SVM) classifier with sparse character and word n-gram features. These models have been found to be successful in earlier instances of VarDial language identification tasks; in fact, they were found to be more effective than more recent neural classifiers (Çöltekin and Rama, 2016; Clematide and Makarov, 2017; Medvedeva et al., 2017). A successful variation of these linear classifiers is an ensemble of classifiers with different n-gram orders used both for language discrimination (Malmasi and Zampieri, 2017b,a), and native language identification (Malmasi and Dras, 2018). Besides the simple, 'flat' concatenation of

Proceedings of VarDial, pages 54–63
Minneapolis, MN, June 7, 2019 ©2019 Association for Computational Linguistics

the overlapping n-gram features, we also used an ensemble approach in some of the tasks, providing a tentative comparison between these two related methods.

An interesting result of last year's VarDial evaluation campaign was SUKI team's success on Indo-Aryan language identification (Jauhiainen et al., 2018b) and GDI (Jauhiainen et al., 2018a) tasks with a rather large margin, which was likely because of the adaptation mechanism they used at prediction time. We adopted a similar adaptation approach to our SVM systems. Besides the curious difference in the GDI data set last year, the adaptation idea is also a good fit for the cross-lingual topic identification task (MRC).

The remainder of this paper introduces the tasks and data sets, describes our systems, and presents the results obtained followed by a brief discussion.

2 Tasks and Data

2.1 CLI: Cuneiform Language Identification

The provided datasets for Cuneiform Language Identification (Jauhiainen et al., 2019) consisted of a training set and a development set. The training data contained cuneiform texts written in Sumerian (SUX) and six Akkadian dialects: Old Babylonian (OLB), Middle Babylonian peripheral (MPB), Standard Babylonian (STB), Neo Babylonian (NEB), Late Babylonian (LTB), and Neo Assyrian (NEA). The data for the shared task contained only Unicode transcriptions of the documents without token boundaries or any other visual features. The data set exhibited a large class imbalance, ranging from 3 803 instances for Old Babylonian to 53 673 instances for Sumerian. The training data contained a total of 139 421 text samples, while the development set contained 668 lines for each language or dialect.

2.2 DMT: Discriminating between Mainland and Taiwan variation of Mandarin

The Discriminating between Mainland and Taiwan variation of Mandarin Chinese (DMT) task consisted of classifying sentences extracted from news articles into classes of two major Mandarin variations: *Putonghua* (Mainland China) and *Guoyu* (Taiwan). The task has two tracks: traditional and simplified.

In Mandarin Chinese, there are many mutually intelligible regional variations. *Putonghua* and *Guoyu* are more distinguishable in spoken language due to systematic phonetic differences, while they are more ambiguous in written text with no overt morphological, syntactic, and lexical preferences in language use, especially in formal text. It is considered challenging even for native speakers to distinguish between them, and since the shared task data offered only textual information with no phonetic transcription, it was particularly interesting to explore possible solutions to the problem.

In contemporary written Chinese, there are two scripts: traditional and simplified. The only distinction between the two writing systems is the visual form of the characters. As the name suggests, characters in simplified Chinese usually appear simpler than their traditional counterparts, while some are identical which may lead to performance variations based on different system designs. A text in traditional Chinese can always be transformed verbatim into its simplified counterpart without any content change and vice versa. Two corpora, one using traditional script and one simplified, were provided to investigate the performance of the discrimination task on the two different scripts, which will be further discussed in Section 5.

The DMT data comes from the news domain for both varieties. The datasets contained a training and development set for both simplified Chinese (McEnery and Xiao, 2003) and traditional Chinese (Chen et al., 1996). The training set consisted of 18 770 samples for both Chinese varieties, whereas the development set contained 2 000 samples each. The texts contained no punctuation and were (automatically) segmented by the task organizers.

2.3 GDI: German Dialect Identification

As in previous years, the GDI data set is based on the corpus introduced in Samardžić et al. (2016), consisting of samples from four regions around Bern (BE), Basel (BS), Lucerne (LU) and Zurich (ZH). Besides transcriptions of the audio recordings, we were also provided with 400-dimensional i-vectors representing the acoustic features of each sample, and automatically obtained normalization data where words are paired with their standard German spelling. In our submissions, we used the text transcripts and i-vectors.

There were 14 279 training and 4 530 development instances. Both training and development sets included a fair amount of class imbalance.

2.4 MRC: Moldavian vs. Romanian Cross-dialect Topic identification

The MRC task involved discrimination between two closely written language varieties, Romanian and Moldavian, and cross-variety topic classification. The first subtask was a binary classification problem, discriminating between the two language varieties. The second and third tasks required classifying the documents in one variety using training data from the other variety into six topics: culture, finance, politics, science, sports and technology. The second subtask used Moldavian as the source language and Romanian as the target language in the transfer task. Task 3 had the same setup, but the source and target languages were swapped. Topic classification tasks are formulated as multi-class problems (in contrast to multi-label classification common in the field), where each text is assigned to only one class. Named entities in the data set were anonymized.

The training data for subtask 1 consisted of 21 701 texts with a slight class imbalance (11 740 Romanian, 9 961 Moldavian), with a development set of 11 834 instances approximately following the same class distribution. Training sets for subtasks 1 and 2 included 9 961 and 11 740 texts, and development sets included 5 432 and 6 402 texts, respectively. All subtasks shared a test set of 5 918 texts, although subtasks 2 and 3 were evaluated on subsets of the test set. Further information on the data can be found in Butnaru and Ionescu (2019).

3 Methods and experimental setting

Our main submissions were based on two SVM systems that differ in the way they combine the n-gram features: SVM with flat feature combinations and SVM ensembles. We employed both character and word n-gram features. Depending on the task, the character n-grams varied between 1 to 9 and the word n-grams varied from 1 to 3. The features were weighted with either tf-idf or BM25 (Robertson et al., 2009) weighting schemes. The flat combination is similar to Çöltekin and Rama (2016) and the ensemble approach is similar to Malmasi and Dras (2015). Both methods were implemented in Python using the scikit-learn library (Pedregosa et al., 2011).

We also experimented with recurrent neural classifiers and considered a system similar to HeLi

(Jauhiainen et al., 2016), which was also used in earlier VarDial evaluation campaigns. However, we only submitted results with the SVM classifiers described in more detail below, and we will limit our discussion to the results obtained by the SVM classifiers.

3.1 SVM with flat combinations of features

For all tasks, we submitted predictions generated by SVM classifiers where a range of overlapping character and word n-grams are combined into a single feature matrix. The features are weighted using BM25, although a plain tf-idf weighing scheme produced similar results on the development set. In all tasks, we optimized the model hyperparameters through random search, using 5-fold cross validation on combined training and development sets. Random search was stopped after approximately 1 000 draws from the space of random parameters, and picking the best average F1-score over the 5 folds. This is simply the same approach taken in a series of earlier VarDial evaluation campaigns (Çöltekin and Rama, 2016; Rama and Çöltekin, 2017; Çöltekin and Rama, 2017; Çöltekin et al., 2018).

Following the adaptation idea used by Jauhiainen et al. (2018a,b) in last year's VarDial evaluation campaign, we also employed an adaptation approach in some of the tasks. At test time, we produced a set of first-level predictions based on the best model tuned for the task on the training/development set, and retrained the model after adding the predictions with high-confidence to the training set. In our case, predictions with high-confidence means the test instances that are farther than a threshold — in this case, 0.50 — from the decision boundary for binary classification, and the instances that are claimed by only one of the one-vs-rest classifiers for the multi-class problems. Intuitively, this is useful for the adaptation subtasks of MRC, and in case the distribution of the test instances diverge from the distribution in the training/development sets.

All tasks we participated in involved text classification. However, the GDI data set also included features extracted from audio samples (i-vectors), as well as normalized spellings of the dialectal words. We did not make use of the normalized spellings, however in our GDI contribution, we used audio features by simply concatenating the i-vectors with the n-gram vectors weighted by BM25, before feeding them to the SVM classifiers. As SVMs are sensitive to the scale of the data, we introduced a weight parameter and searched for its optimum value during tuning.

3.2 SVM ensembles

SVM ensembles are generally considered more robust than single classifiers (Oza and Tumer, 2008). An ensemble system makes use of decisions from multiple classifiers on every input entity. The decisions are congregated through a fusion method, re-evaluated, and a final decision is made. There are various fusion methods (Malmasi and Dras, 2015), but the one we chose was *mean probability rule*, an approach that is considered stable and simple (Kuncheva, 2004) as well as resistant to estimation errors (Kittler, 1998). Each classifier returns a prediction with the probability of each test instance belonging to each label. The final decision is the label with the highest average probability.

Each classifier was trained on the standard training set using single n-gram order. We performed binary search on the DMT simplified training development set in the range of [0, 1000] in order to determine the ideal penalty value C. The F1-score increased with increasing C value, and plateaued when $C \geq 100$, so we adopted $C = 100$ as the optimal value. Table 2 lists the score of each classifier using the DMT simplified development set.

Since SVMs separate classes by maximizing the margin from items to the hyperplane (Burges, 1998), there is no natural probabilistic interpretation of the decision function of an SVM classifier. Therefore, we applied the technique of calibration suggested by Platt et al. (1999), a method that maps the outputs of SVM to probabilities, as implemented in the scikit-learn library.

We used grid search to find the optimal combination of n-gram features for each task. For DMT simplified, the final ensemble system we selected utilized five parallel classifiers, each of them generated with different parameters: character-based bigrams, trigrams, 4-grams, 5-grams, and word-based unigrams. For DMT traditional, the combination additionally included character-based unigrams. For GDI, we used character-based bigrams, trigrams, 4-grams, 5-grams, word-based unigrams, and the audio i-vectors.

task (model)	F1-macro	rank	F1-diff
DMT-S (flat)	87.38	2	−1.91
DMT-S (ens.)	84.45	NA	−4.84
DMT-T (flat)	88.44	3	−2.41
DMT-T (ens.)	85.61	NA	−5.24
GDI (flat)	75.93	1	0.52
GDI (ens.)	65.17	NA	−10.76
MRC 1 (flat)	75.73	5	−13.92
MRC 2 (flat)	61.15	1	5.26
MRC 3 (flat)	55.33	1	13.23
MRC 1 (flat)*	96.20	NA	6.70
MRC 2 (flat)*	69.08	NA	7.93
MRC 3 (flat)*	81.93	NA	26.60
CLI (flat)	76.32	2	−0.63

Table 1: Official results obtained by our models on all tasks we participated. The column F1-diff indicates the macro F1-score difference from the top score if the result is not the top score, or the difference from the second best scores otherwise. Our submissions in the MRC task had an error, causing a shift of labels after a certain index. The scores marked with * are post-evaluation results with the gold labels released by the organizers after the evaluation period.

4 Results

We list the results obtained by our systems on the official test sets in Table 1. The results clearly show that the simple linear classifiers we used are competitive with other (best) participating systems. Furthermore, in our experiments, the flat combination often worked better than the ensemble method. However, we do not provide a more conclusive, systematic comparison at this time. In the remainder of this section, we will first describe some of the interesting results in each task, and also present a series of additional experiments with the adaptation method described above.

4.1 DMT

For both DMT tasks, we submitted at least one classifier with a combined feature matrix (flat) and at least one model with parallel classifiers (ensemble). Our submissions with a combined feature matrix using character n-grams of order 1 to 4 combined with word unigrams and bigrams consistently outperformed the parallel classifiers.

In order to improve accuracy for the ensemble, multiple trials were conducted on the development set to determine the best possible combination of features. Most combinations performed similarly, on the order of approximately 87–89 % accuracy with no significant jump in accuracy using any particular combination. However, the most gains were observed when combining a large number of character n-grams with $1 \leq n \leq 5$ and word unigrams. Word bigrams already resulted in a significant loss of accuracy in the SVM ensemble (possibly overfitting due to large number of features, and large C value selected in the earlier step).

Feature Types	n	F1 macro
character	1	77.41
character	2	83.77
character	3	87.19
character	4	86.99
character	5	83.75
word	1	76.63
word	2	33.33

Table 2: F1 scores achieved by SVM with single features, tested on development set (Simplified Chinese)

During development, we observed that training and testing our model on traditional Chinese consistently performed slightly better than training and testing on simplified Chinese. Combining the traditional training set with the simplified training set did not yield any significant gains and in fact slightly hindered the model's performance.

Our flat SVM model placed second for simplified and third for traditional. Other teams also saw higher F1-scores for traditional compared to simplified which suggests that the traditional script carries more information that proves useful in distinguishing between the two dialects. Despite this, our model misidentified the Taiwanese variant roughly twice as often as its Mainland counterpart using both scripts (simplified: 166 vs. 88, traditional: 151 vs. 80).

4.2 GDI

The same models used for DMT were slightly modified for the German Dialect Identification task. Our flat model using character n-grams of order 1 to 5, word unigrams and bigrams, and the i-vector features achieved first place with an F1-score of 75.93, which was very closely followed by the second and third place entries.

The confusion matrix presented in Figure 1 demonstrates that Basel was most easily identified (recall: 91.99). Lucerne was the dialect most often misclassified (recall: 62.41), usually confused with Bern. Consequently, Bern had the lowest precision (69.39) while Basel and Zurich enjoyed the highest (tied with 80.81). This distribution mirrors the results of last year's GDI task (Ciobanu et al., 2018; Ali, 2018; Benites et al., 2018; Barbaresi, 2018).

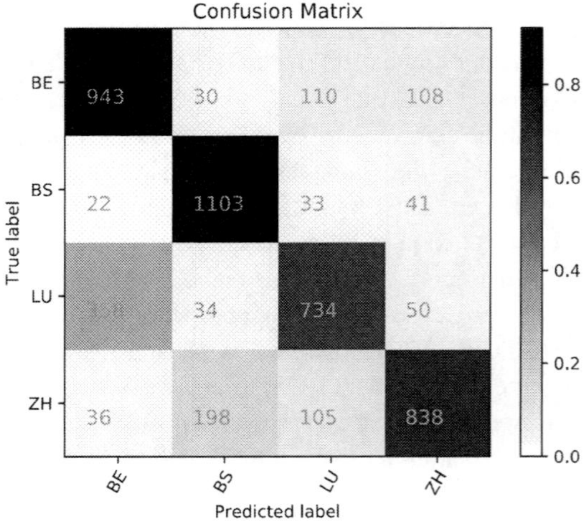

Figure 1: Confusion matrix for GDI. Abbreviation key: Bern (BE), Basel (BS), Lucerne (LU), Zurich (ZH).

In the development set, the SVM ensemble with character n-grams of $2 \leq n \leq 5$, word unigrams, and audio i-vectors outperformed the flat feature combination. The ensemble system yielded an F1-score of 65.35 in comparison to a 44.24 F1-score obtained by the flat combination. This is likely due to the fact that ensemble systems are particularly effective when the individual classifiers are independent, and features from text and audio provide more independent predictions in comparison to the overlapping n-gram features.[1]

4.3 CLI

We submitted predictions using only the flat feature combination for the cuneiform language identification task. Our submission with adaptation came in a close second with an F1-score of 76.32. Since the data did not include any word boundaries, our system combines only character n-grams (of order 1 to 5). We also experimented with two unsupervised segmentation methods (Çöltekin and Nerbonne, 2014; Virpioja et al., 2013). However,

---

[1] Our official score on the test with the flat combination is higher than the ensemble submission. A potential reason for this discrepancy is an error in our submission identified post-evaluation.

using tokens obtained through both segmentation methods as (additional) features did not improve the results on the development set.

On the CLI data, the adaptation method is highly effective. Our submission with no adaptation performed much worse (53.18 F1-score). We will present more results with adaptation in Section 4.5 and discuss it further in Section 5.

The confusion matrix from our official submission is presented in Figure 2, which depicts some effects of the historical proximity of the languages.

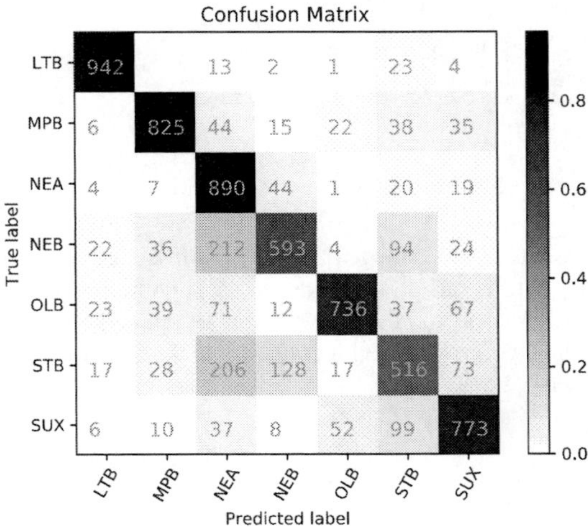

Figure 2: Confusion matrix for CLI. Abbreviations: Late Babylonian (LTB), Middle Babylonian peripheral (MPB), Neo Assyrian (NEA), Neo Babylonian (NEB), Old Babylonian (OLB), Standard Babylonian (STB), Sumerian (SUX).

4.4 MRC

We submitted predictions with only the flat combination for the MRC tasks. Our submissions in this task had an error, causing a shift of labels after a certain index. Despite this shift (with some effort from the organizers to guess the location of the missing predictions) our submissions obtained first rank in subtasks 2 and 3. After rectifying the problem post-evaluation, F1-macro scores increased by up to 30%, reaching 96.20 for subtask 1, 69.08 in subtask 2, and 81.93 in subtask 3. The high rate of success in discriminating between such close linguistic varieties is interesting. However, the primary objective in MRC was cross-lingual learning in the last two subtasks which we discuss further in Section 4.5.

4.5 Adaptation to target data

In this instance of the VarDial evaluation campaign, we employed a method of adaptation to the test data. Among the tasks in which we participated, the clear cases for adaptation are MRC subtasks 2 and 3. These tasks are transfer learning tasks, hence some sort of adaptation is expected to help. In other cases, we do not expect substantial gains from adaptation unless test sets diverge from the training substantially and systematically.

Our official submissions did not always include results from the identical models with and without adaptation, and as such does not clearly indicate the utility of it. Here, we present results from more systematic experiments conducted on the development sets using our SVM model with flat combinations of features. The intuition here is that if the distribution of the test instances diverge from the training set, we can adapt to the test set either by using a small amount of data with gold-labels, or predictions with high confidence at prediction time. The first method (adding gold target data) is not an option during the shared task evaluation. Therefore, we tested both options on the designated development sets. For the second method (adaptation at prediction time), our method is similar to, but simpler than, the method of Jauhiainen et al. (2018a,b). We trained a base classifier on the training data, and re-trained the system after adding the test instances predicted with high-confidence to the training data. For binary tasks, we picked the training instances with a distance greater than 0.50 to the decision boundary. For multi-class classification problems, we picked the instances that are claimed by only one of the one-vs-rest classifiers as confident predictions.

Figure 3 presents five sets of results on all (sub)tasks that we worked on. The first bar in each group represents the average F1-scores obtained with 5-fold cross validation on each training data set. For the rest of the experiments, we split the development set into two equal-sized data sets (after shuffling). The first part is treated as development set, and the second part is treated as test set. The second set of bars (no adapt) represents the F1-scores on the test set (the second part of the respective development sets), after training the model on the training set. The third bar (add) is the first case of adaptation. We add first half of the development set to the training data, and test on the second half. This is compatible in the scenario where we have

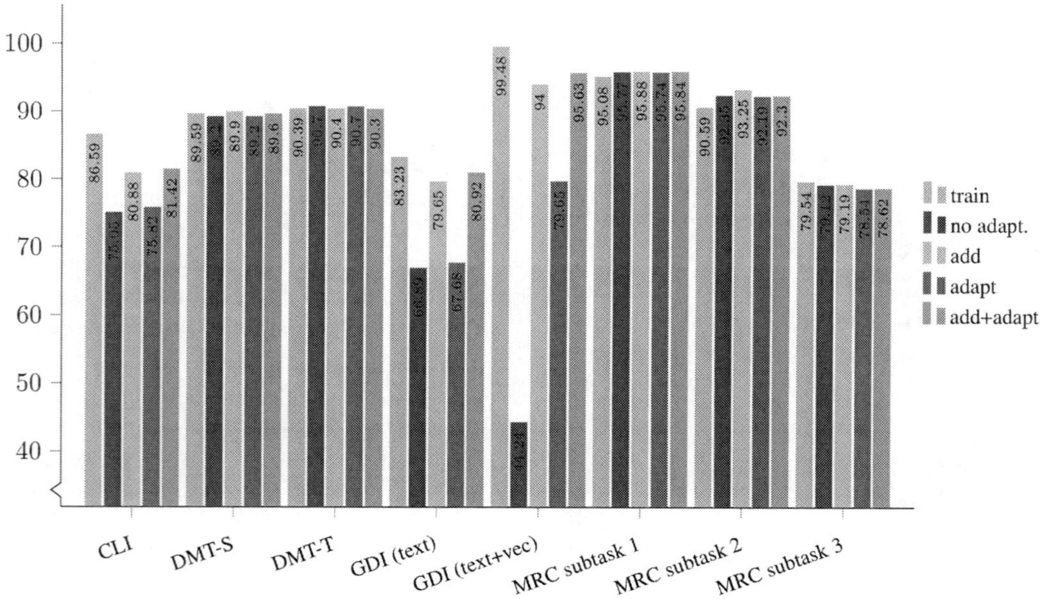

Figure 3: Results of adaptation experiments. The graph presents macro averaged F1-scores of five experiments on each task. 'train' indicates average of 5-fold CV on training set; 'no adapt.' indicates no adaptation, train only on the training set; 'add' indicates adding half of the gold-labeled data from the development set, and testing on the other half; 'adapt' is adaptation during training by adding predictions with high-confidence to the training set and re-training the model; and 'add+adapt' combines the last two options.

a large amount of data from the source domain, with a small amount of data from the target domain. The training instances from the source and target are equally weighted in our experiments. In the fourth set of experiments (adapt), the base classifier is trained on the training data, and testing is done adaptively on the second part of the development set. The final bar (add+adapt) combines the last two. The base system is trained with the combination of the training set and the first half of the development set, and tested on the second part of the development set using adaptation.

The scores illustrated in Figure 3 for both DMT tasks and MRC subtask 1 (language identification) are as expected. The cross-validation scores on the training set are slightly better than scores on the test (part of official development) set, and adaption options give a slight boost in most cases. In MRC subtask 2, the F1-score on the test set is better than the training set. This is particularly interesting, as this is a language transfer task where the test set is expected to diverge. All scores we obtained in this subtask are also much higher than the (corrected) official test set score (69.08) presented in Table 1. Adaptation, however, seems to help if data with gold labels are added. In MRC subtask

3, which reverses the languages in MRC subtask 2, adaptation does not seem to be useful either.

The results of CLI and, especially, GDI tasks are particularly surprising. In these tasks, adaptation, and especially the addition of gold-labeled data, seem to improve the results drastically. The difference likely indicates a systematic difference between the training and development sets (and possibly test). We provide further discussion of these results for the GDI, in Section 5.

5 Summary and Discussion

Thus far we have described our participation in the VarDial 2019 evaluation campaign, where we participated in all text classification tasks using two variants of linear SVM classifiers. Our systems ranked well among other participants, obtaining first place in some tasks, or following the top result with small differences in others. The results show that simple linear classifiers work well in language identification and cross-dialect topic classification. In most of our experiments, a flat combination of features performed better than ensembles. Furthermore, the adaptation system we used seems to be effective, particularly in some of the tasks. In this section, we present our observations on the

DMT task, and discuss the potential reasons for the effectiveness of adaptation methods.

Observations on the DMT task. The relationship from traditional Mandarin to simplified is generally bijective, but there are some cases where the relation is many-to-one. Thus, a machine is better able to predict using traditional over simplified. Consequently, this explains why our model always produced 1-2% better results with the traditional script. To illustrate this, consider the following example: 「雲」 'cloud' and 「云」 'speak' in traditional Mandarin are both written as 「云」 in simplified, which indicates that the simplified character 「云」 carries the meaning of both 'cloud' and 'speak'. In other words, simplified Mandarin has more homonyms, which makes it more difficult for the model to make an accurate prediction.

The texts converted from simplified to traditional are different from traditional to simplified. In traditional Mandarin, both 「后」 and 「後」 can be converted to 「后」 in simplified Mandarin. If we convert the word 「后面」 'in the back' from simplified to traditional, it could be either 「后面」 or 「後面」. Hence, we might erroneously select 「后面」 'the face of a queen', where 「後面」 would be the semantically correct answer. Converting data from traditional to simplified would prevent this type of noise.

Chinese is a language with many compound words, whose tokenization require special attention. Some compounds are used only in Mainland China, but not in Taiwan. However, when split, the individual tokens might all be used in Taiwan, but not the original compound word. Therefore, this would be detrimental to its discrimination accuracy. For example, the word 'microeconomics' is 「個體經濟學」 in Taiwan, but 「微觀經濟學」 on the mainland. It is a compound word composed of 「個體」 and 「經濟學」 in Taiwan and 「微觀」 「經濟學」 in Mainland China. But we should not categorize 「微觀」 and 「經濟學」 as Mainland Chinese, because when they are treated as two tokens, they are two words that are commonly used in Taiwan. This is not a unique example, and similar cases of segmentations of compounds are likely to have detrimental effects on identification.

Adaptation to test set. Another interesting finding in this work is the impact of adaptation in the CLI and GDI tasks, especially when using the i-vectors. A potential explanation for this is the existence of other systematic variation in the data. For the GDI task, our hypothesis is that the second systematic variation is the (limited number of) speakers. Since the data contains multiple utterances from each speaker (and each speaker speaks only one dialect), a classifier relying on speaker specific features in the training set will also do well on identifying his/her dialect. Such a classifier, then, will have difficulty classifying the utterances from different speakers in the test set.

As a result, the scores of the models with no adaptation in Figure 3 drop drastically when they are trained on the training set, and tested on a test set with utterances from different speakers. On the GDI data, this is true of models using text-only and text and i-vector features. However, it becomes more striking when i-vectors are included, as they are well-known for their ability of speaker identification. Although the model can achieve almost perfect dialect identification on the training data, the F1-score drops to 44.24 when tested on different speakers. The success on the training set and the drop on the test set is less drastic for text-only data. In both cases, the models perform clearly better than random. Hence, the models learn something about the dialects as well. However, the success of our (and other participants') adaptation methods, are likely not (only) finding dialectal differences, but rely more on speaker-specific features by incorporating features of otherwise unknown speakers into the training set.

The experiments presented in Figure 3 also indicate a likely additional source of variation in the CLI data as well. Without more information about the data and its division, the source of this variation is not clear. On the other hand, ineffectiveness of the adaptation method on MRC subtasks 2 and 3 is unexpected. However, we are not able to offer a potential explanation at this time.

Future work. Although the flat feature combination worked better in our experiments here, our experiments are far from conclusive. We intend to extend our work on ensemble models to cover different combination methods and more diverse architectures.

Acknowledgments

Some of the experiments reported were run on a Titan Xp donated by the NVIDIA Corporation.

References

Mohamed Ali. 2018. Character Level Convolutional Neural Network for German Dialect Identification. In *Proceedings of the Fifth Workshop on NLP for Similar Languages, Varieties and Dialects (VarDial)*, pages 174–175.

Adrien Barbaresi. 2018. Computationally efficient discrimination between language varieties with large feature vectors and regularized classifiers. In *Proceedings of the Fifth Workshop on NLP for Similar Languages, Varieties and Dialects (VarDial)*, pages 167–168.

Fernando Benites, Ralf Grubenmann, Pius von Daniken, Dirk von Grunigen, Jan Deriu1, and Mark Cieliebak. 2018. Twist Bytes - German Dialect Identification with Data Mining Optimization. In *Proceedings of the Fifth Workshop on NLP for Similar Languages, Varieties and Dialects (VarDial)*, page 224.

Christopher JC Burges. 1998. A tutorial on support vector machines for pattern recognition. *Data mining and knowledge discovery*, 2(2):121–167.

Andrei Butnaru and Radu Tudor Ionescu. 2019. MO-ROCO: The Moldavian and Romanian Dialectal Corpus. *arXiv preprint arXiv:1901.06543*.

Çağrı Çöltekin, Taraka Rama, and Verena Blaschke. 2018. Tübingen-Oslo team at the VarDial 2018 evaluation campaign: An analysis of n-gram features in language variety identification. In *Proceedings of the Fifth Workshop on NLP for Similar Languages, Varieties and Dialects (VarDial 2018)*, pages 55–65.

Çağrı Çöltekin and Taraka Rama. 2016. Discriminating Similar Languages with Linear SVMs and Neural Networks. In *Proceedings of the Third Workshop on NLP for Similar Languages, Varieties and Dialects (VarDial3)*, pages 15–24, Osaka, Japan.

Çağrı Çöltekin and Taraka Rama. 2017. Tübingen system in VarDial 2017 shared task: experiments with language identification and cross-lingual parsing. In *Proceedings of the Fourth Workshop on NLP for Similar Languages, Varieties and Dialects (VarDial)*, pages 146–155, Valencia, Spain.

Keh-Jiann Chen, Chu-Ren Huang, Li-Ping Chang, and Hui-Li Hsu. 1996. SINICA CORPUS : Design Methodology for Balanced Corpora. In *Language, Information and Computation : Selected Papers from the 11th Pacific Asia Conference on Language, Information and Computation : 20-22 December 1996, Seoul*, pages 167–176, Seoul, Korea. Kyung Hee University.

Alina Ciobanu, Shervin Malmasi, and Liviu P. Dinu. 2018. German Dialect Identification Using Classifier Ensembles. In *Proceedings of the Fifth Workshop on NLP for Similar Languages, Varieties and Dialects (VarDial)*, page 291.

Simon Clematide and Peter Makarov. 2017. CLUZH at VarDial GDI 2017: Testing a variety of machine learning tools for the classification of Swiss German dialects. In *Proceedings of the Fourth Workshop on NLP for Similar Languages, Varieties and Dialects (VarDial)*, pages 170–177, Valencia, Spain.

Tommi Jauhiainen, Heidi Jauhiainen, Tero Alstola, and Krister Lindén. 2019. Language and dialect identification of cuneiform texts. In *Proceedings of the Sixth Workshop on NLP for Similar Languages, Varieties and Dialects (VarDial)*.

Tommi Jauhiainen, Heidi Jauhiainen, and Krister Lindén. 2018a. HeLI-based experiments in Swiss German dialect identification. In *Proceedings of the Fifth Workshop on NLP for Similar Languages, Varieties and Dialects (VarDial 2018)*, pages 254–262. Association for Computational Linguistics.

Tommi Jauhiainen, Heidi Jauhiainen, and Krister Lindén. 2018b. Iterative language model adaptation for Indo-Aryan language identification. In *Proceedings of the Fifth Workshop on NLP for Similar Languages, Varieties and Dialects (VarDial 2018)*, pages 66–75. Association for Computational Linguistics.

Tommi Jauhiainen, Krister Lindén, and Heidi Jauhiainen. 2016. HeLI, a Word-Based Backoff Method for Language Identification. In *Proceedings of the Third Workshop on NLP for Similar Languages, Varieties and Dialects (VarDial3)*, pages 153–162, Osaka, Japan.

Tommi Jauhiainen, Marco Lui, Marcos Zampieri, Timothy Baldwin, and Krister Lindén. 2018c. Automatic language identification in texts: A survey. *arXiv preprint arXiv:1804.08186*.

Josef Kittler. 1998. Combining classifiers: A theoretical framework. *Pattern analysis and Applications*, 1(1):18–27.

Ludmila I Kuncheva. 2004. *Combining pattern classifiers: methods and algorithms*. John Wiley & Sons.

Shervin Malmasi and Mark Dras. 2015. Language identification using classifier ensembles. In *Proceedings of the Joint Workshop on Language Technology for Closely Related Languages, Varieties and Dialects (LT4VarDial)*, pages 35–43, Hissar, Bulgaria.

Shervin Malmasi and Mark Dras. 2018. Native language identification with classifier stacking and ensembles. *Computational Linguistics*, 44(3):403–446.

Shervin Malmasi and Marcos Zampieri. 2017a. Arabic dialect identification using iVectors and ASR transcripts. In *Proceedings of the Fourth Workshop on NLP for Similar Languages, Varieties and Dialects (VarDial)*, pages 178–183, Valencia, Spain.

Shervin Malmasi and Marcos Zampieri. 2017b. German dialect identification in interview transcriptions. In *Proceedings of the Fourth Workshop on NLP for Similar Languages, Varieties and Dialects (VarDial)*, pages 164–169, Valencia, Spain.

Shervin Malmasi, Marcos Zampieri, Nikola Ljubešić, Preslav Nakov, Ahmed Ali, and Jörg Tiedemann. 2016. Discriminating between similar languages and Arabic dialect identification: A report on the third dsl shared task. In *Proceedings of the 3rd Workshop on Language Technology for Closely Related Languages, Varieties and Dialects (VarDial)*, Osaka, Japan.

A. M. McEnery and R. Z. Xiao. 2003. The Lancaster corpus of Mandarin Chinese.

Maria Medvedeva, Martin Kroon, and Barbara Plank. 2017. When sparse traditional models outperform dense neural networks: the curious case of discriminating between similar languages. In *Proceedings of the Fourth Workshop on NLP for Similar Languages, Varieties and Dialects (VarDial)*, pages 156–163, Valencia, Spain.

Nikunj C Oza and Kagan Tumer. 2008. Classifier ensembles: Select real-world applications. *Information Fusion*, 9(1):4–20.

Fabian Pedregosa, Gaël Varoquaux, Alexandre Gramfort, Vincent Michel, Bertrand Thirion, Olivier Grisel, Mathieu Blondel, Peter Prettenhofer, Ron Weiss, Vincent Dubourg, et al. 2011. Scikit-learn: Machine learning in Python. *Journal of machine learning research*, 12(Oct):2825–2830.

John Platt et al. 1999. Probabilistic outputs for support vector machines and comparisons to regularized likelihood methods. *Advances in large margin classifiers*, 10(3):61–74.

Taraka Rama and Çağrı Çöltekin. 2017. Fewer features perform well at native language identification task. In *Proceedings of the 12th Workshop on Innovative Use of NLP for Building Educational Applications*, pages 255–260, Copenhagen, Denmark.

Stephen Robertson, Hugo Zaragoza, et al. 2009. The probabilistic relevance framework: BM25 and beyond. *Foundations and Trends® in Information Retrieval*, 3(4):333–389.

Tanja Samardžić, Yves Scherrer, and Elvira Glaser. 2016. ArchiMob – a corpus of spoken Swiss German. In *Proceedings of LREC*.

Sami Virpioja, Peter Smit, Stig-Arne Grönroos, Mikko Kurimo, et al. 2013. Morfessor 2.0: Python implementation and extensions for Morfessor baseline. Technical Report 25/2013.

Marcos Zampieri, Shervin Malmasi, Nikola Ljubešić, Preslav Nakov, Ahmed Ali, Jörg Tiedemann, Yves Scherrer, and Noëmi Aepli. 2017. Findings of the VarDial Evaluation Campaign 2017. In *Proceedings of the Fourth Workshop on NLP for Similar Languages, Varieties and Dialects (VarDial)*, Valencia, Spain.

Marcos Zampieri, Shervin Malmasi, Preslav Nakov, Ahmed Ali, Suwon Shuon, James Glass, Yves Scherrer, Tanja Samardžić, Nikola Ljubešić, Jörg Tiedemann, Chris van der Lee, Stefan Grondelaers, Nelleke Oostdijk, Antal van den Bosch, Ritesh Kumar, Bornini Lahiri, and Mayank Jain. 2018. Language Identification and Morphosyntactic Tagging: The Second VarDial Evaluation Campaign. In *Proceedings of the Fifth Workshop on NLP for Similar Languages, Varieties and Dialects (VarDial)*, Santa Fe, USA.

Marcos Zampieri, Shervin Malmasi, Yves Scherrer, Tanja Samardžić, Francis Tyers, Miikka Silfverberg, Natalia Klyueva, Tung-Le Pan, Chu-Ren Huang, Radu Tudor Ionescu, Andrei Butnaru, and Tommi Jauhiainen. 2019. A report on the third VarDial evaluation campaign. In *Proceedings of the Sixth Workshop on NLP for Similar Languages, Varieties and Dialects (VarDial)*. Association for Computational Linguistics.

Çağrı Çöltekin and John Nerbonne. 2014. An explicit statistical model of learning lexical segmentation using multiple cues. In *Proceedings of EACL 2014 Workshop on Cognitive Aspects of Computational Language Learning*, pages 19–28.

Variation between Different Discourse Types: Literate vs. Oral

Katrin Ortmann
Department of Linguistics
Fakultät für Philologie
Ruhr-Universität Bochum
ortmann@linguistics.rub.de

Stefanie Dipper
Department of Linguistics
Fakultät für Philologie
Ruhr-Universität Bochum
dipper@linguistics.rub.de

Abstract

This paper deals with the automatic identification of literate and oral discourse in German texts. A range of linguistic features is selected and their role in distinguishing between literate- and oral-oriented registers is investigated, using a decision-tree classifier. It turns out that all of the investigated features are related in some way to oral conceptuality. Especially simple measures of complexity (average sentence and word length) are prominent indicators of oral and literate discourse. In addition, features of reference and deixis (realized by different types of pronouns) also prove to be very useful in determining the degree of orality of different registers.

1 Introduction

Halliday distinguishes between two kinds of variation in language: social variation, which he calls *dialect*, and functional variation, which he calls *register* (e.g. Halliday, 1989, p. 44). VarDial's focus is on the first kind of variation, in particular diatopic variation, and addresses topics such as automatic identification of dialects but also includes topics like diachronic language variation. In this paper, we look at variation of the second kind, namely variation between literate/written and oral/spoken language (different registers, as Halliday would call it). However, we assume that the phenomenon of literate/written vs. oral/spoken language interacts with diachronic language change, which, in turn, interacts with diatopic variation (e.g. one dialect becomes more important than another one and has larger impact on the further development of the language). Hence, if we want to understand language change, we have to take into account different kinds of variation.

In general, human language is used in two major forms of representation: written and spoken.

Both discourse modes place different demands on the language user. Spoken discourse has to be processed online by speakers and hearers and, hence, strongly depends on the capacity of the working memory. In contrast, written discourse proceeds independently of production and reading speed, and allows for a rather free and elaborate structuring of texts. This discrepancy can result in quite different utterances.

Moreover, as many linguists have noticed, there is also a high amount of variation *within* written and spoken language (Koch and Oesterreicher, 2007; Halliday, 1989; Biber and Conrad, 2009). For example, the language used in scientific presentations is rather similar to prototypical written language, despite its spoken realization. Chat communication on the other hand, although realized in the written medium, rather resembles spontaneous spoken speech. In other words, independently of their medial realization, language can show characteristics that are typical of the written or spoken mode. As Halliday (1989, p.32) puts it, "'written' and 'spoken' do not form a simple dichotomy; there are all sorts of writing and all sorts of speech, many of which display features characteristic of the other medium".

In the 1980s, Koch and Oesterreicher (1985) proposed to distinguish between *medial and conceptual orality and literacy*. On the medial dimension, an utterance can be realized either phonetically (spoken) or graphically (written), while the conceptual dimension forms a broad continuum between the extremes of conceptual orality and conceptual literacy. Example (1) from Halliday (1989, p.79) illustrates this continuum, from a clear conceptually-literate sentence in (a) to a clear conceptually-oral equivalent in (c).

(1) a. The use of this method of control unquestionably leads to safer and faster train run-

Proceedings of VarDial, pages 64–79
Minneapolis, MN, June 7, 2019 ©2019 Association for Computational Linguistics

ning in the most adverse weather conditions.

b. If this method of control is used trains will unquestionably (be able to) run more safely and faster (even) when the weather conditions are most adverse.

c. You can control the trains this way and if you do that you can be quite sure that they'll be able to run more safely and more quickly than they would otherwise no matter how bad the weather gets.

The work reported here is part of a larger project which investigates syntactic change in German across a long period of time (1000 years). One of the working hypotheses of the project is that certain parts of syntactic change can be attributed to changes in discourse mode: Early writings showed many features of the oral mode. The dense, complex structure which is characteristic of many modern elaborate written texts is the product of a long development.

Interestingly, spoken language has also developed denser structures over time. It is commonly assumed that this is a reflex of the written language, and is due to the increasing amount of written language which became available after the invention of printing and since then has played a prominent role in the society. As Halliday (1989, p.45) argues, this feedback happens "particularly because of the prestige" of written registers.

The aim of the project is to trace these two strands of development, by investigating and comparing texts that are located at different positions of the orality scale. Of course, we do not have records of historical spoken language. Rather, we have to rely on written texts that are as close as possible to the spoken language. So we need to be able to identify conceptually-oral, i.e. spoken-like texts.

The present paper addresses the first step in this enterprise, namely to find means to automatically measure the conceptual orality of a given *modern* text. In particular, we investigate a range of linguistic features that can be automatically determined and seem useful for this task.

The remainder of this paper is structured as follows: Section 2 gives an overview of the related work. In Section 3, features of orality as proposed in the literature are presented, and the set of linguistic features used in the present study is spec-

ified. Section 4 introduces the data and describes their linguistic annotation as well as the way we determine expected orality. In Section 5, results from training a classifier on the linguistc features are discussed. Finally, Section 6 summarizes the results and gives an outlook at future investigations. An appendix provides further details of the analysis.

2   Related Work

Nowadays, the distinction between literate and oral language is widely recognized in linguistics. For instance, in a register analysis of typologically different languages Biber (1995) finds that the distinction between oral and literate language seems to be a dimension that plays a role in all these languages, although it can be expressed in different ways and he could not find "any absolute dichotomies between speech and writing" (p.236).

In the following, we focus on work that deals with features directly related to the difference between literate and oral language.

Koch and Oesterreicher (1985, 2007) list a number of universal characteristics, such as publicity vs. privacy, weak vs. strong emotional involvement, spatial and temporal distance vs. proximity, and monologicity vs. dialogicity. Combining these aspects in different ways results in different degrees of conceptual orality or literacy. Unfortunately, the characteristics are rather abstract and vague, and cannot be operationalized and applied to concrete texts.

To remedy this weakness, Ágel and Hennig (2006) extend the approach of Koch and Oesterreicher and create a framework that allows for objectively measuring the conceptual orality of a given text (in German). For this purpose, they consider a range of diverse linguistic features, e.g. deixis, ellipsis, interjections, number of complete sentences in the text, and compare the observed frequencies to a prototypical conceptually-oral text. The method as described by Ágel and Hennig (2006) requires careful manual inspection of every individual text, though, to determine a large number of linguistic features. Hence, it cannot be applied sensibly to a large amount of data.

A few approaches try to automate the process of feature identification: Rehm (2002) focusses on automatic identification of a small number of features in the restricted domain of computer-mediated communication (CMC) in German, such as websites, emails, etc. The analyzed features include smileys, iterations, emphasis, isolated verb stems like *grins* 'smile', slang expressions or abbreviations, and a few other features like specific punctuation symbols and phonetic contractions marked with an apostrophe.

Following Biber (1995), Biber and Conrad (2009) conduct a register analysis based on automatically-identified co-ocurring linguistic features in English texts. In their analysis, the distinction of oral and literate language makes up the first dimension along which the analyzed registers differ. Biber (1995) showed that if this dimension is broken down, it turns out that it consists of fine-grained dimensions, e.g. dimensions concerning the degree of interactiveness (dialog vs. monolog), production circumstances (on-line vs. careful production), stance (overt marking of personal stance and involvement vs. non-personal/informational), and language-specific functions (e.g. abstract vs. non-abstract style in English, narrative vs. non-narrative in Korean).

3 Features of Orality

The aim of this paper is to identify linguistic features that (i) are useful predictors of the conceptual orality of a given text and (ii) can be recognized fully automatically in texts of any length. Previous work discusses a broad range of features that distinguish between written and spoken mode or literate and oral discourse. As explained above, the medium (written/spoken) and conceptuality (literate/oral) concern different aspects of language, and go hand in hand only in prototypical cases, e.g. edited news (written and literate) or spontaneous colloquial communication (spoken and oral). Researchers often investigate only one of the aspects in their work, and most of them focus on the medial distinction (written vs. spoken), e.g. Chafe (1982), Drieman (1962), Richter (1985), Tomczyk-Popińska (1987). Moreover, many of them consider prototypical cases. As a consequenc, for many features discussed in the literature it is not obvious whether they are indicative of the medium or of conceptuality.

The following presentation does not try to distinguish systematically between the two aspects, and, instead, makes a rough distinction between written/literate on the one hand, and spoken/oral on the other hand. Our study presented in Sec. 5 reveals which of the features correlate with oral conceptuality (whereas the medial aspect is not relevant to our purposes). The focus is on features proposed for English and German.

Reference/deixis As a consequence of the spatial and temporal co-presence of participants, spoken language shows an increased use of pronouns and demonstratives as compared to lexical nouns (Goody, 1987; Diamante and Morlicchio, 2015; Schwitalla and Tiittula, 2009; Tomczyk-Popińska, 1987). There are also some language-specific differences like the use of proper names with a definite article in German (Schwitalla and Tiittula, 2009) as in *der Peter* '(*the) Peter'. This construction is frequent in spoken (and oral) communication but disapproved in written (and literate) language.

Complexity As spoken language is produced and processed in real-time, it is largely dependent on the capacity of the working memory (Weiß, 2005). Therefore, spoken language is less complex than written language in many respects, e.g. it comes with shorter sentences and words (Bader, 2002; Richter, 1985; Tomczyk-Popińska, 1987; Drieman, 1962; Rehm, 2002), less complex noun phrases (Weiß, 2005), less subordination and more coordination (Ágel and Hennig, 2006; Bader, 2002; Müller, 1990; Richter, 1985; Schwitalla and Tiittula, 2009; Sieber, 1998; Speyer, 2013; Tomczyk-Popińska, 1987), which also leads to an increase of sentence-intial use of *and* and *but* (Chafe, 1982).

Moreover, written language shows a nominal style with a higher number of nouns and nominalizations, while spoken language shows a verbal style with a higher proportion of verbs (Bader, 2002; Chafe, 1982; Dürscheid, 2006; Goody, 1987; Halliday, 1989; Sieber, 1998). Finally, written and spoken language differ with respect to the information density, measured as lexical density, i.e. the ratio of lexical vs. functional words: written language uses more lexical words than spoken language (Halliday, 1989).

Syntax Further syntactic features that mark spoken language include a higher ratio of ellipsis (Ágel and Hennig, 2010; Bader, 2002; Fiehler, 2011; Müller, 1990; Richter, 1985; Schwitalla and Tiittula, 2009; Tomczyk-Popińska, 1987), and of parentheses and anacolutha (Müller, 1990; Richter, 1985). Similarly, spoken language shows a clear preference for active instead of passive

Feature	Description
mean_sent	Mean sentence length, without punctuation marks.
med_sent	Median sentence length, without punctuation marks.
mean_word	Mean word length.
med_word	Median word length.
subord	Ratio of subordinating conjunctions (tagged as KOUS or KOUI) to full verbs.
coordInit	Proportion of sentences beginning with a coordinating conjunction.
question	Proportion of interrogative sentences, based on the last punctuation mark of the sentence.
exclam	Proportion of exclamative sentences, based on the last punctuation mark of the sentence.
nomCmplx	Mean number of prenominal dependents for each noun in the dependency tree. This includes determiners but not punctuation marks, prepositions and contractions of prepositions and articles.
V:N	Ratio of full verbs to nouns.
lexDens	Ratio of lexical items (tagged as ADJ.*, ADV, N.*, VV.*) to all words.
PRONsubj	Proportion of subjects which are realized as personal pronouns, based on the head of the subject.
PRON1st	Ratio of 1st person sg. and pl. pronouns with lemmas *ich* 'I' and *wir* 'we' to all words.
DEM	Ratio of demonstrative pronouns (tagged as PDS) to all words.
DEMshort	Proportion of demonstrative pronouns (tagged as PDS) with lemmas *dies* 'this/that' or *der* 'the' which are realized as the short form (lemma *der* 'the').
PTC	Proportion of answer particles (*ja* 'yes', *nein* 'no', *bitte* 'please', *danke* 'thanks') to all words.
INTERJ	Proportion of primary, i.e. one-word interjections (e.g. *ach*, *oh*, *hallo*) to all words.

Table 1: Features used for classification. Tokens tagged as punctuation marks are not counted as words. The POS tags are from the STTS tagset.

structures (Chafe, 1982; Goody, 1987; Richter, 1985), and for analytic instead of synthetic verb forms (Müller, 1990; Richter, 1985; Sieber, 1998; Weiß, 2005) (e.g. past perfect instead of preterite). Finally, the *am*-progressive, as in *Er ist am Arbeiten* 'he is working', is a clear indicator of spoken language (Ágel and Hennig, 2010).

Lexicon   A range of differences between written and spoken language can also be observed by inspecting individual words. Spoken language is characterized by frequent use of various particles, e.g. answer and modal particles in German (Diamante and Morlicchio, 2015; Fiehler, 2011; Müller, 1990; Richter, 1985; Schwitalla and Tiittula, 2009; Weiß, 2005), and interjections (Fiehler, 2011; Richter, 1985; Schwitalla and Tiittula, 2009). Furthermore, spoken language often contains vague expressions and hedges (Chafe, 1982).

Variation   Since written texts can be carefully planned and revised, written language generally shows a high degree of grammatical and lexical variation, e.g. in the form of varying syntactic constructions and high type-token ratios (Drieman, 1962; Dürscheid, 2006; Müller, 1990; Sieber, 1998). In contrast, spoken language contains many repetitions (Diamante and Morlicchio, 2015; Green, 1982; Schwitalla and Tiittula, 2009). On the other hand, spoken language often exhibits a higher variation of sentence types, in that questions and exclamations are more frequent than in

written language (Goody, 1987; Müller, 1990).

Graphical features   Written language can express features of orality with specific graphical means, such as omission of characters, word contractions, or use of ellipsis dots, em dashes or apostrophes (Diamante and Morlicchio, 2015; Tomczyk-Popińska, 1987; Fiehler, 2011; Schwitalla and Tiittula, 2009; Richter, 1985; Rehm, 2002). Especially in the context of CMC, repetition of characters (*aaah*), and repetition of (combinations of) punctuation marks (*!!!*, *!?!?*), as well as capital letters or non-verbal symbols like smileys are clear indicators of orality (Rehm, 2002; Schwitalla and Tiittula, 2009).

Some of these features, such as use of specific particles, are language-dependent while others are language-independent, such as sentence or word length. This is also confirmed by Biber (1995), who shows that certain linguistic features fulfill the same functions in various languages while others are used with a specific function just in one language. In our analysis we mainly include language-independent features.

Not all of the features can be determined automatically. Some features require a detailed and reliable syntactic or semantic analysis, e.g. in the case of anacolutha or ellipsis. The present study only includes features that can be reliably identified based on automatically-created standard linguistic annotations.

Furthermore, it is to be expected that many

of the features correlate, which is precisely how Biber (1995) and Biber and Conrad (2009) identify the relevant features for their register analyses. In our study, we include various features of the different levels presented above, to allow for a broad coverage of features, and leave it to the classifier to determine the relevant ones. For an overview of the features used in the study, see Table 1.[1]

4   The Data

In order to evaluate the selected features for the task at hand, we compiled corpora from five different language registers, which differ with respect to their conceptual orality: newspaper articles (*News*), recited speeches (*Speech*), rehearsed talks (*TED*), chat communication (*Chat*), and spontaneous spoken communication (*Dialog*).

The News register includes various kinds of articles from two German newspapers.[2] In the Speech register, three different genres are considered: speeches and lectures[3] as well as modern Christian sermons.[4] The TED register consists of German transcripts of English TED talks.[5] For the Chat register, chat protocols were extracted from the Dortmunder Chatkorpus[6], including professional as well as informal chats. The texts of the Dialog register were taken from three sources: movie subtitles from the genres romance and drama,[7] subtitles of pranks filmed with a hidden camera from a German TV show[8], and work conversations.[9]

A random subset of texts with about 500,000 tokens was created for each of the five registers. Table 2 gives an overview of the data.

4.1   Preprocessing

To enable automatic identification of the described features, the data was automatically enriched with linguistic annotations. Except for the pre-tokenized texts, all corpora were automatically tokenized using the default NLTK tokenizers.[10] NLTK sentence tokenization was only applied within corpus-specific boundaries.[11]

After tokenization, the texts were tagged for part of speech (POS) with the spaCy tagger.[12] The German model uses the STTS-Tagset (Schiller et al., 1999) and overall achieves high accuracy scores.[13] All texts were automatically lemmatized using output from GermaLemma and the spaCy lemmatizer.[14] Finally, the texts were annotated with syntactic dependencies by the spaCy parser.[15]

---

[1]Besides syntactic features, which are excluded because they cannot be identified easily and reliably, the study also excludes graphical features, as our data includes transcriptions of spoken language which follow different notation conventions.

[2]We included articles from the Tüba-D/Z corpus (http://www.sfs.uni-tuebingen.de/ascl/ressourcen/corpora/tueba-dz.html) and the Tiger corpus (http://www.ims.uni-stuttgart.de/forschung/ressourcen/korpora/tiger.html).

[3]The speeches and lectures were taken from Gutenberg-DE corpus, edition 14 (http://gutenberg.spiegel.de/), including only texts published after 1900, to allow the use of standard annotation tools for automatic processing of the orthographic surface forms.

[4]The sermons were automatically downloaded from the SermonOnline database (http://www.sermon-online.de).

[5]The transcripts were automatically downloaded from the official TED website at https://www.ted.com/talks?language=de.

[6]Release corpus from http://www.chatkorpus.tu-dortmund.de/korpora.html.

[7]The movie subtitles were downloaded from the OpenSubtitles database at http://www.opensubtitles.org/de.

[8]The subtitles were automatically downloaded from the YouTube channel of the show 'Verstehen Sie Spaß?' (https://www.youtube.com/user/VSSpass).

[9]From the Tüba-D/S corpus (http://www.sfs.uni-tuebingen.de/ascl/ressourcen/corpora/tueba-ds.html).

[10]Pre-tokenized texts are from Tiger, TüBa-D/Z and TüBa-D/S. NLTK tokenizer: http://www.nltk.org/api/nltk.tokenize.html. Some tokenizing errors were fixed by heuristic rules, which corrected the tokenization of repeated punctuation marks ('!!!!'), smileys and uses of the @-symbol.

[11]In particular: Movie subtitles were segmented across frames, chat protocols within messages, and lectures and speeches within lines, which usually correspond to paragraphs. In tokenizing TV subtitles, TED talks and sermons, frames or paragraph boundaries were ignored.

[12]https://spacy.io/api/tagger (v2.0). Certain tagging errors were automatically corrected, using word lists and regular expressions (e.g. 'ha+ll+o+', which matches all kinds of spellings of *Hallo* 'hello'). This concerned single-word interjections (ITJ), pronominal adverbs (PAV), and different punctuation types ($(, $, and $.).

[13]An evaluation of a random subset showed accuracy values of over 90% for all registers, except for the chat corpus with an accuracy of 85%. The most frequent confusions occur between nouns and proper names, and between adverbial adjectives, participles and adverbs.

[14]https://github.com/WZBSocialScienceCenter/germalemma, version from February 6, 2019, and https://spacy.io/api/lemmatizer, v2.0.
Words tagged as N.*, V.*, ADJ.* and ADV were lemmatized with GermaLemma. Pronouns (tagged as PPER, PRF and PPOS.*) were lemmatized using custom rules, to preserve information about 1st, 2nd and 3rd person. For all other words, the output of the spaCy lemmatizer was used.

[15]https://spacy.io/api/dependencyparser (v2.0).

Register	#Tokens	#Sentences	#Docs	Corpora
News	500,076	27,375	1,024	679 articles from the newspaper 'taz' (72%), 345 articles from the newspaper 'Frankfurter Rundschau' (28%)
Speech	500,475	18,833	31	11 (collections of) speeches (61%), 5 lectures (28%), 15 sermons (11%)
TED	500,035	30,809	224	224 talk subtitles (100%)
Chat	500,009	58,572	322	322 chat protocols (100%)
Dialog	500,622	66,815	140	30 movie subtitles (51%), 104 TV subtitles (26%), 6 work conversations (23%)

Table 2: Overview of the data. The numbers in brackets after each subcorpus provide the percentage of tokens in the register that stems from the respective subcorpus.

4.2 Expected orality

The features listed in Table 1 are designed for use by a classifier which locates the texts of the different registers on the continuum of conceptual orality. That means that we first have to assign an "index of orality" to each register. Admittedly, as Dürscheid (2006) points out, only individual texts can sensibly be located on the literate-to-oral continuum. However, it is possible to judge the prototypical conceptuality of a register based on its general characteristics. To this end, we establish four *situational characteristics* which allow us to manually determine the expected orality of the registers. The characteristics are based on features proposed by Koch and Oesterreicher (2007), Ágel and Hennig (2006) and Biber and Conrad (2009). The following paragraphs describe the characteristics in detail.

Participants: *many, few* The number of participants in the communication. We only distinguish between many (coded as -1) and few (1) participants, with few participants being an indicator of a higher conceptual orality. The value many refers to communications which usually involve hundreds or thousands of participants, such as public speeches or newspaper articles. In contrast, the value few refers to communications with usually less than ten participants. This characteristic is based on Koch and Oesterreicher (2007)'s distinction of private vs. public. We do not distinguish between addressor(s) and addresse(s), contrary to Biber and Conrad (2009).

Interactiveness: *monolog, dialog* The communication structure which can be either monologous (-1) or dialogous (1), with dialog being the indicator for conceptual orality. Dialogous registers show frequent changes of language producer(s) and recipient(s) while monologous registers are dominated by a single speaker. This characteristic has also been suggested by Koch and Oesterreicher (2007), and it is one of the "relations among participants" described by Biber and Conrad (2009) (the only one that can be determined rather easily and unambiguously).

Production circumstances: *synchronous, quasi-synchronous, asynchronous* The temporal circumstances of the production of utterances, also mentioned by Ágel and Hennig (2006) and Biber and Conrad (2009). Language production can be either synchronous, i.e. real-time production like in spontaneous communication, or asynchronous, i.e. planned production like in writing. As synchronous production is highly dependent on the working memory (Weiß, 2005), it is an indicator of higher conceptual orality. The intermediate value of quasi-synchronous language production was introduced by Dürscheid (2003) and refers to communication situations where the possibility of planning and revising one's utterances is given but possibly not exploited by the speaker, like, e.g., in chat communication or in a well-rehearsed but freely-performed presentation.

Reception circumstances: *synchronous, quasi-synchronous, asynchronous* The temporal circumstances of the reception of utterances, also emphasized by Ágel and Hennig (2006) and Biber and Conrad (2009). Like language production, reception can be either synchronous, when an utterance has to be processed in real time in the moment it is uttered, as in spontaneous communication, or asynchronous like in reading a book, where an utterance can be read multiple times and at any speed. Again, synchronous reception is an indicator of higher conceptual orality. The intermediate value of quasi-synchronous language reception is analogous to the production and refers to communication situations where the possibility of reading the speakers's utterances multiple times is given but possibly not exploited by the participants, like in chat communication, where participants usually want to answer immediately.

Table 3 shows the the five registers used in this study along with their situational characteristics. The characteristics locate the respective registers on a scale from highly literate (News) to highly oral (Dialog). The sum of the individual scores can be interpreted as an index of orality, with high scores indicating orally-oriented registers. It turns out that the two characteristics Participants and Interactiveness split the registers, as considered in the present work, in the same way so that we treat them as one property in the following section.

In order to validate our manual classification, we adapt the approach by Fankhauser et al. (2014), who compare American and British English from the 1960s and 1990s, based on unigram language models. We represent each register by POS unigram language models, which have been smoothed with Jelinek-Mercer smoothing (lambda = 0.005). We compute relative entropy (Kullback-Leiber Divergence, KLD) between each pair of registers as a measure of (dis)similarity of the two registers. In computing KLD, we can use one register as the reference register and compare it with the other four registers.[16] Fig. 1 shows the results for all registers. The plots arrange the registers according to their degree of orality (first bar: News, last bar: Dialog). When a reference register is compared with itself, (e.g. "N–N": News with News), KLD is zero and there is no column.

The plots show that the KLD scores of the orally-adjacent registers are systematically lower than KLD scores of distant registers. For instance, the first plot compares News with all other registers, and KLD is smallest with Speech (first bar) and highest with Dialog (last bar). The second plot compares Speech with all others, and, again, KLD is smallest with its immediate neighbors, News (left) and TED talks (right).[17]

5   Results

As we have seen, the five registers we established in the previous section can be distinguished with regard to (expected) orality, by situational characteristics. The main question of this section is to determine in which way these registers also differ with regard to linguistics features, and which linguistic features can serve as indicators of specific registers and the degree of their conceptual orality.

In a first step, we plot the distribution of all linguistic features listed in Table 1 with regard to the different registers (cf. Fig. 2 in the appendix). The plots show that most of the features quite clearly distinguish between some of the registers. For instance, the feature mean sentence length (1st panel) clearly separates Chat and Dialog data from TED, Speech, and News.

We next train a classifier to determine the registers and their situational characteristics. We use J48 (Quinlan, 1993), a decision-tree classifier, which allows us to inspect the features most prominently used by the classifier.[18]

5.1   Classifying registers

The decision tree resulting from the full dataset is shown in the appendix in Fig. 3.

The major split distinguishes texts with sentences with a mean length of less or more than 10.5. It turns out that this split quite neatly separates oral-oriented registers, i.e. Dialogs and Chats (upper part, with shorter sentences in general), from literate-oriented registers, i.e. TED, Speech, and News (lower part, with longer sentences).

---

[16]For probability distributions p, q, and an event space X, KLD is defined as: $\mathrm{KLD}(p||q) = \sum_{x \in X} p(x) log_2 \frac{p(x)}{q(x)}$. p represents the reference register and q is compared with it.

[17]As mentioned in the beginning of this section, a score of orality should be assigned to individual texts rather than registers. However, of the situational characteristics presented here, Interactiveness is the only one that can be observed in the data itself. All other characteristics would be part of metadata, which is not available. We therefore decided to pick registers with clear prototypical situational characteristics (e.g. TED talks aim at a large number of recipients, sermons are performed by just one speaker, etc.), so that we do not expect individual texts to diverge from the prototypical settings. There are some exceptions, though. For instance, some newspaper articles contain interviews, which are dialogous, whereas newspaper articles in general are monologous. Some movie sequence might feature a lecture, so that this part would have many participants, in contrast to other typical movie sequences (since we selected movies from the genres romance and drama, we expect such exceptional sequences to occur very rarely). Finally, chat data sometimes seem to involve many participants but looking at the data in detail shows that in fact communication takes place between small groups of people only. Hence, we assume that the vast majority of the texts exhibit the prototypical characteristics.

[18]We use J48 as implemented in Weka (Witten et al., 2011), combined with a filter that balances the size of the different classes in the training data. The minimum number of instances per leaf is set to 5, so that the options are set as follows:

```
weka.classifiers.meta.FilteredClassifier
-F "weka.filters.supervised.instance.
ClassBalancer -num-intervals 10" -S 1
-W weka.classifiers.trees.J48 -- -C 0.25
-M 5.
```

Register	Participants		Interactiveness		Production		Reception		Index of Orality
	value	score	value	score	value	score	value	score	score (sum)
News	many	-1	monolog	-1	asynchronous	-1	asynchronous	-1	-4
Speech	many	-1	monolog	-1	asynchronous	-1	synchronous	1	-2
TED	many	-1	monolog	-1	quasi-synchr.	0	synchronous	1	-1
Chat	few	1	dialog	1	quasi-synchr.	0	quasi-synchr.	0	2
Dialog	few	1	dialog	1	synchronous	1	synchronous	1	4

Table 3: Expected orality based on four situational characteristics of the registers. The characteristics rank the registers from highly literate (*News*) to highly oral (*Dialog*).

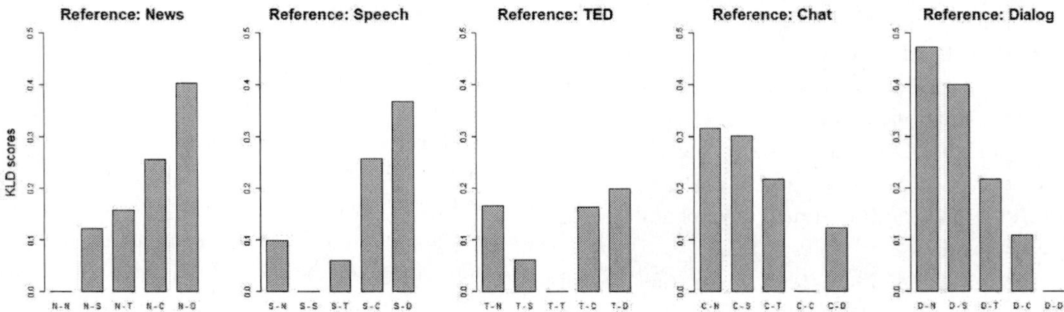

Figure 1: KLD scores of all register pairs.

Class	Precision	Recall	F-Measure
News	0.985	0.913	0.948
Speech	0.486	0.581	0.529
TED	0.731	0.848	0.785
Chat	0.817	0.857	0.836
Dialog	0.752	0.843	0.795
Weighted Avg.	0.894	0.883	0.886

Table 4: Results of classifying registers with the J48 decision-tree classifier.

In both partitions, the feature PRONsubj plays a prominent role: a low rate of pronominal subjects is indicative of News (in both partitions), and singles out certain chats (in the upper part).[19]

A 10-fold cross-validation results in an overall accuracy of 88.28%. Table 4 shows that the News register is classified with high accuracy whereas Speech data is classified with both low precision and low recall.

The confusion matrix in Table 5, which shows the confusions summed over all cross-validations, reveals that Speech data is often confused with News or TED, but very rarely or never with Chat or Dialog. Similarly, other confusions mainly oc-

cur between immediate neighbors, i.e. registers with similar levels of conceptual orality, e.g. Chat and Dialog.

classified as →	News	Speech	TED	Chat	Dialog
News	935	6	46	31	6
Speech	4	18	9	0	0
TED	5	11	190	12	6
Chat	5	0	14	276	27
Dialog	0	2	1	19	118

Table 5: Confusion matrix for the classification of registers.

Manual inspection of confusions shows that erroneous classifications of the Dialog and Chat registers mainly stem from errors in the data, e.g. missing punctuation marks, which result in long sentences or make it impossible to recognize questions automatically. Also, some features relevant to these registers, such as demonstratives, are not present in very short texts.

TED and News are mostly confused with Dialog or Chat data if they contain shorter sentences on average. This is also the main reason for the confusion of Speech data with TED talks.

Confusion of News with more orally-oriented registers (Dialog, Chat, TED) results from specific article types like interviews or literature excerpts, which contain more (first person) pronouns than is

---

[19]The relevance of the feature PRONsubj is also evidenced by the fact that this feature contributes the largest amount of information gain with respect to the class, as shown by Weka's "InfoGainAttributeEval", cf. Table 7 in the appendix.

typical for standard newspaper text.

5.2 Classifying situational characteristics

Since our project ultimately aims at investigating historical language data, we need classifiers that are based on functional, "timeless" features rather than features specific to modern-time registers. To this end, we trained classifiers for the different situational characteristics (see the resulting decision trees in the appendix, Fig. 4–Fig. 6).

Participants/Interactiveness As mentioned above, the registers used in this study only exhibit two combinations of these characteristics: either they are monologs with many participants or dialogs with few participants. Therefore, the resulting decision trees for the two characteristics are identical.

The most important feature for the classification of these characteristics is, again, mean sentence length. However, this time it does not introduce a clear distinction in the tree between oral- (few/dialog) and literate-oriented (many/monolog) characteristics, as we observed it for the registers.

Further relevant features are the ratio of first person pronouns (PRON1st) and questions. A large number of texts with long sentences can be classified by the (almost complete) absence of interjections (INTERJ).

The classifier achieves high scores of overall accuracy (97.13%) and average F-score (0.972, for details see Table 6 in the appendix).

Production and Reception The characteristics of the production and reception circumstances both have three possible values (asynchronous, quasi-synchronous, and synchronous), which are combined pairwise in five different ways by the five registers (see Table 3). Still, there are some interesting similarities between the two classifier trees. For both characteristics, features relating to pronouns (PRON1st for production, PRONsubj for reception) are used as the top-level split. In both cases, all synchronous instances fall into the lower part of the tree, which is marked by a larger number of these pronouns.

For reception, mean sentence length is the second most important feature while for production the mean word length is more discriminating.

It is interesting to note that with both characteristics, binary distinctions at the leaves almost never occur between the values asynchronous and synchronous. Instead, the two values are contrasted individually with quasi-synchronous. This seems to confirm the intermediate status of the quasi-synchronous value. Overall F-score of both characteristics is around 90% (see Table 6 in the appendix). In the case of production, confusions again occur mainly between neighbouring values.

6 Conclusion and Outlook

In this paper, we investigated a range of selected linguistic features, with the aim of automatically identifying conceptually oral and literate texts. It turned out that extremely simple measures of complexity, namely average sentence and word length, are prominent indicators of conceptuality. In addition, features of reference and deixis (realized by different types of pronouns) proved to be useful in determining the degree of orality of different registers.

Even though some of the features did not play major roles in the resulting decision tree, the distribution plots show that all of them are related in some way to oral conceptuality. This is confirmed by the fact that each feature is used at least once in some of the four decision trees. The features occurring least often in the decision trees are subord, exclam, and med_word.

Of course, when languages other than German are investigated, the set of linguistic features might have to be adapted, as features can be used with different functions in different languages (Biber, 1995).

When looking at diachronic data, one also has to consider that the relations between registers, their situational characteristics and the linguistic features might have changed over time. For instance, it is known that English scientific prose used to be closer to the oral mode than it is nowadays (Degaetano-Ortlieb et al., 2019).

Acknowledgments

We would like to thank the anonymous reviewers for very helpful comments. This work was supported by the German Research Foundation (DFG), SFB/CRC 1102 "Information density and linguistic encoding" (Project C6).

References

Vilmos Ágel and Mathilde Hennig. 2006. *Grammatik aus Nähe und Distanz: Theorie und Praxis am Beispiel von Nähetexten 1650-2000*. Niemeyer, Tübingen.

Vilmos Ágel and Mathilde Hennig. 2010. Einleitung. In *Nähe und Distanz im Kontext variationslinguistischer Forschung*, pages 1–22. de Gruyter, Berlin.

Jennifer Bader. 2002. Schriftlichkeit und Mündlichkeit in der Chat-Kommunikation. *NETWORX*, 29. Retrieved from `https://www.mediensprache.net/networx/networx-29.pdf`.

Douglas Biber. 1995. *Dimensions of register variation: a cross-linguistic comparison*. Cambridge University Press.

Douglas Biber and Susan Conrad. 2009. *Register, Genre, and Style*. Cambridge University Press.

Wallace L. Chafe. 1982. Integration and involvement in speaking, writing, and oral literature. In Deborah Tannen, editor, *Spoken and Written Language: Exploring Orality and Literacy*, pages 35–53. Ablex Publishing Corporation, Norwood, NJ.

Stefania Degaetano-Ortlieb, Hannah Kermes, Ashraf Khamis, and Elke Teich. 2019. An information-theoretic approach to modeling diachronic change in scientific English. In Carla Suhr, Terttu Nevalainen, and Irma Taavitsainen, editors, *From Data to Evidence in English Language Research*. Brill, Leiden, NL/Boston, MA.

Grazia Diamante and Elda Morlicchio. 2015. Authentische Dialoge im DaF-Unterricht? In Nicoletta Gagliardi, editor, *Die deutsche Sprache im Gespräch und in simulierter Mündlichkeit*, pages 91–114. Schneider Verlag Hohengehren, Baltmannsweiler.

G. H. J. Drieman. 1962. Differences between written and spoken language: An exploratory study. *Acta Psychologica*, 20:36–57. Doi:10.1016/0001-6918(62)90006-9.

Christa Dürscheid. 2003. Medienkommunikation im Kontinuum von Mündlichkeit und Schriftlichkeit: Theoretische und empirische Probleme. *Zeitschrift für angewandte Linguistik*, 38:37–56.

Christa Dürscheid. 2006. Äußerungsformen im Kontinuum von Mündlichkeit und Schriftlichkeit — Sprachwissenschaftliche und sprachdidaktische Aspekte. In Eva Neuland, editor, *Variation im heutigen Deutsch: Perspektiven für den Sprachunterricht*, pages 375–388. Peter Lang, Frankfurt a. M.

Peter Fankhauser, Jörg Knappen, and Elke Teich. 2014. Exploring and visualizing variation in language resources. In *Proceedings of the 9th LREC*, pages 4125–4128.

Reinhard Fiehler. 2011. Mündliche Verständigung und gesprochene Sprache. In Sandro M. Moraldo, editor, *Deutsch aktuell: 2. Einführung in die Tendenzen der deutschen Gegenwartssprache*, pages 83–107. Carocci, Rome. Retrieved from `https://ids-pub.bsz-bw.de/frontdoor/deliver/index/docId/4338/file/Fiehler_Muendliche_Verstaendigung_und_gesprochene_Sprache_2011.pdf`.

Jack Goody. 1987. *The interface between the written and the oral*. Cambridge University Press.

Georgia M. Green. 1982. Some of my favorite writers are literate: The mingling of oral and literate strategies in written communication. In Deborah Tannen, editor, *Spoken and Written Language: Exploring Orality and Literacy*, pages 239–260. Ablex Publishing Corporation, Norwood, NJ.

Michael A. K. Halliday. 1989. *Spoken and written language*. Oxford University Press.

Peter Koch and Wulf Oesterreicher. 1985. Sprache der Nähe — Sprache der Distanz: Mündlichkeit und Schriftlichkeit im Spannungsfeld von Sprachtheorie und Sprachgeschichte. *Romanistisches Jahrbuch*, 36:15–43.

Peter Koch and Wulf Oesterreicher. 2007. Schriftlichkeit und kommunikative Distanz. *Zeitschrift für germanistische Linguistik*, 35:246–275.

Karin Müller. 1990. *"Schreibe wie du sprichst!" Eine Maxime im Spannungsfeld von Mündlichkeit und Schriftlichkeit: Eine historische und systematische Untersuchung*. Lang, Frankfurt a. M.

Ross Quinlan. 1993. *C4.5: Programs for Machine Learning*. Morgan Kaufmann, San Mateo, CA.

Georg Rehm. 2002. Schriftliche Mündlichkeit in der Sprache des World Wide Web. In Arndt Ziegler and Christa Dürscheid, editors, *Kommunikationsform E-Mail*, pages 263–308. Stauffenburg, Tübingen. Retrieved from `http://www.georg-re.hm/pdf/Rehm-Muendlichkeit.pdf`.

Günther Richter. 1985. Einige Anmerkungen zur Norm und Struktur des gesprochenen Deutsch. *Deutsch als Fremdsprache*, 22(3):149–153.

Anne Schiller, Simone Teufel, Christine Stöckert, and Christine Thielen. 1999. *Guidelines für das Tagging deutscher Textcorpora mit STTS (Kleines und großes Tagset)*. Retrieved from `http://www.sfs.uni-tuebingen.de/resources/stts-1999.pdf`.

Johannes Schwitalla and Liisa Tiittula. 2009. *Mündlichkeit in literarischen Erzählungen: Sprech- und Dialoggestaltung in modernen deutschen und finnischen Romanen und deren Übersetzungen*. Stauffenburg, Tübingen.

Peter Sieber. 1998. *Parlando in Texten: Zur Veränderung kommunikativer Grundmuster in der Schriftlichkeit*. Max Niemeyer, Tübingen.

Augustin Speyer. 2013. Performative Mündlichkeitsnähe als Faktor für die Objektstellung im Mittel- und Frühneuhochdeutschen. *Beiträge zur Geschichte der deutschen Sprache und Literatur*, 135(3):1–36.

Ewa Tomczyk-Popińska. 1987. Linguistische Merkmale der deutschen gesprochenen Standardsprache. *Deutsche Sprache: Zeitschrift für Theorie, Praxis, Dokumentation*, 15:336–375.

Helmut Weiß. 2005. Von den vier Lebensaltern einer Standardsprache. *Deutsche Sprache: Zeitschrift für Theorie, Praxis, Dokumentation*, 33:289–307.

Ian H. Witten, Eibe Frank, and Mark A. Hall. 2011. *Data Mining: Practical Machine Learning Tools and Techniques*, 3rd edition. Morgan Kaufmann, Burlington, MA.

Appendix

Property	Values	#Texts	F-Score
Participants/ Interact.	many/monolog	1,279	0.980
	few/dialog	462	0.947
	weighted avg.		0.972
Production	asynchronous	1,055	0.942
	quasi-synchronous	546	0.838
	synchronous	140	0.795
	weighted avg.		0.898
Reception	asynchronous	1,024	0.951
	quasi-synchronous	322	0.852
	synchronous	395	0.849
	weighted avg.		0.909

Table 6: Results for classifying situational characteristics.

Information Gain	Feature
0.796	PRONsubj
0.738	V.N
0.732	PRON1st
0.69	question
0.676	PTC
0.673	mean_word
0.636	med_sent
0.633	mean_sent
0.508	lexDens
0.494	INTERJ
0.448	med_word
0.442	DEM
0.425	DEMshort
0.404	exclam
0.301	coordInit
0.206	nomCmplx
0.181	subord

Table 7: Ranking of the features according to their Information Gain with respect to the class of registers.

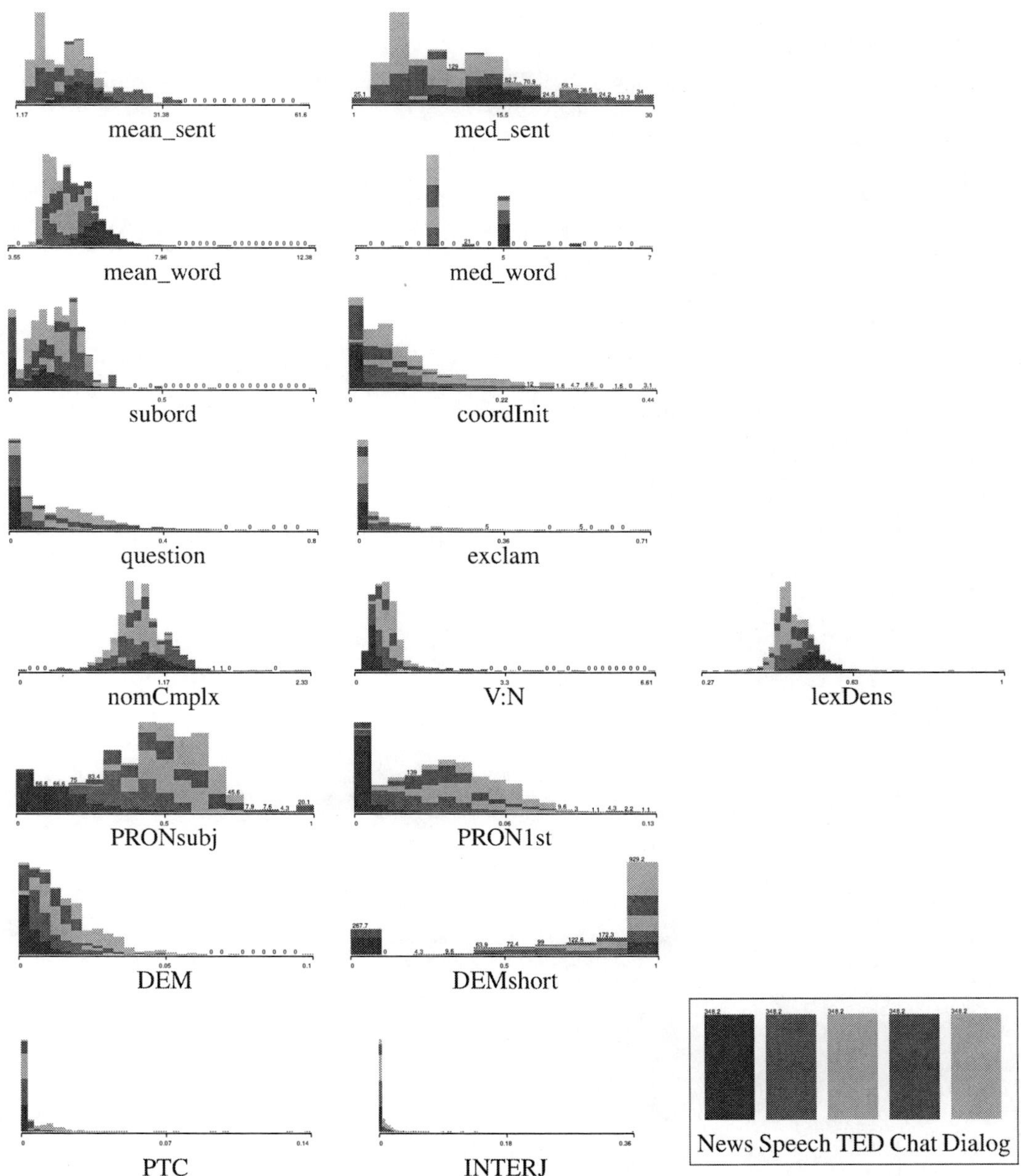

Figure 2: Weka plots for all 17 features investigated in the present study (see Table 1 for descriptions of the features). Registers are balanced and encoded by different colors (blue: *News*, red: *Speech*, cyan: *TED*, green: *Chat*, pink: *Dialog*, see the legend at the bottom right). The graphs plot the distributions of the respective features for each register. For example, the distribution of the feature PRON1st displays a large blue bar (*News*) on the left at value 0, as most newspaper articles do not contain any first person pronouns; the other registers show higher amounts of such pronouns, the pink bars (*Dialog*) achieve top values.

```
mean_sent <= 10.487395
|   PRONsubj <= 0.392857
|   |   question <= 0.066667
|   |   |   PRON1st <= 0.012245: News (34.13/2.16)
|   |   |   PRON1st > 0.012245: Chat (5.01/0.68)
|   |   question > 0.066667: Chat (59.01/1.7)
|   PRONsubj > 0.392857
|   |   DEMshort <= 0.942308: Chat (157.32/16.74)
|   |   DEMshort > 0.942308
|   |   |   V.N <= 1.659091
|   |   |   |   mean_word <= 5.123077
|   |   |   |   |   coordInit <= 0
|   |   |   |   |   |   mean_word <= 4.742631: Dialog (12.87/5.41)
|   |   |   |   |   |   mean_word > 4.742631: Chat (9.73)
|   |   |   |   |   coordInit > 0
|   |   |   |   |   |   question <= 0.277778: Dialog (319.51/13.59)
|   |   |   |   |   |   question > 0.277778
|   |   |   |   |   |   |   DEM <= 0.022727: Chat (9.73)
|   |   |   |   |   |   |   DEM > 0.022727: Dialog (9.95)
|   |   |   |   mean_word > 5.123077
|   |   |   |   |   question <= 0.142395
|   |   |   |   |   |   med_sent <= 5.5: Chat (10.81)
|   |   |   |   |   |   med_sent > 5.5
|   |   |   |   |   |   |   subord <= 0.192308: Dialog (10.63/0.68)
|   |   |   |   |   |   |   subord > 0.192308: Chat (5.41)
|   |   |   |   |   question > 0.142395: Chat (38.32/1.55)
|   |   |   V.N > 1.659091: Chat (30.28)
mean_sent > 10.487395
|   PRONsubj <= 0.232558: News (252.65)
|   PRONsubj > 0.232558
|   |   mean_sent <= 20.653846
|   |   |   lexDens <= 0.514085
|   |   |   |   exclam <= 0.019139
|   |   |   |   |   mean_word <= 4.755344: Speech (15.42/4.19)
|   |   |   |   |   mean_word > 4.755344
|   |   |   |   |   |   DEM <= 0.000745: News (6.58/2.16)
|   |   |   |   |   |   DEM > 0.000745
|   |   |   |   |   |   |   PRON1st <= 0.00905: News (6.32/1.55)
|   |   |   |   |   |   |   PRON1st > 0.00905: TED (298.92/16.01)
|   |   |   |   exclam > 0.019139
|   |   |   |   |   question <= 0.096045
|   |   |   |   |   |   mean_word <= 5.284568
|   |   |   |   |   |   |   lexDens <= 0.449857: TED (7.77)
|   |   |   |   |   |   |   lexDens > 0.449857: Speech (139.45/4.66)
|   |   |   |   |   |   mean_word > 5.284568: TED (10.83/3.06)
|   |   |   |   |   question > 0.096045
|   |   |   |   |   |   PTC <= 0.007194
|   |   |   |   |   |   |   coordInit <= 0.033113: Chat (6.49)
|   |   |   |   |   |   |   coordInit > 0.033113
|   |   |   |   |   |   |   |   lexDens <= 0.482862: TED (15.54)
|   |   |   |   |   |   |   |   lexDens > 0.482862: Chat (8.45/4.13)
|   |   |   |   |   |   PTC > 0.007194: Dialog (5.31/0.34)
|   |   |   lexDens > 0.514085
|   |   |   |   question <= 0.118103: News (28.76/1.55)
|   |   |   |   question > 0.118103: Chat (9.27/1.7)
|   |   mean_sent > 20.653846
|   |   |   question <= 0: Dialog (6.42/3.93)
|   |   |   question > 0
|   |   |   |   question <= 0.097561: Speech (205.1/2.91)
|   |   |   |   question > 0.097561: TED (5.0/0.34)
```

Figure 3: Weka decision tree for classifying registers. Class labels that have been assigned at the leaves are preceded by a colon. The first figure in parentheses states how many instances have been classified at this leaf (the figures do not correspond to actual instances but result from balancing the data, see Footnote 18). The second figure, after the slash, specifies how many instances were classified incorrectly, if any (because the data has missing attribute values, the algorithm used by Weka outputs fractional figures).

```
mean_sent <= 10.681818
|   PRON1st <= 0.008772
|   |   lexDens <= 0.486486: FEW/DIALOG (29.1/2.72)
|   |   lexDens > 0.486486
|   |   |   V.N <= 0.654762: MANY/MONOLOG (74.03/1.88)
|   |   |   V.N > 0.654762: FEW/DIALOG (16.43/1.36)
|   PRON1st > 0.008772
|   |   mean_sent <= 8.4: FEW/DIALOG (632.57/1.36)
|   |   mean_sent > 8.4
|   |   |   question <= 0.204724
|   |   |   |   V.N <= 0.969466
|   |   |   |   |   INTERJ <= 0.005882
|   |   |   |   |   |   med_word <= 4: MANY/MONOLOG (14.14/1.88)
|   |   |   |   |   |   med_word > 4: FEW/DIALOG (8.38/2.72)
|   |   |   |   |   INTERJ > 0.005882: FEW/DIALOG (15.07)
|   |   |   |   V.N > 0.969466: FEW/DIALOG (28.26)
|   |   |   question > 0.204724: FEW/DIALOG (101.75)
mean_sent > 10.681818
|   question <= 0.181024
|   |   INTERJ <= 0.004198: MANY/MONOLOG (744.95/3.77)
|   |   INTERJ > 0.004198
|   |   |   PRONsubj <= 0.473684: MANY/MONOLOG (20.42)
|   |   |   PRONsubj > 0.473684: FEW/DIALOG (5.13/1.36)
|   question > 0.181024
|   |   coordInit <= 0.086957
|   |   |   V.N <= 0.424528: MANY/MONOLOG (5.44)
|   |   |   V.N > 0.424528: FEW/DIALOG (37.16/1.36)
|   |   coordInit > 0.086957: MANY/MONOLOG (8.17)
```

Figure 4: Weka decision tree for classifying the situational characteristics participants or interactiveness. As the registers in the present study are either monologous with many participants or dialogous with few participants, the resulting decision trees for both properties are identical.

```
PRON1st <= 0.011905
|   question <= 0.193878
|   |   mean_sent <= 7.6
|   |   |   lexDens <= 0.501439: QUASI (5.31)
|   |   |   lexDens > 0.501439: ASYNC (12.58/2.13)
|   |   mean_sent > 7.6: ASYNC (499.84/5.31)
|   question > 0.193878
|   |   mean_sent <= 10.818182: QUASI (20.23/1.1)
|   |   mean_sent > 10.818182: ASYNC (5.46/1.06)
PRON1st > 0.011905
|   mean_word <= 5.072603
|   |   DEMshort <= 0.942308
|   |   |   PTC <= 0.034483: QUASI (77.66/2.2)
|   |   |   PTC > 0.034483: SYNC (11.48/3.19)
|   |   DEMshort > 0.942308
|   |   |   V.N <= 1.662281
|   |   |   |   mean_sent <= 9.375
|   |   |   |   |   coordInit <= 0
|   |   |   |   |   |   PRON1st <= 0.022489: SYNC (8.29)
|   |   |   |   |   |   PRON1st > 0.022489
|   |   |   |   |   |   |   PTC <= 0.045455: QUASI (15.94)
|   |   |   |   |   |   |   PTC > 0.045455: SYNC (5.21/1.06)
|   |   |   |   |   coordInit > 0
|   |   |   |   |   |   DEM <= 0.016575
|   |   |   |   |   |   |   question <= 0.263374: SYNC (38.51/5.35)
|   |   |   |   |   |   |   question > 0.263374: QUASI (8.5)
|   |   |   |   |   |   DEM > 0.016575: SYNC (489.24/4.25)
|   |   |   |   mean_sent > 9.375
|   |   |   |   |   PTC <= 0.0071
|   |   |   |   |   |   PRONsubj <= 0.52809
|   |   |   |   |   |   |   INTERJ <= 0.000617: ASYNC (5.46/1.06)
|   |   |   |   |   |   |   INTERJ > 0.000617: QUASI (5.35/1.1)
|   |   |   |   |   |   PRONsubj > 0.52809: QUASI (17.56/0.55)
|   |   |   |   |   PTC > 0.0071: SYNC (13.5/1.06)
|   |   |   V.N > 1.662281
|   |   |   |   med_sent <= 9.5: QUASI (24.45)
|   |   |   |   med_sent > 9.5: SYNC (5.21/1.06)
|   mean_word > 5.072603
|   |   PRONsubj <= 0.264706
|   |   |   PRON1st <= 0.020331: ASYNC (19.8)
|   |   |   PRON1st > 0.020331: QUASI (5.39/2.2)
|   |   PRONsubj > 0.264706
|   |   |   PTC <= 0.015456
|   |   |   |   nomCmplx <= 1.135593
|   |   |   |   |   mean_sent <= 7.429577
|   |   |   |   |   |   nomCmplx <= 1.03125: QUASI (72.83/0.55)
|   |   |   |   |   |   nomCmplx > 1.03125: SYNC (10.42/2.13)
|   |   |   |   |   mean_sent > 7.429577
|   |   |   |   |   |   question <= 0
|   |   |   |   |   |   |   lexDens <= 0.505458: QUASI (13.34/1.65)
|   |   |   |   |   |   |   lexDens > 0.505458: ASYNC (5.5)
|   |   |   |   |   |   question > 0: QUASI (260.38/14.85)
|   |   |   |   nomCmplx > 1.135593
|   |   |   |   |   med_sent <= 16
|   |   |   |   |   |   mean_word <= 5.38497: QUASI (18.07)
|   |   |   |   |   |   mean_word > 5.38497
|   |   |   |   |   |   |   DEMshort <= 0.844828: QUASI (5.86/0.55)
|   |   |   |   |   |   |   DEMshort > 0.844828: ASYNC (9.28/2.13)
|   |   |   |   |   med_sent > 16: ASYNC (8.25)
|   |   |   PTC > 0.015456
|   |   |   |   coordInit <= 0.069565
|   |   |   |   |   question <= 0.05: SYNC (5.21/1.06)
|   |   |   |   |   question > 0.05: QUASI (22.32)
|   |   |   |   coordInit > 0.069565: SYNC (14.56/2.13)
```

Figure 5: Weka decision tree for classifying production circumstances.

```
PRONsubj <= 0.232558
|   mean_sent <= 6.533333
|   |   med_word <= 4.5: QUASI (12.62)
|   |   med_word > 4.5: ASYNC (5.77/1.8)
|   mean_sent > 6.533333: ASYNC (467.55)
PRONsubj > 0.232558
|   mean_sent <= 11.309524
|   |   DEM <= 0.016575
|   |   |   question <= 0.054152
|   |   |   |   DEMshort <= 0.25
|   |   |   |   |   V.N <= 0.481481: ASYNC (9.63)
|   |   |   |   |   V.N > 0.481481: QUASI (24.8/3.17)
|   |   |   |   DEMshort > 0.25: SYNC (21.13/3.5)
|   |   |   question > 0.054152
|   |   |   |   mean_word <= 4.825082
|   |   |   |   |   V.N <= 1.360656
|   |   |   |   |   |   DEM <= 0.012663
|   |   |   |   |   |   |   question <= 0.266667
|   |   |   |   |   |   |   |   PRON1st <= 0.053691: SYNC (7.68/1.8)
|   |   |   |   |   |   |   |   PRON1st > 0.053691: QUASI (10.48/1.47)
|   |   |   |   |   |   |   question > 0.266667: QUASI (19.83)
|   |   |   |   |   |   DEM > 0.012663: SYNC (8.82)
|   |   |   |   |   V.N > 1.360656: QUASI (46.86)
|   |   |   |   mean_word > 4.825082
|   |   |   |   |   mean_sent <= 10.882353: QUASI (284.02/10.07)
|   |   |   |   |   mean_sent > 10.882353
|   |   |   |   |   |   V.N <= 0.726115: QUASI (13.75/1.13)
|   |   |   |   |   |   V.N > 0.726115: SYNC (5.88)
|   |   DEM > 0.016575
|   |   |   mean_word <= 5.072603
|   |   |   |   V.N <= 1.662281
|   |   |   |   |   coordInit <= 0: QUASI (29.97/2.94)
|   |   |   |   |   coordInit > 0: SYNC (194.7/9.58)
|   |   |   |   V.N > 1.662281: QUASI (27.03)
|   |   |   mean_word > 5.072603
|   |   |   |   mean_sent <= 10.3074: QUASI (101.06/7.35)
|   |   |   |   mean_sent > 10.3074: SYNC (6.21/1.8)
|   mean_sent > 11.309524
|   |   lexDens <= 0.511404
|   |   |   coordInit <= 0.003795
|   |   |   |   question <= 0.169811: ASYNC (9.97/1.47)
|   |   |   |   question > 0.169811: QUASI (5.41)
|   |   |   coordInit > 0.003795
|   |   |   |   question <= 0.189189
|   |   |   |   |   PRON1st <= 0.00905
|   |   |   |   |   |   mean_sent <= 23.821429: ASYNC (7.37)
|   |   |   |   |   |   mean_sent > 23.821429: SYNC (5.88)
|   |   |   |   |   PRON1st > 0.00905: SYNC (326.1/17.57)
|   |   |   |   question > 0.189189
|   |   |   |   |   lexDens <= 0.480859: SYNC (11.75)
|   |   |   |   |   lexDens > 0.480859: QUASI (5.97/0.57)
|   |   lexDens > 0.511404
|   |   |   exclam <= 0.047297
|   |   |   |   INTERJ <= 0.000251: ASYNC (44.54/1.47)
|   |   |   |   INTERJ > 0.000251
|   |   |   |   |   nomCmplx <= 1.109966: ASYNC (6.0/1.47)
|   |   |   |   |   nomCmplx > 1.109966: SYNC (5.54/1.13)
|   |   |   exclam > 0.047297
|   |   |   |   question <= 0.209459: ASYNC (7.47/1.8)
|   |   |   |   question > 0.209459: QUASI (7.21)
```

Figure 6: Weka decision tree for classifying reception circumstances.

Neural Machine Translation
Between Myanmar (Burmese) and Rakhine (Arakanese)

Thazin Myint Oo[‡] , **Ye Kyaw Thu**[†] and **Khin Mar Soe**[‡]

Natural Language Processing Lab., University of Computer Studies Yangon, Myanmar[‡]

Language and Semantic Technology Research Team (LST), NECTEC, Thailand [†]

Language and Speech Science Research Lab., Waseda University, Japan [†]

`{thazinmyintoo, khinmarsoe}@ucsy.edu.mm, ka2pluskha2@gmail.com`

Abstract

This work explores neural machine translation between Myanmar (Burmese) and Rakhine (Arakanese). Rakhine is a language closely related to Myanmar, often considered a dialect. We implemented three prominent neural machine translation (NMT) systems: recurrent neural networks (RNN), transformer, and convolutional neural networks (CNN). The systems were evaluated on a Myanmar-Rakhine parallel text corpus developed by us. In addition, two types of word segmentation schemes for word embeddings were studied: Word-BPE and Syllable-BPE segmentation. Our experimental results clearly show that the highest quality NMT and statistical machine translation (SMT) performances are obtained with Syllable-BPE segmentation for both types of translations. If we focus on NMT, we find that the transformer with Word-BPE segmentation outperforms CNN and RNN for both Myanmar-Rakhine and Rakhine-Myanmar translation. However, CNN with Syllable-BPE segmentation obtains a higher score than the RNN and transformer.

1 Introduction

The Myanmar language includes a number of mutually intelligible Myanmar dialects, with a largely uniform standard dialect used by most Myanmar standard speakers. Speakers of the standard Myanmar may find the dialects hard to follow. The alternative phonology, morphology, and regional vocabulary cause some problems in communication. Machine translation (MT) has so far neglected the importance of properly handling the spelling, lexical, and grammar divergences among language varieties. In the Republic of the Union of Myanmar, there are many ethnical groups, and dialectal varieties exist within the standard Myanmar language.

To address this problem, we are developing a Myanmar and Rakhine dialectal corpus with monolingual and parallel text. We conducted statistical machine translation (SMT) experiments and obtained results similar to previous research (Oo et al., 2018).

Deep learning revolution brings rapid and dramatic change to the field of machine translation. The main reason for moving from SMT to neural machine translation (NMT) is that it achieved the fluency of translation that was a huge step forward compared with the previous models. In a trend that carries over from SMT, the strongest NMT systems benefit from subtle architecture modifications and hyperparameter tuning.

NMT models have advanced the state of the art by building a single neural network that can learn representations better (Sutskever et al., 2014a). Other authors (Rikters et al., 2018) conducted experiments with different NMTs for less-resourced and morphologically rich languages, such as Estonian and Russian. They compared the multi-way model performance to one-way model performance, by using different NMT architectures that allow achieving state-of-the-art translation. For the multiway model trained using the transformer network architecture, the reported improvement over the baseline methods was +3.27 bilingual evaluation understudy (BLEU) points.

(Honnet et al., 2017) proposed solutions for the machine translation of a family of dialects, Swiss German, for which parallel corpora are scarcee. The authors presented three strategies for normalizing Swiss German input to address the regional and spelling diversity. The results show that character-based neural machine translation was the most promising strategy for text normalization and that in combination with phrase-based statistical machine translation it achieved 36% BLEU score. In their study, NMT outperformed SMT.

In our study, we performed the first comparative NMT analysis of Myanmar dialectal language with three prominent architectures: recurrent neural network (RNN), convolutional

Proceedings of VarDial, pages 80–88

Minneapolis, MN, June 7, 2019 ©2019 Association for Computational Linguistics

neural network (CNN), and transformer. We investigated the translation quality of the corresponding hyper-parameters (batch size, learning rate, cell type, and activation function) in machine translation between the standard Myanmar and national varieties of the same group of languages. In addition, we used two types of segmentation schemes: word byte pair encoding (Word-BPE) segmentation and syllable byte pair encoding (Syllable-BPE) segmentation. We compared the performance of this method to SMT and NMT experiments with the RNN, transformer, and CNN. We found that the transformer with Word-BPE segmentation outperformed both CNN and RNN for both Myanmar-Rakhine and Myanmar-Rakhine translations. We also found that CNN with Syllable-BPE segmentation obtained a higher score compared with RNN and the transformer.

2   Rakhine Language

Rakhine (Arakanese) is one of the eight national ethnic groups in the Republic of the Union of Myanmar. The Arakan was officially altered to "Rakhine" in 1989 and is located on a narrow coastal strip on the west of Myanmar, 300 miles long and 50 to 20 miles wide. The total population in all countries is nearly 3 million. The Rakhine language has been studied by researchers. L.F-Taylor's "The Dialects of Burmese" described comparative pronunciation, sentence construction, and grammar usage in Rakhine, Dawei, In-tha, Taung-yoe, Danu, and Yae. Professor Denise Bernot, in "The vowel system of Arakanese and Tavoyan," mainly emphasized the vowels of standard Myanmar and Tavoyan (Dawei) in 1965. In "Three Burmese Dialects" (1969), the linguist John Okell studied the spoken language of Myanmar, Dawei, and In-tha: specifically, usage of grammar and vowel differences (OKELL, 1995). Although the Rakhine language used the script as Arakanese or Rakkhawanna Akkhara before at least the 8th century A.D., the current Rakhine script is nearly the same as the Myanmar script. Generally, the Arakanese language is mutually intelligible with the Myanmar language and has the same word order (namely, subject-object-verb (SOV)). Examples of parallel sentences in Myanmar (my) and Rakhine (rk) are given as follows.

rk: ဒယော တစ် ထည် ဇာလောက်လေး ။
my: လုံချည် တစ် ထည် ဘယ်လောက်လဲ ။
("How much for a longyi?" in English)

rk: ကလေချေ တိ ဘောလုံး ကျောက် နီရေ ။
my: ကောင်လေး တွေ ဘောလုံး ကန် နေတယ် ။
("Boys are playing football" in English)

rk: ဇာ ပြော နီချင့် ယင်းသူရို့ ။
my: သူတို့ ဘာ ပြော နေတာလဲ ။
("What are they talking about" in English)

rk: အဘောင်သျှင် စျီး က သပုံ ဝယ် လာတယ် ။
my: အဘွား ဈေး က ဆပ်ပြာ ဝယ် လာတယ် ။
("The grandmother buys soap from the market" in English)

3   Difference between the Rakhine and standard Myanmar language

The Rakhine language is a largely monosyllabic and analytic language, with a SOV word order, and it uses the Myanmar script. It is considered by some to be a dialect of the Myanmar language, though it differs significantly from the standard Myanmar language in its vocabulary and includes loan words from Bengali, Hindi, and English. Compared with the Myanmar language, the speech of the Rakhine language is likely to be closer to the written form. The Rakhine language notably retains an /r/ sound that has become /j/ in the Myanmar language. Rakhine speakers pronounce the medial " ြ" as "Yapint" (i.e., /j/ sound) and the medial "ြ" as "Rayit" (i.e., /r/ sound). Moreover, Myanmar vowel "ေ" (/e/ sound) is pronounced as "ိ" (/i/ sound) in Rakhine language. Thus, for example, the word "dog" in the Myanmar language is written as "ခွေး" (Khwe), and in the Rakhine language it is written as "ခွီး" (khwii). Similarly, Rakhine pronounce "ေး" (/e:/) for Myanmar pronunciation of " ဲ" (/ai/) syllable. Thus, Myanmar word "ပဲဟင်း" (peh-hinn) (pea curry in English) is pronounced "ပေးဟင်း" (pay-hinn) in the Rakhine language. Some Pali words are also used in the Rakhine language. For example, the word "guest" of Myanmar monks "အာဂန္တု" (Agantu) is used in normal speech of Rakhine and it is similar to the normal Myanmar word "guest," "ဧည့်သည်" (Ai thay). In summary, the most significant differences between the Rakhine and Myanmar languages are in their pronunciation and vocabulary; there are no grammatical differences.

4   Segmentation

4.1   Word Segmentation

In both Myanmar and Rakhine texts, spaces are used to separate the phrases for easier reading. The spaces are not strictly necessary and are rarely used in short sentences. There are no clear rules for using spaces. Thus, spaces may (or may not) be inserted between words, phrases, and even between root words and their affixes. Although Myanmar sentences of ASEAN-MT corpus (Boonkwan and Supnithi, 2013) are already segmented, we have to consider some rules for manual word segmentation of Rakhine sentences. We defined Rakhine "word" to be a meaningful unit. Affix, root word, and suffix (s) are separated such as "စား ဗျာယ်", "စား ပီးဗျာယ်", "စား ဖို့ဗျာယ်". Here, "စား" ("eat" in English) is a root word and the others are suffixes for past and future tenses. As Myanmar language, Rakhine plural nouns are identified by the following particle. We added a space between the noun and the following particle: for example a Rakhine word "ကလိန့်မေချေ တိ" (ladies) is segmented as two words "ကလိန့်မေချေ" and the particle "တိ". In Rakhine grammar, particles describe the type of noun and are used after a number or text number. For example, a Rakhine word "အကြိုစေ့နှစ်ခတ်" ("two coins" in English) is segmented as "အကြိုစေ့ နှစ် ခတ်". In our manual word segmentation rules, compound nouns are considered as one word. Thus, a Rakhine compound word "ဖွဲ့သာ" + "အိတ်" ("money" + "bag" in English) is written as one word "ဖွဲ့သာအိတ်" ("wallet" in English). Rakhine adverb words such as "အဂဃောင့်" ("really" in English), "အမြန့်" ("quickly" in English) are also considered as one word. The following is an example of word segmentation for a Rakhine sentence in our corpus, and the meaning is "Among the four air conditioners in our room, two are out of order."

Unsegmented sentence:
အကျွန်ရို့အခန်းထဲမှာဟိရေလီအီးစက်လေးလုံးမှာနှစ်လုံးပျက်နီရေ ။

Segmented sentence:
အကျွန်ရို့ အခန်း ထဲမှာ ဟိ ရေ လီအီးစက် လေး လုံး မှာ နှစ် လုံး ပျက် နီရေ ။

4.2   Syllable Segmentation

Generally, Myanmar words are composed of multiple syllables, and most of the syllables are composed of more than one character. Syllables are also the basic units for pronunciation of Myanmar words. If we only focus on consonant-based syllables, the structure of the syllable can be described with Backus normal form (BNF) as follows:

$$Syllable := CMW[CK][D]$$

Here, C stands for consonants, M for medials, V for vowels, K for vowel killer character, and D for diacritic characters. Myanmar syllable segmentation can be done with a rule-based approach (Maung and Makami, 2008; Thu et al., 2013), finite state automaton (FSA) (Hlaing, 2012), or regular expressions (RE) (https://github.com/ye-kyawthu/sylbreak). In our experiments, we used RE-based Myanmar syllable segmentation tool named "sylbreak."

4.3   Byte-Pair-Encoding

(Sennrich et al., 2016) proposed a method to enable open-vocabulary translation of rare and unknown words as a sequence of subword units representing BPE algorithm (Gage, 1994). The input is a monolingual corpus for a language (one side of the parallel training data, in our case) and starts with an initial vocabulary, the characters in the text corpus. The vocabulary is updated using an iterative greedy algorithm. In every iteration, the most frequent bigram (based on the current vocabulary) in the corpus is added to the vocabulary (the merge operation). The corpus is again encoded using the updated vocabulary, and this process is repeated for a predetermined number of merge operations. The number of merge operations is the only hyperparameter of the system that needs to be tuned. A new word can be segmented by looking up the learnt vocabulary. For instance, a new word "rocket," ဒုံးပျံ may be segmented as ဒ@@ုံး ပျံ after looking up the learnt vocabulary, assuming ဒ and ုံး ပျံ as BPE units learnt during the training.

5   Encoder-Decoder Models for NMT

The core idea is to encode a variable-length input sequence of tokens into a sequence of vector representations, and then decode these representations into a sequence of output tokens. Formally, with a given sentence $X = x_1, ..., x_n$ and target sentence $Y = y_1, ..., y_m$, an

NMT system models $p(Y|X)$ as a target language sequence model, conditioning the probability of target word y_t on target history $Y_{1:t-1}$ and source sentence X. Both x_i and y_t are integer IDs given by the source and target vocabulary mapping, $\mathbf{V}_{src}$ and $\mathbf{V}_{trg}$, built from the training data tokens and represented as one-hot vectors $x_i \in \{0,1\}^{|\mathbf{V}_{src}|}$ and $y_t \in \{0,1\}^{|\mathbf{V}_{trg}|}$. These are embedded into e-dimensional vector representations (Vaswani et al., 2017) $\mathbf{E}_S\mathbf{x}_i$ and $\mathbf{E}_T\mathbf{y}_t$, using embedding matrices $\mathbb{R}^{e\times|\mathbf{V}_{src}|}$ and $\mathbf{E}_T \in \mathbb{R}^{e\times|\mathbf{V}_{trg}|}$. The target sequence is factorized as $p(Y|X;\theta) = \prod_{t=1}^{m} p(y_t|Y_{1:t-1}, X;\theta)$. The model, parameterized by θ, consists of an encoder and decoder part, which vary depending on the model architecture. $p(y_t|Y_{1:t-1}, X;\theta)$ is parameterized via a softmax output layer over some decoder representations $\bar{S}_t$:

$$p(y_t|Y_{1:t-1}, X;\theta) = softmax(\mathbf{W}_o\bar{s}_t+\mathbf{b}_o), \quad (1)$$

where $\mathbf{W}_o$ scales to the dimension of the target vocabulary $\mathbf{V}_{trg}$.

5.1 Stacked RNN with attention

The encoder consists of a bidirectional RNN followed by a stack of unidirectional RNNs. An RNN at layer l produces a sequence of hidden states $\mathbf{h}_1^l \dots \mathbf{h}_n^l$:

$$\mathbf{h}_i^l = f_{enc}(\mathbf{h}_i^{l-1}, \mathbf{h}_{i-1}^l), \quad (2)$$

where f_{rnn} is some non-linear function, such as a gated recurrent unit (GRU) or long short-term memory (LSTM) cell, and $\mathbf{h}_i^{l-1}$ is the output from the lower layer at step i. The bidirectional RNN on the lowest layer uses embeddings $\mathbf{E}_S\mathbf{x}_i$ as input and concatenates the hidden states of a forward and a reverse RNN: $\mathbf{h}_i^0 = [\overrightarrow{\mathbf{h}_i^0}; \overleftarrow{\mathbf{h}_i^0}]$. With deeper networks, learning becomes increasingly difficult (Hochreiter et al., 2001; Pascanu et al., 2012), and residual connections of the form $\mathbf{h}_i^l = \mathbf{h}_i^{l-1} + f_{enc}(\mathbf{h}_i^{l-1}, \mathbf{h}_{i-1}^l)$ become essential (He et al., 2016).

The decoder consists of an RNN to predict one target word at a time through a state vector $\mathbf{s}$:

$$\mathbf{s}_t = f_{dec}([\mathbf{E}_T\mathbf{y}_{t-1}; \bar{\mathbf{s}}_{t-1}], \mathbf{s}_{t-1}), \quad (3)$$

where f_{dec} is a multilayer RNN, $\mathbf{s}_{t-1}$ the previous state vector, and $\bar{\mathbf{s}}_{t-1}$ the source-dependent *attentional vector*. Providing the attentional vector as an input to the first decoder layer is also called *input feeding* (Luong et al., 2015). The initial decoder hidden state is a non-linear transformation of the last encoder hidden state: $\mathbf{s}_0 = \tanh(\mathbf{W}_{init}\mathbf{h}_n + \mathbf{b}_{init})$. The attentional vector $\bar{\mathbf{s}}_t$ combines the decoder state with a *context vector* $\mathbf{c}_t$:

$$\bar{\mathbf{s}}_t = \tanh(\mathbf{W}_{\bar{s}}[\mathbf{s}_t; \mathbf{c}_t]), \quad (4)$$

where $\mathbf{c}_t$ is a weighted sum of encoder hidden states: $\mathbf{c}_t = \sum_{i=1}^{n} \alpha_{ti}\mathbf{h}_i$. The attention vector α_t is computed by an attention network (Bahdanau et al., 2014; Luong et al., 2015):

$$\alpha_{ti} = softmax(score(\mathbf{s}_t, \mathbf{h}_i))$$
$$score(\mathbf{s}, \mathbf{h}) = \mathbf{v}_a^\top \tanh(\mathbf{W}_u\mathbf{s} + \mathbf{W}_v\mathbf{h}). \quad (5)$$

5.2 Self-Attentional Transformer

The transformer model (Vaswani et al., 2017) uses attention to replace recurrent dependencies, making the representation at time step i independent from the other time steps. This requires the explicit encoding of positional information in the sequence by adding fixed or learned positional embeddings to the embedding vectors.

The encoder uses several identical blocks consisting of two core sublayers: self-attention and a feedforward network. The self-attention mechanism is a variation of the dot-product attention (Luong et al., 2015) generalized to three inputs: query matrix $\mathbf{Q} \in \mathbb{R}^{n\times d}$, key matrix $\mathbf{K} \in \mathbb{R}^{n\times d}$, and value $\mathbf{V} \in \mathbb{R}^{n\times d}$, where d denotes the number of hidden units. (Vaswani et al., 2017) further extend attention to multiple *heads*, allowing for focusing on different parts of the input. A single *head u* produces a context matrix

$$\mathbf{C}_u = softmax\left(\frac{\mathbf{Q}\mathbf{W}_u^Q(\mathbf{K}\mathbf{W}_u^K)^T}{\sqrt{d_u}}\right)\mathbf{V}\mathbf{W}_u^V, \quad (6)$$

where matrices $\mathbf{W}_u^Q$, $\mathbf{W}_u^K$, and $\mathbf{W}_u^V$ are in $R^{d\times d_u}$. The final context matrix is given by concatenating the heads, followed by a linear transformation: $\mathbf{C} = [\mathbf{C}_1; \dots; \mathbf{C}_h]\mathbf{W}^O$. The form in Equation 6 suggests parallel computation across all time steps in a single large matrix multiplication. Given a sequence of hidden states $\mathbf{h}_i$ (or input embeddings), concatenated to $\mathbf{H} \in \mathbb{R}^{n\times d}$, the encoder computes self-attention using $\mathbf{Q} = \mathbf{K} = \mathbf{V} = \mathbf{H}$. The second subnetwork of an encoder block is a feedforward network with ReLU activation defined as

$$FFN(\mathbf{x}) = \max(0, \mathbf{x}\mathbf{W}_1 + \mathbf{b}_1)\mathbf{W}_2 + \mathbf{b}_2, \quad (7)$$

which is also easily parallelizable across time steps. Each sublayer, self-attention and feedforward network, is followed by a postprocessing stack of dropout, layer normalization, and residual connection.

The decoder uses the same self-attention and feedforward networks subnetworks. To maintain auto-regressiveness of the model, self-attention is masked out on future time steps according to (Vaswani et al., 2017). In addition to self-attention, a source attention layer, which uses the encoder hidden states as key and value inputs, is added. Given decoder hidden states $\mathbf{S} \in \mathbb{R}^{m \times s}$ and the encoder hidden states of the final encoder layer $\mathbf{H}^l$, source attention is computed as in Equation 5 with $\mathbf{Q} = \mathbf{S}, \mathbf{K} = \mathbf{H}^l, \mathbf{V} = \mathbf{H}^l$. As in the encoder, each sublayer is followed by a postprocessing stack of dropout, layer normalization (Ba et al., 2016), and residual connection.

5.3 Fully Convolutional Models

The convolutional model (Gehring et al., 2017) uses convolutional operations and also dispenses with recurrence. Hence, input embeddings are again augmented with explicit positional encodings.

The convolutional encoder applies a set of (stacked) convolutions that are defined as

$$\mathbf{h}_i^l = v(\mathbf{W}^l[\mathbf{h}_{i-\lfloor k/2 \rfloor}^{l-1}; \ldots ; \mathbf{h}_{i+\lfloor k/2 \rfloor}^{l-1}] + \mathbf{b}^l) + \mathbf{h}_i^{l-1}, \tag{8}$$

where v is a non-linearity such as a gated linear unit (Gehring et al., 2017; Dauphin et al., 2016), and $\mathbf{W}^l \in \mathbb{R}^{d_{cnn} \times kd}$ are the convolutional filters. To increase the context window captured by the encoder architecture, multiple layers of convolutions are stacked. To maintain sequence length across multiple stacked convolutions, inputs are padded with zero vectors.

The decoder is similar to the encoder but adds an attention mechanism to every layer. The output of the target side convolution

$$\mathbf{s}_t^{l*} = v(\mathbf{W}^l[\bar{\mathbf{s}}_{t-k+1}^{l-1}; \ldots ; \bar{\mathbf{s}}_t^{l-1}] + \mathbf{b}^l) \tag{9}$$

is combined to form $\mathbf{S}^*$ and then fed as an input to the attention mechanism of Equation 6 with a single attention head and $\mathbf{Q} = \mathbf{S}^*, \mathbf{K} = \mathbf{H}^l, \mathbf{V} = \mathbf{H}^l$, resulting in a set of context vectors $\mathbf{c}_t$. The full decoder hidden state is a residual combination with the context such that

$$\bar{\mathbf{s}}_t^l = \mathbf{s}_t^{l*} + \mathbf{c}_t + \bar{\mathbf{s}}_t^{l-1} \tag{10}$$

To avoid convolving over future time steps at time t, the input is padded to the left.

6 Experiments

6.1 Corpus Preparation and Statistics

We used 18,373 Myanmar sentences (with no name entity tags) of the ASEAN-MT Parallel Corpus (Boonkwan and Supnithi, 2013), which is a parallel corpus in the travel domain. It contains six main categories: people (greeting, introduction, and communication), survival (transportation, accommodation, and finance), food (food, beverages, and restaurants), fun (recreation, traveling, shopping, and nightlife), resource (number, time, and accuracy), special needs (emergency and health). Manual translation into the Rakhine language was done by native Rakhine students from two Myanmar universities, and the translated corpus was checked by the editor of a Rakhine newspaper. Word segmentation for Rakhine was done manually, and there are exactly 123,018 words in total. We used 14,076 sentences for training, 2,485 sentences for development, and 1,812 sentences for evaluation.

6.2 Moses SMT system

We used the Moses toolkit (Koehn et al., 2007) for training the operation sequence model (OSM) statistical machine translation systems. We did not consider phrase-based statistical machine translation (PBSMT) and hierarchical phrase-based statistical machine translation (HPBSMT), because the OSM approach achieved the highest BLEU (Papineni et al., 2002) and RIBES (Isozaki et al., 2010) scores among three approaches (Oo et al., 2018) for both Myanmar-Rakhine to Rakhine-Myanmar statistical machine translations. The word-segmented (i.e., Syllable-BPE and Word-BPE) source language was aligned with the word-segmented target language using GIZA++. The alignment was symmetrized by *grow-diag-final* and *heuristic*. The lexicalized reordering model was trained with the *msd-bidirectional-fe* option. We used KenLM (Heafield, 2011) for training the 5-gram language model with modified Kneser-Ney discounting. Minimum error rate training (MERT) (Och, 2003) was used to tune the decoder parameters, and the decoding was done using the Moses decoder (version 2.1.1) (Koehn et al., 2007). We used the default settings of Moses for all experiments.

Batch Size	RNN		Transformer		CNN	
	my-rk	rk-my	my-rk	rk-my	my-rk	rk-my
128	79.86	81.44	79.64	82.01	**80.82**	**83.59**
256	80.76	82.94	79.47	81.37	80.33	83.54
512	80.00	82.26	79.47	80.79	79.86	81.38

Table 1: BLEU scores of Syllable-BPE segmentation with different batch sizes for three NMT models

Batch Size	RNN		Transformer		CNN	
	my-rk	rk-my	my-rk	rk-my	my-rk	rk-my
128	60.02	44.44	72.70	72.82	69.03	72.24
256	60.31	46.47	**73.39**	72.45	65.61	68.26
512	42.76	34.93	73.30	**72.95**	67.89	71.68

Table 2: BLEU scores of Word-BPE segmentation with different batch sizes for three NMT models

Learning rate	RNN				Transformer			
	GRU		LSTM		GRU		LSTM	
	my-rk	rk-my	my-rk	rk-my	my-rk	rk-my	my-rk	rk-my
0.0001	79.47	81.37	79.48	80.88	80.76	82.94	80.26	83.02
0.0002	79.82	81.65	**82.85**	82.07	80.88	81.54	80.90	82.99
0.0003	80.22	82.23	80.24	82.13	80.92	82.63	81.78	83.30
0.0004	80.65	82.66	80.85	82.33	81.25	82.54	**81.92**	**84.06**
0.0005	80.41	81.46	81.98	**83.86**	80.57	82.30	80.65	82.51

Table 3: BLEU scores for batch size 256 of Syllable-BPE segmentation with different learning rates and two memory cell types on RNN and the transformer

Learning rate	Batch Size 128				Batch Size 256			
	ReLu		Soft-ReLu		ReLu		Soft-ReLu	
	my-rk	rk-my	my-rk	rk-my	my-rk	rk-my	my-rk	rk-my
0.0001	**81.37**	83.29	80.00	81.97	80.26	81.97	80.03	81.08
0.0002	81.01	82.24	79.89	82.50	80.07	82.29	80.01	81.51
0.0003	80.99	81.59	80.11	**83.34**	81.16	81.69	82.14	**84.08**
0.0004	N/A	N/A	N/A	N/A	79.74	80.87	**83.75**	83.06
0.0005	N/A	N/A	N/A	N/A	79.05	82.43	81.44	83.31

Table 4: BLEU scores for batch sizes 128 and 256 of Syllable-BPE segmentation with different learning rates and two activation functions on CNN

Segmentation	OSM		RNN		Transformer		CNN	
	my-rk	rk-my	my-rk	rk-my	my-rk	rk-my	my-rk	rk-my
Syllable-BPE	82.71	**84.36**	82.03	83.98	82.85	82.65	**83.75**	84.08
Word-BPE	77.12	75.27	60.31	46.47	73.39	72.95	69.03	72.24

Table 5: Comparison of SMT and NMT (top BLEU scores) on two segmentation schemes

6.3 Framework for NMT

An open-source sequence-to-sequence toolkit for NMT written in Python (Hieber et al., 2017) and built on Apache MXNET (Chen et al., 2015), the toolkit offers scalable training and inference for the three most prominent encoder-decoder architectures: attentional recurrent neural network (Schwenk, 2012; Kalchbrenner and Blunsom, 2013; Sutskever et al., 2014b), self-attentional transformers (Vaswani et al., 2017), and fully convolutional networks (Gehring et al., 2017).

6.4 Training Details

We used the Sockeye toolkit, which is based on MXNet, to train NMT models. The initial learning rate is set to 0.0001. If the performance on the validation set has improved for 8 checkpoints, the learning rate is multiplied by 32 checkpoints. All the neural networks have eight layers. For RNN Seq2Seq, the encoder has one bi-directional LSTM and six stacked unidirectional LSTMs, and the encoder is a stack of eight unidirectional LSTMs. The size of hidden states is 512. We apply layer-normalization and label smoothing (0.1) in all models. We tie the source and target embeddings. The dropout rate of the embeddings and transformer blocks is set to (0.1). The dropout rate of RNNs is (0.2). The attention mechanism in the transformer has eight heads.

We applied three different batch sizes (128, 256, and 512) for RNN, Transformer, and CNN network architectures. The learning rate varies from 0.0001 to 0.0005. Two memory cell types GRU and LSTM were used for the RNN and transformer. Moreover, two activation functions were applied to the CNN architecture. The comparison between Syllable-BPE and Word-BPE segmentation schemes was done for both SMT (i.e., OSM) and NMT (RNN, Transformer, and CNN) techniques. All experiments are run on NVIDIA Tesla K80 24GB GDDR5. We trained all models for the maximum number of epochs using the AdaGrad and adaptive moment estimation (Adam) optimizer. The BPE segmentation models were trained with a vocabulary of 8,000.

6.5 Evaluation

We used automatic criteria to evaluate the machine translation output. The metric BLEU (Papineni et al., 2002) measures the adequacy of the translation between language pairs, such as Myanmar and English. The Higher BLEU scores are better. Before computing BLEU, the translations were decomposed into their constituent syllables to ensure that the results are cross-comparable.

7 Results and Discussion

The BLEU score results for three NMT approaches (RNN, Transformer, and CNN) with three batch sizes (128, 256, and 512) for Syllable-BPE segmentation scheme are shown in Table 1. Bold numbers indicate the highest BLEU score among different batch sizes. CNN achieved the highest BLEU scores for both Myanmar-Rakhine and Rakhine-Myanmar translations. However, the transformer architecture achieved the top BLEU scores for Word-BPE segmentation schemes for both Myanmar-Rakhine

and Rakhine-Myanmar neural machine translations (see Table 2).

From the experimental results of Table 1 and Table 2, we noticed that RNN and Transformer NMT with Syllable-BPE have a decreased translation performance for batch size 512. Thus, we used batch size 256 for further experiments with the RNN and transformer architectures. The NMT performance of the RNN and transformer with Syllable-BPE segmentation schemes together with different learning rates (from 0.0001 to 0.0005) and two different memory cell types (GRU and LSTM) can be seen in Table 3. From these BLEU scores of the RNN and transformer approaches, LSTM gave the highest NMT performance for both Myanmar-Rakhine dialect translation and vice versa.

To observe the maximum translation performance of CNN architecture, we extended experiments by using two activation functions (ReLu and Soft-ReLu), two batch sizes (128 and 256), and five learning rates (from 0.0001 to 0.0005) (see Table 4). Here, bold numbers indicate the highest BLEU scores of each batch size. From these results, we can clearly see that Soft-ReLu achieved the highest BLEU scores for both Myanmar to Rakhine and Rakhine to Myanmar translations. We found that the training processes with learning rate 0.0004 and 0.0005 were stopped for the batch size 128 for both ReLu and Soft-ReLu activation functions.

We also made a comparison between SMT and NMT, and the results can be seen in Table 5. In this study, we run only OSM approach for the SMT experiments based on the our previous SMT work (Oo et al., 2018). The Table 5 presents that although CNN achieved the top BLEU score (83.75) for Myanmar to Rakhine translation, OSM gave the best BLEU (84.36) score for Rakhine to Myanmar translation. Furthermore, we also found that Syllable-BPE segmentation scheme is working well for both SMT and NMT for Myanmar-Rakhine dialect language pair.

As shown in the experimental results of Table 1 to Table 5, our dialect NMT experiments give significantly higher BLEU scores than other SMT on different language pairs such as Myanmar-Chinese, Myanmar-German, Myanmar-Japanese, Myanmar-Malaysian, Myanmar-Korean, Myanmar-Spanish, Myanmar-Thai, Myanmar-Vietnamese (Thu et al., 2016), and also for NMT on Myanmar-English (Sin and Soe, 2018). As we discussed in Section 3, Rakhine and Myanmar have the same word order of SOV and also share a lot of vocabulary. For these reasons, we assume that both SMT and NMT systems reach a very high machine translation performance.

8 Conclusion

This paper presents the first study of the neural machine translation between Standard Myanmar and Rakhine (a spoken Myanmar dialect). We implemented three prominent NMT systems: RNN, transformer, and CNN. The systems were evaluated on a Myanmar-Rakhine parallel text corpus that we are developing. We also investigated two types of segmentation schemes (Word-BPE segmentation and Syllable-BPE segmentation). Our results clearly show that the highest performance of SMT and NMT was obtained with Syllable-BPE segmentation for both Myanmar-Rakhine and Rakhine-Myanmar translation. If we only focus on NMT, we find that the transformer with Word-BPE segmentation outperforms CNN and RNN for both Myanmar-Rakhine and Rakhine-Myanmar. We also find that CNN with syllable-BPE segmentation obtains a higher BLEU score compared with the RNN and transformer. In the near future, we plan to conduct a further study with a focus on NMT models with one more subword segmentation scheme SentencePiece for Myanmar-Rakhine NMT. Moreover, we intend to investigate SMT and NMT approaches for other Myanmar dialect languages, such as Myeik and Dawei.

References

Lei Jimmy Ba, Ryan Kiros, and Geoffrey E. Hinton. 2016. Layer normalization. *CoRR*, abs/1607.06450.

Dzmitry Bahdanau, Kyunghyun Cho, and Yoshua Bengio. 2014. Neural machine translation by jointly learning to align and translate. *CoRR*, abs/1409.0473.

Prachya Boonkwan and Thepchai Supnithi. 2013. Technical report for the network-based asean language translation public service project. *Online Materials of Network-based ASEAN Languages Translation Public Service for Members, NECTEC*.

Tianqi Chen, Mu Li, Yutian Li, Min Lin, Naiyan Wang, Minjie Wang, Tianjun Xiao, Bing Xu, Chiyuan Zhang, and Zheng Zhang. 2015. Mxnet: A flexible and efficient machine learning library for heterogeneous distributed systems. *CoRR*, abs/1512.01274.

Yann N. Dauphin, Angela Fan, Michael Auli, and David Grangier. 2016. Language modeling with gated convolutional networks. *CoRR*, abs/1612.08083.

Philip Gage. 1994. A new algorithm for data compression. *C Users J.*, 12(2):23–38.

Jonas Gehring, Michael Auli, David Grangier, Denis Yarats, and Yann N. Dauphin. 2017. Convolutional sequence to sequence learning. *CoRR*, abs/1705.03122.

Kaiming He, Xiangyu Zhang, Shaoqing Ren, and Jian Sun. 2016. Deep residual learning for image recognition. In *2016 IEEE Conference on Computer Vision and Pattern Recognition, CVPR 2016, Las Vegas, NV, USA, June 27-30, 2016*, pages 770–778.

Kenneth Heafield. 2011. Kenlm: Faster and smaller language model queries. In *Proceedings of the Sixth Workshop on Statistical Machine Translation*, WMT '11, pages 187–197, Stroudsburg, PA, USA. Association for Computational Linguistics.

Felix Hieber, Tobias Domhan, Michael Denkowski, David Vilar, Artem Sokolov, Ann Clifton, and Matt Post. 2017. Sockeye: A toolkit for neural machine translation. *CoRR*, abs/1712.05690.

Tin Htay Hlaing. 2012. Manually constructed context-free grammar for myanmar syllable structure. In *In Proceedings of the Student Research Workshop at the 13 th Conference of the European Chapter of the Association for Computational Linguistics (EACL'12)*, pages 32–37.

Sepp Hochreiter, Yoshua Bengio, and Paolo Frasconi. 2001. Gradient flow in recurrent nets: the difficulty of learning long-term dependencies. In J. Kolen and S. Kremer, editors, *Field Guide to Dynamical Recurrent Networks*. IEEE Press.

Pierre-Edouard Honnet, Andrei Popescu-Belis, Claudiu Musat, and Michael Baeriswyl. 2017. Machine translation of low-resource spoken dialects: Strategies for normalizing swiss german. *CoRR*, abs/1710.11035.

Hideki Isozaki, Tsutomu Hirao, Kevin Duh, Katsuhito Sudoh, and Hajime Tsukada. 2010. Automatic evaluation of translation quality for distant language pairs. In *Proceedings of the 2010 Conference on Empirical Methods in Natural Language Processing*, pages 944–952, Cambridge, MA. Association for Computational Linguistics.

Nal Kalchbrenner and Phil Blunsom. 2013. Recurrent continuous translation models. In *Proceedings of the 2013 Conference on Empirical Methods in Natural Language Processing*, pages 1700–1709. Association for Computational Linguistics.

Philipp Koehn, Hieu Hoang, Alexandra Birch, Chris Callison-Burch, Marcello Federico, Nicola Bertoldi, Brooke Cowan, Wade Shen, Christine Moran, Richard Zens, Chris Dyer, Ondřej Bojar, Alexandra Constantin, and Evan Herbst. 2007. Moses: Open source toolkit for statistical machine translation. In *Proceedings of the 45th Annual Meeting of the ACL on Interactive Poster and Demonstration Sessions*, ACL '07, pages 177–180, Stroudsburg, PA, USA. Association for Computational Linguistics.

Minh-Thang Luong, Hieu Pham, and Christopher D. Manning. 2015. Effective approaches to attention-based neural machine translation. *CoRR*, abs/1508.04025.

Zin Maung Maung and Yoshiki Makami. 2008. A rule-based syllable segmentation of myanmar text. In *Proceedings of IJCNLP-08 work-shop of NLP for Less Privileged Language*, pages 51–58.

Franz Josef Och. 2003. Minimum error rate training in statistical machine translation. In *Proceedings of the 41st Annual Meeting on Association for Computational Linguistics - Volume 1*, ACL '03, pages 160–167, Stroudsburg, PA, USA. Association for Computational Linguistics.

John OKELL. 1995. Three burmese dialects. *Papers in Southeast Asian Linguistics No.13, Studies in Burmese Languages*, 13:1–138.

Thazin Myint Oo, Ye Kyaw Thu, and Khin Mar Soe. 2018. Statistical machine translation between myanmar (burmese) and rakhine (arakanese). In *Proceedings of ICCA2018*, pages 304–311.

Kishore Papineni, Salim Roukos, Todd Ward, and Wei-Jing Zhu. 2002. Bleu: A method for automatic evaluation of machine translation. In *Proceedings of the 40th Annual Meeting on Association for Computational Linguistics*, ACL '02, pages 311–318, Stroudsburg, PA, USA. Association for Computational Linguistics.

Razvan Pascanu, Tomas Mikolov, and Yoshua Bengio. 2012. Understanding the exploding gradient problem. *CoRR*, abs/1211.5063.

Matīss Rikters, Mārcis Pinnis, and Rihards Krišlauks. 2018. Training and Adapting Multilingual NMT for Less-resourced and Morphologically Rich Languages. In *Proceedings of the Eleventh International Conference on Language Resources and Evaluation (LREC 2018)*, Miyazaki, Japan. European Language Resources Association (ELRA).

Holger Schwenk. 2012. Continuous space translation models for phrase-based statistical machine translation. In *Proceedings of COLING 2012: Posters*, pages 1071–1080. The COLING 2012 Organizing Committee.

Rico Sennrich, Barry Haddow, and Alexandra Birch. 2016. Neural machine translation of rare words with subword units. In *Proceedings of the 54th Annual Meeting of the Association for Computational Linguistics (Volume 1: Long Papers)*, pages 1715–1725. Association for Computational Linguistics.

Yi Mon Shwe Sin and Khin Mar Soe. 2018. Syllable-based myanmar-english neural machine translation. In *Proceedings of ICCA2018*, pages 228–233.

Ilya Sutskever, Oriol Vinyals, and Quoc V. Le. 2014a. Sequence to sequence learning with neural networks. In *Proceedings of the 27th International Conference on Neural Information Processing Systems - Volume 2*, NIPS'14, pages 3104–3112, Cambridge, MA, USA. MIT Press.

Ilya Sutskever, Oriol Vinyals, and Quoc V. Le. 2014b. Sequence to sequence learning with neural networks. *CoRR*, abs/1409.3215.

Ye Kyaw Thu, Finch Andrew, Win Pa Pa, and Sumita Eiichiro. 2016. A large-scale study of statistical machine translation methods for myanmar language. In *Proceedings of SNLP2016*.

Ye Kyaw Thu, Finch Andrew, Sagisaka Yoshinori, and Sumita Eiichiro. 2013. A study of myanmar word segmentation schemes for statistical machine translation. In *Proceedings of ICCA2013*, pages 167–179.

Ashish Vaswani, Noam Shazeer, Niki Parmar, Jakob Uszkoreit, Llion Jones, Aidan N Gomez, Ł ukasz Kaiser, and Illia Polosukhin. 2017. Attention is all you need. In I. Guyon, U. V. Luxburg, S. Bengio, H. Wallach, R. Fergus, S. Vishwanathan, and R. Garnett, editors, *Advances in Neural Information Processing Systems 30*, pages 5998–6008. Curran Associates, Inc.

Language and Dialect Identification of Cuneiform Texts

Tommi Jauhiainen
Department of Digital Humanities
University of Helsinki
tommi.jauhiainen@helsinki.fi

Heidi Jauhiainen
Department of Digital Humanities
University of Helsinki
heidi.jauhiainen@helsinki.fi

Tero Alstola
Department of Digital Humanities
University of Helsinki
tero.alstola@helsinki.fi

Krister Lindén
Department of Digital Humanities
University of Helsinki
krister.linden@helsinki.fi

Abstract

This article introduces a corpus of cuneiform texts from which the dataset for the use of the Cuneiform Language Identification (CLI) 2019 shared task was derived as well as some preliminary language identification experiments conducted using that corpus. We also describe the CLI dataset and how it was derived from the corpus. In addition, we provide some baseline language identification results using the CLI dataset. To the best of our knowledge, the experiments detailed here represent the first time that automatic language identification methods have been used on cuneiform data.

1 Introduction

We have compiled a corpus of cuneiform texts intended to be used in language identification experiments. As the basis for our corpus, we used the Open Richly Annotated Cuneiform Corpus (Oracc).[1] In Oracc, the texts are stored in transliterated form. We created a tool, Nuolenna, which can transform the transliterations back to the cuneiform script. Selecting all monolingual lines from Oracc and transforming the transliterations into cuneiform, we created a new corpus for Sumerian and six Akkadian dialects.

This corpus was used in the initial experiments where the possibility of language identification in cuneiform texts was verified. In this paper, we report some of the results from the initial experiments. To the best of our knowledge, this is the first time that automatic language identification methods have been used on cuneiform data. The methods we use for language identification utilize mainly character n-grams and their observed probabilities in text.

For the use of the Cuneiform Language Identification (CLI) 2019 shared task[2], we extracted a dataset from the corpus. The dataset is divided into training, development, and test portions to be used in the CLI shared task which is part of the third VarDial Evaluation Campaign. We implemented four baseline language identifiers and evaluated their performance using the CLI dataset. The results of the evaluation are presented here.

2 Related work

So far, no research into language identification using cuneiform texts has been openly reported. Language identification studies involving other contemporary scripts, such as Egyptian hieroglyphs, also seem to be non-existent.

2.1 Cuneiform script and computational methods

In this section, we survey some of the research where computational methods related to language identification have been used with the cuneiform script.

Kataja and Koskenniemi (1988) discuss the description and computational implementation of phonology and morphology for Akkadian. They give examples of the rules in two-level formalism they used with the TWOL rule compiler (Karttunen et al., 1987).

Barthélemy (1998) developed and tested a morphological analyzer for Akkadian verbal forms. The analyzer works with Akkadian represented in Latin encoding (transcription).

Tablan et al. (2006) describe their project, which aims to create a tool for automatic morphological analysis of Sumerian.

---

[1][http://oracc.museum.upenn.edu]

[2][https://sites.google.com/view/vardial2019/campaign]

Proceedings of VarDial, pages 89–98
Minneapolis, MN, June 7, 2019 ©2019 Association for Computational Linguistics

Among several languages, Rao et al. (2009) analyzed Sumerian written in cuneiform using conditional entropy to compare it with the Indus script. Normalized entropy of sign *n-grams* between the two scripts was used as further evidence to indicate the possible linguistic content of the texts written in the Indus script.

Ponti et al. (2013) used the K-means clustering algorithm to cluster transliterated cuneiform texts. The texts analyzed were 51 Old Babylonian letters from Tell Harmal/Šaduppûm. *Term frequency* (TF) and *term frequency - inverse document frequency* (TF-IDF) weighted words were used as features with the clustering methods. Each document was depicted as a feature vector with the length of the whole vocabulary. In K-means, the number of clusters has to be given before the algorithm is applied and Ponti et al. (2013) experimented with 2 to 15 clusters.

Luo et al. (2015) describe an unsupervised Named-Entity Recognition (NER) system for transliterated Sumerian. They compared the use of different lengths of transliterated word *n*-grams in combination with the Decision List CoTrain algorithm, and their evaluations show that word bigrams obtain the highest F1-score. In another article (Liu et al., 2015), they describe how they managed to find unannotated personal names in a corpus and suggest that the NER system could be used as an automated tool for the annotation task. Liu et al. (2016) continue the NER research on Sumerian using a variety of supervised classification methods to detect named entities.

Homburg and Chiarcos (2016) researched automated word segmentation of Akkadian cuneiform script. They used a sign list to restore CDLI[3] transliterations back to cuneiform (represented as UTF-8 characters). This is the only related work we are aware of in which cuneiform texts encoded in Unicode cuneiform have been processed previous to our experiments.

Pagé-Perron et al. (2017) present a project dedicated to creating a pipeline for Sumerian texts. The pipeline is planned to take in transliterated Sumerian and to produce POS tag annotations and lemmatization as well as machine translation into English. Chiarcos et al. (2018) further describe the work done in the project.

In order to measure inter-textual relations, Monroe (2018) calculated the cosine similarity between word vectors consisting of transliterated Late Babylonian words.

Svärd et al. (2018) used Pointwise Mutual Information (PMI) to find collocations and associations between words and word2vec to highlight paradigmatic relationships of the words of interest. They used transliterated and lemmatized Akkadian texts from Oracc.

2.2 Language identification in texts

Automatic language identification is the task of determining the language of a piece of text from the clues in the text itself. The computational methods used in language identification vary from simple wordlists to state-of-the-art deep learning methods. A recent comprehensive survey on language identification was conducted by Jauhiainen et al. (2018c). Language identification for long texts in well-resourced languages is not a difficult task, but it becomes increasingly more challenging when we target short, fragmentary, and multilingual texts in languages where the amount of training material is severely restricted. A separate challenge for language identification is dealing with closely related languages or with several dialects of an individual language. The challenge of discriminating between closely related languages has been investigated in a series of shared tasks that have been organized as part of VarDial workshops (Zampieri et al., 2014, 2015; Malmasi et al., 2016; Zampieri et al., 2017, 2018).

3 Cuneiform texts in Oracc

Our data comes from the Open Richly Annotated Cuneiform Corpus (Oracc). Oracc is an international cooperative effort containing free online editions of cuneiform texts from various projects.[4] Oracc is one of the largest electronic corpora of Sumerian and Akkadian texts, and it is regularly updated. Our data is a snapshot of Oracc from October 2016 from XML files downloaded with the permission of the site administrators. The data is comprised of 13,662 separate texts, most of which were originally written on clay tablets. Some of the texts are duplicates, and before the language identification we removed the duplicates of texts with identical Oracc identification numbers. This procedure removes modern duplicates

---

[3]Cuneiform Digital Library Initiative [https://cdli.ucla.edu]

[4][http://oracc.museum.upenn.edu/doc/about/aboutoracc/index.html]

which have come into existence because a single text has been edited in several Oracc projects. Those duplicates that have different numbers and are thus different ancient manuscripts were not removed. Cuneiform writing does not mark the end of a sentence, and this is not indicated in the XML files either. Our data can, hence, be divided either into lines or texts with one or more lines. Oracc also contains some texts or words written in languages other than Sumerian and Akkadian, such as Hittite, Ugaritic, and Greek, but their number is so small that they were left out of this research.

The metadata of the texts in Oracc contains information about, for example, the provenance (the locality where the text was found), the genre, the time period in which the text was written, and so forth. The basic units in Oracc XML files are the transliterations of words, which are representations of the cuneiform signs in Latin script and which are given even if nothing else is stated about the words. Some of the cuneiform signs have, however, been broken off or are otherwise unreadable on the original tablets. In those cases, the word in question, or part of it, is replaced with an 'x' in the transliteration. The metadata of a word usually indicates its language, and some of the projects have also provided the cuneiform signs for each syllable or word of the transliteration.

The data contains many bilingual documents written in Sumerian and Akkadian. These documents often have the same text in both languages, sometimes on the same line.

3.1 Sumerian and Akkadian

Sumerian and Akkadian are ancient languages which were spoken and written primarily in Mesopotamia, present-day Iraq (Michalowski, 2004; Kouwenberg, 2011). Both languages were written in cuneiform script, but they are not related, Sumerian being a language isolate and Akkadian an East Semitic language. The cuneiform script was originally logographic in essence, then syllabic sign values were introduced to facilitate writing Sumerian, and only later was the script adapted for Akkadian. Consequently, some features of the cuneiform writing system are not ideal for Akkadian and many logograms are used side by side with syllabic spellings of Akkadian words (for further information see Seri, 2010).

Sumerian was one of the first languages ever written, and the oldest texts survive from the turn of the fourth and third millennia before the Common Era (BCE). Akkadian replaced Sumerian as the spoken language during the late third and early second millennia BCE, but Sumerian was used as a liturgical and scholarly language until the end of the cuneiform tradition at the beginning of the Common Era.

Written Akkadian is known from circa 2400 BCE onwards until the first century CE. The Akkadian language had two main dialects, Assyrian and Babylonian, both of which are present in our data. Assyrian was used in northern Mesopotamia and Babylonian in the south. There is written evidence for the simultaneous use of these dialects for 1,400 years, and both of them changed over time. The dialects are, hence, further divided into varieties designated as Old, Middle, and Neo-Assyrian and Old, Middle, and Neo-Babylonian. There was also a literary variety called Standard Babylonian which was used by both Assyrian and Babylonian scribes to write texts in certain genres. In Oracc, Middle-Babylonian is, furthermore, divided into the dialect spoken in Mesopotamia proper and the one spoken outside Mesopotamia. The latter, referred to as Middle Babylonian peripheral, is not a coherent dialect but varies somewhat from site to site. After Assyrian ceased to be a written language around 600 BCE, a variety called Late Babylonian was written for some 700 years. The differences between the dialects and their varieties are relatively small, and after learning a variety one can read the other dialect and varieties as well. In the Oracc metadata, the different dialects and varieties are given for Akkadian words in most cases.

4 Cuneiform representation in Unicode

The effort to provide a standard encoding for cuneiform began in 1999 at Johns Hopkins University as the Initiative for Cuneiform Encoding (ICE). The initiative ended up with an approved proposal for cuneiform Unicode in 2004 (officially accepted into Unicode 5.0 in 2006).[5] The final list of cuneiform signs included is a combination of work done earlier at the University of Chicago, Universität Göttingen, and the University of California, Los Angeles (Cohen et al., 2004).

---

[5]The Unicode Standard Version 11.0 Core Specification [http://www.unicode.org/versions/Unicode11.0.0/appC.pdf]

In the current Unicode standard, there are three blocks of cuneiform signs for the "Sumero-Akkadian" script. The first one is the block covering the base cuneiform signs ranging from U+12000 to U+123FF. The second block, from U+12400 to U+1247F, covers the cuneiform punctuation and numerals and the third, from U+12480 to U+1254F, is an extension containing additional signs for the Early Dynastic period. Unicode has only one character for each sign, even though the signs evolved through the ages. The different ways of writing the signs could be used to determine the language or dialect used or the time period of writing.

The cuneiform texts from the Oracc corpus we use in this research were provided primarily as transliterations using the ASCII Transliteration Format (ATF). ATF was first defined by CDLI and is a standardized way of electronically transliterating cuneiform, following the conventions used by cuneiform scholars in general (Koslova and Damerow, 2003). The data from the Oracc corpus is also available as JSON files in an "XCL" format (Tinney and Robson, 2018)[6], which includes a similar XML representation of the data as the CDLI archival XML format (Koslova and Damerow, 2003). We extracted the individual sign transliterations in Unicode ATF from the XML representation and recreated the transliteration for each line.

There was no available software to automatically transform the transliterations to Unicode cuneiform. As part of Oracc, there is a facility called "Cuneify," which can be used online to transform ATF into Unicode cuneiform.[7] However, it is not possible to download the software and it does not handle the Unicode ATF transliteration. In order to generate the original lines in cuneiform, we implemented a program called "Nuolenna" which takes in the transliteration generated from the XML files and re-produces the lines in Unicode cuneiform.[8] The Nuolenna program uses a list[9] of over 11,000 transliteration-sign pairs. As the base for our sign list, we used a JSON export from the Oracc Global Sign List

(OGSL)[10] provided by Niek Veldhuis, to which we added some missing signs. In order to produce the original cuneiform lines, the program uses *ad hoc* rules to remove any additional annotations related to the signs. For example, sometimes an older or more precise reading can be found within parentheses directly after the reading of a sign. In such cases, we just remove the parentheses and anything between them.

5 Preliminary language identification experiments

To find out to what extent identifying the language of cuneiform text is possible, we performed initial language identification experiments using a state-of-the-art language identification method called HeLI (Jauhiainen et al., 2016). The HeLI method has recently fared well in VarDial shared tasks for Swiss-German dialect and Indo-Aryan language identification (Jauhiainen et al., 2018a,b). The experiments were conducted on individual lines as well as texts spanning several lines.

5.1 Corpus for the preliminary experiments

In Oracc, the transliterated words are separated by whitespaces, which is not the case in the original documents. In order to mimic the original documents, we removed all the whitespaces from each line of cuneiform text. We also ignored any completely broken signs, which were marked with an 'x'.

The individual words in Oracc are tagged with language or dialect information, and sometimes a single line includes words in different languages or dialects. As we set out to do language identification on monolingual texts, we used all those lines which had words in only one language, leaving out multilingual lines. The language tagging in Oracc is not always precise, and therefore some lines in our dataset might still include several languages.

In the preliminary experiments, we experimented with the language identification of both monolingual lines and monolingual texts spanning several lines with the information about line breaks retained. Mostly, each text had the lines of one original document, but if the document was multilingual, it was divided into different texts according to the languages attested.

---

[6][http://oracc.museum.upenn.edu/doc/opendata/]

[7][http://oracc.museum.upenn.edu/doc/tools/cuneify/index.html]

[8][https://github.com/tosaja/Nuolenna]

[9][https://github.com/tosaja/Nuolenna/blob/master/sign_list.txt]

[10][http://oracc.museum.upenn.edu/ogsl/]

We left out the Akkadian varieties of Old and Middle Assyrian as the number of lines available for those dialects was less than 1,000. We had datasets in the Sumerian language as well as the Akkadian varieties of Old Babylonian, Middle Babylonian peripheral, Standard Babylonian, Neo-Babylonian, Late Babylonian, and Neo-Assyrian. The statistics of the corpus used in the preliminary experiments are shown in Table 1.

We were interested in experimenting in both in-domain and out-of-domain test settings as well as with language identification on two different levels: individual lines and texts. In supervised machine learning, the testing data is in-domain if it is similar to the training data. For example, if sentences are from texts that belong to the same genre or collection they are considered more in-domain than if they are not. An even stronger in-domain case is if the sentences are from the same text. Classification of test data which is in-domain with the training data is usually much easier than when it is out-of-domain. The texts in the Oracc export were in the order[11] of "projects," which are collections of texts that have some common theme. The texts in different projects can be considered to be more out-of-domain with each other than those from the same project. The projects from which the texts were extracted are listed in Table 2.

From this corpus, we generated four different test settings. For the out-of-domain experiments, we divided the corpus so that we used the first half of the corpus for training and the second half was divided between development and testing. For the in-domain experiments, we divided the corpus into parts of 20 lines or texts and took the 10 first lines or texts from each part for training, the next 5 for development, and the last 5 for testing. We, thus, ended up with four different datasets,[12] two for lines and two for texts. Each of the datasets had 50% of the material for training, 25% for development, and 25% for testing.

5.2 Results of the preliminary experiments

The HeLI method is a supervised-learning language identification method where the language models are created from a correctly tagged training corpus. The language models consist of words and sign (character) n-grams. When n-grams are extracted from a corpus, the number of unique n-grams is higher the longer the n-grams are. The actual number of occurrences of the longer n-grams is lower than the shorter n-grams. The exact optimal value for n depends on, among many other variables, the size of the training corpus, the length of the text to be identified, and the repertoire of the languages considered. Sometimes the longer n-grams could carry important information even though they are seldom found in the text to be identified. The basic idea in the HeLI method is to score individual words using the longest length n-grams possible. For each individual language, the words are scored first, after which the whole text gets the average score of the individual words. In the case of cuneiform text, as it is not divided into words, we use just sign n-grams and consider a line of text as a word as far as the HeLI method is concerned.

The individual words, or in this case lines, are scored by taking the average score of the found n-grams. Using the notation introduced by Jauhiainen et al. (2018c), the individual n-grams f found from the line to be tested, get a score R as in Equation 1:

$$R_{HeLI}(g, f) = -\log_{10} \frac{c(C_g, f)}{l_{C_g^F}} \qquad (1)$$

where $c(C_g, f)$ is the count of the feature f in the training corpus C_g of the language g and $l_{C_g^F}$ is the total number of occurrences of all the n-grams of the same length in the training corpus. As smoothing, in case the count of a feature is zero in some languages, this version of the HeLI method uses a score $R_{HeLI}(g, f)$ for the count of one multiplied by a penalty multiplier.

Using the development sets, we optimized the sign n-gram range and the penalty multiplier for each setting individually. The results of these experiments are presented in Table 3. As the performance measure, we use the F1-score which is the harmonic mean of precision and recall. The results clearly show how the task of identifying a single line is much harder than that of a complete text. The task of out-of-domain identification is also clearly more difficult than that of in-domain, as was expected.

Quite many of the misclassified lines were very short; many consisted only of one sign and were truly ambiguous and often present in different dialects and even languages. Nevertheless, it was still possible to attain reasonably good language identification results. The hardest test setting was

---

[11]The projects were in the alphabetical order by their abbreviations.

[12]See Table 3.

Language or Dialect (abbreviation in the CLI dataset)	Texts	Lines	Signs
Sumerian (SUX)	5,000	107,345	*c.* 400,000
Old Babylonian (OLB)	527	7,605	*c.* 65,000
Middle Babylonian peripheral (MPB)	365	11,015	*c.* 95,000
Standard Babylonian (STB)	1,661	35,633	*c.* 390,000
Neo-Babylonian (NEB)	1,212	19,414	*c.* 200,000
Late Babylonian (LTB)	671	31,893	*c.* 260,000
Neo-Assyrian (NEA)	3,570	65,932	*c.* 490,000

Table 1: Number of texts, lines, and signs for each language or variety in the corpus.

Project (abbreviation used in Oracc)	SUX	OLB	MPB	STB	NEB	LTB	NEA
Bilinguals in Late Mesopotamian Scholarship (**blms**)	x	x		x			
CAMS/Anzu (**cams-anzu**)				x			
CAMS/Barutu (**cams-barutu**)		x		x			
CAMS/The Standard Babylonian Epic of Etana (**cams-etana**)		x					x
CAMS/Geography of Knowledge Corpus (**cams-gkab**)	x			x		x	x
CAMS/Ludlul (**cams-ludlul**)				x			
CAMS/Seleucid Building Inscriptions (**cams-selbi**)				x			
Cuneiform Commentaries Project on ORACC (**ccpo**)	x			x			
Corpus of Kassite Sumerian Texts (**ckst**)	x				x		
The Amarna Texts (**contrib-amarna**)			x	x			
Cuneiform Texts Mentioning Israelites, Judeans ... (**ctij**)					x	x	x
Lexical Texts in the Royal Libraries at Nineveh (**dcclt-nineveh**)	x			x			
Reading the Signs (**dcclt-signlists**)	x			x			
Digital Corpus of Cuneiform Lexical Texts (**dcclt**)	x	x	x	x			
Digital Corpus of Cuneiform Mathematical Texts (**dccmt**)	x	x		x			
Electronic Text Corpus of Sumerian Royal Inscriptions (**etcsri**)	x						
Corpus of Glass Technological Texts (**glass**)					x		
Hellenistic Babylonia: Texts, Iconography, Names (**hbtin**)						x	
Law and Order: Cuneiform Online Sustainable Tool (**lacost**)	x						
Old Babylonian Model Contracts (**obmc**)	x						
Old Babylonian Tabular Accounts (**obta**)	x	x					
The Inscr. of the Second Dynasty of Isin (**ribo-babylon2**)	x						
The Inscr. of the Period of the Uncertain Dynasties (**ribo-babylon6**)	x						
Rim-Anum: The House of Prisoners (**rimanum**)	x	x					
The Correspondence of Sargon II, Part I (**saao-saa01**)							x
Neo-Assyrian Treaties and Loyalty Oaths (**saao-saa02**)					x	x	x
Court Poetry and Literary Miscellanea (**saao-saa03**)					x		x
Queries to the Sungod (**saao-saa04**)					x		
The Correspondence of Sargon II, Part II (**saao-saa05**)							x
Legal Trns. of the Royal Court of Nineveh, Part I (**saao-saa06**)							x
Imperial Administrative Records, Part I (**saao-saa07**)							x
Astrological Reports to Assyrian Kings (**saao-saa08**)					x	x	x
Assyrian Prophecies (**saao-saa09**)							x
Letters from Assyrian and Babylonian Scholars (**saao-saa10**)					x	x	x
Imperial Administrative Records, Part II (**saao-saa11**)							x
Grants, Decrees and Gifts of the Neo-Assyrian Period (**saao-saa12**)							x
Letters from Assyrian and Babylonian Priests to ... (**saao-saa13**)					x		x
Legal Trns. of the Royal Court of Nineveh, Part II (**saao-saa14**)							x
The Correspondence of Sargon II, Part III (**saao-saa15**)							x
The Political Correspondence of Esarhaddon (**saao-saa16**)							x
The Neo-Babylonian Correspondence of Sargon and ... (**saao-saa17**)					x		
The Babylonian Correspondence of Esarhaddon and ... (**saao-saa18**)					x		
The Correspondence of Tiglath-Pileser III and ... (**saao-saa19**)					x		x

Table 2: The list of Oracc projects from which the texts in the corpus were collected.

where the language of individual out-of-domain lines was to be identified. To us, this seemed to be the most interesting and relevant setting to be used in the CLI shared task, especially if we leave out the extremely short and possibly ambiguous lines.

6 The CLI shared task

The CLI shared task 2019, part of the third VarDial Evaluation Campaign, focused on discriminating between languages and dialects written with cuneiform signs. The task included two different languages: Sumerian and Akkadian. Furthermore,

Type of setting	n-gram range	F1
Lines, out-of-domain	1–3	60
Lines, in-domain	1–3	72
Texts, out-of-domain	1–4	84
Texts, in-domain	1–3	93

Table 3: The F1-scores attained by the HeLI method in the preliminary experiments.

Language or Dialect	Training
Sumerian	53,673
Old Babylonian	3,803
Middle Babylonian peripheral	5,508
Standard Babylonian	17,817
Neo-Babylonian	9,707
Late Babylonian	15,947
Neo-Assyrian	32,966

Table 4: Number of lines for each language or dialect in the training set provided during the VarDial 2019 Evaluation Campaign.

the Akkadian language was divided into six dialects: Old Babylonian, Middle Babylonian peripheral, Standard Babylonian, Neo-Babylonian, Late Babylonian, and Neo-Assyrian. First, we explain how the dataset for the shared task was constructed from the corpus described earlier, and then we present the baseline language identifiers and the results we attained using them.

6.1 The dataset for the shared task

For the CLI task, we created a separate, especially tailored dataset. The participants were given texts for training and development and separate texts were given for testing at the end of the campaign. The training set was exactly the same as the one we used in the preliminary experiments[13] and the number of lines in the training portion for each language or dialect is shown in Table 4.

For the CLI development and test sets, we performed some further operations. The original datasets included duplicate lines, so we first removed all duplicates. Then we filtered out all lines shorter than three characters. After these operations, the smallest sets were those of Old Babylonian including 668 lines in the development set and 985 lines in the test set. As we wanted to make the development and the test sets equal in size between languages and dialects, we randomly selected the same number of lines from the other languages. Thus, in the CLI task, the development sets for each language consisted of 668 lines and

---

[13]In the out-of-domain individual line identification test setting.

the test sets of 985 lines.

6.2 Baseline experiments

We used four of the methods described in the survey by Jauhiainen et al. (2018c) to implement baseline language identifiers for the CLI task. As features, we used sign n-grams of different lengths.

The first method is called simple scoring. In simple scoring, all the n-grams generated from the line to be identified M are compared to the language models and for each n-gram found in a language model $dom(O(C_g))$, the score R of the language g is increased by one. The language gaining the highest score is selected as the predicted language. Jauhiainen et al. (2018c) formulate the method as in Equation 2:

$$R_{simple}(g, M) = \sum_{i=1}^{l_{MF}} \left\{ \begin{array}{ll} 1 & \text{, if } f_i \in dom(O(C_g)) \\ 0 & \text{, otherwise} \end{array} \right. \tag{2}$$

where l_{MF} is the number of individual features in the line M and f_i is its ith feature.

The second method is the sum of relative frequencies where relative frequencies are added to the score of the language. Jauhiainen et al. (2018c) formulate the method as in Equation 3:

$$R_{sum}(g, M) = \sum_{i=1}^{l_{MF}} \frac{c(C_g, f_i)}{l_{C_g^F}} \tag{3}$$

where $c(C_g, f_i)$ is the count of the feature f_i in the training corpus.

The third method is the product of relative frequencies where the relative frequencies are multiplied together. Jauhiainen et al. (2018c) formulate the method as in Equation 4:

$$R_{prod}(g, M) = \prod_{i}^{l_{MF}} \frac{c(C_g, f_i)}{l_{C_g^F}} \tag{4}$$

The actual implementation adds together negative logarithms of the relative frequencies, which produces results with the same ordering. As a smoothing value, we used the negative logarithm of a comparably small relative frequency. The actual value was optimized using the development set. The product of relative frequencies differs from the HeLI method (Equation 1) in that it always uses the full range of available feature types (different length n-grams), as opposed to the HeLI

Method	n-gram range	F1 dev	F1 test
Prod. of rel. freq.	1–4	0.7263	0.7206
Voting Ensemble		0.7222	0.7163
HeLI	1–3 + lines	0.7171	0.7061
Simple scoring	1–10	0.6656	0.6554
Sum of rel. freq.	3–15	0.5984	0.6016

Table 5: The macro F1-scores attained by the baseline methods with the CLI dataset.

Lang.	LTB	MPB	NEA	NEB	OLB	STB	SUX
LTB	*947*	6	9	34	13	25	8
MPB	3	*858*	51	94	84	69	55
NEA	6	26	*780*	185	26	148	26
NEB	4	19	81	*535*	30	160	30
OLB	3	22	12	16	*736*	47	110
STB	17	35	30	113	43	*491*	101
SUX	5	19	22	8	53	45	*655*

Table 6: Confusion matrix for the product of relative frequencies method. The rows indicate the actual languages and the columns indicate predicted languages. Correct identifications are emphasized.

method, which uses only the longest length n-grams applicable.

The fourth method is a majority-voting-based ensemble of the three previous methods.

The parameters and the best possible language models are determined by training the identifier using the training set and evaluating its performance on the development set. Once the best parameters are decided, the texts in the development set can also be added to the training set for the final evaluation against the test set. We used the macro F1-score as the measure for language identification performance. For each of the methods, we evaluated all possible sign n-gram ranges from 1 to 15 using the development set. Table 5 shows the results for all the methods using parameters optimized with the development set. In the voting ensemble, we used the best parameters for the methods from the individual experiments, and in case of a tie, the result from the product of relative frequencies was used.

The product of relative frequencies method is clearly superior to the other two basic methods with an F1-score of 0.7206 using 2.0 as the smoothing value and sign n-grams from one to four. Adding the prediction information from the other two methods in the form of a voting ensemble also fails to improve the result. The F1-score achieved when using the HeLI method does not reach the one from the product of relative frequencies method either. The F1-score gained by the HeLI method is clearly higher than the score attained in the preliminary experiments, which was as expected, as we had filtered out some of the most difficult cases.

Table 5 is a confusion matrix displaying the exact number of identifications. The diagonal values represent correct identifications. Standard Babylonian and Neo-Babylonian were the most difficult varieties to distinguish, mostly being erroneously identified as each other. Late Babylonian was the easiest to identify, with a recall of over 96%.

7 Conclusions and future work

In this paper, we have shown that it is possible to perform language and dialect identification in cuneiform texts encoded in Unicode characters. We have created a dataset to be used in the VarDial Evaluation campaign and evaluated the performance of four baseline identifiers using the dataset.

Some sizeable Oracc projects were left out of the corpus, for example the "Royal Inscriptions of the Neo-Assyrian Period" project, as the exact dialect of the Akkadian language had not been annotated. Furthermore, for the same reason, only the lines in Sumerian could be used from the "Royal Inscriptions of Babylonia online (RiBo)" project. We believe that automatic dialect identification could be useful in making the annotations more detailed and are planning to provide this kind of automatically deduced information as part of the Korp version of Oracc.[14]

Some other avenues for further work are language set identification for the multilingual texts, as well as unsupervised clustering of data without any predefined languages.

Acknowledgments

The research was carried out in the context of the "Semantic Domains in Akkadian Texts" project and the Centre of Excellence in Ancient Near Eastern Empires at the University of Helsinki (ANEE), both funded by the Academy of Finland. This work has also been partly funded by the Kone Foundation and FIN-CLARIN.

We thank Johannes Bach, Mikko Luukko, Aleksi Sahala, and Niek Veldhuis for their valuable comments during the experiments and Raija

---

[14]`http://urn.fi/urn:nbn:fi:lb-2018071121`

Mattila and Saana Svärd for their continued support. We are grateful to Robert Whiting for revising the language of the text and for further insight into the Akkadian and Sumerian languages.

References

François Barthélemy. 1998. A Morphological Analyzer for Akkadian Verbal Forms with a Model of Phonetic Transformations. In *Proceedings of the Workshop on Computational Approaches to Semitic Languages*, pages 73–81. Association for Computational Linguistics.

Christian Chiarcos, Ilya Khait, Émilie Pagé-Perron, Niko Schenk, Christian Fäth, Julius Steuer, William Mcgrath, and Jinyan Wang. 2018. Annotating a Low-Resource Language with LLOD Technology: Sumerian Morphology and Syntax. *Information*, 9.

Jonathan Cohen, Donald Duncan, Dean Snyder, Jerrold Cooper, Subodh Kumar, Daniel Hahn, Yuan Chen, Budirijanto Purnomo, and John Graettinger. 2004. iClay: Digitizing Cuneiform. In *The Proceedings of the 5th International Symposium on Virtual Reality, Archaeology and Cultural Heritage (VAST 2004)*, pages 135–143.

Timo Homburg and Christian Chiarcos. 2016. Akkadian Word Segmentation. In *Proceedings of the 10th International Conference on Language Resource Evaluation (LREC 2016)*, pages 4067–4074.

Tommi Jauhiainen, Heidi Jauhiainen, and Krister Lindén. 2018a. HeLI-based Experiments in Swiss German Dialect Identification. In *Proceedings of the Fifth Workshop on NLP for Similar Languages, Varieties and Dialects (VarDial)*, pages 254–262, Santa Fe, NM.

Tommi Jauhiainen, Heidi Jauhiainen, and Krister Lindén. 2018b. Iterative Language Model Adaptation for Indo-Aryan Language Identification. In *Proceedings of the Fifth Workshop on NLP for Similar Languages, Varieties and Dialects (VarDial)*, pages 66–75, Santa Fe, NM.

Tommi Jauhiainen, Krister Lindén, and Heidi Jauhiainen. 2016. HeLI, a Word-Based Backoff Method for Language Identification. In *Proceedings of the Third Workshop on NLP for Similar Languages, Varieties and Dialects (VarDial3)*, pages 153–162, Osaka, Japan.

Tommi Jauhiainen, Marco Lui, Marcos Zampieri, Timothy Baldwin, and Krister Lindén. 2018c. Automatic Language Identification in Texts: A Survey. *arXiv preprint arXiv:1804.08186*.

Lauri Karttunen, Kimmo Koskenniemi, and Ronald Kaplan. 1987. A compiler for two-level phonological rules. Technical report, Stanford University, Center for the Study of Language and Information.

Laura Kataja and Kimmo Koskenniemi. 1988. Finite-state Description of Semitic Morphology: A Case Study of Ancient Akkadian. In *Proceedings of the 12th International Conference on Computational Linguistics (COLING 1988)*, volume 1, pages 313–315, Budapest, Hungary.

Natalia Koslova and Peter Damerow. 2003. From Cuneiform Archives to Digital Libraries: The Hermitage Museum Joins the Cuneiform Digital Library Initiative. In *Proceedings of the 5th Russian Conference on Digital Libraries (RCDL 2003)*, St.-Petersburg, Russia.

Bert Kouwenberg. 2011. Akkadian in General. In *The Semitic Languages: An International Handbook*, pages 330–340. De Gruyter Mouton.

Yudong Liu, Clinton Burkhart, James Hearne, and Liang Luo. 2015. Enhancing Sumerian Lemmatization by Unsupervised Named-Entity Recognition. In *Proceedings of the Human Language Technologies: The 2015 Annual Conference of the North American Chapter of the Association for Computational Linguistics (HLT-NAACL 2015)*, pages 1446–1451, Denver, Colorado.

Yudong Liu, James Hearne, and Bryan Conrad. 2016. Recognizing Proper Names in UR III Texts through Supervised Learning. In *Proceedings of the Twenty-Ninth International Florida Artificial Intelligence Research Society Conference (Flairs 2016)*, pages 535–540.

Liang Luo, Yudong Liu, James Hearne, and Clinton Burkhart. 2015. Unsupervised Sumerian Personal Name Eecognition. In *Proceedings of the Twenty-Eighth International Florida Artificial Intelligence Research Society Conference (Flairs 2015)*, pages 193–198.

Shervin Malmasi, Marcos Zampieri, Nikola Ljubešić, Preslav Nakov, Ahmed Ali, and Jrg Tiedemann. 2016. Discriminating Between Similar Languages and Arabic Dialect Identification: A Report on the Third DSL Shared Task. In *Proceedings of the Third Workshop on NLP for Similar Languages, Varieties and Dialects*, pages 1–14, Osaka, Japan.

Piotr Michalowski. 2004. Sumerian. In *The Cambridge Encyclopedia of the World's Ancient Languages*, pages 19–59. Cambridge University Press.

M Willis Monroe. 2018. Using Quantitative Methods for Measuring Inter-Textual Relations in Cuneiform. *Digital Biblical Studies*, pages 257–280.

Émilie Pagé-Perron, Maria Sukhareva, Ilya Khait, and Christian Chiarcos. 2017. Machine Translation and Automated Analysis of the Sumerian Language. In *Proceedings of the Joint SIGHUM Workshop on Computational Linguistics for Cultural Heritage, Social Sciences, Humanities and Literature*, pages 10–16, Vancouver, BC. Association for Computational Linguistics.

Giovanni Ponti, Daniela Alderuccio, Giorgio Mencuccini, Alessio Rocchi, Silvio Migliori, Giovanni Bracco, and Paola Negri Scafa. 2013. Data Mining Tools and GRID Infrastructure for Assyriology Text Analysis (an Old-Babylonian Situation Studied Through Text Analysis and Data Mining tools). http://www.eneagrid.enea.it, Published 2017 in: R. De Boer and J. G. Dercksen, editors, *Private and State in the Ancient Near East - Proceedings of the 58th Rencontre Assyriologique Internationale at Leiden, 16–20 July 2012, Eisenbrauns.*

Rajesh P. N. Rao, Nisha Yadav, Mayank N. Vahia, Hrishikesh Joglekar, R. Adhikari, and Iravatham Mahadevan. 2009. Entropic Evidence for Linguistic Structure in the Indus script. *Science*, 324(5931):1165–1165.

Andrea Seri. 2010. Adaptation of Cuneiform to Write Akkadian. In Christopher Woods, editor, *Visible Language. Inventions of Writing in the Ancient middle East and Beyond*, volume 32 of *Oriental Institute Museum Publications*, pages 85–98. The Oriental Institute of the University of Chicago.

Saana Svärd, Heidi Jauhiainen, Aleksi Sahala, and Krister Lindén. 2018. Semantic Domains in Akkadian Texts. In Vanessa Bigot Juloux, Amy Rebecca Gansell, and Alessandro Di Ludovico, editors, *CyberResearch on the Ancient Near East and Neighboring Regions. Case Studies on Archaeological Data, Objects, Texts, and Digital Archiving*, volume 2 of *Digital Biblical Studies*, pages 224–256. Brill.

Valentin Tablan, Wim Peters, Diana Maynard, and Hamish Cunningham. 2006. Creating Tools for Morphological Analysis of Sumerian. In *Proceedings of the 5th Internation Conference on Language Resources and Evaluation (LREC 2006)*, pages 1762–1765, Genoa, Italy.

Steve Tinney and Eleanor Robson. 2018. Oracc Open Data: A brief introduction for programmers. *Oracc: The Open Richly Annotated Cuneiform Corpus*, Oracc.

Marcos Zampieri, Shervin Malmasi, Nikola Ljubeic, Preslav Nakov, Ahmed Ali, Jrg Tiedemann, Yves Scherrer, and Nomi Aepli. 2017. Findings of the VarDial Evaluation Campaign 2017. In *Proceedings of the Fourth Workshop on NLP for Similar Languages, Varieties and Dialects*, pages 1–15, Valencia, Spain.

Marcos Zampieri, Shervin Malmasi, Preslav Nakov, Ahmed Ali, Suwon Shon, James Glass, Yves Scherrer, Tanja Samardžić, Nikola Ljubešić, Jörg Tiedemann, Chris van der Lee, Stefan Grondelaers, Nelleke Oostdijk, Antal van den Bosch, Ritesh Kumar, Bornini Lahiri, and Mayank Jain. 2018. Language Identification and Morphosyntactic Tagging: The Second VarDial Evaluation Campaign. In *Proceedings of the Fifth Workshop on NLP for Similar Languages, Varieties and Dialects (VarDial)*, Santa Fe, USA.

Marcos Zampieri, Liling Tan, Nikola Ljubešić, and Jörg Tiedemann. 2014. A Report on the DSL Shared Task 2014. In *Proceedings of the First Workshop on Applying NLP Tools to Similar Languages, Varieties and Dialects*, pages 58–67, Dublin, Ireland.

Marcos Zampieri, Liling Tan, Nikola Ljubeić, Jrg Tiedemann, and Preslav Nakov. 2015. Overview of the DSL Shared Task 2015. In *Proceedings of the Joint Workshop on Language Technology for Closely Related Languages, Varieties and Dialects (LT4VarDial)*, pages 1–9, Hissar, Bulgaria.

Leveraging Pretrained Word Embeddings for Part-of-Speech Tagging of Code Switching Data

Fahad AlGhamdi [1]**, and Mona Diab**[1,2]

[1] Department of Computer Science, The George Washington University
[2] AWS, Amazon AI
{fghamdi, mtdiab}@gwu.edu

Abstract

Linguistic Code Switching (CS) is a phenomenon that occurs when multilingual speakers alternate between two or more languages/dialects within a single conversation. Processing CS data is especially challenging in intra-sentential data given state-of-the-art monolingual NLP technologies since such technologies are geared toward the processing of one language at a time. In this paper, we address the problem of Part-of-Speech tagging (POS) in the context of linguistic code switching (CS). We explore leveraging multiple neural network architectures to measure the impact of different pre-trained embeddings methods on POS tagging CS data. We investigate the landscape in four CS language pairs, Spanish-English, Hindi-English, Modern Standard Arabic- Egyptian Arabic dialect (MSA-EGY), and Modern Standard Arabic-Levantine Arabic dialect (MSA-LEV). Our results show that multilingual embedding (e.g., MSA-EGY and MSA-LEV) helps closely related languages (EGY/LEV) but adds noise to the languages that are distant (SPA/HIN). Finally, we show that our proposed models outperform state-of-the-art CS taggers for MSA-EGY language pair.

1 Introduction

Code Switching (CS) is a common linguistic behavior where two or more languages/dialects are used interchangeably in either spoken or written form. CS is typically present at various levels of linguistic structure: across sentence boundaries (i.e., inter-sentential), within the same utterances, mixing two or more languages (i.e., intra-sentential), or at the words/morphemes level. The CS phenomenon is noticeable and common in countries that have large immigrant groups, naturally leading to bilingualism. Typically people who code switch master two (or more) languages: a common first language (lang1) and another prevalent language as a second language (lang2). The languages could be completely distinct such as Mandarin and English, or Hindi and English, or they can be variants of one another such as in the case of Modern Standard Arabic (MSA) and Arabic regional dialects (e.g. Egyptian dialect-EGY). CS is traditionally prevalent in the spoken modality but with the ubiquity of the Internet and proliferation of social media, CS is becoming ubiquitous in written modalities and genres (Vyas et al., 2014a; Danet and Herring, 2007; Cárdenas-Claros and Isharyanti, 2009). This new situation has created an unusual deluge of CS textual data on the Internet. This data brings in its wake new opportunities, but it poses serious challenges for different NLP tasks; traditional techniques trained for one language tend to break down when the input text happens to include two or more languages. The performance of NLP models that are currently expected to yield good results (e.g., Part-of-Speech Tagging) would degrade at a rate proportional to the amount and level of mixed-language present. This is a result of out-of-vocabulary words in one language and new hybrid grammar structures, and in some cases shared cognates or ambiguous words that exist in both language lexicons.

POS tagging is a vital component of any Natural Language Understanding system, and one of the first tasks researchers employ to process data. POS tagging is an enabling technology needed by higher-up NLP tools such as chunkers and parsers – syntactic, semantic and discourse level processing; all of which are used for such applications as sentiment analysis and subjectivity, text summarization, information extraction, automatic speech recognition, and machine translation among others. As such, it is crucial that POS taggers be able to process CS textual data.

99

Proceedings of VarDial, pages 99–109
Minneapolis, MN, June 7, 2019 ©2019 Association for Computational Linguistics

In this paper, we address the problem of Part-of-Speech tagging (POS) for CS data on the intra-sentential level for multiple language pairs. We explore the effect of using various embeddings setups and multiple neural network architectures in order to mitigate the problem of the scarcity of CS annotated data. We propose multiple word embedding techniques that could help in tackling POS tagging of CS data.

In order to examine the generalization of our approaches across language pairs, we conduct our study on four different evaluation CS data sets, covering four language pairs: Modern Standard Arabic and the Egyptian Arabic dialect (MSA-EGY), Modern Standard Arabic- and the Levantine Arabic dialect (MSA-LEV), Spanish-English (SPA-ENG) and Hindi-English (HIN-ENG). We use the same POS tag sets for all language pairs, namely, the Universal POS tag set (Petrov et al., 2011). Our contributions are the following: a) We use a state-of-the-art bidirectional recurrent neural networks; b) We explore different strategies to leverage raw textual resources for creating pre-trained embeddings for POS tagging CS data; c) We examine the effect of language identifiers for joint POS tagging and language identification; d) We present the first empirical evaluation on POS tagging with four different language pairs. All of the previous work focused on a single or two language pair combinations.

2   Related Work

Developing CS text processing NLP techniques for analyzing user generated content as well as cater for needs of multilingual societies is vital (Vyas et al., 2014b). Previous studies that address the problem of POS tagging of CS data first attempt to identify the correct language of a word before feeding it into an appropriate monolingual tagger (Solorio and Liu, 2008; Vyas et al., 2014a; AlGhamdi et al., 2016). As is typically the case in NLP, such pipelines suffer from the problem of error propagation; e.g., failure of the language identification will cause problems in the POS tag prediction. Other approaches have trained supervised models on POS-annotated, CS data resources which are expensive to create and unavailable for most language pairs. (AlGhamdi et al., 2016; Solorio and Liu, 2008; Jamatia et al., 2015; Barman et al., 2016) Solorio and Liu (2008), proposed the first statistical approach to POS tagging

of CS data where they employ several heuristics to combine monolingual taggers with limited success, achieving 86% accuracy when choosing the output of a monolingual tagger based on the dictionary language ID of each token. However, an SVM trained on the output of the monolingual taggers performed better than their oracle, reaching 93.48% accuracy. Royal Sequiera (2015) introduces a ML-based approach with a number of new features for HIN-ENG POS tagging for Twitter and Facebook chat messages. The new feature set considers the transliteration problem inherent in social media. Their system achieves an accuracy of 84%. Jamatia et al. (2015) use both a fine-grained and coarse-grained POS tag set in their study. They introduce a comparison between the performance of a combination of language specific taggers and a machine learning based approach that uses a range of different features. They conclude that the machine learning approach failed to outperform the language specific combination taggers. AlGhamdi et al. (2016) examine seven POS tagging strategies to leverage the available monolingual resources for CS data. They conducted their study on two language pairs, namely MSA-EGY and SPA-ENG. The proposed strategies are divided into combined conditions and integrated conditions. Three of the combined conditions consist of running monolingual POS taggers and language ID taggers in a different order and combining the outputs in a single multilingual prediction. The fourth combined condition involved training an SVM model using the output of the monolingual taggers. The three integrated approaches trained a monolingual state-of-the-art POS tagger on a) CS corpus; b) the union of two monolingual corpora of the languages included in the CS; c) the union of the corpora used in a and b. Both combined and integrated conditions outperformed the baseline systems. The SVM approach consistently outperformed the integrated approaches achieving the highest accuracy results for both language pairs. Soto and Hirschberg (2018) propose a new approach to POS tagging for code switching SPA-ENG language pair based on recurrent neural network (RNN) as a way of providing better tools for better code switching data processing, including POS taggers. The authors use an experimental approach of POS tagging for CS utterances entailing use of state-of-the-art bi-directional RNN to extensively study effects of language identi-

100

fiers. For the Boolean features, a bi-directional Long short-term memory (BiLSTM) state-of-the-art neural network with suffix, prefix, and word embeddings, the results show that the neural POS tagging model proposed by the authors performs comparatively higher than other state of the art CS taggers, their system yields a POS tagging accuracy of 96.34%, while joint POS and language ID tagging yields an accuracy of 96.39% for POS tagging and language ID accuracy of 98.78% (Soto and Hirschberg, 2018). Language Modeling (LM) on HIN-ENG language texts has been proposed by (Chandu et al., 2018). (Pratapa et al., 2018) propose the use of a computational technique to create artificial code mixed data that is grammatically valid based on the ECT (Equivalence Constraint Theory) to solve the challenge of scarcity of CS training language models using an experimental approach. (Pratapa et al., 2018) uses two bilingual embedding techniques, namely Bilingual Compositional Model (BiCVM) and Correlation Based Embeddings (BiCCA) (Faruqui and Dyer, 2014; Blunsom and Hermann, 2014). Word embedding results in improved semantic and syntactic CS processing tasks. BiCVM at the sentence level only yields better performance for semantic tasks. BiCCA also only do well on semantic tasks because they make use of word alignments. Furthermore, g-skip embedding outperformed BiCCA and BiCVM, performing well across syntactic and semantic tasks. The study by Pratapa et al. (2018) illustrates that using pretrained embeddings learned from CS data outperforms pretrained embeddings learned from standard bilingual embeddings. Bhat et al. (2018) introduce a dependency parser developed specifically for HIN-ENG CS data. They adopted the neural stacking architecture proposed by (Zhang and Weiss, 2016; Chen et al., 2016) for learning POS tagging and parsing and for transferring the knowledge from bilingual models trained on Hindi and English UD treebanks. The stack-prop tagger, the model proposed by (Zhang and Weiss, 2016), achieves the highest accuracy of 90.53. To identify the language ID, they train a multilayer perceptron (MLP) stacked on top of a recurrent bidirectional LSTM (Bi-LSTM) network. The results of their system is 97.39 %.

3 Approach

Pretrained word embeddings enable models to exploit the raw textual data which is in all languages larger than annotated data. In recent times, there has been some interest in embedding approaches, e.g., multilingual embeddings and bilingual word embeddings, where two monolingual embeddings of two languages are mapped to a shared embeddings space. The main advantage of bilingual and multilingual embeddings is in solving tasks involving reasoning across two languages, such as Machine Translation (MT) (Vulić and Moens, 2016; Zou et al., 2013), as well as enabling transfer of models learned on a resource-rich language onto a resource-poor language (Adams et al., 2017). One of the potential applications of bilingual and multilingual embeddings is in the processing of code switching language. In this section, we compare leveraging multiple neural network architectures for POS tagging CS data. Moreover, we explore different embedding setups to investigate the optimal way of tackling the POS tagging of CS data. First, we illustrate the tool used for training the embeddings layer. Second, we present the neural network models. Then we list the embedding setups.

Pretrained Word Embedding Model Most successful methods for learning word embeddings (Mikolov et al., 2013c; Pennington et al., 2014; Bojanowski et al., 2017) rely on the distributional hypothesis (Mikolov et al., 2013b), i.e., words occurring in similar contexts tend to have similar meanings. Among all word embedding techniques, we choose the FastText tool developed by Facebook (Bojanowski et al., 2017). Our choice of FastText is motivated by the fact that social media networks are the primary source of our unlabeled data. This type of data exhibits huge variations of spelling and misspellings. FastText takes advantage of subword (i.e., n-gram) information. It creates vector representations for misspelling replacement candidates absent from the trained embedding space, by summing the vectors of the character n-grams. All word embedding techniques aim to capture the relation of the words that tend to appear in similar context. These relations occur on the sentential level for most of the NLP applications trained for monolingual data. However, the lack of having sufficient context in CS data makes learning these kinds of relations a difficult task as they occur on the sub-sentential (intra-sentential) level. Hence, we resort to using Fast-Text due to its principle approach of leveraging subword (i.e., n-gram) information. The n-gram approach resolves the problem of modeling languages with rare word inflections by using character n-grams. On the other hand, other embedding techniques, e.g., word2vec and glove, lack subword information and hence struggle with morphologically rich languages such as Arabic and noisy data such as Twitter data (Mikolov et al., 2013a; Pennington et al., 2014).

A Model for Neural POS Tagging For our experiments we use three neural networks architectures: a) a BiLSTM-CRF architecture similar to the one proposed by (Reimers and Gurevych, 2017) for POS tagging; b) a multi-task learning model for learning jointly POS tagging for related language pairs; and, c) a multi-task learning model for learning jointly POS and Language ID tagging.

- We train a BiLSTM network with a conditional random field objective (Reimers and Gurevych, 2017) that obtain the probability distribution over all labels by jointly modeling the probability of the entire tag sequence score. We initialize the embedding layer with the pre-trained FastText word embeddings and feed the output sequence from this layer to the BiLSTM layer. The BiLSTM hidden layer has 200 units for each direction and dropout of 0.2. We use early stopping (Chollet et al., 2015) based on performance on validation sets. We refer to this model as BiLSTM-CRF POS Tagger for the rest of the article and in our tables.

- Our second model is a multi-task learning model that learns simultaneously POS tagging for related code switching language pairs. The architecture of this model follows the BiLSTM-CRF architecture (Reimers and Gurevych, 2017). We add a second CRF output layer for predicting the POS tag for the related language pair (e.g., MSA-LEV), while the first CRF output layer is for predicting the POS tag for the other related language pair (e.g., MSA-EGY). The two output layers of POS tagging tasks for the two language pairs are independent and are connected by their weight matrices to the hidden layer, and both loss functions are given the same weight. We

refer to this model as MTL-POS Tagger for the rest of the article and in our tables.

- The third model is a multi-task learning model. The model learns simultaneously POS and language id tags with the aim of boosting the performance of POS tagging task. The architecture of this model follows MTL-POS Tagger architecture. The difference is that one output layer is for predicting the POS tagging, and the other output layer is for predicting language id task. This model is referred to as MTL-POS+LID Tagger.

Experimental Conditions

Monolingual embedding (baseline): We train word embeddings using the monolingual corpora for each language involved in the four language pairs. The results of this approach are six separate pre-trained embeddings, MSA, EGY, LEV, ENG, SPA, and HIN pre-trained embeddings. For each language, we train a BiLSTM-CRF model using one of the six pre-trained embeddings. We consider these models as baseline systems. The baseline performance is the POS tagging accuracy of the monolingual models with no special training for CS data.

Merged Bilingual embeddings:

Combined filtered monolingual corpora (CFM): To leverage the inter-sentential code switching type, we train a model using a pre-trained word embedding trained on monolingual data only. The assumption is that the data in MSA is purely MSA and that in EGY is purely EGY. This condition yields an inter-sentential CS pre-trained embeddings. None of the sentences reflect intra-sentential CS data.

Pure Code switched corpora (PCS): To leverage the intra-sentential code switching type, we train a model using a pre-trained word embedding trained on CS data only. The assumption is that the data used to train the embeddings exhibit the CS phenomenon. This condition yields an intra-sentential CS type. None of the sentences reflect inter-sentential CS data.

(Pseudo) Combined monolingual and CS corpora (PseudoCS): To address both code switching types, the intra-sentential and inter-sentential, we combine the pure code switched corpora and combined filtered monolingual corpora to form unified to be used to train a unified word embeddings.

Dataset	Train	Dev	Test
ARZ (MSA-EGY)	133,357	21,146	20,464
LEV (MSA-LEV)	45,167	5,749	5,779
Miami Bangor (SPA-ENG)	268,464	67,114	67,114
UD-HIN-ENG	19,695	3,339	3,190

Table 1: Datasets distribution for the four language pairs

Merged multilingual embeddings: We train a multilingual embedding for language pairs that have one language in common (pivot language). To do so, we combine the corpora used to train the word embeddings of the language pairs that share one common language. For MSA-EGY and MSA-LEV language pairs, we have a common language, which is MSA, while ENG is a common language between SPA-ENG and HIN-ENG. To leverage this commonality between each of the two language pairs, we merge all the previous corpora: PCS, Mono, and PseudoCS for each language pair to form one corpus used to train merged multilingual embeddings model for MSA-EGY-LEV languages and another corpus for SPA-HIN-ENG. The intuition of this embeddings is to capture word usage in the context of each language and eliminates the ambiguity for the words that have the same surface form in multiple languages.

Projected bilingual embedding Projected bilingual embeddings are vector representations of two languages mapped into shared space, such that translated word pairs have similar vectors. There are three approaches to learn bilingual embeddings: 1) by mapping the space of both monolingual embeddings into a single shared space; 2) monolingual adaptation of one language's embedding space into another's; 3) Bilingual Training by bootstrapping the target representations learned from well-trained embeddings space of a source language. We train individual CS and monolingual embedding models separately before mapping them into a shared embedding space. To do so, We use MUSE (Conneau et al., 2017), state-of-the-art model for creating a projected bilingual embedding that uses the monolingual adaptation technique to create the shared space embedding. MUSE is equipped to learn either via supervision or no supervision. In our study, we utilize the unsupervised version of MUSE.

4   Evaluation

4.1   Data sets

Throughout our experiments, we use one evaluation dataset for each language pair and various corpora for training the embeddings layer. Table-1 shows the distribution of the evaluation data sets.

MSA-EGY We use the LDC Egyptian Arabic Treebanks 1-5 (ARZ1-5) (Maamouri et al., 2012). The ARZ1-5 data is from the discussion forums genre mostly in the Egyptian Arabic dialect (EGY). The total number of sentences in the corpus is 13,698 while the number of words is 174,967 words.

To train pre-trained embeddings, we crawl Egyptian tweets from some of the Egyptian public figures' Twitter accounts. The rest of the Egyptian raw textual data comes from the following sources: (Zaidan and Callison-Burch, 2011)'s Egyptian online news commentary corpus, the Egyptian tweets used in the CS shared tasks (Solorio et al., 2014; Molina et al., 2016; Aguilar et al., 2018), portion of MSA Gigaword (Parker et al., 2011), and LDC Arabic tree bank corpora (MSA) (Maamouri et al., 2004; Diab et al., 2013). To identify the language id of MSA-EGY tokens, we use the Automatic Identification of Dialectal Arabic (AIDA2) tool (Al-Badrashiny et al., 2015) to perform token level language identification for the EGY and MSA tokens in context.

MSA-LEV We use the Curras Corpus of Palestinian Arabic as the MSA-LEV textual CS data (Jarrar et al., 2017). Palestinian Arabic is a subdialect of Levantine Arabic. The corpus comprises 57,000 words, half of which come from transcripts of a TV show and the rest of which comes from various sources such as Facebook, discussing forums, Twitter, and blogs. The corpus is morphologically annotated by Eskander et al. (2016) using the same guidelines utilized for annotating the Egyptian ARZ corpus. We annotate the MSA-LEV evaluation data set with language id using the guidelines and tool proposed by (Diab et al., 2016; AlGhamdi and Diab, 2018).

To train pre-trained embeddings, we crawl tweets from Levantine public figures. Moreover, we compile Levantine and MSA raw textual data from multiple resources: online news commentary corpus from (Zaidan and Callison-Burch, 2011), weblogs from COLABA (Diab et al., 2010), commentaries and tweets from Cotterell and Callison-Burch (2014), the Levantine portion of the PADIC data set (Meftouh et al., 2015), portion of MSA Gigaword (Parker et al., 2011), and LDC Arabic tree bank corpora (MSA) (Maamouri et al., 2004; Diab et al., 2013).

SPA-ENG   The Miami Bangor (MB) corpus is a conversational speech corpus recorded from bilingual Spanish-English speakers living in Miami, FL. It includes 56 conversations recorded from 84 speakers (Soto and Hirschberg, 2017). The corpus consists of 242,475 words (333,069 including punctuation tokens) and 35 hours of recorded conversation. The language markers in the corpus were manually annotated.

To train pre-trained embeddings for Spanish and English language, we use the English Universal Dependencies (UD) corpus (Silveira et al., 2014) and the Spanish UD corpus (McDonald et al., 2013). Universal Dependencies (UD) is a project to develop cross-linguistically consistent treebank annotations for many languages. Moreover, we use some other English monolingual data from various resources. The English monolingual data contains around 250M sentences.

HIN-ENG   The Hindi-English Code switching treebank is based on CS tweets of Hindi and English multilingual speakers (mostly Indian) (Bhat et al., 2017). The treebank is manually annotated using UD scheme. The corpus contains data from Twitter. The corpus contains 1,852 tweets and 26,224 tokens. To train pre-trained embeddings for Hindi and English language, we use the English Universal Dependencies (UD) corpus (Silveira et al., 2014) and the Hindi UD corpus (Bhat et al.; Palmer et al., 2009). Also, we use some other Hindi monolingual data from various resources. The word representations are learned using Skip-gram model with negative sampling which is implemented in FastText toolkit for all language.

Baseline Results   The baseline performance is the POS tagging accuracy of the monolingual models with no special training for CS data. Therefore, our baselines are the neural network models trained using the monolingual embeddings. If CS data do not pose any particular challenge to monolingual POS taggers, then we should not expect a major degradation in performance.

Table-2 shows the performance of the different baseline POS tagging systems on the test data. For each language pair, there are two baseline systems.

For MSA-EGY, the baseline accuracies are 85.40 when the baseline system utilizes the MSA pre-trained embeddings, and 81.06 when BiLSTM-CRF uses the EGY pre-trained embeddings. Similarly, we report the baseline results for MSA-LEV, SPA-ENG and HIN-ENG language pairs.

4.2   Results

In this section, we present the results of our experiments using the neural network models and embeddings approach introduced in Section 3 and the datasets from Section 4.1. Also, we show the results of three neural network models when the embeddings are randomly initialized. Table-2 shows the POS tagging accuracy results of all language pairs, while Table-3 shows the LID accuracy results of all language pairs using MTL-POS+LID Tagger. To evaluate the performance of our approaches we report the accuracy of each condition by comparing the output POS tags generated from each condition against the available gold POS tags for each data set. We consistently apply the different experimental conditions on the same test set per language pair: for MSA-EGY we report results on MSA-EGY test set, for MSA-LEV we report results on MSA-LEV test set, and for SPA-ENG, we report results on Miami Bangor corpus (SPA-ENG) test set, and finally for HIN-ENG, we report on UD-HIN-ENG (HIN-ENG) test set. The highest accuracy results for MSA-EGY and MSA-LEV language pairs are 92.90% and 92.92%, respectively. These results are achieved by MTL-POS Tagger+Merged Bilingual PseudoCS embeddings. Our best model for MSA-EGY outperform state-of-the-art system by ∼ 2% (AlGhamdi et al., 2016). We could not compare our best system for MSA-LEV language pair to any previous systems as we map the original POS tag set (Buckwalter POS tag set) of the MSA-LEV dataset into UD POS tag set. BiLSTM-CRF+Merged Bilingual PseudoCS embeddings yield the highest accuracy results for both SPA-ENG and HIN-ENG language pairs. The SPA-ENG model's accuracy, 96.55%, is comparable to the state-of-the-art system, 96.63% (Soto and Hirschberg, 2018). On the other hand, the accuracy of our best HIN-ENG model (86.01%) underperforms the state-of-the-

Embedding Condition	MSA-EGY	MSA-LEV	SPA-ENG	HIN-ENG
BiLSTM-CRF Tagger (1) + Random-Initi-Embed	89.12	88.90	95.33	69.87
(1) + mono (MSA/SPA/HIN) (Baseline)	85.40	83.25	50.30	63.30
(1) + mono (EGY/LEV/ENG) (Baseline)	81.06	80.21	71.21	67.11
(1)+ Merged Bilingual CFM	90.00	89.41	95.40	85.98
(1)+Merged Bilingual PCS	89.06	88.94	94.22	83.31
(1)+Merged Bilingual PseudoCS	91.96	91.92	*96.55*	*86.01*
(1)+ Merged Multilingual Embeddings(pivot)	92.81	92.91	94.81	85.87
(1)+Projected Bilingual	89.24	87.60	91.31	83.02
MTL-POS Tagger (2) + Random-Initi-Embed	89.91	90.02	92.89	79.51
(2)+Merged Bilingual PCS	90.01	90.51	93.21	84.30
(2)+Merged Bilingual PseudoCS	*92.90*	*92.92*	94.14	84.33
MTL-POS+LID Tagger (3) + Random-Initi-Embed	88.96	89.79	92.65	78.51
(3)+ Merged Bilingual CFM	90.00	89.01	95.42	84.01
(3)+Merged Bilingual PCS	90.41	90.48	95.29	84.41
(3)+Merged Bilingual PseudoCS	91.89	91.92	96.50	85.91
(3)+Projected Bilingual	88.61	88.09	92.91	82.39
State-of-the-art	90.56	–	**96.63**	**91.90**

Table 2: POS tagging accuracy (%) on the four corpora. Average over five runs with different random seeds. Bold and italics font indicates the best result in our experiments, while bold font indicates the best results compared to the state-of-the-art systems. We refer to BiLSTM-CRF Tagger as (1), MTL-POS Tagger that learns POS tag for related languages as (2), and MTL-POS+LID that learns jointly POS tagging and language identification as (3). Random-Initi-Embed refers to Random initialized embedding

Embedding Condition	MSA-EGY	MSA-LEV	SPA-ENG	HIN-ENG
MTL-POS+LID Tagger: (3) + Random-Initi-Embed	80.71	79.29	96.42	78.41
(3) + mono (MSA/SPA/HIN) (baselines)	77.41	78.08	88.11	71.46
(3) + mono (EGY/LEV/ENG) (baselines)	71.51	76.37	85.09	74.80
(3)+ Merged Bilingual CFM	80.06	78.39	95.49	92.54
(3)+Merged Bilingual PCS	81.33	79.28	95.02	93.20
(3)+Merged Bilingual PseudoCS	**82.15**	**81.32**	*97.20*	*94.92*
(3)+Projected Bilingual	78.17	79.11	90.01	87.69
State-of-the-art	–	–	**98.78**	**97.39**

Table 3: LID accuracy (%) on the four corpora. Average over five runs with different random seeds. Bold and italics font indicates the best result in our experiments, while bold font indicates the best results compared to the state-of-the-art systems. We refer to MTL-POS+LID that learns jointly POS tagging and language identification as (3). Random-Initi-Embed refers to Random initialized embeddings

art system (91.90%) (Bhat et al., 2018). For LID task, all our models underperform the state-of-the-art systems. Since there are no state-of-the-art systems for MSA-EGY and MSA-LEV, we compare the performance of our models against the baseline systems.

5   Discussion

Multilingual embedding (e.g., MSA-EGY and MSA-LEV) helps closely related languages (EGY/LEV) but adds noise to the languages that are distant (SPA/HIN). Similarly, learning jointly POS tagging for closely related languages yields the highest accuracy results for MSA-EGY and MSA-LEV as opposed to the languages that are distant (SPA/HIN). The accuracy results of MSA-EGY and MSA-LEV language pairs are the highest results in all experimental setups. The improvement could be attributed to the significant number of homographs some of which are cognates.

The CS behavior can be different depending on the medium of communication, topic, speakers (or authors), and the languages being mixed among other factors. Hence, we believe that the difference in the genre of the evaluation data sets of SPA-ENG and HIN-ENG language pairs is one of the potential reasons that make both language pairs not to benefit from the multilingual embedding and learning jointly POS tagging for both language pairs. On the other hand, the MTL-POS-LID Tagger that learns simultaneously POS and language id tags with the aim of boosting the performance of POS tagging task benefit distant (SPA/HIN) more than closely related languages (EGY/LEV). We define code switching points as the points within a sentence where the languages of the words on the two sides are dif-

MSA-EGY		MSA-LEV		SPA-ENG		HIN-ENG	
Error Type	**Percentage**	**Error Type**	**Percentage**	**Error Type**	**Percentage**	**Error Type**	**Percentage**
ADJ >NOUN	19%	ADJ >NOUN	21%	NOUN >ADJ	10%	NOUN >VERB	27%
VERB >NOUN	15%	VERB >NOUN	19%	NOUN >PRON	8%	VERB >NOUN	24%
NOUN >VERB	11%	NOUN >ADJ	16%	VERB >NOUN	7%	NOUN >ADJ	19%
NOUN >ADJ	8%	NOUN >VERB	9%	ADJ >PRON	5%	ADJ >VERB	14%

Table 4: Most common errors for the best systems for all language pairs (Gold-POS > Predicted-POS)

ferent. We observe a sharp jump in the accuracy for SPA-ENG corpus. We believe the major factor of this jump is the low percentage of the CS points, $\sim 6\%$, while the percentage of CS points in the MSA-EGY, MSA-LEV, and HIN-ENG datasets are relatively high, 38.78%, 30.12%, and 15.17%. The low percentage of CS points in the SPA-ENG corpus leads the models that address the inter-sentential code switching type (BiLSTM-CRF+Merged BilingualMerged Bilingual CFM and MTL+Merged BilingualMerged Bilingual CFM) to score the second highest accuracy results, 95.40% and 95.42%.

The two key advantages of the Merged Bilingual PseudoCS embeddings and Multilingual embeddings are, 1) it enables the learned embeddings to capture the interactions between the words in different languages; 2) It captures the word usage in the context of each language and eliminates the ambiguity for the words that have the same surface form in multiple languages. Hence, the OOV percentage and ambiguity of words are reduced. Using multilingual embeddings for MSA-EGY and MSA-LEV, reduced the percentage of OOV of MSA-EGY and MSA-LEV from 10% and 13% to 8% and 10%, respectively. Similarly, with SPA-ENG and HIN-ENG language pairs, the rate of OOV is decreased from 12% and 15% to 9% and 11%, respectively.

One of the common CS intra-sentential patterns we notice in our data sets is insertion patterns. This pattern involves inserting material (lexical items, or entire constituents) from one language into a structure from the other language (Muysken et al., 2000). To evaluate the effect of the CS insertion pattern we define the CS fragment (CSF) of those test sentences. We define a CSF as the minimum contiguous span of words where a CS occurs (Soto and Hirschberg, 2018). The average length of the CS fragments in the SPA-ENG test set is 2.16, and 6.1 in the HIN-ENG test set. The average length of the CS fragments is 5.1 in MSA-LEV, and 5.8 in MSA-EGY test set. We observe that the length of the CS fragments impacts the overall performance of the classifiers. For example, short CS fragments confuse the best classifiers of almost all language pairs. We noticed that a majority of CS sentences that have one or two lexical elements inserted had been miss-classified by almost all models in all language pairs.

Using bilingual embeddings outperform the baseline systems, but it did not achieve the highest results achieved by the other proposed models for all language pairs. The experiment results show a promising direction towards obtaining bilingual embeddings for CS tasks. Our explanation for this performance is that the sense distribution of polysemous words can differ widely between a monolingual (mono) corpus and Merged Bilingual PseudoCS corpus. For instance, the word 'bank' in English has several meanings such as (a) the land alongside or sloping, (b) a financial institution, and (c) a set or series of similar things. However, in a Spanish dominant sentence or corpus, 'bank' is primarily, if not only, used in sense (a). Our experiments show that standard bilingual embeddings are not well suited, in general, for CS tasks; embeddings learned from CS data yield better results which are aligned with our findings (Pratapa et al., 2018).

Table 4 shows the most common errors for the best systems for each language pairs. We observe almost the same trends across both MSA-EGY and MSA-LEV language pairs, while the common errors are relatively different between SPA-ENG and HIN-ENG.

6   Conclusion

In this paper, we present a detailed study of various strategies for POS tagging of CS data in four language pairs. We explore multiple strategies of measuring the impact of pretrained embeddings on POS tagging of CS data. We find that related language pairs, e.g., MSA-EGY and MSA-LEV, benefit from both jointly learning POS tagging as well as merged multilingual embeddings (i.e., pivot embedding), while distant language pairs, e.g., SPA-ENG and HIN-ENG, benefit from a multi-task learning model that learns two different tasks, e.g., POS tagging and language identification. Furthermore, we compared our results to the previous state-of-the-art POS tagger for MSA-EGY, SPA-ENG, and HIN-ENG and showed that our classifiers outperform the MSA-EGY state-of-the-art system in every configuration (AlGhamdi et al., 2016). The results achieved by BiLSTM-CRF+Merged Bilingual PseudoCS embeddings model is comparable to Soto and Hirschberg (2018). We will explore several directions in the future. First, we will study the theoretical aspects of word embedding learning. Second, we will investigate the proposed word embeddings on other downstream NLP applications, such as segmentation and parsing.

Acknowledgments

We would like to thank the four anonymous reviewers for their valuable comments and suggestions.

References

Oliver Adams, Adam Makarucha, Graham Neubig, Steven Bird, and Trevor Cohn. 2017. Cross-lingual word embeddings for low-resource language modeling. In *Proceedings of the 15th Conference of the European Chapter of the Association for Computational Linguistics: Volume 1, Long Papers*, volume 1, pages 937–947.

Gustavo Aguilar, Fahad AlGhamdi, Victor Soto, Mona Diab, Julia Hirschberg, and Thamar Solorio. 2018. Named entity recognition on code-switched data: Overview of the calcs 2018 shared task. In *Proceedings of the Third Workshop on Computational Approaches to Linguistic Code-Switching*, pages 138–147. Association for Computational Linguistics.

Mohamed Al-Badrashiny, Heba Elfardy, and Mona T. Diab. 2015. Aida2: A hybrid approach for token and sentence level dialect identification in arabic. In *Proceedings of the 19th Conference on Computational Natural Language Learning, CoNLL 2015, Beijing, China, July 30-31, 2015*, pages 42–51. ACL.

Fahad AlGhamdi and Mona Diab. 2018. Wasa: A web application for sequence annotation. In *Proceedings of the 11th Language Resources and Evaluation Conference*, Miyazaki, Japan. European Language Resource Association.

Fahad AlGhamdi, Giovanni Molina, Mona T. Diab, Thamar Solorio, Abdelati Hawwari, Victor Soto, and Julia Hirschberg. 2016. Part of speech tagging for code switched data. In *Proceedings of the Second Workshop on Computational Approaches to Code Switching@EMNLP 2016, Austin, Texas, USA, November 1, 2016*.

Utsab Barman, Joachim Wagner, and Jennifer Foster. 2016. Part-of-speech tagging of code-mixed social media content: Pipeline, stacking and joint modelling. In *Proceedings of the Second Workshop on Computational Approaches to Code Switching*, pages 30–39. Association for Computational Linguistics.

Irshad Bhat, Riyaz A Bhat, Manish Shrivastava, and Dipti Sharma. 2017. Joining hands: Exploiting monolingual treebanks for parsing of code-mixing data. In *Proceedings of the 15th Conference of the European Chapter of the Association for Computational Linguistics: Volume 2, Short Papers*, volume 2, pages 324–330.

Irshad Ahmad Bhat, Riyaz Ahmad Bhat, Manish Shrivastava, and Dipti Misra Sharma. 2018. Universal dependency parsing for Hindi-English code-switching. *arXiv preprint arXiv:1804.05868*.

Riyaz Ahmad Bhat, Rajesh Bhatt, Annahita Farudi, Prescott Klassen, Bhuvana Narasimhan, Martha Palmer, Owen Rambow, Dipti Misra Sharma, Ashwini Vaidya, Sri Ramagurumurthy Vishnu, et al. The hindi/urdu treebank project. In *Handbook of Linguistic Annotation*. Springer Press.

Phil Blunsom and Karl Moritz Hermann. 2014. Multilingual models for compositional distributional semantics.

Piotr Bojanowski, Edouard Grave, Armand Joulin, and Tomas Mikolov. 2017. Enriching word vectors with subword information. *Transactions of the Association for Computational Linguistics*, 5:135–146.

Mónica Stella Cárdenas-Claros and Neny Isharyanti. 2009. Code-switching and code-mixing in internet chatting: Betweenyes,'yes' , 'ya' , and 'si' a case study. *The Jalt Call Journal*, 5(3):67–78.

Khyathi Chandu, Thomas Manzini, Sumeet Singh, and Alan W. Black. 2018. Language informed modeling of code-switched text. In *Proceedings of the Third Workshop on Computational Approaches to Linguistic Code-Switching*, pages 92–97. Association for Computational Linguistics.

Hongshen Chen, Yue Zhang, and Qun Liu. 2016. Neural network for heterogeneous annotations. In *Proceedings of the 2016 Conference on Empirical Methods in Natural Language Processing*, pages 731–741.

François Chollet et al. 2015. Keras. https://github.com/fchollet/keras.

Alexis Conneau, Guillaume Lample, Marc'Aurelio Ranzato, Ludovic Denoyer, and Hervé Jégou. 2017. Word translation without parallel data. *arXiv preprint arXiv:1710.04087*.

Ryan Cotterell and Chris Callison-Burch. 2014. A multi-dialect, multi-genre corpus of informal written Arabic. In *Proceedings of the Ninth International Conference on Language Resources and Evaluation (LREC-2014)*. European Language Resources Association (ELRA).

Brenda Danet and Susan C Herring. 2007. *The multilingual Internet: Language, culture, and communication online*. Oxford University Press.

Mona Diab, Mahmoud Ghoneim, Fahad AlGhamdi, Nada AlMarwani, and Mohamed Al-Badrashiny. 2016. Creating a large multi-layered representational repository of linguistic code switched arabic data. In *10th International Conference on Language Resources and Evaluation (LREC'16)*, Portorož, Slovenia. European Language Resources Association (ELRA).

Mona Diab, Nizar Habash, Owen Rambow, Mohamed Altantawy, and Yassine Benajiba. 2010. COLABA: Arabic dialect annotation and processing. In *Lrec workshop on semitic language processing*, pages 66–74.

Mona Diab, Nizar Habash, Owen Rambow, and Ryan Roth. 2013. LDC Arabic treebanks and associated corpora: Data divisions manual. *arXiv preprint arXiv:1309.5652*.

Ramy Eskander, Nizar Habash, Owen Rambow, and Arfath Pasha. 2016. Creating resources for dialectal Arabic from a single annotation: A case study on egyptian and levantine. In *Proceedings of COLING 2016, the 26th International Conference on Computational Linguistics: Technical Papers*, pages 3455–3465. The COLING 2016 Organizing Committee.

Manaal Faruqui and Chris Dyer. 2014. Improving vector space word representations using multilingual correlation. In *Proceedings of the 14th Conference of the European Chapter of the Association for Computational Linguistics*, pages 462–471.

Anupam Jamatia, Björn Gambäck, and Amitava Das. 2015. Part-of-speech tagging for code-mixed English-Hindi Twitter and Facebook chat messages. *RECENT ADVANCES IN*, page 239.

Mustafa Jarrar, Nizar Habash, Faeq Alrimawi, Diyam Akra, and Nasser Zalmout. 2017. Curras: an annotated corpus for the Palestinian Arabic dialect. *Language Resources and Evaluation*, 51(3):745–775.

Mohamed Maamouri, Ann Bies, Tim Buckwalter, and Wigdan Mekki. 2004. The penn Arabic treebank: Building a large-scale annotated Arabic corpus. In *NEMLAR conference on Arabic language resources and tools*, volume 27, pages 466–467. Cairo.

Mohamed Maamouri, Ann Bies, Seth Kulick, Dalila Tabessi, and Sondos Krouna. 2012. Egyptian Arabic Treebank pilot.

Ryan McDonald, Joakim Nivre, Yvonne Quirmbach-Brundage, Yoav Goldberg, Dipanjan Das, Kuzman Ganchev, Keith Hall, Slav Petrov, Hao Zhang, Oscar Täckström, Claudia Bedini, Núria Bertomeu Castelló, and Jungmee Lee. 2013. Universal dependency annotation for multilingual parsing. In *Proceedings of the 51st Annual Meeting of the Association for Computational Linguistics (Volume 2: Short Papers)*, pages 92–97. Association for Computational Linguistics.

Karima Meftouh, Salima Harrat, Salma Jamoussi, Mourad Abbas, and Kamel Smaili. 2015. Machine translation experiments on padic: A parallel Arabic dialect corpus. In *Proceedings of the 29th Pacific Asia Conference on Language, Information and Computation*, pages 26–34.

Tomas Mikolov, Kai Chen, Greg Corrado, and Jeffrey Dean. 2013a. Efficient estimation of word representations in vector space. *CoRR*, abs/1301.3781.

Tomas Mikolov, Quoc V Le, and Ilya Sutskever. 2013b. Exploiting similarities among languages for machine translation. *arXiv preprint arXiv:1309.4168*.

Tomas Mikolov, Ilya Sutskever, Kai Chen, Greg S Corrado, and Jeff Dean. 2013c. Distributed representations of words and phrases and their compositionality. In *Advances in neural information processing systems*, pages 3111–3119.

Giovanni Molina, Fahad AlGhamdi, Mahmoud Ghoneim, Abdelati Hawwari, Nicolas Rey-Villamizar, Mona Diab, and Thamar Solorio. 2016. Overview for the second shared task on language identification in code-switched data. In *Proceedings of the Second Workshop on Computational Approaches to Code Switching*, pages 40–49. Association for Computational Linguistics.

Pieter Muysken, Carmen Pena Díaz, Pieter Cornelis Muysken, et al. 2000. *Bilingual speech: A typology of code-mixing*, volume 11. Cambridge University Press.

Martha Palmer, Rajesh Bhatt, Bhuvana Narasimhan, Owen Rambow, Dipti Misra Sharma, and Fei Xia. 2009. Hindi syntax: Annotating dependency, lexical predicate-argument structure, and phrase structure. In *The 7th International Conference on Natural Language Processing*, pages 14–17.

Robert Parker, David Graff, Ke Chen, Junbo Kong, and Kazuaki Maeda. 2011. Arabic Gigaword fifth edition LDC2011t11. *Philadelphia: Linguistic Data Consortium*.

Jeffrey Pennington, Richard Socher, and Christopher Manning. 2014. Glove: Global vectors for word representation. In *Proceedings of the 2014 conference on empirical methods in natural language processing (EMNLP)*, pages 1532–1543.

Slav Petrov, Dipanjan Das, and Ryan T. McDonald. 2011. A Universal Part-of-Speech Tagset. *CoRR*, abs/1104.2086.

Adithya Pratapa, Monojit Choudhury, and Sunayana Sitaram. 2018. Word embeddings for code-mixed language processing. In *Proceedings of the 2018 Conference on Empirical Methods in Natural Language Processing*, pages 3067–3072. Association for Computational Linguistics.

Nils Reimers and Iryna Gurevych. 2017. Reporting Score Distributions Makes a Difference: Performance Study of LSTM-networks for Sequence Tagging. In *Proceedings of the 2017 Conference on Empirical Methods in Natural Language Processing (EMNLP)*, pages 338–348, Copenhagen, Denmark.

Kalika Bali Royal Sequiera, Monojit Choudhury. 2015. POS tagging of Hindi-English Code Mixed Text from Social Media: Some Machine Learning Experiments. In *Proceedings of International Conference on NLP*. NLPAI.

Natalia Silveira, Timothy Dozat, Marie-Catherine de Marneffe, Samuel Bowman, Miriam Connor, John Bauer, and Chris Manning. 2014. A Gold Standard Dependency Corpus for English. In *Proceedings of the Ninth International Conference on Language Resources and Evaluation (LREC-2014)*. European Language Resources Association (ELRA).

Thamar Solorio, Elizabeth Blair, Suraj Maharjan, Steven Bethard, Mona Diab, Mahmoud Gohneim, Abdelati Hawwari, Fahad AlGhamdi, Julia Hirschberg, Alison Chang, and Pascale Fung. 2014. Overview of the first shared task on language identification in code-switched data. In *First Workshop on Computational Approaches to Code Switching, EMNLP-2014*, Doha, Qatar. Association for Computational Linguistics.

Thamar Solorio and Yang Liu. 2008. Part-of-speech tagging for English-Spanish code-switched text. In *Proceedings of the Conference on Empirical Methods in Natural Language Processing*, pages 1051–1060. Association for Computational Linguistics.

Victor Soto and Julia Hirschberg. 2017. Crowdsourcing Universal Part-Of-Speech tags for Code-Switching. In *Interspeech 2017*, pages 77–81.

Victor Soto and Julia Hirschberg. 2018. Joint part-of-speech and language id tagging for code-switched data. In *Proceedings of the Third Workshop on Computational Approaches to Linguistic Code-Switching*, pages 1–10. Association for Computational Linguistics.

Ivan Vulić and Marie-Francine Moens. 2016. Bilingual distributed word representations from document-aligned comparable data. *Journal of Artificial Intelligence Research*, 55:953–994.

Yogarshi Vyas, Spandana Gella, Jatin Sharma, Kalika Bali, and Monojit Choudhury. 2014a. Pos tagging of English-Hindi code-mixed social media content. In *Proceedings of the 2014 Conference on Empirical Methods in Natural Language Processing (EMNLP)*, pages 974-979, Doha, Qatar. Association for Computational Linguistics.

Yogarshi Vyas, Spandana Gella, Jatin Sharma, Kalika Bali, and Monojit Choudhury. 2014b. Pos tagging of English-Hindi code-mixed social media content. In *Proceedings of the 2014 Conference on Empirical Methods in Natural Language Processing (EMNLP)*, pages 974–979. Association for Computational Linguistics.

Omar F Zaidan and Chris Callison-Burch. 2011. The Arabic online commentary dataset: an annotated dataset of informal Arabic with high dialectal content. In *Proceedings of the 49th Annual Meeting of the Association for Computational Linguistics: Human Language Technologies: short papers-Volume 2*, pages 37–41. Association for Computational Linguistics.

Yuan Zhang and David Weiss. 2016. Stack-propagation: Improved representation learning for syntax. *arXiv preprint arXiv:1603.06598*.

Will Y Zou, Richard Socher, Daniel Cer, and Christopher D Manning. 2013. Bilingual word embeddings for phrase-based machine translation. In *Proceedings of the 2013 Conference on Empirical Methods in Natural Language Processing*, pages 1393–1398.

Toward a deep dialectological representation of Indo-Aryan

Chundra A. Cathcart
Department of Comparative Linguistics
University of Zurich
chundra.cathcart@uzh.ch

Abstract

This paper presents a new approach to disentangling inter-dialectal and intra-dialectal relationships within one such group, the Indo-Aryan subgroup of Indo-European. I draw upon admixture models and deep generative models to tease apart historic language contact and language-specific behavior in the overall patterns of sound change displayed by Indo-Aryan languages. I show that a "deep" model of Indo-Aryan dialectology sheds some light on questions regarding inter-relationships among the Indo-Aryan languages, and performs better than a "shallow" model in terms of certain qualities of the posterior distribution (e.g., entropy of posterior distributions), and outline future pathways for model development.

1 Introduction

At the risk of oversimplifying, quantitative models of language relationship fall into two broad categories. At a wide, family-level scale, phylogenetic methods adopted from computational biology have had success in shedding light on the histories of genetically related but significantly diversified speech varieties (Bouckaert et al., 2012). At a shallower level, the subfield of dialectometry has used a wide variety of chiefly distance-based methodologies to analyze variation among closely related dialects with similar lexical and typological profiles (Nerbonne and Heeringa, 2001), though this work also emphasizes the importance of hierarchical linguistic relationships and the use of abstract, historically meaningful features (Prokić and Nerbonne, 2008; Nerbonne, 2009). It is possible, however, that neither methodology is completely effective for for language groups of intermediate size, particularly those where certain languages have remained in contact to an extent that blurs the phylogenetic signal, but have expe-

rienced great enough diversification that dialectometric approaches are not appropriate. This paper presents a new approach to disentangling inter-dialectal and intra-dialectal relationships within one such group, the Indo-Aryan subgroup of Indo-European.

Indo-Aryan presents many interesting puzzles. Although all modern Indo-Aryan (henceforth NIA) languages descend from Sanskrit or Old Indo-Aryan (henceforth OIA), their subgrouping and dialectal interrelationships remain somewhat poorly understood (for surveys of assorted problems, see Emeneau 1966; Masica 1991; Toulmin 2009; Smith 2017; Deo 2018). This is partly due to the fact that these languages have remained in contact with each other, and this admixture has complicated our understanding of the languages' history. Furthermore, while most NIA languages have likely gone through stages closely resembling attested Middle Indo-Aryan (MIA) languages such as Prakrit or Pali, no NIA language can be taken with any certainty to be direct descendants of an attested MIA variety, further shrouding the historical picture of their development.

The primary goal of the work described in this paper is to build, or work towards building, a model of Indo-Aryan dialectology that incorporates realistic assumptions regarding historical linguistics and language change. I draw upon admixture models and deep generative models to tease apart historic language contact and language-specific behavior in the overall patterns of sound change displayed by Indo-Aryan languages. I show that a "deep" model of Indo-Aryan dialectology sheds some light on questions regarding inter-relationships among the Indo-Aryan languages, and performs better than a "shallow" model in terms of certain qualities of the posterior distribution (e.g., entropy of posterior distributions). I provide a comparison with other met-

110

Proceedings of VarDial, pages 110–119
Minneapolis, MN, June 7, 2019 ©2019 Association for Computational Linguistics

rics, and outline future pathways for model development.

2 Sound Change

The notion that sound change proceeds in a regular and systematic fashion is a cornerstone of the comparative method of historical linguistics. When we consider cognates such as Greek $p^h er\bar{o}$ and Sanskrit *bharā(mi)* 'I carry', we observe regular sound correspondences (e.g., p^h:*bh*) which allow us to formulate sound changes that have operated during the course of each language's development from their shared common ancestor. Under ideal circumstances, these are binary yes/no questions (e.g., Proto-Indo-European $*b^h$ > Greek p^h). At other times, there is some noise in the signal: for instance, OIA *kṣ* is realized as *kh* in most Romani words (e.g., *akṣi-* 'eye' > *jakh*), but also as *čh* (*kṣurikā-* > *čhuri* 'knife'), according to Matras (2002, 41). This is undoubtedly due to relatively old language contact (namely lexical borrowing) between prehistoric Indo-Aryan dialects, as opposed to different conditioning environments which trigger a change *kṣ* > *kh* in some phonological contexts but *kṣ* > *čh* in others. The idea that Indo-Aryan speech varieties borrowed forms from one another on a large scale is well established (Turner, 1975 [1967], 406), as is often the case in situations where closely related dialects have developed in close geographic proximity to one another (cf. Bloomfield, 1933, 461–495). An effective model of Indo-Aryan dialectology must be able to account this sort of admixture. Phylogenetic methods and distance-based methods provide indirect information regarding language contact (e.g., in the form of uncertain tree topologies), but do not explicitly model intimate borrowing.

A number of studies have used mixed-membership models such as the Structure model (Pritchard et al., 2000) in order to explicitly model admixture between languages (Reesink et al., 2009; Syrjänen et al., 2016). Under this approach, individual languages receive their linguistic features from latent ancestral components with particular feature distributions. A key assumption of the Structure model is the relative invariance and stability of the features of interest (e.g., allele frequencies, linguistic properties). However, sound change is a highly recurrent process, with many telescoped and intermediate changes, and it is not possible to treat sound changes that have operated as stable, highly conservative features.[1]

Intermediate stages between OIA and NIA languages are key for capturing similarities in cross-linguistic behavior, and we require a model that teases apart dialect group-specific trends and language-level ones. Consider the following examples:

- Assamese /x/, the reflex of OIA *s, ś, ṣ*, is thought to develop from intermediate **ś* (Kakati, 1941, 224). This isogloss would unite it with languages like Bengali, which show /ʃ/ for OIA *s, ś, ṣ*.

- Some instances of NIA *bh* likely come from an earlier **mh* (Tedesco 1965, 371; Oberlies 2005, 48) (cf. Oberlies 2005:48).

- The Marathi change *ch* > *s* affects certain words containing MIA **ch* < OIA *kṣ* as well as OIA *ch* (Masica, 1991, 457); *ch* ~ *kh* < OIA *kṣ* variation is of importance to MIA and NIA dialectology (compare the Romani examples given above).

In all examples, a given NIA language shows the effects of chronologically deep behavior which serves as an isogloss uniting it with other NIA languages, but this trend is masked by subsequent language-specific changes.[2] Work on probabilistic reconstruction of proto-word forms explicitly appeals to intermediate chronological stages where linguistic data are unobserved (Bouchard-Côté et al., 2007); however, unlike the work cited, this paper does not assume a fixed phylogeny, and hence I cannot adopt many of the simplifying conventions that the authors use.

3 Data

I extracted all modern Indo-Aryan forms from Turner's (1962–1966) *Comparative Dictionary of the Indo-Aryan Languages* (henceforth CDIAL),[3]

---

[1]Cathcart (to appear) circumvents this issue in a mixed-membership model of Indo-Aryan dialectology by considering only sound changes thought *a priori* in the literature to be relatively stable and of importance to dialectology.

[2]Some similar-looking sound changes can be shown to be chronologically shallow. For instance, the presence of *ș* for original *kh* in Old Braj, taken by most scholars to represent a legitimate sound change and not just an orthographic idiosyncrasy, affects Persian loans such as *șaracu* 'expense' ← Modern Persian *xirč* (McGregor, 1968, 125). This orthographic behavior is found in Old Gujarati as well (Baumann, 1975, 9). For further discussion of this issue, see Strnad 2013, 16ff.

[3]Available online at http://dsal.uchicago.edu/dictionaries/soas/

along with the Old Indo-Aryan headwords (henceforth ETYMA) from which these reflexes descend. Transcriptions of the data were normalized and converted to the International Phonetic Alphabet (IPA). Systematic morphological mismatches between OIA etyma and reflexes were accounted for, including stripping the endings from all verbs, since citation forms for OIA verbs are in the 3sg present, while most NIA reflexes give the infinitive. I matched each dialect with corresponding languoids in Glottolog (Hammarström et al., 2017) containing geographic metadata, resulting in the merger of several dialects. I excluded cognate sets with fewer than 10 forms, yielding 33231 modern Indo-Aryan forms. I preprocessed the data, first converting each segment into its respective sound class, as described by List (2012), and subsequently aligning each converted OIA/NIA string pair via the Needleman-Wunsch algorithm, using the Expectation-Maximization method described by Jäger (2014), building off of work by Wieling et al. (2012). This yields alignments of the following type: e.g., OIA /aːntra/ 'entrails' > Nepali /aːnØro/, where Ø indicates a gap where the "cursor" advances for the OIA string but not the Nepali string. Gaps on the OIA side are ignored, yielding a one-to-many OIA-to-NIA alignment; this ensures that all aligned cognate sets are of the same length.

4   Model

The basic family of model this paper employs is a Bayesian mixture model which assumes that each word in each language is generated by one of K latent dialect components. Like Structure (and similar methodologies like Latent Dirichlet Allocation), this model assumes that different elements in the same language can be generated by different dialect components. Unlike the most basic type of Structure model, which assumes a two-level data structure consisting of (1) languages and the (2) features they contain, our model assumes a three-level hierarchy, where (1) languages contain (2) words, which display the operation of different (3) sound changes; latent variable assignment happens at the word level.

I contrast the behavior of a DEEP model with that of a SHALLOW model. The deep model draws inspiration from Bayesian deep generative models (Ranganath et al., 2015), which incorporate intermediate latent variables which mimic the ar-

chitecture of a neural network. This structure allows us to posit an intermediate representation between the sound patterns in the OIA etymon and the sound patterns in the NIA reflex, allowing the model to pick up on shared dialectal similarities between forms in languages as opposed to language-specific idiosyncrasies. The shallow model, which serves as a baseline of sorts, conflates dialect group-level and language-level trends; it contains a flat representation of all of the sound changes taking place between a NIA word and its ancestral OIA etymon, and in this sense is halfway between a Structure model and a Naïve Bayes classifier (with a language-specific rather than global prior over component membership).

4.1   Shallow model

Here, I describe the generative process for the shallow model, assuming W OIA etyma, L languages, K dialect components, I unique OIA inputs, O unique NIA outputs, and aligned OIA-NIA word pair lengths $T_w : w \in \{1, ..., W\}$. For each OIA etymon, an input $x_{w,t}$ at time point $t \in \{1, ..., T_w\}$ consists of a trigram centered at the timepoint in question (e.g., ntr in OIA /aːntra/ 'entrails'), and the NIA reflex's output $y_{w,l,t}$ contains the segment(s) aligned with timepoint t (e.g., Nepali Ø). $x_{w,t} : t = 0$ is the left word boundary, while $x_{w,t} : t = T_w + 1$ is the right word boundary. Accordingly, sound change in the model can be viewed as a rewrite rule of the type A > B / C _ D. The model has the following parameters:

- Language-level weights over dialect components: $U_{l,k}; l \in \{1, ..., L\}, k \in \{1, ..., K\}$

- Dialect component-level weights over sound changes: $W_{k,i,o}; k \in \{1, ..., K\}, i \in \{1, ..., I\}, o \in \{1, ..., O\}$

The generative process is as follows:

For each OIA etymon $x_w \in \{1, ..., W\}$

  For each language $l \in \{1, ..., L\}$ in which the etymon survives, containing a reflex $y_{w,l}$

    Draw a dialect component assignment $z_{w,l} \sim \text{Categorical}(f(U_{l,.}))$

    For each time point $t \in \{1, ..., T_w\}$

      Draw a NIA sound $y_{w,l,t} \sim \text{Categorical}(f(W_{z_{w,l}, x_{w,t}, .}))$

All weights in U and W are drawn from a Normal distribution with a mean of 0 and standard deviation of 10; $f(\cdot)$ represents the softmax function (throughout this paper), which transforms these weights to probability simplices. The generative process yields the following joint log likelihood of the OIA etyma $\boldsymbol{x}$ and NIA reflexes $\boldsymbol{y}$ (with the discrete latent variables $\boldsymbol{z}$ marginalized out:

$$P(\boldsymbol{x}, \boldsymbol{y}|U, W) =$$

$$\prod_{w=1}^{W} \prod_{l=1}^{L} \sum_{k=1}^{K} \left[f(U_{l,k}) \prod_{t=1}^{T_w} f(W_{k,x_{w,l,t},y_{w,l,t}}) \right] \quad (1)$$

As readers will note, this model weights all sound changes equally, and makes no attempt to distinguish between dialectologically meaningful changes and noisy, idiosyncratic changes.

4.2 Deep model

The deep model, like the shallow model, is a mixture model, and as such retains the language-level weights over dialect component membership U. However, unlike the shallow model, in which the likelihood of an OIA etymon and NIA reflex under a component assignment $z = k$ is dependent on a flat representation of edit probabilities between OIA trigrams and NIA unigrams associated with dialect component k. Here, I attempt to add some depth to this representation of sound change by positing a hidden layer of dimension J between each $x_{w,t}$ and $y_{w,l,t}$. The goal here is to mimic a "noisy" reconstruction of an intermediate stage between OIA and NIA represented by dialect group k. This reconstruction is not an explicit, linguistically meaningful string (as in Bouchard-Côté et al. 2007, 2008, 2013); furthermore, it is re-generated for each individual reflex of each etymon, and not shared across data points (such a model would introduce deeply nested dependencies between variables, and enumerating all possible reconstructions would be computationally infeasible).

For parsimony's sake, I employ a simple Recurrent Neural Network (RNN) architecture to capture rightward dependencies (Elman, 1990). Figure 1 gives a visual representation of the network, unfolded in time. This model exchanges W, the dialect component-level weights over sound changes, for the following parameters:

- Dialect component-level weights governing hidden layer unit activations by OIA sounds:

$W_{k,i,j}^{x}; k \in \{1, ..., K\}, i \in \{1, ..., I\}, j \in \{1, ..., J\}$

- Dialect component-level weights governing hidden layer unit activations by previous hidden layers: $W_{k,i,j}^{h}; k \in \{1, ..., K\}, i \in \{1, ..., J\}, j \in \{1, ..., J\}$

- Language-level weights governing NIA output activations by hidden layer units: $W_{l,j,o}^{y}; l \in \{1, ..., L\}, j \in \{1, ..., J\}, o \in \{1, ..., O\}$

For a given mixture component $z = k$, the activation of the hidden layer at time t, h_t, depends on two sets of parameters, each associated with component k: the weights $W_{k,x_{x_t},\cdot}^{x}$, associated with the OIA input at time t; and W_k^h, the weights associated with the previous hidden layer h_{t-1}'s activations, for all $t > 1$. Given a hidden layer h_t, the weights W^l can be used to generate a probability distribution over possible outcomes in NIA language l. The forward pass of this network can be viewed as a generative process, denoted $\boldsymbol{y}_{w,t} \sim \mathsf{RNN}(\boldsymbol{x}_{w,l}, W_k^x, W_k^h, W^l)$ under the parameters for component k and language l; under such a process, the likelihood of $\boldsymbol{y}_{w,l}$ can be computed as follows:

$$P_{\mathsf{RNN}}(\boldsymbol{y}_{w,l}|\boldsymbol{x}_w, W_k^x, W_k^h, W^l) = \prod_{t=1}^{T_w} f(h_t^{\top} W^l)_{y_{w,l,t}} \quad (2)$$

where

$$h_t = \begin{cases} f(W_{k,x_{w,t},\cdot}^{x}), & \text{if } t = 1 \\ f(h_{t-1}^{\top} W^h \oplus W_{k,x_{w,t},\cdot}^{x}), & \text{if } t > 1 \end{cases} \quad (3)$$

The generative process for this model is nearly identical to the process described in the previous sections; however, after the dialect component assignment ($z_{w,l} \sim \mathrm{Categorical}(f(U_{l,\cdot}))$) is drawn, the NIA string $\boldsymbol{y}_{w,l}$ is sampled from $\mathsf{RNN}(\boldsymbol{x}_w, W_{z_{w,l}}^x, W_{z_{w,l}}^h, W^l)$. The joint log likelihood of the OIA etyma $\boldsymbol{x}$ and NIA reflexes $\boldsymbol{y}$ (with the discrete latent variables $\boldsymbol{z}$ marginalized out is the following:

$$P(\boldsymbol{x}, \boldsymbol{y}|U, W^x, W^h, W^y) = \prod_{w=1}^{W} \prod_{l=1}^{L}$$
$$\sum_{k=1}^{K} \left[f(U_{l,k}) P_{\mathsf{RNN}}(\boldsymbol{y}_{w,l}|\boldsymbol{x}_w, W_k^x, W_k^h, W^l) \right] \quad (4)$$

The same $\mathcal{N}(0, 10)$ prior as above is placed over U, W^x, W^h, W^y. J, the dimension of the hidden layer, is fixed at 100. This model bears some similarities to the mixture of RNNs described by Kim et al. (2018).

I have employed a simple RNN (rather than a more state-of-the art architecture) for several reasons. The first is that I am interested in the consequences of expanding a flat mixture model to contain a simple, slightly deeper architecture. Additionally, I believe that the fact that the hidden layer of an RNN can be activated by a softmax function is more desirable from the perspective of representing sound change as a categorical or multinomial distribution, as all layer unit activations sum to one, as opposed to the situation with Long Short-Term Memory (LSTM) and Gated Recurrent Units (GRU), which traditionally use sigmoid or hyperbolic tangent functions to activate the hidden layer. Furthermore, long-distance dependencies are not particularly widespread in Indo-Aryan sound change, lessening the need for more complex architectures. At the same time, the RNN is a crude approximation to the reality of language change. RNNs and related models draw a single arc between a hidden layer at time t and the corresponding output. It is perhaps not appropriate to envision this single dependency unless the dimensionality of the hidden layer is large enough to absorb potential contextual information that is crucial to sound change. To put it simply, emission probabilities in sound change are sharper than transitions common in most NLP applications (e.g., sentence prediction), and it may not be correct to envision y_t given $h_{t'<t}, h_t$ as a function of an additive combination of weights, though in practice, I find it too computationally costly to enumerate all possible value combinations the hidden layer at multiple consecutive time points. This issue requires further exploration, and I employ what seems to be the most computationally tractable approach for the moment.

5   Results

I learn each model's MAP configuration using the Adam optimizer (Kingma and Ba, 2015) with a learning rate of $.1$.[4] I run the optimizer for 10000 iterations over three random initializations, fitting the model on mini-batches of 100 data points, and

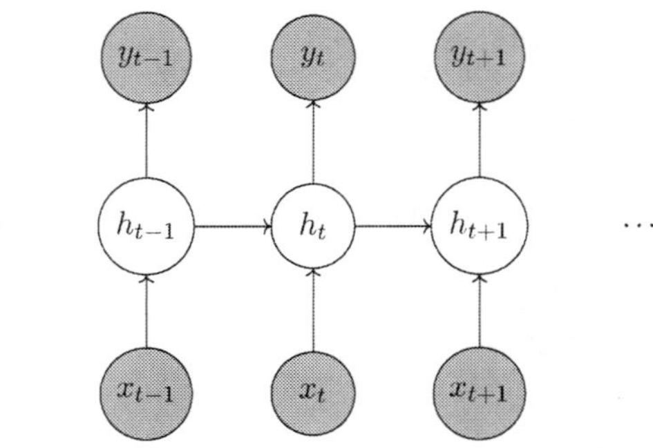

Figure 1: RNN representation, unfolded in time: hidden layers depend on OIA inputs $x_1, ..., x_{T_w}$ and previous hidden layers (for $t > 1$); NIA outputs $y_1, ..., y_{T_w}$ depend on hidden layers. Hidden layer activations are dependent on dialect component-specific parameters, while activations of the output layer are dependent on individual NIA language-specific parameters.

monitor convergence by observing the trace of the log posterior (Figure 2).

The flat model fails to pick up on any major differences between languages, finding virtually identical posterior values of $f(U_l)$, the language-level distribution over dialect component membership, for all $l \in \{1, ..., L\}$. According to the MAP configuration, each language draws forms from the same dialect group with $> .99$ probability, essentially undergoing a sort of "component collapse" that latent variable models sometimes encounter (Bowman et al., 2015; Dinh and Dumoulin, 2016). It is likely that bundling together sound change features leads to component-level distributions over sound changes with high entropy that are virtually indistinguishable from one another.[5] While this particular result is disappointing in the lack of information it provides, I observe some properties of our models' posterior values in order to diagnose problems that can be addressed in future work (discussed below).

The deep model, on the other hand, infers highly divergent language-level posterior distributions over cluster membership. Since these distributions are not identical across initializations due to the label-switching problem, I compute the Jensen-Shannon divergence between the language-level posterior distributions over cluster membership for each pair of languages in our sample for each initialization. I then average these divergences across initializations. These averaged

---

[4] Code for all experiments can be found at `https://github.com/chundrac/IA_dial/VarDial2019`.

[5] I made several attempts to run this model with different specifications, including different prior distributions, but achieved the same result.

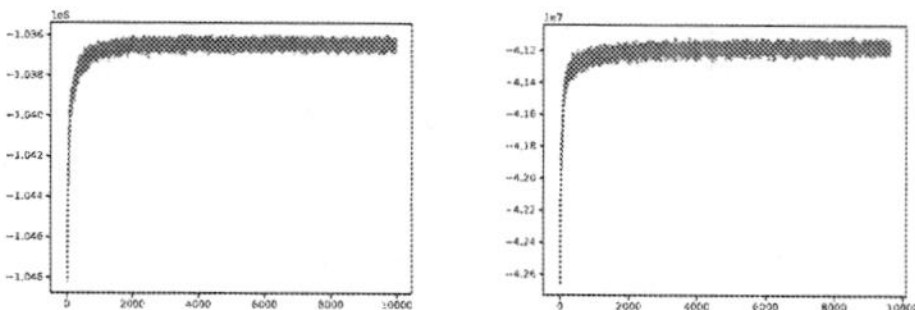

Figure 2: Log posteriors for shallow model (left) and deep model (right) for 10000 iterations over three random initializations.

divergences are then scaled to three dimensions using multidimensional scaling. Figure 3 gives a visualization of these transformed values via the red-green-blue color vector, plotted on a map; languages with similar component distributions display similar colors. With a few exceptions (that may be artifacts of the fact that certain languages have only a small number of data points associated with them), a noticieable divide can be seen between languages of the main Indo-Aryan speech region on one hand, and languages of northwestern South Asia (dark blue), the Dardic languages of Northern Pakistan, and the Pahari languages of the Indian Himalayas, though this division is not clear cut. Romani and other Indo-Aryan varieties spoken outside of South Asia show affiliation with multiple groups. While Romani dialects are thought to have a close genetic affinity with Hindi and other Central Indic languages, it was likely in contact with languages of northwest South Asian during the course of its speakers' journey out of South Asia (Hamp, 1987; Matras, 2002). However, this impressionistic evaluation is by no means a confirmation that the deep model has picked up on linguistically meaningful differences between speech varieties. In the following sections, some comparison and evaluation metrics and checks are deployed in order to assess the quality of these models' behavior.

5.1 Entropy of distributions

I measure the average entropy of the model's posterior distributions in order to gauge the extent to which the models are able to learn sparse, informative distributions over sound changes, hidden state activations, or other parameters concerning transitions through the model architecture. Normalized entropy is used in order to make entropies of distributions of different dimension comparable; a distribution's entropy can be normalized by dividing by its maximum possible entropy.

As mentioned above, our data set consists of OIA trigrams and the NIA segment corresponding to the second segment in the trigram, representing rewrite rules operating between OIA and the NIA languages in our sample. It is often the case that more than one NIA reflex is attested for a given OIA trigram. As such, the sound changes that have operated in an NIA language can be represented as a collection of categorical distributions, each summing to one. I calculate the average of the normalized entropies of these sound change distributions as a baseline against which to compare entropy values for the models' parameters. The pooled average of the normalized entropies across all languages is .11, while the average of averages for each language is .063.

For the shallow model, the parameter of interest is $f(V)$, the dialect component-level collection of distributions over sound changes, the mean normalized entropy of which, averaged across initializations but pooled across components within each initialization, is 0.91 (raw values range from 0.003 to 1). For the deep model, the average entropy of the dialect-level distributions over hidden-layer activations, $f(W^x)$, is only slightly lower, at 0.86 (raw values range from close to 0 to 1).

For each $k \in \{1, ..., K\}$, I compute the forward pass of $\mathrm{RNN}(x_{w,l}, W_k^x, W_k^h, W^l)$ for each etymon w and each language l in which the etymon survives using the inferred values for W_k^x, W_k^h, W^l and compute the entropy of each $f(h_t^\top W^l)$, yielding an average of .74 (raw values range from close to 0 to 1). While these values are still very high, it is clear that the inclusion of a hidden layer has learned sparser, potentially more meaningful distributions than the flat approach, and that increasing the dimensionality of the hidden layer will likely bring about even sparser, more meaningful distributions. The entropies cited here are considerably higher than the average entropy of languages' sound change distributions, but the latter distributions do little to tell us about the internal clustering of the languages.

5.2 Comparison with other linguistic distance metrics

Here, I compare the cluster membership inferred by this paper's models against other measures of linguistic distance. Each method yields a pairwise inter-language distance metric, which can be compared against a non-linguistic measure. I measure

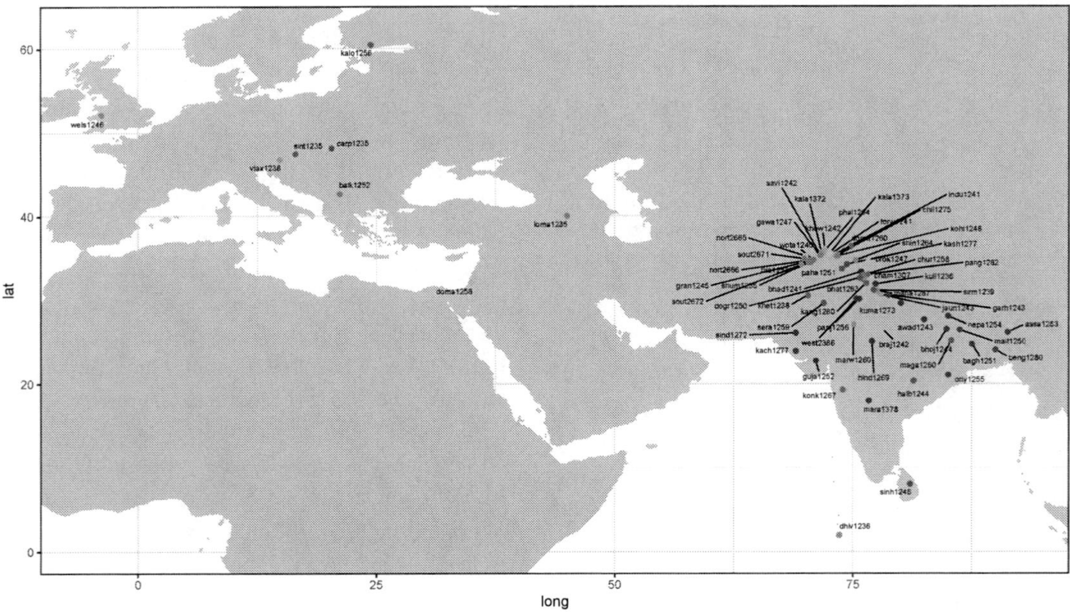

Figure 3: Dialect group makeup of languages in sample under deep model

the correlation between each linguistic distance measure as well as great circle geographic distance and patristic distance according to the Glottolog phylogeny using Spearman's ρ.

5.2.1 Levenshtein distance

Borin et al. (2014) measure the normalized Levenshtein distances (i.e., the edit distance between two strings divided by the length of the longer string) between words for the same concept in pairs of Indo-Aryan languages, and find that average normalized Levenshtein distance correlates significantly with patristic distances in the Ethnologue tree. This paper's dataset is not organized by semantic meaning, so for comparability, I measure the average normalized Levenshtein distance between cognates in pairs of Indo-Aryan languages, which picks up on phonological divergence between dialects, as opposed to both phonological and lexical divergence.

5.2.2 Jensen-Shannon divergence

Each language in our dataset attests one or more (due to language contact, analogy, etc.) outcomes for a given OIA trigram, yielding a collection of sound change distributions, as described above. For each pair of languages, I compute the Jensen-Shannon divergence between sound change distributions for all OIA trigrams that are continued in both languages, and average these values. This

gives a measure of pairwise average diachronic phonological divergence between languages.

5.2.3 LSTM Autoencoder

Rama and Çöltekin (2016) and Rama et al. (2017) develop an LSTM-based method for representing the phonological structure of individual word forms across closely related speech varieties. Each string is fed to a unidirectional or bidirectional LSTM autoencoder, which learns a continuous latent multidimensional representation of the sequence. This embedding is then used to reconstruct the input sequence. The latent values in the embedding provide information that can be used to compute dissimilarity (in the form of cosine or Euclidean distance) between strings or across speech varieties (by averaging the latent values for all strings in each dialect or language). I use the bidirectional LSTM Autoencoder described in the work cited in order to learn an 8-dimensional latent representation for all NIA forms in the dataset, training the model over 20 epochs on batches of 32 data points using the Adam optimizer to minimize the categorical cross-entropy between the input sequence and the NIA reconstruction predicted by the model. I use the learned model parameters to generate a latent representation for each form. The latent representations are averaged across forms within each language, and pairwise linguistic Euclidean distances are computed between each av-

	Geographic	Genetic
Shallow JSD	−0.01	−0.03
Deep JSD	0.147*	0.008
LDN	0.346*	0.013
Raw JSD	0.302*	−0.051*
LSTM AE	0.158*	−0.068*
LSTM ED	0.084*	0.0001

Table 1: Spearman's ρ values for correlations between each linguistic distance metric (JSD = Jensen-Shannon Divergence, LDN = Levenshtein Distance Normalized, AE = Autoencoder, ED = Encoder-Decoder) and geographic and genetic distance. Asterisks represent significant correlations.

eraged representation.

5.2.4 LSTM Encoder-Decoder

For the sake of completeness, I use an LSTM encoder-decoder to learn a continuous representation for every OIA-NIA string pair. This model is very similar to the LSTM autoencoder, except that it takes an OIA input and reconstructs an NIA output, instead of taking an NIA form as input and reconstructing the same string. I train the model as described above.

5.3 Correlations

Table 1 gives correlation coefficients (Spearman's ρ) between linguistic distance metrics and non-linguistic distance metrics. In general, correlations with Glottolog patristic distance are quite poor. This is surprising for Levenshtein Distance Normalized, given the high correlation with patristic distance reported by Borin et al. (2014). Given that the authors measured Levenshtein distance between identical concepts in pairs of languages, and not cognates, as I do here, it is possible that lexical divergence carries a stronger genetic signal than phonological divergence, at least in the context of Indo-Aryan (it is worth noting that I did not balance the tree, as described by the authors; it is not clear that this would have yielded any improvement). On the other hand, the Levenshtein distance measured in this paper correlates significantly with great circle distance, indicating a strong geographic signal. Average Jensen-Shannon divergence between pairs of languages' sound change distributions shows a strong association with geographic distance as well.

Divergence/distances based on the deep model, the LSTM Autoencoder, and the LSTM Encoder-Decoder show significant correlations with geospatial distance, albeit lower ones. It is not entirely clear what accounts for this disparity. Intuitively, we expect more shallow chronological features to correlate with geographic distance. It is possible that the LSTM and RNN architectures are picking up on chronologically deeper information, and show a low geographic signal for this reason, though this highly provisional idea is not borne out by any genetic signal.

It is not clear how to assess the meaning of these correlations at this stage. Nevertheless, deep architectures provide an interesting direction for future research into sound change and language contact, as they have the potential to disaggregate a great deal of information regarding interacting forces in language change that is censored when raw distance measures are computed directly from the data.

6 Outlook

This paper explored the consequences of adding hidden layers to models of dialectology where the languages have experienced too much contact for phylogenetic models to be appropriate, but have diversified to the extent that traditional dialectometric approaches are not applicable. While the model requires some refinement, its results point in a promising direction. Modifying prior distributions could potentially produce more informative results, as could tweaking hyperparameters of the learning algorithms employed. Additionally, it is likely that the model will benefit from hidden layers of higher dimension J, as well as bidirectional approaches, and despite the misgivings regarding LSTM and GRUs stated above, future work will probably benefit from incorporating these and related architectures (e.g., attention). Additionally, the models used in this paper assumed discrete latent variables, attempting to be faithful to the traditional historical linguistic notion of intimate borrowing between discrete dialect groups. However, continuous-space models may provide a more flexible framework for addressing the questions asked in this paper (cf. Murawaki, 2015).

This paper provides a new way of looking at dialectology and linguistic affiliation; with refinement and expansion, it is hoped that this and related models can further our understanding of the history of the Indo-Aryan speech community and can generalize to new linguistic scenarios. It is hoped that methodologies of this sort can join forces with similar tools designed to investigate interaction of regularly conditioned sound change and chronologically deep language contact in individual languages' histories.

References

George Baumann. 1975. *Drei Jaina-Gedichte in Alt-Gujarātī: Edition, Übersetzung, Grammatik, und Glossar*. Franz Steiner, Wiesbaden.

Leonard Bloomfield. 1933. *Language*. Holt, Rinehart and Winston, New York.

Lars Borin, Anju Saxena, Taraka Rama, and Bernard Comrie. 2014. Linguistic landscaping of south asia using digital language resources: Genetic vs. areal linguistics. In *Ninth International Conference on Language Resources and Evaluation (LREC'14)*, pages 3137–3144.

Alexandre Bouchard-Côté, David Hall, Thomas L. Griffiths, and Dan Klein. 2013. Automated reconstruction of ancient languages using probabilistic models of sound change. *Proceedings of the National Academy of Sciences*, 110:4224–4229.

Alexandre Bouchard-Côté, Percy Liang, Thomas Griffiths, and Dan Klein. 2007. A probabilistic approach to diachronic phonology. In *Proceedings of the 2007 Joint Conference on Empirical Methods in Natural Language Processing and Computational Natural Language Learning (EMNLP-CoNLL)*, pages 887–896, Prague. Association for Computational Linguistics.

Alexandre Bouchard-Côté, Percy S Liang, Dan Klein, and Thomas L Griffiths. 2008. A probabilistic approach to language change. In *Advances in Neural Information Processing Systems*, pages 169–176.

R. Bouckaert, P. Lemey, M. Dunn, S. J. Greenhill, A. V. Alekseyenko, A. J. Drummond, R. D. Gray, M. A. Suchard, and Q. D. Atkinson. 2012. Mapping the origins and expansion of the Indo-European language family. *Science*, 337(6097):957–960.

Samuel R Bowman, Luke Vilnis, Oriol Vinyals, Andrew M Dai, Rafal Jozefowicz, and Samy Bengio. 2015. Generating sentences from a continuous space. *Proceedings of the Twentieth Conference on Computational Natural Language Learning (CoNLL)*.

Chundra Cathcart. to appear. A probabilistic assessment of the Indo-Aryan Inner-Outer Hypothesis. *Journal of Historical Linguistics*.

Ashwini Deo. 2018. Dialects in the Indo-Aryan landscape. In Charles Boberg, John Nerbonne, and Dominic Watt, editors, *The Handbook of Dialectology*, pages 535–546. John Wiley & Sons, Oxford.

Laurent Dinh and Vincent Dumoulin. 2016. Training neural Bayesian nets. `http://www.iro.umontreal.ca/bengioy/cifar/NCAP2014-summerschool/slides/Laurent_dinh_cifar_presentation.pdf`.

Jeffrey Elman. 1990. Finding structure in time. *Cognitive Science*, 14(2):179–211.

Murray B. Emeneau. 1966. The dialects of Old-Indo-Aryan. In Jaan Puhvel, editor, *Ancient Indo-European dialects*, pages 123–138. University of California Press, Berkeley.

Harald Hammarström, Robert Forkel, and Martin Haspelmath. 2017. Glottolog 3.3. Max Planck Institute for the Science of Human History.

Eric P Hamp. 1987. On the sibilants of romani. *Indo-Iranian Journal*, 30(2):103–106.

Gerhard Jäger. 2014. Phylogenetic inference from word lists using weighted alignment with empirically determined weights. In *Quantifying Language Dynamics*, pages 155–204. Brill.

Banikanta Kakati. 1941. *Assamese, its formation and development*. Government of Assam, Gauhati.

Yoon Kim, Sam Wiseman, and Alexander M Rush. 2018. A tutorial on deep latent variable models of natural language. *arXiv preprint arXiv:1812.06834*.

Diederik P. Kingma and Jimmy Ba. 2015. Adam: A method for stochastic optimization. In *International Conference on Learning Representations (ICLR)*.

Johann-Mattis List. 2012. SCA. Phonetic alignment based on sound classes. In M. Slavkovik and D. Lassiter, editors, *New directions in logic, language, and computation*, pages 32–51. Springer, Berlin, Heidelberg.

Colin P. Masica. 1991. *The Indo-Aryan languages*. Cambridge University Press, Cambridge.

Yaron Matras. 2002. *Romani – A Linguistic Introduction*. Cambridge University Press, Cambridge.

R. S. McGregor. 1968. *The language of Indrajit of Orcha*. Cambridge University Press, Cambridge.

Yugo Murawaki. 2015. Continuous space representations of linguistic typology and their application to phylogenetic inference. In *Proceedings of the 2015 Conference of the North American Chapter of the Association for Computational Linguistics: Human Language Technologies*, pages 324–334.

John Nerbonne. 2009. Data-driven dialectology. *Language and Linguistics Compass*, 3(1):175–198.

John Nerbonne and Wilbert Heeringa. 2001. Computational comparison and classification of dialects. *Dialectologia et Geolinguistica*, 9:69–83.

Thomas Oberlies. 2005. *A historical grammar of Hindi*. Leykam, Graz.

Jonathan K. Pritchard, Matthew Stephens, and Peter Donnelly. 2000. Inference of population structure using multilocus genotype data. *Genetics*, 155(2):945–959.

Jelena Prokić and John Nerbonne. 2008. Recognising groups among dialects. *International journal of humanities and arts computing*, 2(1-2):153–172.

Taraka Rama and Çağrı Çöltekin. 2016. Lstm autoencoders for dialect analysis. In *Proceedings of the Third Workshop on NLP for Similar Languages, Varieties and Dialects (VarDial3)*, pages 25–32.

Taraka Rama, Çağrı Çöltekin, and Pavel Sofroniev. 2017. Computational analysis of gondi dialects. In *Proceedings of the Fourth Workshop on NLP for Similar Languages, Varieties and Dialects (VarDial)*, pages 26–35.

Rajesh Ranganath, Linpeng Tang, Laurent Charlin, and David Blei. 2015. Deep exponential families. In *Artificial Intelligence and Statistics*, pages 762–771.

Ger Reesink, Ruth Singer, and Michael Dunn. 2009. Explaining the linguistic diversity of Sahul using population models. *PLoS Biology*, 7:e1000241.

Caley Smith. 2017. The dialectology of Indic. In Jared Klein, Brian Joseph, and Matthias Fritz, editors, *Handbook of Comparative and Historical Indo-European Linguistics*, pages 417–447. De Gruyter, Berlin, Boston.

Jaroslav Strnad. 2013. *Morphology and Syntax of Old Hindi*. Brill, Leiden.

Kaj Syrjänen, Terhi Honkola, Jyri Lehtinen, Antti Leino, and Outi Vesakoski. 2016. Applying population genetic approaches within languages: Finnish dialects as linguistic populations. *Language Dynamics and Change*, 6:235–283.

Paul Tedesco. 1965. Turner's Comparative Dictionary of the Indo-Aryan Languages. *Journal of the American Oriental Society*, 85:368–383.

Matthew Toulmin. 2009. *From linguistic to sociolinguistic reconstruction: the Kamta historical subgroup of Indo-Aryan*. Pacific Linguistics, Research School of Pacific and Asian Studies, The Australian National University, Canberra.

Ralph L. Turner. 1962–1966. *A comparative dictionary of Indo-Aryan languages*. Oxford University Press, London.

Ralph L. Turner. 1975 [1967]. Geminates after long vowel in Indo-aryan. In *R.L. Turner: Collected Papers 1912–1973*, pages 405–415. Oxford University Press, London.

Martijn Wieling, Eliza Margaretha, and John Nerbonne. 2012. Inducing a measure of phonetic similarity from pronunciation variation. *Journal of Phonetics*, 40(2):307–314.

Naive Bayes and BiLSTM Ensemble for Discriminating between Mainland and Taiwan Variation of Mandarin Chinese

Li Yang
Tongji University
Shanghai
China
li.yang@tongji.edu.cn

Yang Xiang
Tongji University
Shanghai
China
shxiangyang@tongji.edu.cn

Abstract

Automatic dialect identification is a more challenging task than language identification, as it requires the ability to discriminate between varieties of one language. In this paper, we propose an ensemble based system, which combines traditional machine learning models trained on bag of n-gram fetures, with deep learning models trained on word embeddings, to solve the Discriminating between Mainland and Taiwan Variation of Mandarin Chinese (DMT) shared task at VarDial 2019. Our experiments show that a character bigram-trigram combination based Naive Bayes is a very strong model for identifying varieties of Mandarin Chinense. Through further ensemble of Navie Bayes and BiLSTM, our system (team: *itsalexyang*) achived an macro-averaged F1 score of 0.8530 and 0.8687 in two tracks.

1 Introduction

Dialect identification, which aims at distinguishing related languages or varieties of a specific language, is a special case of language identification. Accurate detection of dialects is an important step for many NLP piplines and applications, such as automatic speech recognition, machine translation and multilingual data acquisition. While there are effective solutions to language identification, dialect identification remains a tough problem to be tackled. As linguistic differences among related languages are less obvious than those among different languages, dialect identification is more subtle and complex, and therefore has become an attractive topic for many researchers in recent years.

Mandarin Chinese is a group of related varieties of Chinese spoken across many different regions. The group includes *Putonghua*, the offical language of Mainland China, and *Guoyu*, another

Term	Mainland China	Taiwan
taxi	出租车	計程車
bicycle	自行车	腳踏車
software	软件	軟體
program	程序	程式
kindergarten	幼儿园	幼稚園

Table 1: Different expressions with the same meaning used in Mainland China and Taiwan.

Mandarin variant widely spoken in Taiwan. However related they are, there are still some difference between these two varieties. First, the most notable one is the character set they use. Mainland Chinese uses simplified Chinese characters, as opposed to the traditional Chinense characters used by Taiwanese. Take *"natural language processsing"* for example - its simplified character form adopted in Mainland China is "自然语言处理", while the traditional character form in Taiwan is "自然語言處理". Second, some vocabularies differ. Although some terms are mutually intelligible, they are preferred in one region. Table 1 lists some examples. Apart from character form and vocabularies, pronunciations, especially intonations, are also different. But we don't discuss this aspect, as it is irrelevant to the task.

The DMT task, first introduced by VarDial evaluation campagin (Zampieri et al., 2019) this year, aims at determining whether a sentence belongs to news articles from Mainland China or from Taiwan. The organizers prepare two versions of the same corpus, traditional and simplified, and ask participants to predict the labels for text instances in both tracks. For that reason, character form can not be used to discriminate between these two language varieties. Mainstream approach to dialect identification is to regard it as a text classification task and use a linear support vector ma-

Proceedings of VarDial, pages 120–127
Minneapolis, MN, June 7, 2019 ©2019 Association for Computational Linguistics

chine (SVM) with bag of n-gram features as input to slove it. However, we seek to find out what's the best classification algorithm for DMT task. Therefore, we experiment with serveral classical machine learning models trained on different word or character level n-gram features and feature combinatons. Besides, deep learning methods have currently achieve remakable sucess in many NLP tasks, including question answering, sentiment analysis, machine translation and natural language inference. To inverstigate how much deep neural neworks can help identify language varieties, we test 7 different deep learning models, including CNN based, RNN based and CNN-RNN hybrid models. Thorough performance comparison to machine learning models is also conducted. Finally, we explore different ways to ensemble the classifiers we discuss before.

2   Related Work

A number of works have devoted to differentiate between language varieties or related languages, especially since the series of VarDial evaluation campaigns (Zampieri et al., 2017, 2018, 2019). (Lui and Cook, 2013) studies on English dialect identification and presents serveral classification approaches to classify Australia, British and Caniadian English. (Zampieri and Gebre, 2012) utilizes a character n-gram and a word n-gram language model for automatic classificaton of two written varieties of Portuguese: European and Brazilian. (Ciobanu and Dinu, 2016) conducts an intial study on the dialects of Romanian and proposes using the orthographic and phonetic features of the words to build a dialect classifier. (Clematide and Makarov, 2017) uses a majority-vote ensemble of the Navie Bayes, CRF and SVM systems for Swiss German dialects identification. (Kreutz and Daelemans, 2018) uses two SVM classifiers: one trained on word n-grams fewtures and one trained on Pos n-grams to determine whether a document is in Flemish Dutch or Netherlandic Dutch. (Çöltekin et al., 2018) uses a unified SVM model based on character and word n-grams features with careful hyperparameter tuning for 4 language/dialect identification tasks.

Methods to discriminate between varieties of Mandarin Chinese haven't been well studied. (Huang and Lee, 2008) uses a top-bag-of-word similarity based contrastive approach to reflect distance among three varieties of Mandarin: Mainland China, Singapore and Taiwan. (Xu et al., 2016) deals with 6 varieties of Mandarin: Maninland, Hong Kong, Taiwan, Macao, Malaysia and Singapore. They discover that character bigram and word segmentation based feature work better than traditional character unigram, and some features such as character form, PMI-based and word alignment-based features can help improve performance. However, a thorough comparison of different algorithms and architectures has yet to be conducted.

3   Data and Methodology

3.1   Data

The DMT task is provided with labeled sentences from news published in Mainland China or in Taiwan (Chen et al., 1996; McEnery and Xiao, 2003). They are composed of 18770 instances for training set, 2000 for validation set and 2000 for test set. As shown in Table 2, the DMT dataset has a perfectly balanced class distribution. The avergae sentence lengths (in word level) of two varieties are almost the same. It's worth mentioning that the organizers have prepared two version of the same dataset: traditional and simplified version, which means we can't utilize character form feature to discriminate between these two language varieties. Since the sentences have been tokenized and punctuation has been removed from the texts, we don't apply any preprocessing on the dataset.

3.2   Traditional Machine Learning Models

Traditional machine learning models based on feature engineering are the most common methods for dialect identification. In this paper, we experiment with 3 different classifiers: (1) logistic regression (**LR**), (2) linear support vector machine (**SVM**), and (3) multinomial Naive Bayes (**MNB**) based on bag of n-gram features. We also examine other Navie Bayes models such as Gaussian Navie Bayes and Bernoulli Naive Bayes, but they are inferior to multinomial Naive Bayes on the validation set. The bag of n-gram features include word and character level n-grams with sizes ranging from 1 to a specific number. We conduct a set of experiments to fully explore the most contributing feature and feature combination for the DMT task, and the results are shown in next Section.

Variety	Number of instances			Sentence length			
	train	valid	test	min	max	avg	st.dev.
Mainland China	9385	1000	1000	5	66	9.63	3.73
Taiwan	9385	1000	1000	6	48	9.24	3.30

Table 2: Statistics of dataset for each variety. Sentence lengths are calculated based on word-level tokens from training and validation set.

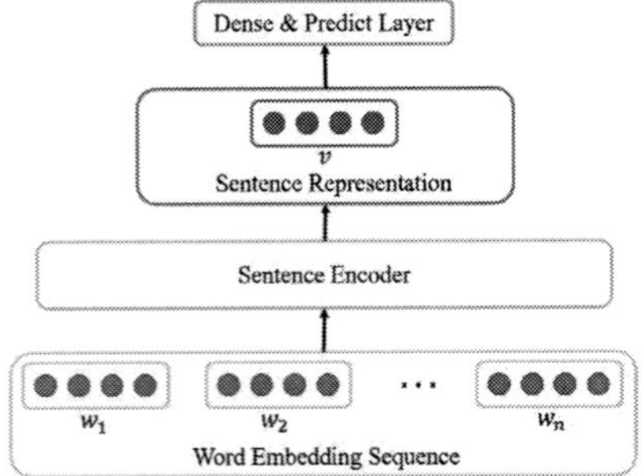

Figure 1: The overall framework of deep models.

3.3 Deep Learning Models

Deep neural networks (DNNs) are of growing interest for their capacity to learn text representation from data without careful engineering of features. For short-text classification task, Convolution neural network (CNN) and recurrent neural network (RNN) are two mainstream DNN architectures. In this paper, we examine a number of deep learning models based on a common framework to solve the DMT task. Figure 1 shows a high-level view of the framework. Vertically, the figure depicts 3 major components: (1) **Input Embedding Layer**. Suppose a sentence has n tokens, we use a pre-trained embedding method Word2vec (Mikolov et al., 2013) trained on training data to represent it in a sequence of word embeddings:

$$S = (\mathbf{w_1}, \mathbf{w_2}, \cdots \mathbf{w_n}) \tag{1}$$

where w_i is a vector representing a d dimentional word embedding for the i-th word in the sentence. S is thus a concatenation of all word embeddings. We do try using character embeddings and other pre-trained embedding methods such as Glove (Pennington et al., 2014) and Fasttext (Bojanowski et al., 2017) but observed no further improvement on validation set. (2) **Sentence Encoder Layer**. The sentence encoder, specified by different deep learning models, processes the input word embedding sequence and outputs a high level sentence representation:

$$v = encode\,(S) \tag{2}$$

(3) **Output Layer**. After obtaining sentence vector, we feed it through one hidden dense layer with 256 units and a final predict dense layer:

$$\hat{y} = \sigma\left(\mathbf{W_p}\gamma\left(\mathbf{W_h}v + \mathbf{b_h}\right) + \mathbf{b_p}\right) \tag{3}$$

where $\mathbf{W_h}$ and $\mathbf{b_h}$ are the parameters for hidden layer, $\mathbf{W_p}$ and $\mathbf{b_p}$ are the parameters for predict layer, γ and σ are relu and sigmoid activation function respectively, $\hat{\mathbf{y}} \in \mathbb{R}$ represents the predicted score for postive class. During training process, we minimize the binary cross-entropy loss defined as follow:

$$L = -\frac{1}{N}\sum_{i=1}^{N}\left(y_i \log \hat{y}_i + (1 - y_i)\log\left(1 - \hat{y}_i\right)\right) \tag{4}$$

where y_i is the ground-truth.

We examine 7 different deep learning models to encode sentences into fixed-size vectors, including CNN-based, RNN-based and CNN-RNN hybrid neural networks.

- **CNN:** First introduced by (Kim, 2014), the convolution network applies a concolution operation with a filter $\mathbf{W_c} \in \mathbb{R}^{hd}$ to a window of h words to produce a new feature:

$$c_i = f\left(\mathbf{W_c} \cdot \mathbf{w}_{i:i+h-1} + b\right) \tag{5}$$

  After applying this filter to each possible window of words in a sentence, a feature map can be produced. In this paper, we use 300 filters with window sizes ranging from 2 to 5 to extract four 300 dimensional feature maps. After that, we apply max-over-time pooling operation by taking the highest value for each feature map to capture the most important feature, then concatanate all the features to represent the input sentence.

- **DCNN:** (Kalchbrenner et al., 2014) use a dynamic convolution neural network (DCNN) that alternates wide concolution layers and dynamic k-Max pooling layers for sentence modeling. Through a k-Max pooling operation, a feature graph over the sentence can be induced, which explicitly captures both short and long-range relations.

- **DPCNN:** (Johnson and Zhang, 2017) propose a deep concolutional neural network by stacking concolution blocks (two concolution layers and a shortcut connection) interleaved with pooling layers with stride 2 for downsampling. The 2-stride downsampling reduces the size of the internal represenation of each text by half, enabling efficient representation of long-range association in the text. The shortcut connection ensures training of deep networks. DPCNN has been shown powerful in many text classification task.

- **BiLSTM:** LSTM is an effective neural network for sentence modeling for its ability to capture long-term dependencies. BiLSTM use a forward and a backward LSTM to process sequence, so that each produced hidden state can contain information from context in two opposite direction. Specifically, at each time step t, hidden state h_t is the concatenation of results from forward and backward LSTM:

$$
\begin{aligned}
\overrightarrow{h_t} &= \overrightarrow{\mathrm{LSTM}}\left(\mathbf{w_1}, \mathbf{w_2}, \ldots, \mathbf{w_t}\right) \\
\overleftarrow{h_t} &= \overleftarrow{\mathrm{LSTM}}\left(\mathbf{w_n}, \mathbf{w_{n-1}}, \ldots, \mathbf{w_t}\right) \\
h_t &= \left[\overrightarrow{h_t}, \overleftarrow{h_t}\right]
\end{aligned}
\tag{6}
$$

  After obtaining hidden state squence, we apply max-over-time pooling operation to form a fixed-size vector as sentence representation.

- **Self-attentive BiLSTM:** Attention mechanism is most comonly used in sequence-to-sequence models to attend to encoder states (Bahdanau et al., 2014; Vaswani et al., 2017). In this paper, we make use of attention, more specifically, self-attention (Lin et al., 2017) to obtain a distribution over features learned from BiLSTM (a.k.a hidden states). Suppose H is the output hidden states of BiLSTM: $H = (\mathbf{h_1}, \mathbf{h_2}, \cdots \mathbf{h_n})$, we can calculate the attention vector α and the final sentence representation v as follows:

$$
\begin{aligned}
e_t &= \mathbf{U}_a^\top \tanh\left(\mathbf{W}_a \mathbf{h}_t\right) \\
\alpha_t &= \frac{\exp\left(e_t\right)}{\sum_{i=1}^{T} \exp\left(e_i\right)} \\
v &= \Sigma_{i=1}^{T} \alpha_i h_i
\end{aligned}
\tag{7}
$$

where $\mathbf{W}_a \in \mathbb{R}^{2d \times 2d}$ and $\mathbf{U}_a \in \mathbb{R}^{2d \times 1}$ are parameters of the attention layer (we use d units for LSTM, thus h_t being a $2d$ dimensional vector). Using self-attention allows a sentence to attend to itself, therefore we can extract the most relevant information.

- **CNN-BiLSTM:** Similar as (Zhou et al., 2015), we first use CNN to extract a higher-level sequence representations from word embedding sequences, and then feed them into BiLSTM to obtain final sentence representation. By combing CNN and BiLSTM, we are able to capture both local features of phrases and global informantion of sentences.

- **BiLSTM-CNN:** We also use BiLSTM layer as feature extrator first and then feed the hidden states to the CNN layer, which we call BiLSTM-CNN.

3.4 Ensemble Models

Classifier ensemble is a way of combining different models with the goal of improving overall peformance through enhanced decision making, which has been shown to achieve better results than a single classifier. In this paper, we explore 4 ensemble strategies to intergrate outputs (predicted labels or probabilities) from models introduced above and reach a final decision.

- **Mean Probability:** Simply take an average of predictions from all the models and use it to make the final prediction.

- **Highest Confidence:** The class label that recieves vote with the highest probability is selected as the final prediction.

- **Majority Voting:** Each classifier votes for a single class label. The votes are summed and the label with majority votes (over 50%) wins. In case of a tie, the ensemble result falls back to the prediction by the model with highest peformance on validation set.

- **Meta-Classifier:** Use the individual classifier outputs along with training labels to train a second-level meta-classifier. The second meta-classifier then predicts the final prediction. Meta-Classifier is also refered to as Classifier Stacking.

While the first three strategies use a simple fusion method to combine models, Meta-Classifier has parameters to train, which attempts to learn the collective knowledge represented by base classifiers. As for choosing estimators for meta-classfier, we test with a wide range of learning algorithms including not only the ones mentioned in Section 3.2, but also random forest, GBDT, XG-Boost and so on. It turns out Gaussian Navie Bayes is the most competitive model, which will be the only meta classifer discusssed in next Section.

4 Experiments

4.1 Experimental Setup

We use scikit-learn library[1] for the implementation of the n-gram features based models and the ensemble meta-classifier. As for deep learning models, we implement them using Keras[2] library with Tensorflow backend. We used Adam (Kingma and Ba, 2014) method as the optimizer, setting the first momentum to be 0.9 , the second momentum 0.999 and the initial learning 0.001. The bacth size is 32. All hidden states of LSTMs, feature maps of CNNs and word embeddings have 300 dimensions. Word embeddings are fine tuned during training process. All models are trained separately on dataset of traditional and simplified version, and evaluated using macro-weighted f1 score. Our code for all experiments is publicly available[3].

4.2 Contribution of Single N-gram Feature

To find the most contributing individual n-gram feature for discriminating between Mandarin Chinese varieties. We run a number of experiments with the three classifiers using one single n-gram at a time, and the results are shown in Figure 2. In terms of n-gram features, for dataset of both simplified and traditional version, performances of 3 models all drop sharply as n-gram size increases, especially for word level n-grams. The

most contributing character level ngram is character trigram, which is slightly better than character bigram. Word unigram is the best among word level n-grams, but no better than character bigram or trigram. As for the 3 models, although SVM has been the most preferred method for dialect identification, in our experiment, MNB outperforms LR and SVM. Lastly, for all models, performance on the traditional version dataset is slightly better than that on the simplified version dataset.

4.3 Combination of N-gram Features

Table 3 shows the results of combining individual feature on each dataset. The performances of individual feature are also listed for direct comparison. As indicated from the table, feature combination does bring a performance gain. MNB with character bigram and trigram combination achieves the highest macro-weighted f1 scores, 0.9080 for the simplified version and 0.9225 for the traditional version.

4.4 Performance of Deep Learning Models

To fully compare deep learning methods with machine learning methods for the DMT task, we evaluate 7 deep learning models. Results are listed in Table 4. Among these models, BiLSTM stands out from the others with macro-weighted f1 scores of 0.9000 and 0.9115. All deep learning models outperform LR and SVM, but are inferior to MNB, which shows again MNB is a very strong classifier for discriminating between varieties of Mandarin Chinese.

4.5 Performance of Ensemble Models

We also try to achieve a better result by aggregating outputs of the models we have implemented. As presented in Table 5, no single ensemble strategy performs consistently better than the others. The best choice for ensemble model is using MNB and BiLSTM as base classifier, and Mean Probability or Highest Confidence as fusion method. (When there are only 2 base classifiers, results of Mean Probability and Highest Confidence are always the same.)

4.6 Results of Shared Task

We submit 3 systems for the evalution of test set: MNB, BiLSTM and their ensemble. The official results of our submissons show the same pattern observed on the validation set (see Table 6). MNB performs better than BiLSTM, especially for the

---

[1] https://scikit-learn.org/stable/
[2] https://github.com/keras-team/keras
[3] https://github.com/AlexYangLi/DMT

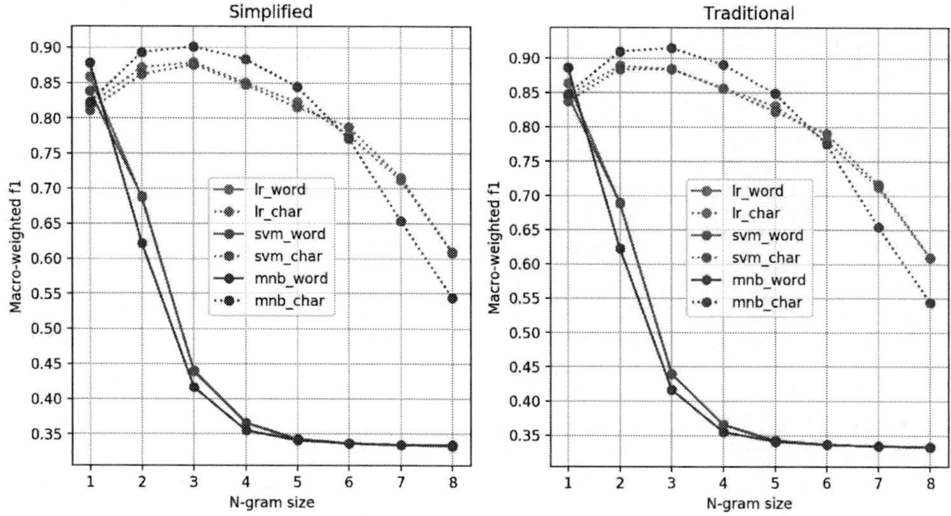

Figure 2: Macro-weighted f1 scores of LR (red lines), SVM (green lines), MNB (blue lines) using character (dotted lines) or word level (solid lines) n-gram of different sizes as input, both on dataset of simplified (left) and traditional (right) version.

Feature	Simplified			Traditional		
	LR	SVM	MNB	LR	SVM	MNB
Individual feature						
word uigram	0.8590	0.8384	0.8784	0.8634	0.8460	0.8860
char bigram	0.8720	0.8620	0.8935	0.8890	0.8840	0.9100
char trigram	0.8790	0.8760	0.9015	0.8840	0.8845	0.9150
char 4gram	0.8504	0.8474	0.8835	0.8570	0.8559	0.8910
Combined feature						
char bigram+trigram	0.8865	0.8830	**0.9080**	0.8960	0.8925	**0.9225**
char bigram+trigram+4gram	0.8880	0.8835	0.9030	0.8945	0.8920	0.9170
char bigram+char trigram+word unigram	0.8875	0.8835	0.9055	0.8990	0.8940	0.9200

Table 3: Macro-weighted f1 scores of LR, SVM, MNB using individual or combined features as input, both on dataset of simplified and traditional version.

Model	Simplfied	Traditional
CNN-based		
CNN	0.8964	0.9090
DCNN	0.8970	0.9080
DPCNN	0.8925	0.9070
RNN-based		
BiLSTM	**0.9000**	**0.9115**
Self-attentive BiLSTM	0.8915	0.9020
CNN-RNN hybrid		
CNN-BiLSTM	0.8935	0.9080
BiLSTM-CNN	0.8950	0.9095

Table 4: Macro-weighted f1 scores of deep learning models using word embeddings as input, both on dataset of simplified and traditional version.

Ensemble Strategy	Simplfied			Traditional		
	all ML*	all DL*	MNB + BiLSTM	all ML*	all DL*	MNB + BiLSTM
Mean Probability	0.9025	0.9050	**0.9130**	0.9170	0.9215	**0.9240**
Highest Confidence	0.9080	0.9015	**0.9130**	0.9225	0.9100	**0.9240**
Majority Voting	0.8880	0.9060	-	0.8985	0.9195	-
Meta-Classifier	0.8915	0.9025	0.9050	0.906	0.9130	0.9215

Table 5: Macro-weighted f1 scores of 4 ensemble strategies combining different base classifiers, both on dataset of simplified and traditional version. "all ML" and "all DL" refer to combine all machine learning models and deep learning models respectively. All machine learning models use character bigram-trigram combination as input.

Submission	Simplified	Traditional
BiLSTM	0.8118	0.8450
MNB	0.8499	0.8650
MNB + BiLSTM	**0.8530**	**0.8687**

Table 6: Macro-weighted f1 scores of 3 submissions on test sets (team: *itsalexyang*).

simplified version of test data. In addition, the MNB-BiLSTM ensemble achieves a higher score than a single model for both versions of test data. Overall, our models' performance is consistently lower on the test set than on the validation set. We believe tuning parameters with k-fold cross validation or applying other overfitting prevention strategies may help yield better results on unseen data.

5 Conclusion

In this paper, we describes our submission for the DMT task. Our experiments show that multinomial Naive Bayes is a very strong model for discrinating between Mandarin varieties, which works better than the most commonly used SVM and popular deep learning models. For MNB, character trigram is the most contributing feature. Further performance gain can be achieved by combining character trigram and bigram feature. We also explore different ways to ensemble models, and find that average ensemble (or highest confidence ensemble) of MNB and BiLSTM is the best model for the DMT task.

In future work, we would like to apply our model to deal with more varieties of Mandarin Chinese (e.g. Hong Kong, Taiwan, Macao, Singapore and Malaysia) to examine its effectiveness.

References

Dzmitry Bahdanau, Kyunghyun Cho, and Yoshua Bengio. 2014. Neural machine translation by jointly learning to align and translate. *CoRR*, abs/1409.0473.

Piotr Bojanowski, Edouard Grave, Armand Joulin, and Tomas Mikolov. 2017. Enriching word vectors with subword information. *Transactions of the Association for Computational Linguistics*, 5:135–146.

Keh-Jiann Chen, Chu-Ren Huang, Li-Ping Chang, and Hui-Li Hsu. 1996. SINICA CORPUS : Design Methodology for Balanced Corpora. In *Language, Information and Computation : Selected Papers from the 11th Pacific Asia Conference on Language, Information and Computation : 20-22 December 1996, Seoul*, pages 167–176, Seoul, Korea. Kyung Hee University.

Alina Maria Ciobanu and Liviu P. Dinu. 2016. A computational perspective on the romanian dialects. In *Proceedings of Language Resources and Evaluation (LREC)*.

Simon Clematide and Peter Makarov. 2017. Cluzh at vardial gdi 2017: Testing a variety of machine learning tools for the classification of swiss german dialects. In *Proceedings of the Fourth Workshop on NLP for Similar Languages, Varieties and Dialects (VarDial)*, pages 170–177. Association for Computational Linguistics.

Çağrı Çöltekin, Taraka Rama, and Verena Blaschke. 2018. Tübingen-oslo team at the vardial 2018 evaluation campaign: An analysis of n-gram features in language variety identification. In *Proceedings of the Fifth Workshop on NLP for Similar Languages, Varieties and Dialects (VarDial 2018)*, pages 55–65. Association for Computational Linguistics.

Chu-Ren Huang and Lung-Hao Lee. 2008. Contrastive approach towards text source classification based on top-bag-of-word similarity. In *Proceedings of the 22nd Pacific Asia Conference on Language, Information and Computation*.

Rie Johnson and Tong Zhang. 2017. Deep pyramid convolutional neural networks for text categorization. In *Proceedings of the 55th Annual Meeting of the Association for Computational Linguistics (Volume 1: Long Papers)*, pages 562–570. Association for Computational Linguistics.

Nal Kalchbrenner, Edward Grefenstette, and Phil Blunsom. 2014. A convolutional neural network for modelling sentences. In *Proceedings of the 52nd Annual Meeting of the Association for Computational Linguistics (Volume 1: Long Papers)*, pages 655–665. Association for Computational Linguistics.

Yoon Kim. 2014. Convolutional neural networks for sentence classification. In *Proceedings of the 2014 Conference on Empirical Methods in Natural Language Processing (EMNLP)*, pages 1746–1751. Association for Computational Linguistics.

Diederik P. Kingma and Jimmy Ba. 2014. Adam: A method for stochastic optimization. *CoRR*, abs/1412.6980.

Tim Kreutz and Walter Daelemans. 2018. Exploring classifier combinations for language variety identification. In *Proceedings of the Fifth Workshop on NLP for Similar Languages, Varieties and Dialects (VarDial 2018)*, pages 191–198. Association for Computational Linguistics.

Zhouhan Lin, Minwei Feng, Cícero Nogueira dos Santos, Mo Yu, Bing Xiang, Bowen Zhou, and Yoshua Bengio. 2017. A structured self-attentive sentence embedding. *CoRR*, abs/1703.03130.

Marco Lui and Paul Cook. 2013. Classifying english documents by national dialect. In *Proceedings of the Australasian Language Technology Association Workshop 2013 (ALTA 2013)*, pages 5–15.

A. M. McEnery and R. Z. Xiao. 2003. The lancaster corpus of mandarin chinese.

Tomas Mikolov, Kai Chen, Greg Corrado, and Jeffrey Dean. 2013. Efficient estimation of word representations in vector space. *CoRR*, abs/1301.3781.

Jeffrey Pennington, Richard Socher, and Christopher D. Manning. 2014. Glove: Global vectors for word representation. In *Empirical Methods in Natural Language Processing (EMNLP)*, pages 1532–1543.

Ashish Vaswani, Noam Shazeer, Niki Parmar, Jakob Uszkoreit, Llion Jones, Aidan N. Gomez, Lukasz Kaiser, and Illia Polosukhin. 2017. Attention is all you need. *CoRR*, abs/1706.03762.

Fan Xu, Mingwen Wang, and Maoxi Li. 2016. Sentence-level dialects identification in the greater china region. *International Journal on Natural Language Computing (IJNLC)*, 5(6).

Marcos Zampieri and Binyam Gebrekidan Gebre. 2012. Automatic identification of language varieties: The case of portuguese. In *Proceedings of KONVENS*.

Marcos Zampieri, Shervin Malmasi, Nikola Ljubešić, Preslav Nakov, Ahmed Ali, Jörg Tiedemann, Yves Scherrer, and Noëmi Aepli. 2017. Findings of the vardial evaluation campaign 2017. In *Proceedings of the Fourth Workshop on NLP for Similar Languages, Varieties and Dialects (VarDial)*, pages 1–15. Association for Computational Linguistics.

Marcos Zampieri, Shervin Malmasi, Preslav Nakov, Ahmed Ali, Suwon Shon, James Glass, Yves Scherrer, Tanja Samardžić, Nikola Ljubešić, Jörg Tiedemann, Chris van der Lee, Stefan Grondelaers, Nelleke Oostdijk, Dirk Speelman, Antal van den Bosch, Ritesh Kumar, Bornini Lahiri, and Mayank Jain. 2018. Language identification and morphosyntactic tagging: The second vardial evaluation campaign. In *Proceedings of the Fifth Workshop on NLP for Similar Languages, Varieties and Dialects (VarDial 2018)*, pages 1–17. Association for Computational Linguistics.

Marcos Zampieri, Shervin Malmasi, Yves Scherrer, Tanja Samardžić, Francis Tyers, Miikka Silfverberg, Natalia Klyueva, Tung-Le Pan, Chu-Ren Huang, Radu Tudor Ionescu, Andrei Butnaru, and Tommi Jauhiainen. 2019. A Report on the Third VarDial Evaluation Campaign. In *Proceedings of the Sixth Workshop on NLP for Similar Languages, Varieties and Dialects (VarDial)*. Association for Computational Linguistics.

Chunting Zhou, Chonglin Sun, Zhiyuan Liu, and Francis C. M. Lau. 2015. A C-LSTM neural network for text classification. *CoRR*, abs/1511.08630.

BAM: A combination of deep and shallow models for German Dialect Identification.

Andrei M. Butnaru

Department of Computer Science, University of Bucharest

14 Academiei, Bucharest, Romania

butnaruandreimadalin@gmail.com

Abstract

In this paper, we present a machine learning approach for the German Dialect Identification (GDI) Closed Shared Task of the DSL 2019 Challenge. The proposed approach combines deep and shallow models, by applying a voting scheme on the outputs resulted from a Character-level Convolutional Neural Networks (Char-CNN), a Long Short-Term Memory (LSTM) network, and a model based on String Kernels. The first model used is the Char-CNN model that merges multiple convolutions computed with kernels of different sizes. The second model is the LSTM network which applies a global max pooling over the returned sequences over time. Both models pass the activation maps to two fully-connected layers. The final model is based on String Kernels, computed on character p-grams extracted from speech transcripts. The model combines two blended kernel functions, one is the presence bits kernel, and the other is the intersection kernel. The empirical results obtained in the shared task prove that the approach can achieve good results. The system proposed in this paper obtained the fourth place with a macro-F_1 score of 62.55%.

1 Introduction

Being at its third edition, the 2019 VarDial Evaluation Campaign (Zampieri et al., 2019) includes two shared tasks on dialect identification which proves that researchers are still interested in this challenging NLP task. For example, in the 2018 GDI Shared Task (Zampieri et al., 2018), a system (Jauhiainen et al., 2018) that uses a series of language models based on character n-grams achieves state-of-the-art with a macro-F_1 score near 69%, in a 4-way classification setting. For the 2019 GDI Shared Task, the organizers have included audio features together with speech transcripts, and also provided a word-level normal-

ization for each transcript. For solving this task, we propose a combination of deep and shallow models, by applying a voting scheme on the outputs resulted from a Character-level Convolutional Neural Networks (Char-CNN), a Long Short-Term Memory (LSTM) network, and a model based on String Kernels. In the 2019 GDI Shared Task, the participants had to discriminate between four German dialects, in a 4-way classification setting. A number of 6 participants have submitted their results, and the model proposed in this paper obtained 4th place with an accuracy of 62.95%, and macro-F_1 score of 62.55%.

The best scoring system that we submitted for the GDI Shared Task is an ensemble that combines both deep and shallow models. The system uses features from two deep models, Char-CNNs and LSTMs, and also from a shallow model that combines several kernels using multiple kernel learning. The Char-CNN model merges convolutions computed with kernels of different sizes to learn a first group of features. The LSTM network learns the second group of features by applying a global max pooling over the returned sequences over time. For the String Kernel model, we combined two kernel functions. The first kernel used is the p-grams presence bits kernel[1] which takes into account only the presence of p-grams instead of their frequencies. The second kernel is the histogram intersection kernel[2], which was first used in a text mining task by (Ionescu et al., 2014). This kernel functions proved useful in previous dialect identification shared tasks (Ionescu and Popescu, 2016; Ionescu and Butnaru, 2017; Butnaru and Ionescu, 2018).

There are two steps in the learning process. In

---

[1] The p-grams presence bits kernel was computed using the code available at http://string-kernels.herokuapp.com.

[2] The intersection string kernel was computed using the code available at http://string-kernels.herokuapp.com.

Proceedings of VarDial, pages 128–137

Minneapolis, MN, June 7, 2019 ©2019 Association for Computational Linguistics

the first step, the deep models are trained individually using the Adam optimization algorithm (Kingma and Ba, 2015). In the second step, the string kernel model is learned by applying Kernel Ridge Regression (KRR) (Shawe-Taylor and Cristianini, 2004). Finally, a voting schema is applied to obtain the final class for a test sample. Before deciding the final system, we tuned each model for the task. First of all, we tuned the string kernels model by trying out p-grams of various lengths, including blended variants of string kernels as well. Besides blended variants, we evaluated individual kernels, and also various kernel combinations. Second of all, we tuned the Char-CNN model, by trying out various convolution lengths, number of filters and depths. Finally, we tuned the LSTM model by seeking the best number of output units.

The paper is organized as follows. Work related to German dialect identification, models based on Character-Level Convolutional Neural Networks, Long Short-Term Memory Networks, and methods based on string kernels is presented in Section 2. Section 3 presents Char-CNNs, LSTMs and the string kernel models used in this approach. In this section, we also present the ensemble model. Details about the German dialect identification experiments are provided in Section 4. Finally, we draw the conclusion in Section 5.

2 Related Work

2.1 German Dialect Identificaion

German dialect identification is not a widely researched task, but we can observe an increased interest in it within recent years. In 2010, a system for written dialect identification was proposed (Scherrer and Rambow, 2010) , and it was based on an automatically generated Swiss German lexicon that maps word forms with their geographical extensions. During test time, they split a sentence into words and look up their geographical extension in the lexicon. Another method (Hollenstein and Aepli, 2015) was proposed for solving the Swiss German dialect identification task based on trigrams. For each dialect, a language model was trained, and each test sentence was scored against every model. The predicted dialect is chosen based on the lowest perplexity. In 2016, a corpus (Samardžić et al., 2016) that can be used for GDI was presented, which was later used to evaluate the participants in the GDI Shared Task of the DSL 2017 Challenge. One of the partici-

pants in the previously mentioned shared task, defined a system (Ionescu and Butnaru, 2017) that is based on multiple string kernels. The team used a Kernel Ridge Regression classifier trained on a kernel combination of a blended presence bits kernel based on $3 - 6$-grams, a blended intersection kernel based on $3-6$-grams, and a kernel based on LRD with $3 - 5$-grams. The winning team of the GDI Shared Task of the VarDial 2018 Workshop defined a system (Jauhiainen et al., 2018) that is based on language models defined on character 4-grams, and having on top the HeLI method.

2.2 String Kernels

In the past years, we can find that techniques that approach text at the character level proved remarkable performance levels in various text analysis tasks (Lodhi et al., 2002; Sanderson and Guenter, 2006; Kate and Mooney, 2006; Escalante et al., 2011; Popescu and Grozea, 2012; Popescu and Ionescu, 2013; Ionescu et al., 2014, 2016; Giménez-Pérez et al., 2017; Popescu et al., 2017; Cozma et al., 2018; Ionescu and Butnaru, 2018a). String kernels are a natural way of using character level information to generate features that are helpful in solving various areas of tasks. They are a particular case of the more general convolution kernels (Haussler, 1999). Since the beginning of the 21st century, researchers applied string kernels on document categorization (Lodhi et al., 2002), obtaining excellent results. String kernels were also successfully used in authorship identification (Sanderson and Guenter, 2006; Popescu and Grozea, 2012). For example, the first ranked team of the PAN 2012 Traditional Authorship Attribution task, used a system (Popescu and Grozea, 2012) based on string kernels. In recent years, various blended string kernels reached state-of-the-art accuracy rates for native language identification (Ionescu et al., 2016; Ionescu and Popescu, 2017), Arabic dialect identification (Ionescu and Popescu, 2016; Ionescu and Butnaru, 2017; Butnaru and Ionescu, 2018), polarity classification (Giménez-Pérez et al., 2017; Popescu et al., 2017), automatic essay scoring (Cozma et al., 2018), and cross-domain text classification (Ionescu and Butnaru, 2018a,b).

2.3 Character-Level CNN Networks

Convolutional networks (LeCun et al., 1998) have proven to be very efficient in solving various computer vision tasks (Krizhevsky et al., 2012; Szegedy et al., 2015; Ren et al., 2015). Therefore, many researchers decided to apply CNNs in their primary area of interest. For example, in the NLP domain, Convolutional Neural Networks (LeCun et al., 1998; Krizhevsky et al., 2012) were successfully applied on several NLP tasks such as part-of-speech tagging (Santos and Zadrozny, 2014), text categorization (Kim, 2014; Zhang et al., 2015; Johnson and Zhang, 2015), dialect identification (Belinkov and Glass, 2016; Ali, 2018), machine translation (Gehring et al., 2017) and language modeling (Kim et al., 2016; Dauphin et al., 2017). Word embeddings (Mikolov et al., 2013; Pennington et al., 2014) had a significant impact on NLP due to their ability to learn semantic and syntactic latent features. Because of this, researchers developed many CNN-based methods that rely on word embeddings. Trying to eliminate the pre-trained word embeddings from the pipeline, some researchers have tried to build end-to-end models using characters as input, in order to solve text classification (Zhang et al., 2015; Belinkov and Glass, 2016), language modeling (Kim et al., 2016) or dialect identification (Butnaru and Ionescu, 2019) tasks. Using characters as features can help the model learn unusual character sequences such as misspellings or take advantage of unseen words during test time. Working at the character-level can prove useful in solving the dialect identification task, since some state-of-the-art dialect identification methods (Ionescu and Butnaru, 2017; Butnaru and Ionescu, 2018) use character n-grams as features.

2.4 Long-Short Term Memory Networks

Recurrent Neural Networks (RNNs) (Elman, 1990) have the ability to process fixed length sequences and learn short-term dependencies between items from the sequence (Lin et al., 1996). A limitation of the RNN model is that it cannot learn long-distance correlations between items within a sequence (Hochreiter and Schmidhuber, 1997; Hochreiter et al., 2001). Long Short-Term Memory (LSTMs) (Hochreiter and Schmidhuber, 1997) have been proposed as a solution for the RNNs issue, introducing a memory cell inside the network. LSTMs have become more popular after being successfully applied in statistical machine translation (Sutskever et al., 2014). Besides this, researchers employed LSTMs in various areas,

from speech recognition (Graves et al., 2013a,b; Amodei et al., 2016), to language modelling (Kim et al., 2016), and text classification (Zhang et al., 2015).

2.5 Ensemble Learning

Ensemble learning combines a number of previously trained classifiers to classify new data samples by applying a voting schema on their predictions. Ensemble methods have been successfully employed in various machine learning tasks, including feature selection (Saeys et al., 2008), sentiment analysis (Xia et al., 2011; Wang et al., 2014), complex word identification (Malmasi et al., 2016), and dialect identification (Malmasi and Dras, 2015; Malmasi and Zampieri, 2017).

3 Method

The model presented in this paper combines the results obtained from three different learning algorithms: Kernel Ridge Regression over String Kernels, Character-level Convolutional Neural Networks, and a Long Short-Term Memory Network. The intuition to use three different learning algorithms comes from the idea that each trained model can discover from the same input different discriminant features, thus combining them will increase the accuracy of each and any model. String Kernels uses a function to compute a similarity matrix that carries the correlation between all pairs of samples. Based on the similarity between the samples (that is held in the similarity matrix) the KRR can learn a function that discriminates between them. Character-level Convolutional Neural Networks can learn to discriminate between samples by discovering patterns at character-level. The intuition in using this method comes from the idea that the same words in different dialects can have small character differences. Besides small character differences, there can be connections between words within a text. Having this in mind we propose to employ an LSTM netowrk to learn patterns between words within texts from the same dialect.

3.1 String Kernels

Kernel functions (Shawe-Taylor and Cristianini, 2004) have the ability to capture the concept of similarity between objects within a specific domain. The kernel function gives kernel methods the power to naturally handle input data that is not in the form of numerical vectors, for example strings. There are many kernel functions that can be applied on strings, with significant impact in domains such as computational biology and computational linguistics. String kernels embed the texts in a very large feature space, given by all the substrings of length p, and leave the job of selecting important (discriminative) features for the specific classification task to the learning algorithm, which assigns higher weights to the important features (character p-grams). Perhaps one of the most natural ways to measure the similarity of two strings is to count how many substrings of length p the two strings have in common. This gives rise to the p-spectrum kernel. Formally, for two strings over an alphabet Σ, $s, t \in \Sigma^*$, the p-spectrum kernel is defined as:

$$k_p(s, t) = \sum_{v \in \Sigma^p} \text{num}_v(s) \cdot \text{num}_v(t),$$

where $\text{num}_v(s)$ is the number of occurrences of string v as a substring in s. The feature map defined by this kernel associates to each string a vector of dimension $|\Sigma|^p$ containing the histogram of frequencies of all its substrings of length p (p-grams). A variant of this kernel can be obtained if the embedding feature map is modified to associate to each string a vector of dimension $|\Sigma|^p$ containing the presence bits (instead of frequencies) of all its substrings of length p. Thus, the character p-grams presence bits kernel is obtained:

$$k_p^{0/1}(s, t) = \sum_{v \in \Sigma^p} \text{in}_v(s) \cdot \text{in}_v(t),$$

where $\text{in}_v(s)$ is 1 if string v occurs as a substring in s, and 0 otherwise.

In computer vision, the (histogram) intersection kernel has successfully been used for object class recognition from images (Maji et al., 2008; Vedaldi and Zisserman, 2010). Ionescu et al. (2014) have used the intersection kernel as a kernel for strings, in the context of native language identification. The intersection string kernel is defined as follows:

$$k_p^{\cap}(s, t) = \sum_{v \in \Sigma^p} \min\{\text{num}_v(s), \text{num}_v(t)\}.$$

For the p-spectrum kernel, the frequency of a p-gram has a very significant contribution to the kernel, since it considers the product of such frequencies. On the other hand, the frequency of a p-gram is completely disregarded in the p-grams presence bits kernel. The intersection kernel lies somewhere in the middle between the p-grams presence bits kernel and the p-spectrum kernel, in the sense that the frequency of a p-gram has a moderate contribution to the intersection kernel. In other words, the intersection kernel assigns a high score to a p-gram only if it has a high frequency in both strings, since it considers the minimum of the two frequencies. The p-spectrum kernel assigns a high score even when the p-gram has a high frequency in only one of the two strings. Thus, the intersection kernel captures something more about the correlation between the p-gram frequencies in the two strings. Based on these comments, in the experiments we use only the p-grams presence bits kernel and the intersection string kernel.

Data normalization helps to improve machine learning performance for various applications. Since the value range of raw data can have large variations, classifier objective functions will not work properly without normalization. After normalization, each feature has an approximately equal contribution to the similarity between two samples. To obtain a normalized kernel matrix of pairwise similarities between samples, each component is divided by the square root of the product of the two corresponding diagonal components:

$$\hat{K}_{ij} = \frac{K_{ij}}{\sqrt{K_{ii} \cdot K_{jj}}}.$$

To ensure a fair comparison among strings of different lengths, normalized versions of the p-grams presence bits kernel and the intersection kernel were used in the experiments. Taking into account p-grams of different lengths and summing up the corresponding kernels, new kernels, termed *blended spectrum kernels*, can be obtained. Various blended spectrum kernels were used in the experiments in order to find the best combination.

3.2 Character-Level CNN

Convolutional Neural Networks can discover patterns within the data. These patterns are then later used to classify new data samples. Character-level CNNs learn such patterns in texts by searching through sequences of characters. The inspiration for this model is drawn from Kim (2014), but instead of using word embeddings as inputs, we use character encodings. This means that every character from an alphabet of size t is mapped to a

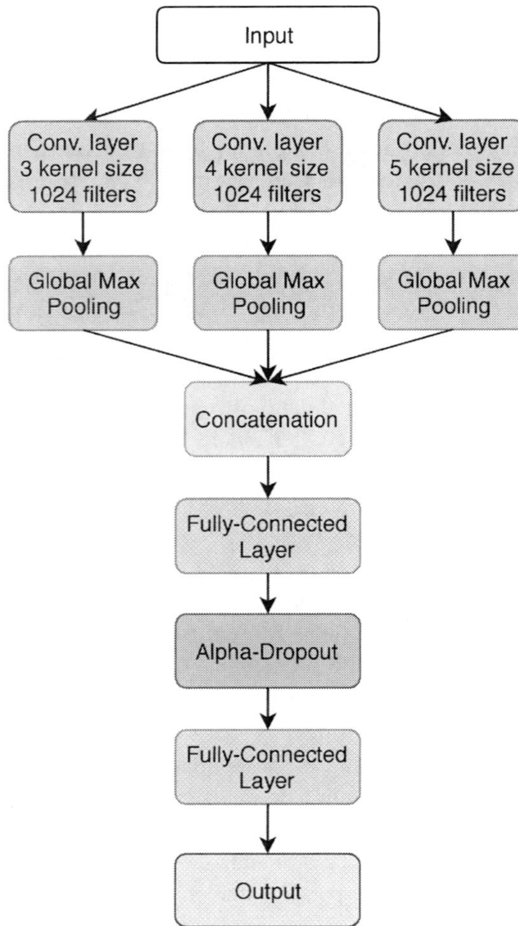

Figure 1: The architecture of the Character-level CNN model.

one-hot vector. For example, having the alphabet $\Sigma = \{a, b, c\}$, the encoding for character a is $[1, 0, 0]$, for b is $[0, 1, 0]$, and for c is $[0, 0, 1]$. Each character from the input text is encoded, and only a fixed size l of the input is kept. In the experiments presented in this paper, l was set to 270 characters. The documents that are under the length were zero-padded. The alphabet was extracted from the dataset and it contains a total of 32 characters from which 26 are the lower case letters of the English alphabet, plus 6 Swiss-German diacritics (such as ã, ä, õ, ö, ü, ẽ). Characters that do not appear in the alphabet are encoded as a blank character.

As illustrated in Figure 1, the architecture is 5 layers deep. The first layer is composed of three different convolutional layers, each followed by a global max-pooling layer. The third layer concatenates the features extracted from the global max-pooling layers, then passes the concatenation to two fully-connected layers. The convolutional layers are based on one-dimensional filters, one with filter size 3, another one with filter size 4, and the last one with filter size 5. After the concatenation step, the activation maps pass through a fully-connected layer having ReLU activation and after that, through an alpha dropout layer with the drop probability of 0.1. The last fully-connected layer has a softmax activation, which provides the final output. All convolutional layers have 1024 filters, and the first fully-connected layer has 256 neurons. The network is trained with the Adam optimizer using categorical cross-entropy as loss function, and a learning rate of 0.001.

3.3 Long Short-Term Memory Network

Long Short-Term Memory networks (LSTMs) have the capacity to learn long-term dependencies from a sequence. When applied on text, LSTMs can discover connections between words within a sentence or a text. Those connections can help the learning algorithm to find patterns that can later be used to solve a specific task. For example, discovering such connections can be useful to say if a text belongs to one class or another. Based on this idea, this paper proposes an LSTM model that can learn to discriminate between different dialects.

The input for this model is the same as the input used for the Char-CNN model. Characters were chosen as input because of the idea that between dialects, there are subtle character differences that makes a word belong to one dialect or another. The other reason is that there might be connections between substrings within the whole text of a specific dialect. The LSTM model defined for the GDI task is illustrated in Figure 2. The architecture consists of an LSTM layer, with the number of cells equal to 256, followed by a global max-pooling layer over the hidden state of each input character. The activation maps then pass through a fully-connected layer with 128 neurons, having ReLU activation. Finally, the predictions are computed by another fully-connected layer. The network is trained with the Adam optimizer using categorical cross-entropy as loss function, and a learning rate of 0.01.

3.4 Ensemble Model

Ensemble methods combine multiple learning algorithms to obtain a new model that has better performance than any individual model used in the ensemble. In this paper, a simple ensemble

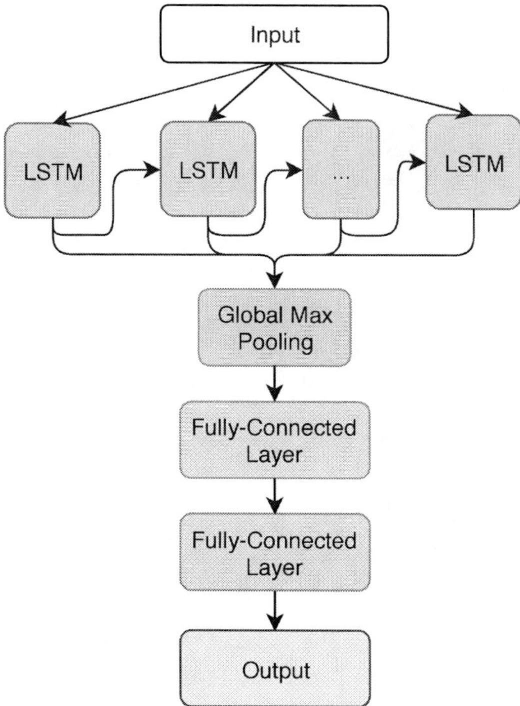

Figure 2: The architecture of the LSTM model.

method is employed. A voting schema is applied over the predictions from the Char-CNN, LSTM and String Kernel model. The vote from each model has equal weight. The class voted by the majority of the models is the final class for a sample data. If there is a tie, the class is chosen between the prediction of the Char-CNN model or the LSTM model, whichever prediction has the highest confidence among the outputs of the two models.

4 Experiments

4.1 Data Set

The 2019 GDI Shared Task data set (Zampieri et al., 2019) contains manually annotated transcripts of Swiss German speech, acoustic features for each transcript, and word-level normalization for each text. The task is to discriminate between Swiss German dialects from four different areas: Basel (BS), Bern (BE), Lucerne (LU), Zurich (ZH). As the samples are almost evenly distributed, an accuracy of 27.10% can be obtained with a majority class baseline on the test set. In our experiments, we used only the text transcripts to generate features.

4.2 Parameter and System Choices

The approach presented in this paper treats transcripts as strings. Because the approach works at the character level, there is no need to split the texts into words or to do any NLP-specific processing before computing the string kernels or feed the data to the deep networks. One thing to mention here is that for the deep networks the characters were mapped to one-hot encodings.

In order to tune the parameters and find the best system choices, the development set was used. Each model used in the ensemble was tuned. For tuning the parameters of the String Kernel method, we carried out a set of preliminary experiments to determine the optimal range of p-grams for each string kernel. We fix the learning method to KRR and evaluated all p-grams in the range $2 - 7$. The best accuracy (63.99%) is obtained with 4-grams. Having set the optimal number of p-grams, we experimented with different blended kernels to find out if combining p-grams of different lengths will improve the accuracy. For both kernels, presence and intersection, the best accuracy was obtained by combining p-grams with the length in range $3 - 5$.

After determining the optimal range of p-grams for each kernel function, we conducted further experiments by combining the presence bits kernel with the intersection kernel. When multiple kernels are combined, the features are actually embedded in a higher-dimensional space. As a consequence, the search space of linear patterns grows, which helps the classifier to select a better discriminant function. The most natural way of combining two or more kernels is to sum them up. The process of summing up kernels or kernel matrices is equivalent to feature vector concatenation. The results obtained by the individual kernels and also with the combined version are reported in Table 1. We can notice that even the individual kernels yield similar accuracy, when combined, the accuracy increases by a small amount.

After tuning the String Kernel method, we tuned the Character-level CNN. With the information discovered while tuning the String Kernels, we fixed the kernel size for the convolutional layers within the same range. Having the kernel size fixed, one convolution layer with kernel size 3, one with kernel size 4 and one with kernel size 5, we carried out further experiments in order to find the optimal number of filters and fully-connected lay-

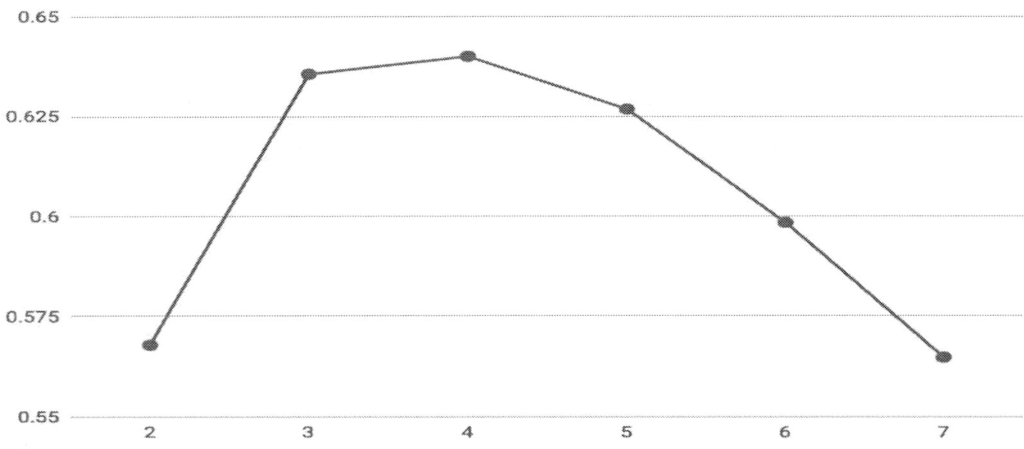

Figure 3: Accuracy rates of the KRR based on the presence bits kernel with p-grams in the range $2-7$.

Model	Accuracy
$\hat{k}_{3-5}^{0/1}$	66.05%
$\hat{k}_{3-5}^{\cap}$	66.00%
$\hat{k}_{3-5}^{0/1} + \hat{k}_{3-5}^{\cap}$	66.09%
$Char - CNN$	66.09%
$LSTM$	65.39%
$\hat{k}_{3-5}^{0/1} + \hat{k}_{3-5}^{\cap} + Char - CNN + LSTM$	67.95%

Table 1: Accuracy rates of various models used in experiments. The results are obtained over the development set.

System	Accuracy	Macro-F_1
Run 1	62.66%	62.19%
Run 2	62.83%	62.38%
Run 3	62.96%	62.55%

Table 2: Results on the test set of the 2019 GDI Shared Task (closed training) of the method described in this paper.

ers. From those experiments, we discovered that having 1024 filters on each convolutional layer, and one fully-connected layer having 256 neurons employs the best result (66.09%). In the experiments, the model was trained using Adam optimizer having the learning rate set at 0.001 and with mini-batches of 64 samples. The network was trained for 25 epochs.

The last defined model was the LSTM model. For this model, we fixed the length of the hidden cell to be a number that is a power of two and close to the maximum length of a sample. Because the maximum length of a sample was set to 270 characters, we fixed the hidden cell number to be 256. The fully-connected layer was also fixed to 128 neurons from the beginning. For this model, we tuned the learning rate and the mini-batch size used for training. Through experiments, we fixed the learning rate to 0.01 and the mini-batch size to 32. This model was also trained using Adam optimizer. The best accuracy obtained with this model was 65.39% and it was obtained after training the model for 25 iterations.

Applying a voting schema over the three mod-

els, we observe an increase of almost 2% over the best individual model.

4.3 Results

Table 2 presents our results for the German Dialect Identification Closed Shared Task for the 2019 VarDial Evaluation Campaign. The only difference between the three runs is the regularization parameter used in training the string kernel method. On the first run, the regularization parameter was set to 10^{-3}, on the second one it was set to 10^{-4}, and on the last run it was set to 10^{-5}. Among the submitted systems, the best performance is obtained when the KRR regularization parameter, for the String Kernel model, is set to 10^{-5}. The String Kernel model used in the three runs was trained on both training and development set. The submitted systems were ranked by their macro-F_1 scores and among the 6 participants, the best model that we submitted obtained the fourth place with a macro-F_1 score of 62.55%. The confusion matrix for the model is presented in Figure 4. The confusion matrix reveals that the system wrongly predicted over 400 samples of the Lucerne dialect as part of the Bern dialect. Furthermore, it has some difficulties in distinguish-

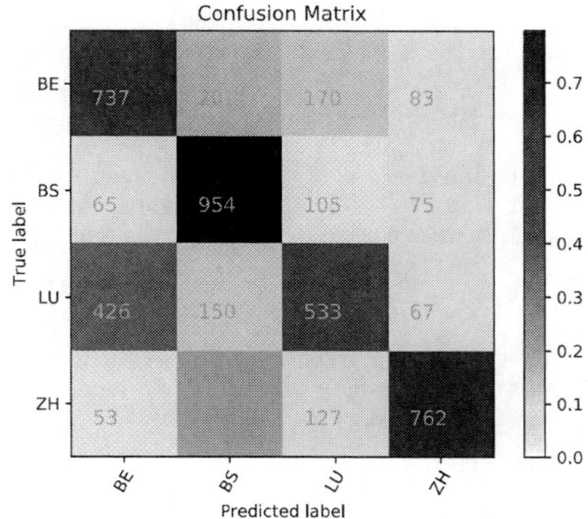

Figure 4: The confusion matrix of our best submission (run 3).

ing the Zurich dialect from the Basel dialect on one hand, and the Bern dialect from the Basel dialect on the other hand. Overall, the results look good, as the main diagonal scores dominate the other matrix components.

5 Conclusion

In this paper, we presented an approach for the GDI Shared Task of the DSL 2019 Challenge (Zampieri et al., 2019). The approach is based on an ensemble model that combines using a voting scheme results from three different models: Character-level Convolutional Neuronal Networks, Long Short-Term Memory network, and a String Kernel model. The approach obtained the fourth place.

References

Mohamed Ali. 2018. Character level convolutional neural network for arabic dialect identification. In *Proceedings of VarDial*, pages 122–127.

Dario Amodei, Sundaram Ananthanarayanan, Rishita Anubhai, Jingliang Bai, Eric Battenberg, Carl Case, Jared Casper, Bryan Catanzaro, Qiang Cheng, Guoliang Chen, et al. 2016. Deep speech 2: End-to-end speech recognition in english and mandarin. In *International conference on machine learning*, pages 173–182.

Yonatan Belinkov and James Glass. 2016. A Character-level Convolutional Neural Network for Distinguishing Similar Languages and Dialects. In *Proceedings of VarDial*, pages 145–152.

Andrei M. Butnaru and Radu Tudor Ionescu. 2018. UnibucKernel Reloaded: First Place in Arabic Dialect Identification for the Second Year in a Row. In *Proceedings of VarDial*, pages 77–87.

Andrei M Butnaru and Radu Tudor Ionescu. 2019. Moroco: The moldavian and romanian dialectal corpus. *arXiv preprint arXiv:1901.06543*.

Mădălina Cozma, Andrei M. Butnaru, and Radu Tudor Ionescu. 2018. Automated essay scoring with string kernels and word embeddings. In *Proceedings of ACL*, pages 503–509.

Yann Dauphin, Angela Fan, Michael Auli, and David Grangier. 2017. Language Modeling with Gated Convolutional Networks. In *Proceedings of ICML*, pages 933–941.

Jeffrey L Elman. 1990. Finding structure in time. *Cognitive science*, 14(2):179–211.

Hugo Jair Escalante, Thamar Solorio, and Manuel Montes-y-Gómez. 2011. Local Histograms of Character N-grams for Authorship Attribution. In *Proceedings of ACL: HLT*, volume 1, pages 288–298.

Jonas Gehring, Michael Auli, David Grangier, and Yann Dauphin. 2017. A Convolutional Encoder Model for Neural Machine Translation. In *Proceedings of ACL*, pages 123–135.

Rosa M. Giménez-Pérez, Marc Franco-Salvador, and Paolo Rosso. 2017. Single and Cross-domain Polarity Classification using String Kernels. In *Proceedings of EACL*, pages 558–563.

Alex Graves, Navdeep Jaitly, and Abdel-rahman Mohamed. 2013a. Hybrid speech recognition with deep bidirectional lstm. In *2013 IEEE workshop on automatic speech recognition and understanding*, pages 273–278. IEEE.

Alex Graves, Abdel-rahman Mohamed, and Geoffrey Hinton. 2013b. Speech recognition with deep recurrent neural networks. In *2013 IEEE international conference on acoustics, speech and signal processing*, pages 6645–6649. IEEE.

David Haussler. 1999. Convolution Kernels on Discrete Structures. Technical Report UCS-CRL-99-10, University of California at Santa Cruz, Santa Cruz, CA, USA.

Sepp Hochreiter, Yoshua Bengio, Paolo Frasconi, Jürgen Schmidhuber, et al. 2001. Gradient flow in recurrent nets: the difficulty of learning long-term dependencies.

Sepp Hochreiter and Jürgen Schmidhuber. 1997. Long short-term memory. *Neural computation*, 9(8):1735–1780.

Nora Hollenstein and Noëmi Aepli. 2015. A resource for natural language processing of swiss german dialects. In *GSCL*, pages 108–109.

Radu Tudor Ionescu and Andrei M. Butnaru. 2017. Learning to Identify Arabic and German Dialects using Multiple Kernels. In *Proceedings of VarDial*, pages 200–209.

Radu Tudor Ionescu and Andrei M. Butnaru. 2018a. Improving the results of string kernels in sentiment analysis and Arabic dialect identification by adapting them to your test set. In *Proceedings of EMNLP*, pages 1084–1090.

Radu Tudor Ionescu and Andrei Madalin Butnaru. 2018b. Transductive learning with string kernels for cross-domain text classification. In *International Conference on Neural Information Processing*, pages 484–496. Springer.

Radu Tudor Ionescu and Marius Popescu. 2016. UnibucKernel: An Approach for Arabic Dialect Identification based on Multiple String Kernels. In *Proceedings of VarDial*, pages 135–144.

Radu Tudor Ionescu and Marius Popescu. 2017. Can string kernels pass the test of time in native language identification? In *Proceedings of BEA-12*, pages 224–234.

Radu Tudor Ionescu, Marius Popescu, and Aoife Cahill. 2014. Can characters reveal your native language? A language-independent approach to native language identification. In *Proceedings of EMNLP*, pages 1363–1373.

Radu Tudor Ionescu, Marius Popescu, and Aoife Cahill. 2016. String kernels for native language identification: Insights from behind the curtains. *Computational Linguistics*, 42(3):491–525.

Tommi Jauhiainen, Heidi Jauhiainen, and Krister Lindén. 2018. Heli-based experiments in swiss german dialect identification. In *Proceedings of the Fifth Workshop on NLP for Similar Languages, Varieties and Dialects (VarDial 2018)*, pages 254–262.

Rie Johnson and Tong Zhang. 2015. Effective Use of Word Order for Text Categorization with Convolutional Neural Networks. In *Proceedings of NAACL*, pages 103–112.

Rohit J. Kate and Raymond J. Mooney. 2006. Using String-kernels for Learning Semantic Parsers. In *Proceedings of ACL*, pages 913–920, Stroudsburg, PA, USA. Association for Computational Linguistics.

Yoon Kim. 2014. Convolutional Neural Networks for Sentence Classification. In *Proceedings of EMNLP*, pages 1746–1751.

Yoon Kim, Yacine Jernite, David Sontag, and Alexander M. Rush. 2016. Character-Aware Neural Language Models. In *Proceedings of AAAI*, pages 2741–2749.

Diederik P. Kingma and Jimmy Ba. 2015. Adam: A method for stochastic optimization. In *Proceedings of ICLR*.

Alex Krizhevsky, Ilya Sutskever, and Geoffrey E. Hinton. 2012. ImageNet Classification with Deep Convolutional Neural Networks. In *Proceedings of NIPS*, pages 1106–1114.

Yann LeCun, Leon Bottou, Yoshua Bengio, and Pattrick Haffner. 1998. Gradient-based learning applied to document recognition. *Proceedings of the IEEE*, 86(11):2278–2324.

Tsungnan Lin, Bill G Horne, Peter Tino, and C Lee Giles. 1996. Learning long-term dependencies in narx recurrent neural networks. *IEEE Transactions on Neural Networks*, 7(6):1329–1338.

Huma Lodhi, Craig Saunders, John Shawe-Taylor, Nello Cristianini, and Christopher J. C. H. Watkins. 2002. Text classification using string kernels. *Journal of Machine Learning Research*, 2:419–444.

Subhransu Maji, Alexander C. Berg, and Jitendra Malik. 2008. Classification using intersection kernel support vector machines is efficient. *Proceedings of CVPR*, pages 1–8.

Shervin Malmasi and Mark Dras. 2015. Language identification using classifier ensembles. In *Proceedings of the Joint Workshop on Language Technology for Closely Related Languages, Varieties and Dialects*, pages 35–43.

Shervin Malmasi, Mark Dras, and Marcos Zampieri. 2016. Ltg at semeval-2016 task 11: Complex word identification with classifier ensembles. In *Proceedings of the 10th International Workshop on Semantic Evaluation (SemEval-2016)*, pages 996–1000.

Shervin Malmasi and Marcos Zampieri. 2017. Arabic Dialect Identification Using iVectors and ASR Transcripts. In *Proceedings of the VarDial*, pages 178–183.

Tomas Mikolov, Ilya Sutskever, Kai Chen, Gregory S. Corrado, and Jeffrey Dean. 2013. Distributed Representations of Words and Phrases and their Compositionality. In *Proceedings of NIPS*, pages 3111–3119.

Jeffrey Pennington, Richard Socher, and Christopher D. Manning. 2014. GloVe: Global Vectors for Word Representation. In *Proceedings of EMNLP*, pages 1532–1543.

Marius Popescu and Cristian Grozea. 2012. Kernel methods and string kernels for authorship analysis. In *Proceedings of CLEF (Online Working Notes/Labs/Workshop)*.

Marius Popescu, Cristian Grozea, and Radu Tudor Ionescu. 2017. HASKER: An efficient algorithm for string kernels. Application to polarity classification in various languages. In *Proceedings of KES*, pages 1755–1763.

Marius Popescu and Radu Tudor Ionescu. 2013. The Story of the Characters, the DNA and the Native Language. *Proceedings of the Eighth Workshop on Innovative Use of NLP for Building Educational Applications*, pages 270–278.

Shaoqing Ren, Kaiming He, Ross Girshick, and Jian Sun. 2015. Faster R-CNN: Towards Real-Time Object Detection with Region Proposal Networks. In *Proceedings of NIPS*, pages 91–99.

Yvan Saeys, Thomas Abeel, and Yves Van de Peer. 2008. Robust feature selection using ensemble feature selection techniques. In *Joint European Conference on Machine Learning and Knowledge Discovery in Databases*, pages 313–325. Springer.

Tanja Samardžić, Yves Scherrer, and Elvira Glaser. 2016. ArchiMob–A corpus of spoken Swiss German. In *Proceedings of LREC*, pages 4061–4066.

Conrad Sanderson and Simon Guenter. 2006. Short Text Authorship Attribution via Sequence Kernels, Markov Chains and Author Unmasking: An Investigation. In *Proceedings of EMNLP*, pages 482–491, Sydney, Australia. Association for Computational Linguistics.

Cicero D. Santos and Bianca Zadrozny. 2014. Learning character-level representations for part-of-speech tagging. In *Proceedings of ICML*, pages 1818–1826.

Yves Scherrer and Owen Rambow. 2010. Word-based dialect identification with georeferenced rules. In *Proceedings of the 2010 Conference on Empirical Methods in Natural Language Processing*, pages 1151–1161. Association for Computational Linguistics.

John Shawe-Taylor and Nello Cristianini. 2004. *Kernel Methods for Pattern Analysis*. Cambridge University Press.

Ilya Sutskever, Oriol Vinyals, and Quoc V Le. 2014. Sequence to sequence learning with neural networks. In *Advances in neural information processing systems*, pages 3104–3112.

Christian Szegedy, Wei Liu, Yangqing Jia, Pierre Sermanet, Scott Reed, Dragomir Anguelov, Dumitru Erhan, Vincent Vanhoucke, and Andrew Rabinovich. 2015. Going Deeper With Convolutions. In *Proceedings of CVPR*.

Andrea Vedaldi and Andrew Zisserman. 2010. Efficient additive kernels via explicit feature maps. *Proceedings of CVPR*, pages 3539–3546.

Gang Wang, Jianshan Sun, Jian Ma, Kaiquan Xu, and Jibao Gu. 2014. Sentiment classification: The contribution of ensemble learning. *Decision support systems*, 57:77–93.

Rui Xia, Chengqing Zong, and Shoushan Li. 2011. Ensemble of feature sets and classification algorithms for sentiment classification. *Information Sciences*, 181(6):1138–1152.

Marcos Zampieri, Shervin Malmasi, Preslav Nakov, Ahmed Ali, Suwon Shon, James Glass, Yves Scherrer, Tanja Samardžić, Nikola Ljubešić, Jörg Tiedemann, Chris van der Lee, Stefan Grondelaers, Nelleke Oostdijk, Antal van den Bosch, Ritesh Kumar, Bornini Lahiri, and Mayank Jain. 2018. Language Identification and Morphosyntactic Tagging: The Second VarDial Evaluation Campaign. In *Proceedings of VarDial*, pages 1–17.

Marcos Zampieri, Shervin Malmasi, Yves Scherrer, Tanja Samardžić, Francis Tyers, Miikka Silfverberg, Natalia Klyueva, Tung-Le Pan, Chu-Ren Huang, Radu Tudor Ionescu, Andrei Butnaru, and Tommi Jauhiainen. 2019. A Report on the Third VarDial Evaluation Campaign. In *Proceedings of the Sixth Workshop on NLP for Similar Languages, Varieties and Dialects (VarDial)*. Association for Computational Linguistics.

Xiang Zhang, Junbo Zhao, and Yann LeCun. 2015. Character-level Convolutional Networks for Text Classification. In *Proceedings of NIPS*, pages 649–657.

The R2I_LIS Team Proposes Majority Vote for VarDial's MRC Task

Adrian-Gabriel Chifu
Aix-Marseille Université
Université de Toulon
CNRS, LIS, Marseille, France
`adrian.chifu@univ-amu.fr`

Abstract

This article presents the model that generated the runs submitted by the R2I_LIS team to the VarDial2019 evaluation campaign, more particularly, to the binary classification by dialect sub-task of the Moldavian vs. Romanian Cross-dialect Topic identification (MRC) task. The team proposed a majority vote-based model, between five supervised machine learning models, trained on forty manually-crafted features. One of the three submitted runs was ranked second at the binary classification sub-task, with a performance of 0.7963, in terms of macro-F1 measure. The other two runs were ranked third and fourth, respectively.

1 Introduction

The term "dialect" is used to capture two different types of linguistic phenomena: a variety of a language specific to a particular group of the language's speakers (Oxford Living Dictionaries) and a socially subordinated language with respect to a regional or national standard language, but not actually derived from the standard language (Maiden and Parry, 2006). In the case of the latter usage, the standard language it is not considered a "dialect", since it is the dominant language in state or a region.

The dynamics and the characteristics of the language variations are interesting for many research disciplines, Computer Science included. The Workshop on NLP for Similar Languages, Varieties and Dialects (VarDial) represents a series of workshops focused on studying diatopic language variations from a computational perspective. The first workshop was in 2014, co-located with the COLING conference (Zampieri et al., 2014) and VarDial2019 is co-located with the NAACL2019 conference (Zampieri et al., 2019).

Since 2017, evaluation campaigns are proposed for the VarDial workshops. Four or five tasks are proposed every year. One of the VarDial2019 evaluation campaign (Zampieri et al., 2019) tasks is the Moldavian vs. Romanian Cross-dialect Topic identification (MRC) closed training shared task.

The proposed approach tackles the first sub-task of the MRC task (binary classification between dialects). We show how 40 simple features can be effective for a simple supervised machine learning architecture. The features are fed to five learning models and a majority vote between the decisions of the five classifiers is charged with the final decision.

The motivation behind this approach is to prove that simple features, thus faster to compute, are effective for the discrimination task. Another point is that the majority vote helps improving the performance and also stabilizes the model, making it more robust, with respect to various train data splits.

The rest of the article is structured as follows. Section 2 positions the article with respect to VarDial evaluation campaigns and presents the related work that provided the data set for the evaluation task. Section 3 describes the method, while Section 4 presents the implementation details and the experimental framework. In Section 5 the results are presented and discussed. Section 6 concludes the paper.

2 Related Work

Our research fits in the context of the VarDial evaluation campaigns. As for other evaluation campaigns, the tasks evolve from one edition to another. While some tasks are recurrent, others are not re-conducted, leaving place for new ones.

The 2017 campaign (Zampieri et al., 2017) had four tasks: Arabic Dialect Identification (ADI),

138

Proceedings of VarDial, pages 138–143
Minneapolis, MN, June 7, 2019 ©2019 Association for Computational Linguistics

Cross-lingual Dependency Parcing (CLP), Discriminating between Similar Languages (DSL) and German Dialect Identification (GDI).

In 2018, the evaluation campaign (Zampieri et al., 2018) had five tasks, the continuation of the ADI and GDI tasks and the Morphosyntactic Tagging of Tweets (MTT), the Discriminating between Dutch and Flemish in Subtitles (DFS) and the Indo-Aryan Language Identification (ILI).

The latest evaluation campaign, VarDial2019 has also five shared tasks: the continuation of the German Dialect Identification (GDI) task, the Cross-lingual Morphological Analysis (CMA) task, the Discriminating between Mainland and Taiwan variation of Mandarin Chinese (DMT) task, the Moldavian vs. Romanian Cross-dialect Topic identification (MRC) task and the Cuneiform Language Identification (CLI) task.

We participated at the MRC task, more specifically at the sub-task that focuses on the discrimination between Romanian and Moldavian news texts. To the best of our knowledge, there is no related work for these specific dialects, except for the MOROCO data set paper (Butnaru and Ionescu, 2019), in which the authors describe the collected corpus and present empirical studies on several classification tasks. Some experiments using a shallow string kernels-based approach and a deep approach, based on character-level CNNs with Squeeze-and-Excitation blocks are conducted. The authors also present and analyze the impact of the named entities. In the final data set, the named entities are removed.

3 Method

The proposed method is based on forty manually-crafted features that are fed to five supervised machine learning models for binary classification. The final output represents a majority vote that decides whether a text is written in Romanian or in Moldavian ("RO/MD?"). The architecture of the model is presented in Figure 1.

3.1 Features

The features we considered for this method are handcrafted and meant to be straightforward, simple to understand, thus easy and fast to compute. The forty features are of five types: token statistics-based, character-based, punctuation-based, word-based and named entity-based features, respectively. We believe that frequencies of some characters, or words may be discriminant for the classification between the two dialects.

3.1.1 Token Statistics Features

In order to compute these features, the text was pre-processed. Sentences have been extracted, based on the punctuation. In order to obtain tokens, the punctuation was removed and the remaining text was split by spaces. All tokens are transformed to lowercase.

For a given text, we considered three such features: the average number of tokens per sentence, the total number of tokens and the average number of characters of a token.

3.1.2 Character Features

The character-based features consider the text at the character level. A character feature represents the number of occurrences of the character in the text. We took into account fifteen such features. The considered characters are: all the vowels in Romanian (a, e, i, o u, ă, â and î) and some Romanian consonants (b, c, d, m, n and ş and ţ). Except for the "ş" and "ţ", which are specific for the Romanian language, the choice of the other consonants was completely empirical.

Regarding the character "î", we have considered an extra feature that represents the number of occurrences of this character inside a token (not at the beginning). For instance, the character occurrence in the word "dînsa" was counted, while the occurrence in the word "început" was not. This is very specific to the Moldavian dialect, since in the Romanian dialect, the character "î" does not generally appear (there are a few exceptions) in the interior of words, being replaced by the character "â".

3.1.3 Punctuation Features

The punctuation features concern some punctuation signs (space was also considered here). The number of occurrences of a punctuation sign represents a the feature value. Five such features were considered: space, dot, double quotes, exclamation points and question marks.

3.1.4 Word Features

The word features take into account some words that we considered as potentially discriminant, such as prepositions, or dialect/regional words. The number of occurrences of the selected words represent the feature values. There are fifteen such features: "ci", "mai", "cu", "care", "la", "în", "o"

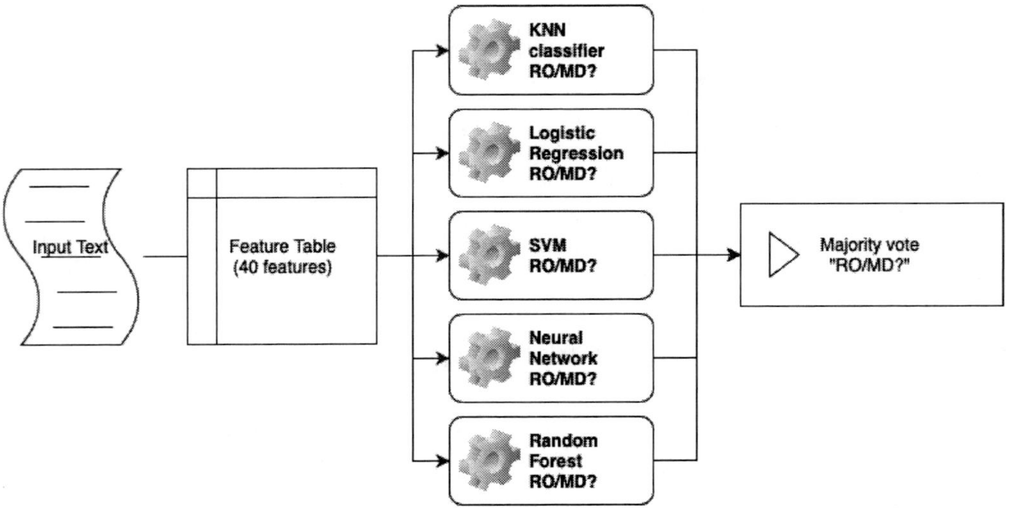

Figure 1: The architecture of the majority vote-based proposed model.

(the single character between two spaces), "un", "de", "pe", "şi", "dînsa", "dînsul", "dînşii" and "dînsele".

3.1.5 Named Entity Feature

In the data set for the MRC task (Butnaru and Ionescu, 2019), the name entities are identified and replaced by "NE". We decided to take this information into account, thus the number of occurrences of "NE" represent the feature value for our named entity-based feature.

3.2 Models

The features are fed to five supervised machine learning models. We have chosen the following models:

- a KNN classifier (called KNN here);

- a Logistic Regression classifier (called LR here);

- a SVM Classifier (called SVM here);

- a Neural Network classifier (called NN here);

- a Random Forest classifier (called RF here).

The hyperparameters of each model are presented later, in Section 4.2.

3.3 Majority Vote

The five models output their respective classification decisions. The final decision is made by a simple majority vote between the five aforementioned decisions. Having an odd number of votes will not yield any ex aequo final decisions. For instance, if three of the models decided in favor of Romanian and two models decided in favor of Moldavian, the final decision is Romanian.

4 Experiments

In this section we present the data set, the model parameters, as well as the submitted runs with their respective particularities.

4.1 Data Set

For the VarDial2019's (Zampieri et al., 2019) MRC task, the MOROCO data set (Butnaru and Ionescu, 2019) is proposed. We focus on the data provided for the binary classification sub-task, that is to say the first sub-task, in which a classification model is required to discriminate between the Moldavian and the Romanian dialects.

The data set contains Moldavian (MD) and Romanian (RO) samples of text collected from the news domain. The training set (called "train") contains 21719, the development set (called "dev") contains 11845 samples and the test set (called "test") contains 5923 samples. A summary of the data set, containing the class distribution is presented in Table 1.

Since the training type for this task is a closed one, only subsets of provided train data have been used, without any external resources.

4.1.1 Environment

The proposed architecture was implemented in python (version 3.7.2) and the five supervised

140

# samples	Total	RO	MD
train	21719	11751	9968
dev	11845	6410	5435
test	5923	3205	2718

Table 1: MRC task data set summary.

machine learning models were implemented with the sklearn library (version 0.20.2). The implemented features have been scaled with a model from sklearn (StandardScaler), based on training features and then applied to both training and testing feature sets.

4.2 Model Parameters

We describe here the sklearn hyperparameter settings for each of the five supervised machine learning models used in the proposed architecture. We mention that the hyperparameter settings were chosen empirically. Most of the models are standard models with slim modifications. A more robust cross-validation is left as a perspective for the future work.

KNN. Besides the default configuration, the number of neighbors was set to five.

LR. Besides the default configuration, the random state was set to zero, the solver was "newton-cg", the maximum number of iterations was set to one thousand and the multi-class parameter was set to "auto".

SVM. Besides the default configuration, the gamma parameter was set to "scale".

NN. Besides the default configuration, the solver was set to "adam", the activation function was set to "tanh", the maximum number of iterations was set to one thousand, the alpha was set to $1e-5$, the size of the hidden layer was set to one hundrend, the random state was set to one and the warm start was set as "True".

RF. Besides the default configuration, the number of estimators was set to three hundred, the maximum depth was set to two and the random state was set to zero.

4.3 Runs

The MRC task allows three runs per sub-task. We describe below the particularities of the three runs that we submitted to the first sub-task.

Run1. For this run, the forty features are computed as described in Section 3.1 and the training data was represented by the "train" and the "dev" texts, concatenated.

Run2. For this run, the forty features are computed as described in Section 3.1 and the training data was represented only by the "train" texts.

Run3. For this run, the forty features are computed as described in Section 3.1, with one modification: the character features, the punctuation features and the word features were normalized by dividing them by the total number of characters in the corresponding text. The training data was represented by the "train" and the "dev" texts, concatenated.

5 Results and Discussion

We present here the F1-score results and the confusion matrices of the submitted runs. We discuss the results both with respect with train and test data. Finally, we present the relative performance of our runs that were ranked second, third and fourth, with respect to the other participants to the first sub-task of the MRC task.

5.1 F1-scores

The macro-averaged F1-score was the ranking criterion for the MRC task. The values obtained by the three submitted runs are presented in Table 2. We present the performance both on train and on test and with respect to the five models of the architecture. The final decision majority vote (called "Majority" here) performances are displayed on the last line of the table. One can clearly notice that the best performing run, Run3, obtains the best performance in the case of the most models (except for RF and test data of NN). Run1 only gets the best performance on test data for the NN model. Run2 has the best performance for the RF model. However, overall, Run1 has a slightly better performance (Majority on test: 0.7781) than Run2 (Majority on test: 0.7762).

Run3 has the normalized features. Thus, as expected, the normalized features are performing better than the unnormalized features.

Run1 and Run3 are trained on the concatenated "train" and "dev" texts. Thus, as expected, the best performances are achieved when training on the most data possible.

Since there are not many differences in terms of performance between train and test, we may hypothesise that overfitting is not present. The only exception is for the NN models, for the three runs, where the absolute difference between train and

Runs	Run1		Run2		Run3	
Model/Split	train	test	train	test	train	test
KNN	0.8367	0.7551	0.8318	0.7467	**0.8476**	**0.7732**
LR	0.7248	0.7204	0.7272	0.7218	**0.7327**	**0.7315**
SVM	0.7884	0.7765	0.7857	0.7718	**0.8305**	**0.8039**
NN	0.8502	**0.7889**	0.8727	0.7646	**0.8933**	0.7821
RF	0.6896	0.6973	**0.7078**	**0.7151**	0.6994	0.7049
Majority	0.8092	0.7781	0.8117	0.7762	**0.8379**	**0.7964**

Table 2: The macro-averaged F1 score for the three runs, by split (train/test) and by model. The best values per line, for train and test, respectively, are displayed in bold.

Model/Split			train		test	
			predicted		predicted	
			MD	*RO*	*MD*	*RO*
KNN	true	*MD*	12861	2542	2072	646
		RO	2537	15624	690	2515
LR	true	*MD*	10070	5333	1805	913
		RO	3467	14694	652	2553
SVM	true	*MD*	11717	3686	1991	727
		RO	1889	16262	413	2792
NN	true	*MD*	13113	2290	2016	702
		RO	1247	16914	575	2630
RF	true	*MD*	7738	7665	1383	1335
		RO	1751	16410	297	2908
Majority	true	*MD*	11570	3833	1928	790
		RO	1484	16677	389	2816

Table 3: Confusion matrices for Run3, by method and by split (train/test).

test performance is of about 0.1.

5.2 Confusion Matrices

To focus on the best submitted run, we present the confusion matrices for Run3 in Table 3. In this table, we present the detailed confusion matrices for each of the five models, as well as for the Majority, both for train and test.

One can notice that the most balanced in terms of false positives is KNN, while the most unbalanced seems to be RF. Even though the examples in the data set are quite balanced with respect to the number of samples per class, our model has a tendency to predict much more texts for the label "RO". For instance, the false positives for the "RO" class are more than twice as many as for the "MD" class. This occurs for Majority, both for train and test.

In Figure 2 we display the confusion matrices for the test data, for the three runs. One can notice that Run2 has the most false positives for the class "MD". On the other hand, Run1 has the most false positives for the class "RO".

5.3 Other Participants

The ranking of all participants at the first sub-task of MRC are presented in Table 4. One can notice that the runner-up, our Run3 is at a significant distance from the winner (about 0.1 in absolute difference between the macro-averaged F1-scores).

6 Conclusion

We presented here the approach that generated the three runs we submitted at VarDial's MRC task, most specifically at the first sub-task that aims to discriminate news texts written in Moldavian and Romanian dialects. The architecture is based on forty features and a majority vote between five supervised machine learning models. The submitted runs ranked second, third and fourth, respectively. We thus showed that a simple architecture, based on features simple to compute can still be effective and competitive.

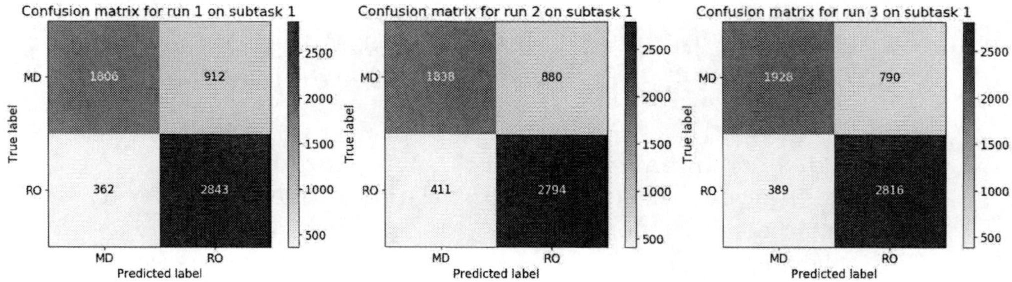

Figure 2: The confusion matrices for the three submitted runs.

Rank	Team	Run	Macro-F1	Weighted-F1	Micro-F1 (accuracy)
1	DTeam	1	0.8950	0.8960	0.8965
2	**R2I_LIS (Run3)**	3	**0.7964**	**0.7989**	**0.8009**
3	**R2I_LIS (Run1)**	1	**0.7781**	**0.7813**	**0.7849**
4	**R2I_LIS (Run2)**	2	**0.7762**	**0.7792**	**0.7820**
5	tearsofjoy	1	0.7573	0.7592	0.7596
6	lonewolf	2	0.7354	0.7332	0.7381
7	SC-UPB	1	0.7088	0.7114	0.7121
8	lonewolf	1	0.6560	0.6646	0.6877
9	lonewolf	3	0.6077	0.5997	0.6319
10	SC-UPB	2	0.5081	0.5131	0.5156

Table 4: The ranking of all participants at the MRC's first sub-task. The runs from this paper are shown in bold.

As future work, we plan to set up a more rigorous cross-validation protocol for the hyperparameter setup, in order to obtain more robust models. Another lead is to apply a feature selection method in order to identify the most useful features.

References

Andrei Butnaru and Radu Tudor Ionescu. 2019. MO-ROCO: The Moldavian and Romanian Dialectal Corpus. *arXiv preprint arXiv:1901.06543*.

Martin Maiden and Mair Parry. 2006. *The dialects of Italy*. Routledge.

Marcos Zampieri, Shervin Malmasi, Nikola Ljubešić, Preslav Nakov, Ahmed Ali, Jörg Tiedemann, Yves Scherrer, and Noëmi Aepli. 2017. Findings of the vardial evaluation campaign 2017. In *Proceedings of the Fourth Workshop on NLP for Similar Languages, Varieties and Dialects (VarDial)*, pages 1–15, Valencia, Spain. Association for Computational Linguistics.

Marcos Zampieri, Shervin Malmasi, Preslav Nakov, Ahmed Ali, Suwon Shon, James Glass, Yves Scherrer, Tanja Samardžić, Nikola Ljubešić, Jörg Tiedemann, Chris van der Lee, Stefan Grondelaers, Nelleke Oostdijk, Antal van den Bosch, Ritesh Kumar, Bornini Lahiri, and Mayank Jain. 2018. Language identification and morphosyntactic tagging: The second VarDial evaluation campaign. In *Proceedings of the Fifth Workshop on NLP for Similar Languages, Varieties and Dialects (VarDial)*, Santa Fe, USA.

Marcos Zampieri, Shervin Malmasi, Yves Scherrer, Tanja Samardžić, Francis Tyers, Miikka Silfverberg, Natalia Klyueva, Tung-Le Pan, Chu-Ren Huang, Radu Tudor Ionescu, Andrei Butnaru, and Tommi Jauhiainen. 2019. A Report on the Third VarDial Evaluation Campaign. In *Proceedings of the Sixth Workshop on NLP for Similar Languages, Varieties and Dialects (VarDial)*. Association for Computational Linguistics.

Marcos Zampieri, Liling Tan, Nikola Ljubešić, and Jörg Tiedemann. 2014. A report on the dsl shared task 2014. In *Proceedings of the First Workshop on Applying NLP Tools to Similar Languages, Varieties and Dialects*, pages 58–67, Dublin, Ireland. Association for Computational Linguistics and Dublin City University.

Initial Experiments In Data-Driven Cross-Lingual Morphological Analysis Using Morpheme Segmentation

Vladislav Mikhailov
National Research University
Higher School of Economics
School of Linguistics
Moscow
vnmikhaylov@edu.hse.ru

Lorenzo Tosi
National Research University
Higher School of Economics
School of Linguistics
Moscow
ltosi@edu.hse.ru

Anastasia Khorosheva
National Research University
Higher School of Economics
School of Linguistics
Moscow
aakhorosheva@edu.hse.ru

Oleg Serikov
National Research University
Higher School of Economics
School of Linguistics
Moscow
oaserikov@edu.hse.ru

Abstract

The paper describes initial experiments in data-driven cross-lingual morphological analysis of open-category words using a combination of unsupervised morpheme segmentation, annotation projection and an LSTM encoder-decoder model with attention. Our algorithm provides lemmatisation and morphological analysis generation for previously unseen low-resource language surface forms with only annotated data on the related languages given. Despite the inherently lossy annotation projection, we achieved the best lemmatisation F1-score in the VarDial 2019 Shared Task on Cross-Lingual Morphological Analysis for both Karachay-Balkar (Turkic languages, agglutinative morphology) and Sardinian (Romance languages, fusional morphology).

1 Introduction

This paper describes our submission to the VarDial 2019 Shared Task on Cross-Lingual Morphological Analysis (Zampieri et al., 2019). It is the task of producing lemma, part-of-speech tag and morphosyntactic annotations for previously unseen surface forms based on annotated data in related languages. Since surface forms are likely to be ambiguous, morphological analysis systems are supposed to produce a complete list of all possible and only valid analyses. These may represent not only multiple sets of morphosyntactic features, but also distinct lemmas and part-of-speech tags. For example, given a Turkish word *girdi* 'to enter, entry', the morphological analyzer should generate a full set of morphological readings the word can attain. (see Table 1).

In this paper we explore the task of data-driven cross-lingual morphological analysis. We apply this to two relatively low-resource languages: Karachay-Balkar and Sardinian; the former is Turkic with agglutinative morphology, while the latter is Romance and has fusional morphology.

We believe that it is possible to transfer morphology across related languages by exploiting cross-lingual inflection patterns despite language-specific morphological features inventories. For example, we can observe orthography specific common substring in *NOUN* surface forms in multiple related languages which stores the same tag values set *Case = Loc, Number = Plur, Number[psor] = {Sing, Plur}, Person[psor] = 3* (see Table 2).

Our method is inspired by previous approaches to neural-network based morphological analysis using inflection patterns for Polish (Jędrzejowicz and Strychowski, 2005), to cross-lingual morphological tagging for low-resource

Proceedings of VarDial, pages 144–152
Minneapolis, MN, June 7, 2019 ©2019 Association for Computational Linguistics

iso	word form	lemma	POS	MSD
tur	girdi	gir	VERB	Aspect = Perf, Number = Plur, Person = 3, Tense = Past, Valency = 1, VerbForm = Fin
tur	girdi	girdi	NOUN	Case = Nom
tur	girdi	gir	VERB	Aspect = Perf, Number = Plur, Person = 3, Tense = Past, Valency = 2, VerbForm = Fin

Table 1: **A complete set of morphological annotations for the Turkish word form** *girdi*, **meaning** *gir-* '(to) enter', *girdi-* 'entry'.

iso	word form	lemma	POS	MSD
tur	kenarlarında	kenar	NOUN	Case = Loc, Number = Plur, Number[psor] = {Sing, Plur}, Person[psor] = 3
kir	клеткаларында	клетка	NOUN	Case = Loc, Number = Plur, Number[psor] = {Sing, Plur}, Person[psor] = 3
tat	мәктәпләрендә	мәктәп	NOUN	Case = Loc, Number = Plur, Number[psor] = {Sing, Plur}, Person[psor] = 3
bak	далаларында	дала	NOUN	Case = Loc, Number = Plur, Number[psor] = {Sing, Plur}, Person[psor] = 3
kaz	аңғарларында	аңғар	NOUN	Case = Loc, Number = Plur, Number[psor] = {Sing, Plur}, Person[psor] = 3

Table 2: **An example of morphological grapheme level pattern for a set of NOUN tag values:** *-ләрендә* (tat), *-larında* (tur) **and** *-ларында* (kir, bak, kaz).

languages (Buys and Botha, 2016) and to data-driven morphological analysis for Finnish (Silfverberg and Hulden, 2018). In contrast to these approaches, our algorithm[1] produces full morphological analyses for previously unseen surface forms: it provides both morphological tags and lemmas as output and it can return multiple alternative analyses for one input word form.

We now give a brief description of our algorithm. First, we orthographically normalize and automatically transliterate both source and target language data into a joint orthographic representation using lookup tables. We model morpheme-to-tag inventory for each language family employing unsupervised morpheme segmentation with Morfessor (Virpioja, 2013). After this, we cluster all the target surface forms by making predictions over only part-of-speech tag with Morphnet (Silfverberg and Tyers, 2019), an LSTM encoder-decoder model with attention implemented using the OpenNMT neural machine translation toolkit (Klein et al., 2017). Within each cluster, we apply a greedy annotation algorithm using the cross-

lingual morpheme-to-tag inventory. The next step is the annotation projection based on string intersections between source language data and target language data. Finally, we transliterate the analyzed target language data back to its non-normalized format.

2 Related works

Our method is similar to alignment-based distant supervision approach, where the aim is to train a morphological tagger in the low-resource language through annotations projected across aligned bilingual text corpora with a high-resource language. (Buys and Botha, 2016) propose an embedding-based model using Wsabie, a shallow neural network that makes predictions at each token independently. To project annotations onto the target language, one uses type and token constraints across parallel text corpora. However, we transfer morphology for target surface forms only through the same language family without manual constraint implementation, and cover lemmatisation with ambiguous annotations produced.

Another trend in cross-lingual morphological analysis is transfer learning. The key idea is to employ multi-task learning,

---

[1] Code available at https://github.com/NIS-2018-CROSS-M/vardial-cma

treating each individual language as a single task and train a joint model for all the tasks. All learned representations are jointly embedded into a shared vector space to transfer morphological knowledge in a language-to-language manner. (Cotterell and Heigold, 2017) propose a character-level recurrent neural morphological tagger to learn language specific features by forcing character embeddings for both high-resource language and low-resource language to share the same vector space. In contrast to the projection-based approach, this model requires a minimal amount of annotated data in the low-resource target language. However, we do not use the target language annotated data and morphological tagging datasets provided by the Universal Dependencies (UD) treebanks; and our algorithm generates lemmas and multiple sets of morphosyntactic annotations.

Our work is most closely related to the Morphnet model in (Silfverberg and Tyers, 2019). The essential idea is to analyze previously unseen surface forms using a corpus of morphologically annotated data in the related language. This can represent the solution to low coverage inherent in rule-based morphological analyzers. They don't require constant updating to keep working, but need to be updated to cover new surface forms. In our algorithm, we use Morphnet to cluster target words by predicting over part-of-speech tags and then to generate a full set of morphological readings for words not being analyzed with the greedy annotation algorithm. However, we do not use the Universal Dependencies (UD) treebanks and learn the algorithm to analyze four open class words: nouns, verbs, adjectives and adverbs.

3 Data

The data used in the experiments consisted of tab separated files with five columns: language code, surface form, lemma, part-of-speech tag and morphosyntactic description (MSD). We used unannotated data for two Turkic target languages (Crimean Tatar, Karachay-Balkar) and for two Romance target languages (Asturian, Sardinian). We also used annotated data for five Turkic source languages (Bashkir, Kazakh, Kyrgyz, Tatar, Turkish) and for five Romance source languages (Catalan, French, Italian, Portuguese, Spanish). We compiled a corpus of segmented target language surface forms with Morfessor.

3.1 Normalization

We discarded all the diacritics in the Romance languages set, e.g. a Portuguese word *seqüência* 'sequence' becomes *sequencia*. In the Turkic languages set, the Turkish data was transliterated from Latin into Cyrillic, e.g. *gelen* 'coming' becomes *гелен*. In the Karachay-Balkar data, we discarded grapheme 'ъ' , e.g. *чыкъгъанды* 'appeared' becomes *чыкганды*. We also discarded all the diacritics in the Bashkir, Kazakh, Kyrgyz and Tatar data, e.g. Kazakh word *шығармалардың* 'complete works' becomes *шыгармалардын*.

3.2 Morpheme segmentation

We employed default recursive training of the Morfessor model. In recursive training, the current split for the processed surface form is removed from the model and its morphemes are updated accordingly. After this, all possible splits are tried by choosing one split and running the algorithm recursively on the created morphemes. The best split is selected and the training continues with the next surface form. We did not tune the Morfessor model with the average morpheme length and the approximate number of desired morpheme types because we want to use the algorithm unsupervised. To train the model, we split the data into 80% train data and 20% test data. Consider an example of the output for the following input Karachay-Balkar surface forms, where the $+$ sign implies the morpheme boundary:

пюзюрлеринде	*пюзюр+леринде*
экземпляр	*эк+з+е+м+п+ля+р*
политикасында	*политика+сында*

4 Methodology

In this section we describe our approach to data-driven cross-lingual morphological analysis implemented specifically for the Turkic languages. We refer to the source language annotated data as *Source*, to the target language unannotated data as *Target* and to the corpus of segmented target surface forms as *Morf. POS* is always one of *NOUN*, *VERB*, *ADJ*, or *ADV*.

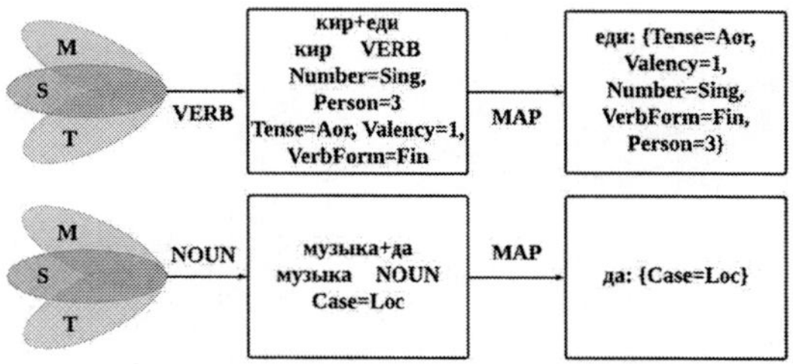

Figure 1: A graphical structure for modeling cross-lingual morpheme-to-tag inventory for Turkic languages. Source, Target and Morf are represented as S, T and M, respectively.

4.1 Morpheme-to-tag inventory

The key idea of modeling cross-lingual morpheme-to-tag inventory is automatic revealing of cross-lingual inflection patterns using unsupervised morpheme segmentation and string intersections between *Source*, *Target* and *Morf.*

We assume the morpheme-to-tag inventory to be specific to each part-of-speech tag and we do not merge the inventories in the experiments. We also do not compile the inventory for *ADJ* and *ADV* surface forms, since the latter do not store any morphosyntactic description in *Source*, e.g. *борын* 'langsyne' (word form), *борын* (lemma), *ADV* (POS), '_' (MSD). 116 out of 4146 (2%) *ADJ* surface forms in *Source* store only one tag value *Degree=Comp* which we consider to be statistically insignificant for model performance.

In agglutinative languages (Turkic family) the stem is invariant across different word forms. We generate distinct morphosyntactic features with a single root-word and map morphemes with morphological features, e.g. morpheme *лар* stores the feature *Number=Plur* for nouns and verbs. We represent each word as a grapheme level sequence $stem_i + m_{1i} + ... + m_{ni}$, so that $stem_i$ is a $lemma_i$ for $word\ form_i$. For example, the stem of a word *нюзюрлеринде* is *нюзюр* 'promise' and the lemma is *нюзюр*. We also refer to the first morpheme m_1 in each morphologically segmented word form $m_1, ..., m_n$ in *Morf* as the Morfessor lemma. Consider the segmented word form *нюзюр+леринде* with the Morfessor lemma *нюзюр* and m_2 *леринде*.

The overall scheme for modeling *NOUN* and *VERB* cross-lingual morpheme-to-tag inventories is outlined in Figure 1, where the respective string intersections between *Source*, *Target* and *Morf* are found. Here, we first compute the word form intersection between *Source* and *Target*, and the lemma intersection between *Source* and *Morf*. If the word form in *Target* can be found in *Source* and if the respective lemma in *Morf* can be found in *Source*, we generate the following unit sequence: *Target word form, segmented Target word form, Morfessor lemma, Source word form, Source lemma, Source POS and Source MSD*. Within each unit sequence in the intersection, we project the *Source MSD* of the word form onto the second morpheme m_2 in the *Target* segmented word form. Finally, we create the respective morpheme-to-tag pair.

For example, we have the following analysis in *Source*: *музыкада* (word form), *музыка* 'music' (lemma), *NOUN* (POS), *Case=Loc* (MSD). We can also find the same word form *музыкада* in *Target* and the respective segmented word form *музыка+да* in *Morf* (the Morfessor lemma is *музыка* and the segmented morpheme is *да*). On the basis of the word form intersection and the lemma intersection, we project the MSD *Case=Loc* onto the morpheme *да*. Thus, we create the morpheme-to-tag pair *да : Case=Loc*.

Since a single morpheme-to-tag pair can represent a concatenated string of distinct morphemes mapped with a set of morphological tag values, we additionally retrieve morpheme-to-tag pairs within each cross-lingual inventory. It is achieved by computing the difference between the morpheme strings and the difference between the tag values sets. For example, *NOUN* morpheme-to-tag inventory stores the following pairs:

ларын   *Case=Acc,*
    Number=Plur,   *Number[psor]=*
    {Sing, Plur}, Person[psor]=3

ын   *Case=Acc,   Number[psor]={Sing,*
    Plur}, Person[psor]=3

In this case, we compute the difference between the two morpheme-to-tag pairs, i.e.

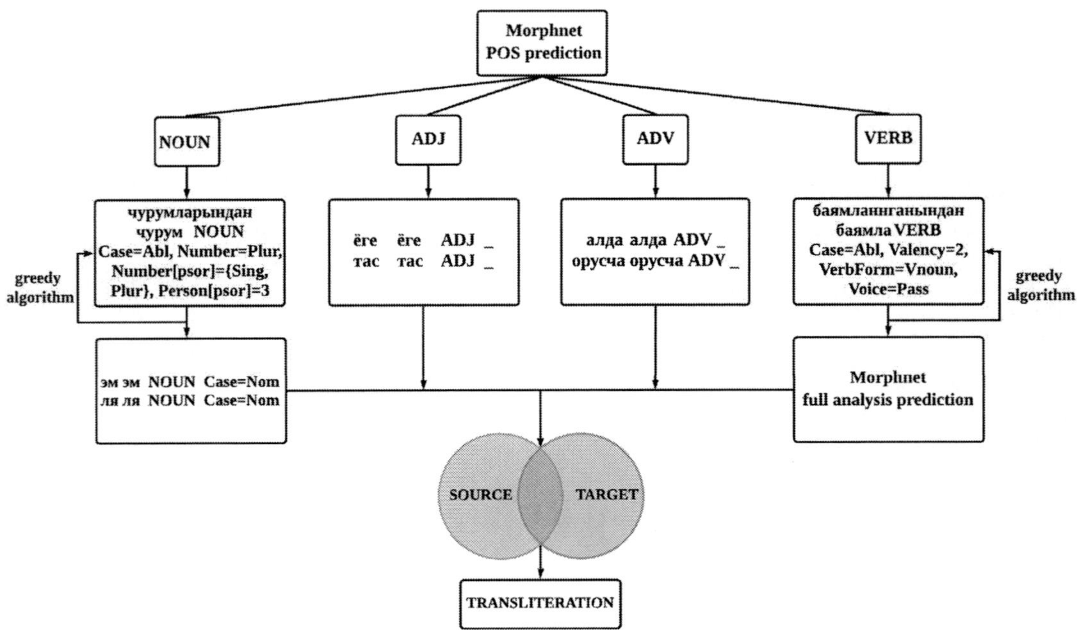

Figure 2: A graphical structure for morphological analysis of Karachay-Balkar surface forms.

$$\text{ларын} - \text{ын} \rightarrow$$

$$\left\{\begin{array}{l} Case = Acc, \\ Number = Plur, \\ Number[psor] = \\ \{Sing, Plur\}, \\ Person[psor] = 3 \end{array}\right\} \setminus \left\{\begin{array}{l} Case = Acc, \\ Number[psor] = \\ \{Sing, Plur\}, \\ Person[psor] = 3 \end{array}\right\}$$

As a result, we map previously unretrieved morpheme *лар* with the tag value *Number=Plur*.

4.2 A greedy annotation algorithm

We cluster all the target surface forms by making predictions over only part-of-speech tags with Morphnet trained through *Source*. Each target surface form is processed in the following manner (see Figure 2). Due to the reasons described in Section 4, we consider *word form$_i$* to be *lemma$_i$* and *MSD$_i$* to be '_' for all the surface forms in *ADJ* and *ADV* clusters.

In *NOUN* and *VERB* clusters, we apply a greedy annotation algorithm to inflect a lemma and a morphosyntactic description for each surface form, which we now describe.

All morpheme-to-tag pairs in *NOUN* and *VERB* cross-lingual inventories are sorted by the morpheme length in the descending order. First, the longest cross-lingual morpheme is matched with a substring of the processed surface form starting from its end. If match, the respective inflection pattern is projected onto the surface form. If it fails to match, the next surface form is processed. After this, we deinflect a lemma by computing the difference between the surface form string and the matched morpheme string.

For example, one of the longest morphemes *ларындан* (*Case=Abl*, *Number=Plur*, *Number[psor]={Sing, Plur}, Person[psor]=3*) is matched with a target surface form *ызларындан*. The respective inflection pattern is projected onto the surface form. The inflected lemma is the difference *ызларындан − ларындан → ыз* 'trace'. Finally, we get a full analysis set: *ызларындан* (word form), *ыз* (lemma), *NOUN* (POS), *{Case=Abl, Number=Plur, Number[psor]= {Sing, Plur}, Person[psor]=3}* (MSD).

Out-of-vocabulary cross-lingual morpheme-to-tag pairs and ambiguous target surface forms are the potential weak points of the greedy algorithm. If the analysis with the greedy algorithm fails:

- we consider non-analyzed $NOUN$ surface forms to have the following analysis. Since a zero affix stores *'Case=Nom'* tag value, we assume *wordform* string to be the respective *lemma* and MSD to be *'Case=Nom'*. For example, *юг* 'South' (word form), *юг* (lemma), $NOUN$ (POS), '_' (MSD).

- we give non-analyzed $VERB$ surface forms to Morphnet as the input. The output is a full morphological analysis with ambiguous annotations, merged with the previously analyzed surface forms.

To correct the analyses acquired with the greedy algorithm and Morphnet predictions, we project annotations from *Source* across *Target* on the basis of string intersection (one-to-one orthographic match). We suppose that the intersection keeps loan words and cognates, which share the same set of morphological annotations. Finally, we employ transliteration of the analyzed target data back to its non-normalized format.

5 Experiments and results

We present results for six experiments and compare the performance of our algorithm on the VarDial 2019 CMA Shared Task with the baseline system. Since analyzed surface forms can have multiple morphological analyses, the results are evaluated on precision, recall and F1-score (Silfverberg and Tyers, 2019).

5.1 Experiment on Test Data

We performed four experiments in the orthographically non-normalized and normalized data scenarios on each language family.

Experiment 1. Turkic languages, normalized data
Source: Bashkir (bak), Kazakh (kaz), Kyrgyz (kir), Tatar (tat), Turkish (tur).
Target: Crimean Tatar (crh).

Experiment 2. Turkic languages, non-normalized data
Source: Bashkir (bak), Kazakh (kaz), Kyrgyz (kir), Tatar (tat), Turkish (tur).
Target: Crimean Tatar (crh).

Experiment 3. Romance languages, normalized data
Source: Catalan (cat), French (fra), Italian (ita), Portuguese (por), Spanish (spa).
Target: Asturian (ast).

Experiment 4. Romance languages, non-normalized data
Source: Catalan (cat), French (fra), Italian (ita), Portuguese (por), Spanish (spa).
Target: Asturian (ast).

5.2 Experiment on Surprise Language

In these experiments the target languages were unknown before the data release. We performed two experiments only in the orthographically normalized data scenario since the normalization improved the performance on the test data.

Experiment 5. Turkic languages, normalized data
Source: Bashkir (bak), Kazakh (kaz), Kyrgyz (kir), Tatar (tat), Turkish (tur).
Target: Karachay-Balkar (krc).

Experiment 6. Romance languages, normalized data
Source: Catalan (cat), French (fra), Italian (ita), Portuguese (por), Spanish (spa).
Target: Sardinian (srd).

Tables 3, 4, 5, 6 show the results on complete analyses including lemma, part-of-speech tag and morphosyntactic description. Our algorithm delivers the best F1-score on lemma prediction for Karachay-Balkar and Sardinian languages.

6 Discussion

Our approach of representing a surface form as a grapheme level sequence of stem and morphemes, along with retrieving cross-lingual inflection patterns improves performance on lemmatisation comparing to the baseline system. Despite the fact that this approach naively appears suitable only for agglutinative morphology, we yet achieve the best results for Sardinian (fusional morphology) in the VarDial 2019 Shared Task on CMA.

We looked at the analyses for the Karachay-Balkar language and classified the errors into nine categories: (1) Out-of-vocabulary morpheme-to-tag pairs; (2) Boundary between stem and morphemes; (3) Part-of-speech tag prediction; (4) Analysis overgeneration; (5) Insufficient analysis set; (6) Statistical assumption based error; (7) Back transliteration; (8) Substandard forms; (9) Derivational morphemes.

A common source of first-category errors is found in lemmatisation and morphosyntactic description of the surface forms storing out-of-vocabulary morphemes. For example, the morpheme *ла* was not retrieved when modeling the cross-lingual inventory. As a result, the algorithm produced the lemma **эмиратла* and the MSD **Case=Acc* of the *NOUN* *эмиратланы* rather than *эмират* 'emirate' and *Case=Acc, Number=Plur*.

The algorithm also generated both correct and incorrect annotations for the same input form; this can be considered as the second error category. For example, we get one correct analysis for the word *башланды* with the lemma *башлан* 'beginning' and the incorrect one with the lemma **башла*. It can be explained as the overenthusiastic greedy annotation when the cross-lingual morpheme being a substring of the lemma string.

For the third error category consider the *VERB* *юлеширге* 'to divide' analyzed with Morphnet as **NOUN*. Consequently, the algorithm produced the lemma **юлешир* and the incorrect MSD **Case=Dat* instead of *юлеш* and *Case=Dat, Tense=Aor, Valency=2, VerbForm=Vnoun*.

The fourth error category includes superfluous analysis generation, e.g. we get two analyses for the *VERB* *эта* (a form of the auxiliary verb 'to be') with the correct morphosyntactic annotation *Aspect=Imp, Valency=1, VerbForm=Conv* and the redundant one **Aspect=Imp, Valency=2, VerbForm=Conv*. This error can also occur when one surface form is predicted with two different part-of-speech tags, e.g. the word *къарачай-малкъар* 'Karachay-Balkar' is analyzed as both *NOUN* and **VERB*.

For errors of the fifth type we have the *NOUN* *джолларын* (lemma *джол*, meaning 'road') given only one correct annotation *Case=Acc, Number=Plur, Number[psor]={Sing, Plur}, Person[psor]=3* instead of two possible. Moreover, there are ambiguous morphemes which store more than one tag value set. Consider the compound *NOUN* *премьер-министрни* with the lemma *премьер-министр*, 'prime-minister' having two correct MSDs *Case=Acc* and *Case=Gen*. In contrast, our algorithm provided only one correct MSD *Case=Acc*.

Errors of the seventh category can be

model	Recall	Precision	F1
experiment 1	66.91	33.32	44.49
experiment 2	25.07	9.88	14.17
experiment 3	62.09	31.82	42.07
experiment 4	67.70	13.83	22.97
baseline crh	36.43	44.74	40.16
baseline ast	66.64	70.73	68.62
experiment 5	43.01	35.59	38.95
experiment 6	74.58	37.15	49.60
baseline krc	39.59	50.94	44.55
baseline srd	66.42	67.28	66.85

Table 3: Results for morphosyntactic description prediction.

model	Recall	Precision	F1
experiment 1	76.75	34.85	47.94
experiment 2	32.43	13.15	18.72
experiment 3	35.34	21.02	26.36
experiment 4	58.53	13.43	21.85
baseline crh	56.87	59.66	58.23
baseline ast	62.28	59.90	61.07
experiment 5	63.30	51.82	56.99
experiment 6	48.07	32.55	38.82
baseline krc	54.90	56.91	55.89
baseline srd	35.73	35.59	35.66

Table 4: Results for lemma prediction.

model	Recall	Precision	F1
experiment 1	87.72	67.47	76.27
experiment 2	80.29	33.94	47.71
experiment 3	75.66	61.09	67.60
experiment 4	73.71	23.16	35.25
baseline crh	77.37	79.38	78.36
baseline ast	75.40	73.53	74.45
experiment 5	87.87	67.61	76.42
experiment 6	87.29	62.28	72.69
baseline krc	77.38	79.13	78.25
baseline srd	68.12	68.60	68.36

Table 5: Results for POS prediction.

model	Recall	Precision	F1
experiment 1	58.39	25.53	35.53
experiment 2	24.93	9.13	13.36
experiment 3	26.15	12.76	17.15
experiment 4	49.22	9.54	15.99
baseline crh	29.29	36.04	32.32
baseline ast	44.56	44.26	44.41
experiment 5	39.57	32.38	35.61
experiment 6	36.54	17.08	23.28
baseline krc	34.77	44.94	39.21
baseline srd	26.85	26.10	26.47

Table 6: Results for full analysis prediction: lemma + POS + MSD.

found in the lemmas containing mismatched graphemes *къ* and *гъ*. For example, the *NOUN де-факто* 'de facto' receives the lemma **де-факъто* instead of *де-факто*.

The eighth error category is represented by substandard attested word forms, e.g. the generated lemma **энтта* for the *ADV энтма* is confused with the correct lemma *энтда* 'again'.

Errors of the ninth category are considered to be the incorrect lemmas for the word forms containing the derivational morphemes *ду*, *ды*, and *ди*. These can be found specifically in *ADJ* and do not store any morphosyntactic description. The algorithm produced the lemma **джокъзду* for the *ADJ джокъзду* 'no' derived from the underlying stem and the actual lemma *джокъз* 'nothingness'.

We suggest that the rate of errors in the first and the second categories can probably be reduced by applying GBUSS algorithm (Shalonova et al., 2009) which proved to perform better than Morfessor. Another approach is to include the morphological information on lemma and suffixes into the character-based word representations learned by the bi-LSTMs (Özateş et al., 2018). The errors of the third, fourth and fifth categories might be partially resolved with the Morphnet hyperparameters tuning, e.g. increasing a probability threshold and adjusting the maximal number of output candidates specifically for each POS cluster. Back transliteration errors can be reduced by employing byte-pair encoding (BPE) which allows to eliminate the orthographic normalization. Finally, semi-supervised learning and retrieving *ADJ* cross-lingual morpheme-to-tag pairs might solve the sixth, eighth and ninth error categories.

Future Work

In future work we are planning to experiment with Slavic languages (fusional morphology).

Hard attention models for morphological analysis are the object of our further exploration since these proved to deliver a better performance in the low-resource language scenario (Cotterell et al., 2018).

Another direction is to make use of cognate identification as it might improve morphology transferring across the single language family. Cognates tend to share the same language knowledge, e.g. English *tooth* and German *Zahn* have the same semantic meaning and morphosyntactic features. This can be achieved with applying phoneme level Siamese convolutional networks (Rama, 2016) or generating multilingual cognate tables by clustering surface forms from existing lexical resources (Wu and Yarowsky, 2018).

Conclusion

In this paper we proposed an approach for data-driven cross-lingual morphological analysis in a low-resource language setting based on a combination of unsupervised morpheme segmentation, annotation projection and an LSTM encoder-decoder model with attention. Despite the morphological differences between agglutinative and fusional languages, our algorithm obtains the best performance on lemmatisation for Karachay-Balkar and Sardinian languages in the VarDial 2019 Shared Task on CMA.

Acknowledgements

We wish to thank the anonymous reviewers for helpful comments and suggestions.

References

Jan Buys and Jan A Botha. 2016. Cross-lingual morphological tagging for low-resource languages. *arXiv preprint arXiv:1606.04279*.

Ryan Cotterell and Georg Heigold. 2017. Cross-lingual, character-level neural morphological tagging. *arXiv preprint arXiv:1708.09157*.

Ryan Cotterell, Christo Kirov, John Sylak-Glassman, Géraldine Walther, Ekaterina Vylomova, Arya D McCarthy, Katharina Kann, Sebastian Mielke, Garrett Nicolai, Miikka Silfverberg, et al. 2018. The conll–sigmorphon 2018 shared task: Universal morphological reinflection. *arXiv preprint arXiv:1810.07125*.

Piotr Jędrzejowicz and Jakub Strychowski. 2005. A neural network based morphological analyser of the natural language. In *Intelligent Information Processing and Web Mining*, pages 199–208. Springer.

Guillaume Klein, Yoon Kim, Yuntian Deng, Jean Senellart, and Alexander M. Rush. 2017. OpenNMT: Open-source toolkit for neural machine translation. In *Proc. ACL*.

Şaziye Betül Özateş, Arzucan Özgür, Tunga Gungor, and Balkız Öztürk. 2018. A morphology-based representation model for lstm-based dependency parsing of agglutinative languages. In *Proceedings of the CoNLL 2018 Shared Task: Multilingual Parsing from Raw Text to Universal Dependencies*, pages 238–247.

Taraka Rama. 2016. Siamese convolutional networks for cognate identification. In *Proceedings of COLING 2016, the 26th International Conference on Computational Linguistics: Technical Papers*, pages 1018–1027.

Ksenia Shalonova, Bruno Golénia, and Peter Flach. 2009. Towards learning morphology for under-resourced fusional and agglutinating languages. *IEEE Transactions on Audio, Speech, and Language Processing*, 17(5):956–965.

Miikka Silfverberg and Mans Hulden. 2018. Initial experiments in data-driven morphological analysis for finnish. In *Proceedings of the Fourth International Workshop on Computational Linguistics of Uralic Languages*, pages 98–105.

Miikka Silfverberg and Francis Tyers. 2019. Data-driven morphological analysis for uralic languages. In *Proceedings of the Fifth International Workshop on Computational Linguistics for Uralic Languages*, pages 1–14.

Peter; Grönroos Stig-Arne; Kurimo Mikko Virpioja, Sami; Smit. 2013. Morfessor 2.0: Python implementation and extensions for morfessor baseline. D4 julkaistu kehittämis- tai tutkimusraportti tai -selvitys.

Winston Wu and David Yarowsky. 2018. Creating large-scale multilingual cognate tables. In *Proceedings of the Eleventh International Conference on Language Resources and Evaluation (LREC-2018)*.

Marcos Zampieri, Shervin Malmasi, Yves Scherrer, Tanja Samardžić, Francis Tyers, Miikka Silfverberg, Natalia Klyueva, Tung-Le Pan, Chu-Ren Huang, Radu Tudor Ionescu, Andrei Butnaru, and Tommi Jauhiainen. 2019. A Report on the Third VarDial Evaluation Campaign. In *Proceedings of the Sixth Workshop on NLP for Similar Languages, Varieties and Dialects (VarDial)*. Association for Computational Linguistics.

Neural and Linear Pipeline Approaches to
Cross-lingual Morphological Analysis

Çağrı Çöltekin
University of Tübingen
Department of Linguistics
`ccoltekin@sfs.uni-tuebingen.de`

Jeremy Barnes
University of Oslo
Department of Informatics
`jeremycb@ifi.uio.no`

Abstract

This paper describes Tübingen-Oslo team's participation in the cross-lingual morphological analysis task in the VarDial 2019 evaluation campaign. We participated in the shared task with a standard neural network model. Our model achieved analysis F1-scores of 31.48 and 23.67 on test languages Karachay-Balkar (Turkic) and Sardinian (Romance) respectively. The scores are comparable to the scores obtained by the other participants in both language families, and the analysis score on the Romance data set was also the best result obtained in the shared task. Besides describing the system used in our shared task participation, we describe another, simpler, model based on linear classifiers, and present further analyses using both models. Our analyses, besides revealing some of the difficult cases, also confirm that the usefulness of a source language in this task is highly correlated with the similarity of source and target languages.

1 Introduction

Morphological analysis is one of the basic tasks in natural language processing (NLP). The need for morphological analysis becomes particularly important in processing morphologically rich languages, where analysis of words can both be challenging and fruitful. Morphological analysis can be useful in downstream NLP tasks as well as being useful for (linguistic) research.

Traditionally, morphological analyzers have been developed using finite state transducers (FSTs). Finite-state morphological analyzers define a lexicon and a set of rules to specify both morphotactics and morpho-phonological (or orthographic) alternations. The resulting rule-based system is compiled into a finite state transducer which is capable of analyzing a given word to an underlying linguistic representation. The resulting FSTs are fast, and can be used for a range of tasks from stemming/lemmatization to full morphological analysis. As well as transducing word forms to a linguistic analysis, they can also be used in reverse to generate the word form(s) of a given linguistic representation.

Finite-state morphological analyzers have been used successfully for a broad range of NLP tasks, and are available for most of the world's major languages. Finite-state analyzers also exist for all of the languages that are featured in this shared task (examples of such analyzers include, Tzoukermann and Liberman, 1990; Altintas and Cicekli, 2001; Armentano-Oller et al., 2006; Çöltekin, 2010; Kessikbayeva and Cicekli, 2014; Washington et al., 2014; Forcada et al., 2011; Tyers et al., 2010). On the downside, developing these analyzers requires substantial expert effort,[1] which in some cases may not even exist, e.g., for languages with few speakers where experts are also hard to find. A potential solution to aid developing morphological analysis tools is to use unsupervised methods. Earlier attempts to develop unsupervised morphological analysis tools, mostly within Morpho Challenge shared tasks (Kurimo et al., 2010), returned rather mixed, often sub-optimal results (see Hammarström and Borin, 2011, for a survey).

Another approach for obtaining morphological analyses for languages without a morphological analyzer is based on transfer learning, which has become a widespread approach in NLP and related disciplines rather recently (Yarowsky et al., 2001; Faruqui and Kumar, 2015; Johnson et al., 2017; Barnes et al., 2018). The general idea is to train a supervised machine learning model that predicts analyses of word forms in a target language using gold-standard analyses that exist in other related languages.

---

[1] Access to an analyzer for a closely-related language may reduce the development time and effort considerably (Washington et al., 2014).

Proceedings of VarDial, pages 153–164
Minneapolis, MN, June 7, 2019 ©2019 Association for Computational Linguistics

The present shared task, cross-lingual morphological analysis, takes the second approach. Track 1 of the task that we participated in aims to analyze words in a 'surprise' language, given gold-standard analyses of words in languages in the same language family. The second track included some additional resources (see Zampieri et al. (2019) for further details about the task).

The present task is also strongly related to the series of SIGMORPHON (re)inflection tasks (Cotterell et al., 2017, 2018), where the emphasis is in generation of the inflected forms rather than producing an analysis. Another difference between the present task and the inflection tasks is also the level of ambiguity. In inflection tasks, especially in context, ambiguity level is rather low, making it less pressing to produce multiple results, while dealing with ambiguity is more important in morphological analysis.

We developed multiple systems for the task. Our main system was a neural encoder–decoder architecture, where we used a recurrent network as encoder and lemma decoder, but unlike many earlier examples, we do not consider POS tags and morphological features as part of the output sequence. Although they share the encoder, the tags are predicted by multi-layer feed-forward neural classifiers. The second, simpler method is a set of linear SVM classifiers. Besides describing both models, we report further experiments and analyses, including a comparison of the models, a detailed error analysis, and a set of experiments investigating the roles of individual source languages in transfer learning.

2   Models

2.1   Linear baseline

Recently, the dominating approaches to morphology learning tasks have been neural models, particularly recurrent neural networks. However, linear models provide surprisingly good performance in some tasks (e.g., Çöltekin and Rama, 2016, 2018), with the added advantage that they are computationally cheaper to train and tune, and often exhibit less variance than modern neural architectures. Although our submissions were recurrent encoder/decoder architectures, we also implemented a fully linear approach to solve the task.

Our linear model is a pipeline model with components for predicting lemma, POS, and morphological features separately. After having experimented with different orders, our final pipeline first predicts the lemma, then POS tags, and finally the morphological features. In all parts, we use (multi-class) linear SVM models.

Lemma prediction is a two-step process, using two separate classifiers. The first classifier predicts the stem, the prefix shared by both the word form and the lemma. Subsequently, the second classifier predicts the possibly null string to be added to the lemma. For example, for the word *uçağını* 'his/her/their airplane-ACC' (Crimean Tatar), whose lemma is *uçaq*, the first classifier segments the word form as *uça·ğını*, and the second classifier predicts the string '*q*' to be appended to the stem. The features for both classifiers are the overlapping character n-grams, before and after the segmentation point.

POS tag prediction is also based on a classifier with character n-gram features. The n-grams for the (predicted) lemma and the suffixes after the segmentation point are used as features for a multi-class linear classifier.

Morphological tag prediction is similar to the POS tag prediction. In the linear model reported here, we treat the whole feature string as class labels. We have also experimented with multiple classifiers per feature, and a standard multi-label approach predicting individual Feature=Value pairs. However, in our preliminary experiments the monolithic single classifier yielded better performance on the development sets. In addition, it also offers an easier way to obtain n-best predictions during decoding.

Decoding follows the above order for the complete analysis of a given word form. At each step, we use a threshold value to pick n-best results. All predictions with a distance from the decision boundary larger than the threshold is produced, and passed to the next predictor in the pipeline.

2.2   Recurrent encoder/decoder

Our neural model follows a similar pipeline approach, again, predicting lemma, POS tag and morphological features one by one. The overall architecture is presented in Figure 1. The order of components are different from the linear model.[2] Another notable difference from the linear model

---

[2]The choice is due to computational convenience. We did not investigate the effects of the order of components on the overall prediction performance.

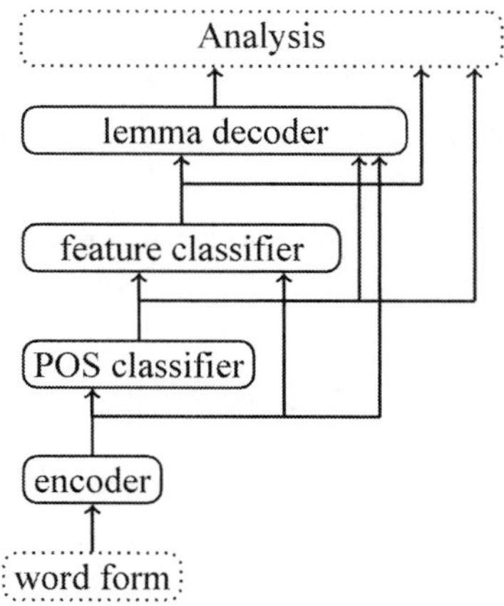

Figure 1: Overall architecture of the neural model.

is that the neural model shares some components during training, where components of the linear model are all trained/tuned individually.

The encoder is a bidirectional recurrent networks with gated-recurrent units (GRU, Cho et al., 2014) operating on input characters. Characters are passed through an embedding layer before being fed to the recurrent encoder. In this study, the embeddings are trained within the task, we do not use pre-trained character embeddings. We do not use intermediate representations of the input word either. Only the final representation, concatenation of forward and backward RNNs, is fed into the other parts of the network.

The POS classifier is a feed-forward component with two hidden layers with relu units followed by a softmax classifier.

The morphological feature classifier consists of multiple feed-forward networks for each morphological feature. Similar to the POS classifier we use two hidden layers with relu activation, followed by a softmax classifier for each morphological feature. The target values for each morphological feature are the feature values observed in the training data as well as a special 'not applicable' value. The morphological feature classifiers are trained jointly.

The lemma decoder is a recurrent decoder with GRU units. The initial symbol to the network is a special 'end of sequence symbol' and otherwise predictions of the previous time step are fed to the recurrent unit as input. The hidden state of the recurrent unit is initialized with the final output of the

encoder. Similar to the encoder, the characters are embedded as continuous vectors before being fed into the recurrent layer. The embedding layers of the encoder and the lemma decoder are not shared. The output of the encoder, along with the tag predictions are fed to a softmax classifier at each step, which outputs the characters of the lemma.

We train the model in multiple steps. First the model is trained to guess POS tags, then morphological features, and finally the lemmas. While training a model further in the pipeline we initialize the encoder (and embedding) weights with the weights from the previous step, but freeze the weights of the classifier(s) of the previous step(s).

During decoding, we follow the same order. For POS tags we predict all POS tags until the total probability assigned by the softmax classifier exceeds a particular threshold. During the lemma prediction, we predict a lemma whenever probability of end-of-sequence symbol reaches to a defined threshold. We do not predict multiple values for the morphological features.

3 Experimental setup

3.1 Data and preprocessing

The CMA task included data from two language families, Romance (ROA) and Turkic (TRK). Since we participate only on track 1, we only make use of morphological analyses released by the shared task organizers. The reader is referred to Zampieri et al. (2019) for detailed description of the data set. We give a brief description of the data set here.

The Turkic (TRK) data consisted of training samples from Bashkir (bak), Kazakh (kaz), Kyrgyz (kir), Tatar (tat) and Turkish (tur), Turkic development data came from Crimean Tatar (crh), and test data was from Karachay-Balkar (krc). The Romance (ROA) data consisted of training samples from Catalan (cat), French (fra), Italian (ita), Portuguese (por) and Spanish (spa). Romance development and test data were from Asturian (ast) and Sardinian (srd) respectively. The number of word forms along with the number of lemmas, tags (POS and morphological feature combinations) and analyses per word form for each language is presented in Table 2.

For both language families, the task involves predicting possibly multiple analyses consisting of a lemma, a POS tag, and a set of morphological feature–value pairs for each word form (examples

word form	lemma	POS	morphological features
desgaste	*desgaste* 'wear'	NOUN	`Gender=Masc|Number=Sing`
	desgastar 'to wear (out)'	VERB	`Mood=Sub|Number=Sing|Person=3|Tense=Pres|VerbForm=Fin`
karın	*kar* 'snow'	NOUN	`Case=Gen`
	kar 'snow'	NOUN	`Case=Nom|Number[psor]=Sing|Person[psor]=2`
	kar 'snow'	VERB	`Mood=Imp|Number=Plur|Person=2|Valency=2|VerbForm=Fin`
	karı 'wife'	NOUN	`Case=Nom|Number[psor]=Sing|Person[psor]=2`
	karın 'stomach'	NOUN	`Case=Nom`

Table 1: Examples taken from Spanish (ROA track) and Turkish (TRK track) training data for the morphological prediction task.

family	lcode	words	analysis	lemma	pos	tag
TRK	bak	9 999	1.46	1.10	1.08	1.38
	kaz	9 995	1.67	1.18	1.18	1.59
	kir	10 000	1.41	1.11	1.09	1.32
	tat	10 000	1.42	1.10	1.08	1.37
	tur	9 990	1.97	1.20	1.11	1.95
(dev)	crh	999	1.25	1.05	1.03	1.23
(test)	krc	8 768				
ROA	cat	10 000	1.44	1.15	1.28	1.43
	fra	9 986	1.67	1.15	1.29	1.66
	ita	9 998	1.55	1.21	1.35	1.54
	por	9 999	1.41	1.08	1.11	1.41
	spa	9 999	1.39	1.15	1.28	1.39
(dev)	ast	1 000	1.46	1.13	1.26	1.44
(test)	srd	9 998				

Table 2: Statistics on individual languages of CMA analysis data. The column 'words' is the number of word forms, the other columns indicate the ambiguity, e.g., 'pos' indicates number of part-of-speech tags per word form. 'analysis' indicate the full-analysis ambiguity, 'tag' indicates ambiguity of full morphological tag (combination of the POS and morphological features).

shown in Table 1). The POS tag set used for both languages consist of nouns, adjectives, adverbs, and verbs. The number of unique morphological feature–value combinations is 89 in the ROA training set, and 1 013 in the TRK training set.

3.1.1 Transliteration

The Turkic data set includes languages that use two different scripts. Turkish and Crimean Tatar uses the Latin script, while the other languages in this data set are written with the Cyrillic script. To our knowledge there are no standard way to transliterate between Turkic languages.[3] As a result, we

used a rather ad hoc transliteration that tries to keep similarly-sounding letters of Cyrillic used in the languages of the training set, and the version of the Latin script used in Turkish and Crimean Tatar.

3.2 Evaluation

Following the official evaluation script, we report precision, recall and F1-scores, for lemmas, tags (combination of POS tags and morphological features) and full analysis (combination of all) for each word form. In some experiments we also report separate scores for POS tags and morphological features. We compare our models against the competition baseline, which is a neural machine translation model (Silfverberg and Tyers, 2019).

3.3 Linear model

All classifiers in our linear models are linear SVM classifiers. For multi-class classifiers (all except the stemmer), we use one-vs-rest multi-class strategy. All models were implemented in scikit-learn Python library (Pedregosa et al., 2011) using liblinear back end (Fan et al., 2008).

We tuned each classifier separately using random search on the development set, where all languages in the training set were used without any weighting scheme. Tuning involved classifier regularization parameter, maximum n-gram order used as features and threshold parameter for each classifier that affect the number of predictions produced during decoding. The resulting parameter values are listed in Table 3. The threshold of 0.00 in Table 3 indicates a single prediction, which means the configuration chosen by our tuning procedure produces only a single-best analysis on the Turkic data set, and producing multiple predictions only for the POS tags on the Romance data.

---

[3]Standard/documented transliteration methods from Cyrillic to Latin script exists for most languages. However, these methods are often developed better readability of the resulting text in English, which often diverges from the version of Latin script used in the Turkic languages.

Classifier	parameter	Romance	Turkic
POS	C	0.08	0.70
	threshold	−0.50	0.00
	n-grams	5	9
Lemma	C (seg)	0.02	0.02
	C (suffix)	3.70	0.52
	seg. threshold	0.00	0.00
	n-grams	5	7
Features	C	0.70	4.80
	threshold	0.00	0.00
	n-grams	10	5

Table 3: Hyperparameter for the linear model determined with a random search through the parameter space. A threshold value of 0.00 means only a single prediction. Values for n-grams are the maximum n-gram order used as features.

3.4 Neural model

For the neural model, we fixed the model architecture after initial experimentation. We used an embedding size of 64. Both forward and backward GRU layers in the encoder learned 512-dimensional representations, resulting in 1 024 hidden units in the lemma decoder. We used a dropout of 0.50 before the encoder (after embeddings) and before each classifier. We tuned the models using random search for optimum threshold values, selecting the model that resulted in the best overall analysis F1-score on the development set. The best scores were obtained for both language families with a POS tag threshold of 0.70 and a lemma threshold of 0.50. The neural model was implemented with Tensorflow (Abadi et al., 2015) using Keras API (Chollet et al., 2015).

4 Results and discussion

4.1 Performance on test and dev sets

Official evaluation results of submitted (neural) system in comparison to the shared-task baseline provided by the organizers are presented in Table 4. The system obtained good results on the ROA test set (Sardinian) in comparison to the baseline and the other participants. It predicted the tags particularly well, which also lead to the best analysis score despite lower lemma scores. The results on the TRK test set (Karachay-Balkar) are below shared-task baseline which was the clear winner on this language family by surpassing the scores of the other participants as well.

family/model	Analysis	Lemma	Tag
ROA			
NN	23.67	31.36	61.33
Baseline	22.94	31.56	51.88
TRK			
NN	31.53	52.74	38.93
Baseline	39.79	54.94	44.56

Table 4: Official results obtained by our neural model in comparison to the shared-task baseline. The scores are F1-scores.

The scores of our submitted model, the linear baseline described in Section 2.1, and the baseline results as reported by the organizers are presented in Table 5 with some additional detail. Since our models were tuned to perform well on the development set without exploiting the similarities or differences between the training and the test languages, it is not surprising that the test set results are substantially lower than the scores we obtained on the development set. However, the result on Table 5 also offers a few interesting observations.

Our NN model obtains better scores than the competition baseline on both language families. In contrast to the test set, on the development set the difference on the Turkic data is more pronounced. Our model yields an analysis F1-score approximately 16 percentage points (pp.) higher than the baseline on the dev set, while this difference is approximately 8 pp. in favor of the baseline on the test set. A likely reason for the difference is the tuning procedure. An untuned model is likely to be more general, and hence may do better on a surprise language. Another potential reason for the difference can be related to the transliteration process (see Section 4.2 for further discussion).

In comparison to the neural model, the linear model performs worse on the ROA data set. However, it performs competitively on the TRK data set, even yielding better lemma predictions than the neural model. The linear pipeline predicts the lemmas first, while neural model also makes use of the earlier POS and feature predictions during predicting lemmas. Although propagation of the error may affect the lemma predictions of the neural model adversely, it also has more information.

The difference in performance between linear and neural models across language families may also be due to their morphological typol-

family	Analysis			Lemma			Tag			POS			Morphology		
model	P	R	F	P	R	F	P	R	F	P	R	F	P	R	F
ROA															
NN	41.14	45.12	43.04	60.07	60.82	60.44	60.61	65.62	63.01	87.58	79.70	83.45	66.56	73.78	69.99
Linear	32.99	42.54	37.16	53.00	60.00	56.29	49.38	62.84	55.30	63.05	70.34	66.50	61.86	75.33	67.94
Baseline	42.57	43.33	42.94	55.91	60.60	58.16	60.13	59.50	59.81	–	–	–	–	–	–
TRK															
NN	47.84	53.36	50.45	72.33	73.59	72.95	55.70	62.07	58.71	87.80	81.67	84.63	55.91	62.88	59.19
Linear	43.86	53.95	48.38	78.53	82.38	80.41	47.80	58.76	52.72	82.15	84.28	83.20	47.84	58.76	52.74
Baseline	31.24	38.44	34.47	56.30	59.06	57.65	38.52	47.35	42.48	–	–	–	–	–	–

Table 5: Detailed results on the development set in comparison to the our linear baseline (Linear) as well as the competition baseline (Baseline). Besides the F1 scores (F) we also present precision and recall. Last two groups, 'POS' and 'Morphology' columns are a breakdown of the 'Tag' scores to part of speech tags and morphological features, respectively.

ogy. Predicting agglutinating morphology of Turkic languages with linear models may be easier, due to more transparent mappings between the morph(eme)s and relevant tags. On the other hand, the more fusional nature of Romance languages may require combining multiple pieces of information (possibly non-linearly) for successful predictions.

4.2 Effect of source language

In transfer learning, a natural question to ask is how useful a particular source language, or combination of source languages can be for a given target language. To test the effects of the source language in analyzing a target language, we used all individual languages in the training set as source, and tested on all training and development languages for both families. Due to computational convenience, we performed these experiments using only the linear model. The results of this 'cross-training' experiments are presented in Figure 2. The presented scores are the overall best analysis F1-scores obtained after a random search through the space of hyperparameters listed in Table 3. The diagonal presents the results of tests on the training languages, hence, only useful for an approximate upper bound achievable by the model on the given language.

An interesting observation from Figure 2 is that while analyzing the Romance development data (Asturian), the score obtained using only Spanish (40.79) is better than the results we obtained using the complete training set (37.16). In Turkic languages, no single language is better than the overall score we obtained. However, using only Kazakh as training data gets close to what we

	test					
train	ast	cat	fra	ita	por	spa
cat	30.99	73.42	22.76	21.31	24.35	32.45
fra	15.91	20.72	69.61	17.10	14.24	15.23
ita	14.10	16.10	4.85	69.14	19.72	22.48
por	20.43	29.11	18.36	22.12	73.11	45.28
spa	40.79	32.99	21.17	22.59	44.57	78.68

train	crh	bak	kaz	kir	tat	tur
bak	28.19	75.47	34.60	26.13	48.82	19.28
kaz	44.10	39.29	67.67	38.07	40.02	25.94
kir	35.91	29.35	35.77	82.10	36.62	27.54
tat	31.45	38.56	28.10	24.78	78.02	20.60
tur	31.02	18.02	19.55	21.52	25.11	59.16

Figure 2: Analysis F1-scores for cross-training languages with another single language in the family: (top) Romance, (bottom) Turkic. All results are obtained using the linear model.

obtained using the complete training data set. It seems the choice of source language(s) is important, and more data, if not appropriate, may even hurt performance depending on the model setup. It is also worth noting that the usefulness of a language as a source language for another exhibits a fair level of asymmetry. Even though the performance matrices presented in Figure 2 (after removing the development set columns) are close to symmetric matrices, there are clear cases of asymmetry as well. For example, using Italian to train a morphological analyzer for French is less useful than using French to train a morphological analyzer for Italian.

Presumably due to distances within the family, French and Italian seem less useful than the other language in the Romance data set. On Turkic data set, the same seems to be true for Turkish. Excluding Crimean Tatar, Turkish is the least useful language for predicting others. This may also be part of the reason for the difference between the shared task baseline and our systems on the development and test set. Since the baseline system does not transliterate the source languages, it does not benefit from training languages except Turkish. On the other hand, while predicting analysis for the test language Karachay-Balkar, which is written in Cyrillic, the baseline system does not make use of data from Turkish. Not making use of a rather noisy part of the input may in fact be an advantage. Hence, our model outperforms the baseline on the development set by benefiting from all the data. However, for the test language, it gets mislead by a less useful source language that the baseline system simply ignores.

In general, however, the similarity of languages seem to help. The cross-testing results are better for similar languages in Figure 2 in comparison to less-similar ones. In fact, the average performance obtained using language pairs on Romance data correlates highly ($r = 0.83$) with linguistic similarities based on shared cognates (Dellert, 2017), indicating, as expected, usefulness of source languages more similar to the target language.

4.3 Error analysis

In this section, we look at the errors made by the systems on the development set more carefully. As well as reporting the rates of some of the quantifiable aspects of errors, we provide some qualitative analysis of the types of mistakes made by different models.

Most POS tag errors are confusions between POS tags NOUN and VERB, which may also be largely due to the fact these are also the most frequent POS classes in the data. Otherwise, for both families major confusions are either due to missing some of the ambiguous analyses, or, to a lesser extent, predicting additional (wrong) POS tags. We present confusion tables of POS tags sets of the neural model in Table 8 in Appendix. The tables also show that POS ambiguity is more common in Romance data set.

Given large number of morphological feature–value pairs, a similar analysis is not easy for the morphological features. We count true positive (TP) and false positive (FP) errors, i.e., number of instances of a feature–value pair in gold data miss-

Feature	FP rate	FN rate
Person[psor]	0.09	0.07
Number[psor]	0.14	0.11
Case	0.15	0.14
Number	0.28	0.03
Voice	0.38	0.20
Aspect	0.54	0.10
Tense	0.61	0.33
Valency	0.62	0.46
Mood	0.63	0.50
VerbForm	0.71	0.30
Person	0.76	0.19
Deriv	0.79	0.40
Missing	1.00	1.00
Polarity	1.00	0.00

Table 6: False positive (FP) and false negative (FN) error rates on feature–value pairs on Turkic development set. The rates are aggregated over the feature label.

Feature	FP rate	FN rate
Number	0.03	0.04
Gender	0.12	0.13
Aspect	0.22	0.14
VerbForm	0.24	0.29
Tense	0.39	0.31
Mood	0.48	0.26
Person	0.49	0.24
Possessive	1.00	0.00

Table 7: False positive (FP) and false negative (FN) error rates on feature–value pairs on Romance development set. The rates are aggregated over the feature label.

ing from the predictions and number of pairs that are predicted but not in the gold data. We present the rates aggregated by each feature label in Table 6 and 7, Turkic and Romance development sets respectively (more detailed versions, reporting error rates for each feature–value pair are presented in Table 10 and 9 in Appendix).

In both families, the nominal features seem to be easier to predict than verbal ones. Besides features that are difficult to interpret, e.g., Missing in Turkic data, very high error rates happen with features that are observed only a few times and those with ambiguity. For example, Possessive occurs only twice on Asturian data. To exemplify a case with ambiguity of the mapping between the surface strings and the features, we look at Crimean Tatar suffix -*me*/-*ma*, which is ambiguous between negative and infinitive markers. This ambiguity is the likely cause of complete failure of the model in predicting the `Polarity` features, as well as being responsible for some of the errors for `VerbForm=Vnoun`. We present further (mostly qualitative) error analyses on both development sets below.

ROA   Regarding the Asturian development data, both of our models lead to fewer overall predictions than the gold data contains: 1 133 for the linear model and 1 389 for the neural model compared to the 1 461 predictions in the development data, suggesting that our models are conservative when predicting POS tags. This is especially noticeable with the linear model, where 65 % of the POS tag predictions where for `NOUN`. The neural approach gives a similar distribution over POS tags as the gold standard, which suggests that neural models may be better at capturing the ambiguity inherent in morphological prediction.

Both cross-lingual models fail on examples of morphological paradigms that are not found in the training data. An example from Asturian is the formation of the past participles, where the infinitive ending (-*ar*, -*er*, -*ir*) is removed and replaced by the participle ending (-*áu*, -*íu*). Our linear model incorrectly predicts that these are nouns and predicts the same form as the lemma, while the neural model is better able to predict the POS tags, but cannot consistently predict the correct lemma, often choosing a similar lemma from Spanish.

When the POS prediction is correct, the average Levenshtein difference between the predicted and gold lemmas is respectable (0.46 for the linear model, 0.42 for the neural model).

TRK   Similar to the ROA development set, both our models make fewer predictions on average than the gold standard predictions provided for Crimean Tatar. As noted in Section 3 the (optimum) linear model makes only a single prediction for each of the 999 word forms. The linear model predicts more with 1 196 analyses in total, close to, but still less than 1 245 gold-standard analyses.

In Turkic development set, systematic errors in lemmatization involve missing multiple lemmas for a form where one of the lemmas is a derived form of another. For example, both models miss the alternative lemma *kiriş* 'to interfere' for the word *kirişti* 'interfered / entered (cooperatively)',

predicting only the simpler form *kir* 'to enter'. Common prediction errors also include segmenting words at common suffixes. *biznesi* 'his/her business' is lemmatized as *bizne*, as -*si* is a common allomorph of the third person singular possessive suffix across Turkic languages, while the loan-word *biznes* is probably an unlikely sequence of letters for a Turkic lemma despite a few occurrences in the training data. Another, possibly fixable, problem for the neural model is due to the letters that do not occur in the training set. For example, the Crimean Tatar data includes the letter *â* which is always predicted as another letter that is most probable in context.

As expected from the overall lemma prediction scores on the Turkic data, when the POS prediction is correct, the average edit difference between the predicted and gold lemmas are lower for the linear model (0.27) than the neural model (0.46).

5   Conclusions

We have presented our submission for the cross-lingual morphological prediction task, which achieved the best tag and analysis scores in the Romance track. We trained both linear and neural morphological analyzers in a pipeline fashion and demonstrated that these models can take advantage of labeled data in source languages to predict the morphological analysis in a similar target language.

While the results presented here are competitive with others obtained in this shared task, the analysis scores are admittedly low. However, there are multiple ways to improve the results as our models do not incorporate much in terms of cross-lingual signal. In the future, it would be worth integrating this cross-lingual signal in the form of pre-trained cross-lingual word embeddings (Artetxe et al., 2016; Lample et al., 2018) or sub-word, e.g., character, embeddings (Chaudhary et al., 2018; Sofroniev and Çöltekin, 2018), as this could lead to better generalization to new languages. Similarly, typological distance between source and target language often correlates with performance (Cotterell and Heigold, 2017), which could be exploited for weighting the contribution of source-language examples when learning a multilingual model.

Acknowledgments

Some of the experiments reported here were run on a Titan Xp donated by the NVIDIA Corporation.

References

Martín Abadi, Ashish Agarwal, Paul Barham, Eugene Brevdo, Zhifeng Chen, Craig Citro, Greg S. Corrado, Andy Davis, Jeffrey Dean, Matthieu Devin, Sanjay Ghemawat, Ian Goodfellow, Andrew Harp, Geoffrey Irving, Michael Isard, Yangqing Jia, Rafal Jozefowicz, Lukasz Kaiser, Manjunath Kudlur, Josh Levenberg, Dan Mané, Rajat Monga, Sherry Moore, Derek Murray, Chris Olah, Mike Schuster, Jonathon Shlens, Benoit Steiner, Ilya Sutskever, Kunal Talwar, Paul Tucker, Vincent Vanhoucke, Vijay Vasudevan, Fernanda Viégas, Oriol Vinyals, Pete Warden, Martin Wattenberg, Martin Wicke, Yuan Yu, and Xiaoqiang Zheng. 2015. TensorFlow: Large-scale machine learning on heterogeneous systems. Software available from tensorflow.org.

Kemal Altintas and Ilyas Cicekli. 2001. A morphological analyser for Crimean Tatar. In *Proceedings of the 10th Turkish Symposium on Artificial Intelligence and Neural Networks (TAINN'2001)*, pages 180–189.

Carme Armentano-Oller, Rafael C Carrasco, Antonio M Corbí-Bellot, Mikel L Forcada, Mireia Ginestí-Rosell, Sergio Ortiz-Rojas, Juan Antonio Pérez-Ortiz, Gema Ramírez-Sánchez, Felipe Sánchez-Martínez, and Miriam A Scalco. 2006. Open-source Portuguese–Spanish machine translation. In *International Workshop on Computational Processing of the Portuguese Language*, pages 50–59. Springer.

Mikel Artetxe, Gorka Labaka, and Eneko Agirre. 2016. Learning principled bilingual mappings of word embeddings while preserving monolingual invariance. In *Proceedings of the 2016 Conference on Empirical Methods in Natural Language Processing (EMNLP 2016)*, pages 2289–2294.

Jeremy Barnes, Roman Klinger, and Sabine Schulte im Walde. 2018. Bilingual sentiment embeddings: Joint projection of sentiment across languages. In *Proceedings of the 56th Annual Meeting of the Association for Comutational Linguistics (Volume 1: Long Papers)*, pages 2483–2493.

Çağrı Çöltekin. 2010. A freely available morphological analyzer for Turkish. In *Proceedings of the 7th International Conference on Language Resources and Evaluation (LREC 2010)*, pages 820–827.

Çağrı Çöltekin and Taraka Rama. 2016. Discriminating similar languages with linear SVMs and neural networks. In *Proceedings of the Third Workshop on NLP for Similar Languages, Varieties and Dialects (VarDial3)*, pages 15–24, Osaka, Japan.

Çağrı Çöltekin and Taraka Rama. 2018. Tübingen-Oslo at SemEval-2018 task 2: SVMs perform better than RNNs at emoji prediction. In *Proceedings of the 12th International Workshop on Semantic Evaluation (SemEval-2018)*, pages 34—38, New Orleans, LA, United States. Association for Computational Linguistics.

Aditi Chaudhary, Chunting Zhou, Lori Levin, Graham Neubig, David R. Mortensen, and Jaime Carbonell. 2018. Adapting word embeddings to new languages with morphological and phonological subword representations. In *Proceedings of the 2018 Conference on Empirical Methods in Natural Language Processing*, pages 3285–3295. Association for Computational Linguistics.

Kyunghyun Cho, Bart van Merrienboer, Caglar Gulcehre, Dzmitry Bahdanau, Fethi Bougares, Holger Schwenk, and Yoshua Bengio. 2014. Learning phrase representations using RNN encoder–decoder for statistical machine translation. In *Proceedings of the 2014 Conference on Empirical Methods in Natural Language Processing (EMNLP)*, pages 1724–1734. Association for Computational Linguistics.

François Chollet et al. 2015. Keras. `https://github.com/fchollet/keras`.

Ryan Cotterell and Georg Heigold. 2017. Cross-lingual character-level neural morphological tagging. In *Proceedings of the 2017 Conference on Empirical Methods in Natural Language Processing*, pages 748–759. Association for Computational Linguistics.

Ryan Cotterell, Christo Kirov, John Sylak-Glassman, Géraldine Walther, Ekaterina Vylomova, Arya D. McCarthy, Katharina Kann, Sebastian Mielke, Garrett Nicolai, Miikka Silfverberg, David Yarowsky, Jason Eisner, and Mans Hulden. 2018. The CoNLL–SIGMORPHON 2018 shared task: Universal morphological reinflection. In *Proceedings of the CoNLL SIGMORPHON 2018 Shared Task: Universal Morphological Reinflection*, pages 1–27. Association for Computational Linguistics.

Ryan Cotterell, Christo Kirov, John Sylak-Glassman, Géraldine Walther, Ekaterina Vylomova, Patrick Xia, Manaal Faruqui, Sandra Kübler, David Yarowsky, Jason Eisner, and Mans Hulden. 2017. CoNLL-SIGMORPHON 2017 shared task: Universal morphological reinflection in 52 languages. In *Proceedings of the CoNLL SIGMORPHON 2017 Shared Task: Universal Morphological Reinflection*, pages 1–30. Association for Computational Linguistics.

Johannes Dellert. 2017. *Information-Theoretic Causal Inference of Lexical Flow*. Ph.D. thesis, University of Tübingen.

Rong-En Fan, Kai-Wei Chang, Cho-Jui Hsieh, Xiang-Rui Wang, and Chih-Jen Lin. 2008. LIBLINEAR: A library for large linear classification. *Journal of Machine Learning Research*, 9:1871–1874.

Manaal Faruqui and Shankar. Kumar. 2015. Multilingual open relation extraction using cross-lingual projection. In *Proceedings of the 2016 Conference of the North American Chapter of the Association for Computational Linguistics: Human Language Technologies*, Proceedings of the 2018 Conference

161

of the North American Chapter of the Association for Computational Linguistics: Human Language Technologies, Volume 2 (Short Papers), pages 1351–1356.

Mikel L Forcada, Mireia Ginestí-Rosell, Jacob Nordfalk, Jim O'Regan, Sergio Ortiz-Rojas, Juan Antonio Pérez-Ortiz, Felipe Sánchez-Martínez, Gema Ramírez-Sánchez, and Francis M Tyers. 2011. Apertium: a free/open-source platform for rule-based machine translation. *Machine translation*, 25(2):127–144.

Harald Hammarström and Lars Borin. 2011. Unsupervised learning of morphology. *Computational Linguistics*, 37(2):309–350.

Melvin Johnson, Mike Schuster, Quoc V. Le, Maxim Krikun, Yonghui Wu, Zhifeng Chen, Nikhil Thorat, Fernanda Viégas, Martin Wattenberg, Greg Corrado, Macduff Hughes, and Jeffrey Dean. 2017. Google's multilingual neural machine translation system: Enabling zero-shot translation. *Transactions of the Association for Computational Linguistics*, 5:339–351.

Gulshat Kessikbayeva and Ilyas Cicekli. 2014. Rule based morphological analyzer of Kazakh language. In *Proceedings of the 2014 Joint Meeting of SIGMORPHON and SIGFSM*, pages 46–54.

Mikko Kurimo, Sami Virpioja, Ville Turunen, and Krista Lagus. 2010. Morpho Challenge competition 2005–2010: evaluations and results. In *Proceedings of the 11th Meeting of the ACL Special Interest Group on Computational Morphology and Phonology*, pages 87–95. Association for Computational Linguistics.

Guillaume Lample, Alexis Conneau, Marc'Aurelio Ranzato, Ludovic Denoyer, and Hervé Jégou. 2018. Word translation without parallel data. In *International Conference on Learning Representations*.

F. Pedregosa, G. Varoquaux, A. Gramfort, V. Michel, B. Thirion, O. Grisel, M. Blondel, P. Prettenhofer, R. Weiss, V. Dubourg, J. Vanderplas, A. Passos, D. Cournapeau, M. Brucher, M. Perrot, and E. Duchesnay. 2011. Scikit-learn: Machine learning in Python. *Journal of Machine Learning Research*, 12:2825–2830.

Miikka Silfverberg and Francis Tyers. 2019. Data-driven morphological analysis for Uralic languages. In *Proceedings of the Fifth International Workshop on Computational Linguistics for Uralic Languages*, pages 1–14. Association for Computational Linguistics.

Pavel Sofroniev and Çağrı Çöltekin. 2018. Phonetic vector representations for sound sequence alignment. In *Proceedings of the 15th SIGMORPHON Workshop on Computational Research in Phonetics, Phonology, and Morphology*, page (to appear).

Francis Tyers, Felipe Sánchez-Martínez, Sergio Ortiz-Rojas, and Mikel Forcada. 2010. Free/open-source resources in the Apertium platform for machine translation research and development. *The Prague Bulletin of Mathematical Linguistics*, 93:67–76.

Evelyne Tzoukermann and Mark Y Liberman. 1990. A finite-state morphological processor for Spanish. In *Proceedings of the 13th conference on Computational linguistics-Volume 3*, pages 277–282. Association for Computational Linguistics.

Jonathan Washington, Ilnar Salimzyanov, and Francis M Tyers. 2014. Finite-state morphological transducers for three Kypchak languages. In *LREC*, pages 3378–3385.

David Yarowsky, Grace Ngai, and Richard Wicentowski. 2001. Inducing multilingual text analysis tools via robust projection across aligned corpora. In *Proceedings of the first international conference on Human language technology research*, pages 1–8. Association for Computational Linguistics.

Marcos Zampieri, Shervin Malmasi, Yves Scherrer, Tanja Samardžić, Francis Tyers, Miikka Silfverberg, Nat alia Klyueva, Tung-Le Pan, Chu-Ren Huang, Radu Tudor Ionescu, Andrei Butnaru, and Tommi Jauhiainen. 2019. A Report on the Third VarDial Evaluation Campaign. In *Proceedings of the Sixth Workshop on NLP for Similar Languages, Varieties and Dialects (VarDial)*. Association for Computational Linguistics.

A   Appendix

	A	J	N	V	AN	JN	JV	NV	ANV	JAN	JNV
A	9	0	0	1	0	1	1	0	1	1	0
J	0	85	1	2	0	37	2	2	0	0	2
N	0	1	237	24	1	42	4	43	1	0	8
V	0	4	12	197	0	4	12	18	0	0	4
AN	0	0	0	0	0	0	0	0	0	1	0
JA	0	1	1	0	0	1	0	0	0	0	0
JN	0	14	14	2	0	102	3	3	0	0	2
JV	0	1	1	7	0	4	12	4	0	0	1
NV	0	1	13	3	0	0	0	31	0	0	0
JNV	0	0	2	3	0	4	1	7	0	0	4

	A	J	N	V	AN	JA	JN	JV	NV
A	0	0	2	1	1	0	0	0	0
J	0	8	18	2	0	0	13	0	5
N	0	2	662	15	1	1	15	0	24
V	0	3	51	116	1	0	4	3	25
AN	0	0	3	0	1	0	0	0	0
JA	0	0	1	0	0	0	0	0	0
JN	0	0	2	0	1	0	0	0	0
JV	0	1	0	2	0	0	0	0	0
NV	0	0	5	2	0	0	2	0	6

Table 8: Confusion matrix for Asturian (left) and Crimean Tatar (right) data sets for all POS combinations. The letters in the column and row labels are adverb (A) adjective (J), noun (N) and verb (V), where combination of letters indicate words that are assigned all indicated POS tags in the gold standard (rows) or predictions (columns). Columns and rows with all zeros were removed.

Feature=Value	FP	NP	FP rate	FN	NN	FN rate
VerbForm=Ger	0	22	0.00	0	22	0.00
VerbForm=Inf	0	48	0.00	4	52	0.08
Number=Plur	6	324	0.02	4	322	0.01
Number=Sing	22	619	0.04	27	624	0.04
Gender=Fem	28	326	0.09	28	326	0.09
Gender=Masc	44	363	0.12	53	372	0.14
Aspect=Perf	7	56	0.13	11	60	0.18
VerbForm=Fin	35	198	0.18	60	223	0.27
Gender=Masc,Fem	20	109	0.18	21	110	0.19
Person=3	41	161	0.25	22	142	0.15
Tense=Past	57	167	0.34	48	158	0.30
Mood=Ind	66	173	0.38	32	139	0.23
Aspect=Imp	11	27	0.41	0	16	0.00
Tense=Pres	50	108	0.46	26	84	0.31
Mood=Sub	24	50	0.48	15	41	0.37
Mood=Cnd	3	6	0.50	0	3	0.00
Number=Sing,Plur	2	4	0.50	4	6	0.67
Mood=Imp	19	36	0.53	8	25	0.32
VerbForm=Part	51	87	0.59	46	82	0.56
Person=1	23	39	0.59	2	18	0.11
Person=2	48	67	0.72	24	43	0.56
Possessive=Yes	2	2	1.00	0	0	0.00

Table 9: False positive (FP) and false negative (FN) error rates of the neural model on the Romance development set (Asturian). NP indicate number of instance of the feature-value pair in the gold data, NN indicate the total number of instances in the predictions.

Feature=Value	FP	NP	FP rate	FN	NN	FN rate
Case=Abl	0	50	0.00	31	81	0.38
Case=Gen	0	79	0.00	0	79	0.00
Case=Loc	0	82	0.00	3	85	0.04
Case=Acc	2	79	0.03	6	83	0.07
Person[psor]=3	17	356	0.05	25	364	0.07
Number=Plur	12	225	0.05	1	214	0.00
Number[psor]=Sing,Plur	32	356	0.09	23	347	0.07
Case=Nom	76	441	0.17	76	441	0.17
Case=Dat	20	106	0.19	5	91	0.05
Case=Sim	2	6	0.33	0	4	0.00
Voice=Pass	21	56	0.38	9	44	0.20
Valency=2	54	140	0.39	74	160	0.46
Tense=Past	38	79	0.48	3	44	0.07
Aspect=Imp	14	28	0.50	1	15	0.07
Aspect=Perf	37	68	0.54	4	35	0.11
VerbForm=Fin	67	119	0.56	20	72	0.28
VerbForm=Conv	49	80	0.61	3	34	0.09
Mood=Imp	10	14	0.71	4	8	0.50
Person=3	75	102	0.74	5	32	0.16
Number=Sing	81	107	0.76	7	33	0.21
Deriv=Coop	11	14	0.79	2	5	0.40
VerbForm=Vnoun	88	110	0.80	7	29	0.24
Tense=Aor	34	42	0.81	12	20	0.60
Person[psor]=1	15	18	0.83	0	3	0.00
VerbForm=Part	37	44	0.84	2	9	0.22
Person=2	14	16	0.88	2	4	0.50
Valency=1	87	95	0.92	5	13	0.38
Aspect=Prog	2	2	1.00	0	0	0.00
Case=Ins	29	29	1.00	1	1	1.00
Missing=ger_abst	21	21	1.00	1	1	1.00
Missing=ger_fut	3	3	1.00	0	0	0.00
Number[psor]=Plur	7	7	1.00	7	7	1.00
Number[psor]=Sing	13	13	1.00	12	12	1.00
Person=1	2	2	1.00	0	0	0.00
Person[psor]=2	2	2	1.00	2	2	1.00
Polarity=Neg	22	22	1.00	0	0	0.00
Tense=Fut	5	5	1.00	0	0	0.00

Table 10: False positive (FP) and false negative (FN) error rates of the neural model on the Turkic development set (Crimean Tatar). NP indicate number of instance of the feature-value pair in the gold data, NN indicate the total number of instances in the predictions.

Ensemble Methods to Distinguish Mainland and Taiwan Chinese

Hai Hu[*][†]   **Wen Li**[*][†]   **He Zhou**[*][†]   **Zuoyu Tian**[†]   **Yiwen Zhang**[†]   **Liang Zou**[‡]

Department of Linguistics, Indiana University[†]
Courant Institute of Mathematical Sciences, New York University[‡]
{huhai,wl9,hzh1,zuoytian,yiwezhan}@iu.edu, lz1904@nyu.edu

Abstract

This paper describes the IUCL system at VarDial 2019 evaluation campaign for the task of discriminating between Mainland and Taiwan variation of mandarin Chinese. We first build several base classifiers, including a Naive Bayes classifier with word n-gram as features, SVMs with both character and syntactic features, and neural networks with pre-trained character/word embeddings. Then we adopt ensemble methods to combine output from base classifiers to make final predictions. Our ensemble models achieve the highest F1 score (0.893) in simplified Chinese track and the second highest (0.901) in traditional Chinese track. Our results demonstrate the effectiveness and robustness of the ensemble method.

1 Introduction

Like many other languages in the world, Mandarin has several varieties among different speaking communities, mainland China, Taiwan, Malaysia, Indonesia, etc. Previous research on these varieties are mainly focused on language differences and integration (Yan-bin, 2012). Discriminating between the Mainland and Taiwan variations of Mandarin Chinese (DMT) is one of the shared tasks at VarDial evaluation campaign 2019, aiming to determine if a given sentence is taken from news articles from Mainland China or Taiwan (Zampieri et al., 2019). This task not only serves as a platform to test various models, but also encourages linguists to rethink the different linguistic features among those varieties.

This paper describes the IUCL (Indiana University Computational Linguistics) systems and submissions at VarDial 2019. We first build several base classifiers: a Naive Bayes classifier with word n-gram as features, Support Vector Machines (SVM) using both character and syntactic features,

and neural networks such as LSTM and BERT. We then build ensemble models by using the maximum probability among all base classifiers, or choosing the class with maximum average probability, or training another SVM on top of the output of base classifiers. We apply the three ensemble models for both the simplified Chinese track and the traditional Chinese track, which also correspond to our three submissions on both tracks. As shown in the official evaluation results, our SVM ensemble is ranked the first place on the simplified Chinese test data with a macro-averaged F1 score of 0.893, and our ensemble model using maximum probability from base classifiers ranked second on the traditional Chinese test data with a macro-averaged F1 score of 0.901.

In this paper, we will briefly review related work in Section 2, describe our single classifiers and three ensemble methods in Section 3, and finally present and discuss our results in Section 4, with a conclusion in Section 5.

2 Related Work

Discriminating between similar languages (DSL) is one of the main challenges faced by language identification systems (Zampieri et al., 2017, 2015). Since 2014, the DSL shared task provided a platform for researchers to evaluate language identification methods with standard dataset and evaluation methodology. Previous shared tasks on DSL have differentiated a wide range of languages, including similar languages, such as Bosnian, Croatian and Serbian, and one language spoken in different language societies, such as Brazilian vs. European Portuguese. In these shared tasks, SVMs are probably the most widely used classifier, while logistic regression and naive Bayes also performed well. More recently, Convolutional Neural Networks and Recurrent Neural Networks are also

---

[*]Equal contribution

165

Proceedings of VarDial, pages 165–171
Minneapolis, MN, June 7, 2019 ©2019 Association for Computational Linguistics

implemented with byte-level, character-level or word-level embeddings. Regarding features in this task, character and word n-grams are most frequently used (Zampieri et al., 2015; Malmasi et al., 2016; Zampieri et al., 2017, 2018). Besides, ensemble methods are also used widely in DSL to improve results beyond those of the individual base classifiers, for example, majority voting between a classifier trained with different features, majority voting to combine several classifiers, polarity voting with SVMs, etc. (Jauhiainen et al., 2018).

Like many languages studied in the literature of DSL, Mandarin Chinese also has several varieties among its speaking communities. Previous work on this was done by proposing a top-bag-of-word similarity measures for classifying texts from different variants of the same language (Huang and Lee, 2008). A top-bag-of-word, similarity-based contrastive approach was adopted to solve the text source classification problem. That is, the classification process adopted similar heuristics to generate determined intervals between classes. Then a contrastive elimination algorithm is used that simple majority voting mechanism is employed for determining the final classification results. LDC's Chinese Gigaword Corpus (Huang, 2009) was used as the comparable corpora, which is composed of three varieties of Chinese from Mainland China, Singapore, and Taiwan. Experimentation shows that the contrastive approach using similarity to determine the classes is a reliable and robust tool.

3 Methodology and Data

3.1 Base Classifiers

In this section, we describe each of the classifiers that are included in our final ensemble model.

3.1.1 Naive Bayes Classifier (NB)

Naive Bayes is a simple yet effective probabilistic model that works quite well on various text classification tasks, including sentiment analysis (Narayanan et al., 2013), spam detection (Kim et al., 2006), email classification, and authorship attribution. It has two simplifying assumptions: bag-of-words assumption and conditional independence assumption (Jurafsky and Martin, 2014).

This task can be considered as a binary text classification problem, since an instance is labelled with either M or T. A sentence is treated as a sequence of words, and it is assumed that each word is generated independent of each other. Here we construct features with word unigram, bigram, and trigram, and train a Bernoulli Naive Bayes classifier. Since we have finite number of words, i.e., 18,769 sentences in training set, the classifier is likely to encounter unseen words in development set, therefore smoothing is needed. We iterate the additive smoothing parameter α in range between 0 and 1 for 100 times on training data of both simplified Chinese and traditional Chinese, finding the best α value 0.42 for simplified Chinese and 0.51 for traditional Chinese.

3.1.2 Classifier with Syntactic Features (SYN)

Syntactic features have been shown to be helpful in various text classification tasks, e.g. authorship attribution (Baayen et al., 1996; Gamon, 2004), native language identification (Bykh and Meurers, 2014), and detecting translationese (Hu et al., 2018).

For this task, we employ two types of syntactic features. The first is context-free grammar rules that are not terminal rules. The second is dependency triples (`John_ate_nsubj`). We use the linear SVM classifier from scikit-learn (Pedregosa et al., 2011). The syntactic features are obtained using Stanford CoreNLP with their default models (Manning et al., 2014).

3.1.3 Sequential Model Classifier (SEQ)

We create a classifier based on the multi-layer neutral network model using Keras (Chollet et al., 2015).

First, we prepare the data using bag-of-words model to generate vectors from texts. We create a vocabulary of all the unique words in the test sentences and create a feature vector representing the count of each word. Then we preprocess the data by padding sentences into the same input length of 50.

We build a sequential model including a linear stack of layers. The first layer takes an integer matrix of the size of the vocabulary and shapes the output embedding as 16. The second layer is a global average pooling layer which returns a fixed-length output vector for each example by averaging over the sequence dimension. Then the output vector is piped through a dense layer with 16 hidden units. This model uses the Rectifier activation function, which has been proven to generate good results. The last layer is a dense layer with a single output node using sigmoid activation function. Each value is transformed to a float between 0 and 1, representing probability.

To update weights and find the best parameters in the model, we configure the learning process using the Adam optimizer and the binary cross entropy loss function, which are commonly used for binary classification tasks. Then we train the model by running the iteration for 40 epochs with a batch size of 512.

We use the development set to evaluate the model and make predictions on the test data.

3.1.4 Word-Level Long Short-Term Memory (LSTM)

Long short-term memory is an efficient, gradient-based model (Hochreiter and Schmidhuber, 1997), which is widely used in NLP tasks. We choose as features the most frequent 5000 words in combined training and development data. We transform sentences with one-hot encoder, followed by a 128-dimension embedding layer as well as 64 hidden layers. The batch size and input length are both 32, and we train the model with 7 epochs. To avoid overfitting, we set the dropout rate equal to 0.5.

3.1.5 Classifier with Pretrained Chinese Word Embeddings (EMB)

Word embeddings are dense vector representations of words (Collobert and Weston, 2008; Mikolov et al., 2013). Compared with bag-of-word features, word embeddings are better at capturing semantic and syntactic information in the context. In this task, we choose 300-dimension skip-gram with negative sampling word embeddings trained on People's Daily Newspaper (Li et al., 2018).

The pre-trained embeddings are chosen for the following reasons. First, the training data may not be large enough for building robust word embedding, since subtle semantic relations and infrequent phrases could be overlooked due to the limited data size. The pre-trained embeddings are trained on news over 70 years with 668 million tokens in total, covering the majority of words used in the news genre. Second, the language of People's Daily is quite similar to the Mainland Mandarin data in this task, which also comes from a Chinese official news agency.

We initialise the weights of the projection layer with this 300-dimension pre-trained word embeddings, and keep this layer frozen during the following fine-tuning. Then we feed the output sequentially into a convolutional layer, a max pooling layer and LSTM layer. Finally, two dense layers with sigmoid activation are used.

3.1.6 Bidirectional Encoder Representations from Transformers (BERT)

Bidirectional Encoder Representations from Transformers (Devlin et al., 2018) have shown state-of-art performance in many NLP tasks. The pre-trained model supports multiple languages, and we adapt the Chinese model for classification in this task. Since the model tends to overfit on small dataset, during fine tuning we experiment with 1-3 training epochs. We set the maximum sequence length to be 32, since most of the sentences in training and development data have no more than 32 words. We train the model with two epochs for official submission, since it performs the best when evaluating on development data.

3.2 Ensemble Classifiers

Ensemble models have been widely adopted in various text classification tasks and machine learning applications (e.g., Liu et al., 2016). Ensemble learning can combine weak learners into a strong learner to improve the performance, and it also helps to reduce the variance of models prone to overfitting.

Each classifier outputs the probabilities for the input sentence to be of class M and T. These probabilities are then passed on to an ensemble model which makes the final decision. We experiment with three ensemble models.

MaxProb The MaxProb ensemble simply looks at the max probability of an input sentence. That is, the classifier that is most confident of its decision will have the final say.

MaxMeanProb The MaxMeanProb ensemble computes the average probability for the two classes (M, T) across all classifiers and returns the label with higher average probability.

SVM Classifier stacking is often used in ensemble learning to integrate different models to produce the final output (e.g., Li and Zou, 2017). We concatenate the probabilities produced by base classifiers and feed them into SVM to get the final label.

3.3 Data

The training, development and test data all come from two sources: Chen et al. (1996) for news text in traditional Chinese and McEnery and Xiao (2003) for simplified Chinese. There are 18,769 sentences for training, 2,000 sentences for development, and 2,000 sentences for test. The datasets are balanced across two classes.

4 Results and Discussion

We report the results of each base classifier and the ensemble models on both the development set and the test set.

4.1 Results on Dev Set

The results for development set are presented in Table 1. Most of the base classifiers achieve an F-measure between 0.87 and 0.90. In particular, a word n-gram Naive Bayes (NB) model can reach 0.88 F-score. Using syntactic features (SYN) produces slightly worse results, likely due to the sentence-based nature of the task. That is, the syntactic features are very sparse, unlike in related tasks where the classification is on the document level (Bykh and Meurers, 2014; Hu et al., 2018). Models based on word level neural networks (LSTM and SEQ) have similar results, while adding pre-trained word embeddings improves the results (EMB). BERT with pre-trained character embeddings gives comparable results as EMB.

The best results are achieved using our ensemble models described in section 3.2. They are able to improve the F score by 0.01-0.02 over the best preforming base classifier, illustrating the robustness of ensemble models.

4.2 Results on Test Set

For the campaign, we submit the predictions of the three ensemble models. The results are presented in Table 2. The MaxProb and SVM ensemble models have similar performance, with an accuracy around 0.92. Our system is ranked as the first place for the simplified Chinese track and second place for the traditional Chinese track.

The confusion matrix of our best performing models are shown in Figure 1 and Figure 2. There seems to be a bias of predicting Taiwan sentences as Mainland sentences, the reason for which calls for further exploration.

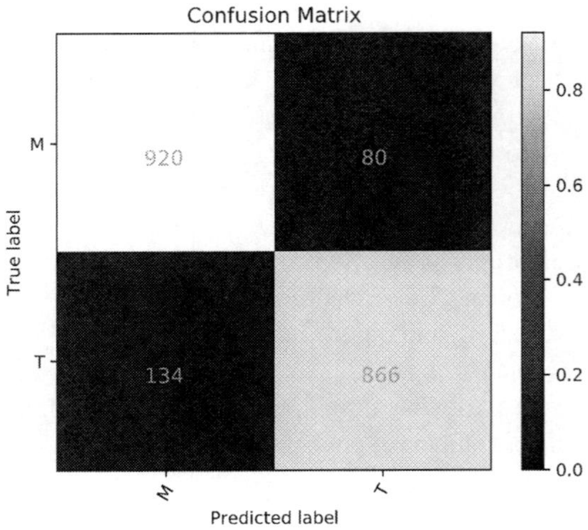

Figure 1: Sub-task DMT-simplified, Ensemble SVM

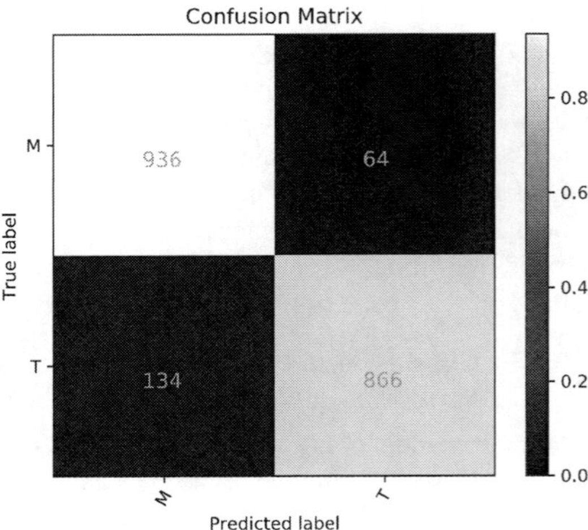

Figure 2: Sub-task DMT-traditional, Ensemble Max-Prob

4.3 Prominent Features in Mainland and Taiwan Text

Now we examine word unigram features of the classes more closely. Using Information Gain described in Liu et al. (2016), we rank all the word unigram features. The top 20 features are shown in Table 3. First we notice proper nouns that are understandably distinctive, e.g., the word "Taiwan" appears more frequent in Taiwan news, while "Shenzhen"–a city in Mainland China–shows up only in Mainland news. Some other words have to do with the political system in Mainland, e.g., "comrade" and "socialism" occur only in Mainland news.

	BERT	LSTM	SEQ	EMB	NB	SYN	Ensemble MaxProb	Ensemble MaxMeanProb	Ensemble SVM
Simp.	**0.900**	0.874	0.878	0.893	0.881	0.854	0.917	0.910	0.921
Trad.	0.905	0.879	0.891	**0.907**	0.888	0.884	0.924	0.920	0.934

Table 1: Macro-averaged F score on **development** set for simplified and traditional Chinese. BERT: classifier using BERT pre-trained Chinese model. LSTM: word-level LSTM. SEQ: word-level sequential model classifier. EMB: neural network using pre-trained Chinese word embeddings. NB: word-level Naive-Bayes model. SYN: SVM with syntactic features.

System	Simplified	Traditional
Ensemble MaxProb	0.892	**0.901**
Ensemble MaxMeanProb	0.872	0.878
Ensemble SVM	**0.893**	0.899

Table 2: Macro-averaged F score on test set for simplified and traditional Chinese using ensemble models.

rank	ig_value	word	translation	freq Mainland	freq Taiwan
1	0.00237293	一个	one	290	0
2	0.00122218	学生	student	28	234
3	0.00118379	经济	economy	254	29
4	0.00094773	这个	this	116	0
5	0.00092902	台湾	Taiwan	19	172
6	0.00090684	全国	whole country	111	0
7	0.00079236	同志	comrade	97	0
8	0.0006871	网路	internet	0	77
9	0.00065798	我们	we	325	104
10	0.00061201	就是	be	82	1
11	0.00060674	资讯	information	0	68
12	0.00060137	改革	reform	102	6
13	0.00059619	深圳	Shenzhen (city)	73	0
14	0.00059442	使用	use	11	107
15	0.00058054	人们	people	106	8
16	0.00057632	记者	journalists	142	21
17	0.00054397	企业	enterprises	232	66
18	0.00053899	社会主义	socialism	66	0
19	0.00052829	人民	masses	127	18
20	0.00052387	为了	in order to	71	1

Table 3: Top 20 features selected by information gain

However, the top ranking feature 一个 (one) appears to be a segmentation error. It turns out that it is segmented as two words in Taiwan news, i.e., 一|个, but it is one word in Mainland news. In fact, it appears 143 times in the Taiwan training data (still half the frequency of Mainland news). The same goes for 这个 (this) and 全国 (whole country), which is segmented as two words in Taiwan news, but one in Mainland news.

Perhaps the only interesting lexical variations between Mainland and Taiwan in the top 20 features are 网路 (internet) and 资讯 (information), which are immediately recognized by the authors as Taiwan Mandarin. In Mainland China, they would be 网络 (internet) and 信息 (information).

5 Conclusion

In this paper we have described the IUCL ensemble models that distinguish Mainland and Taiwan Mandarin Chinese. We show that neural networks using pre-trained character/word embeddings outperform traditional *n*-gram models, and ensemble models can further improve the results over base classifiers. Although neural networks produce strong empirical results, traditional classifiers like SVM still play an important role when we need to investigate the importance of different features.

6 Acknowledgement

He Zhou and Hai Hu are funded by China Scholarship Council.

References

Harald Baayen, Hans Van Halteren, and Fiona Tweedie. 1996. Outside the cave of shadows: Using syntactic annotation to enhance authorship attribution. *Literary and Linguistic Computing*, 11(3):121–132.

Serhiy Bykh and Detmar Meurers. 2014. Exploring syntactic features for native language identification: A variationist perspective on feature encoding and ensemble optimization. In *Proceedings of COLING 2014, the 25th International Conference on Computational Linguistics: Technical Papers*, pages 1962–1973.

Keh-Jiann Chen, Chu-Ren Huang, Li-Ping Chang, and Hui-Li Hsu. 1996. SINICA CORPUS : Design Methodology for Balanced Corpora. In *Language, Information and Computation : Selected Papers from the 11th Pacific Asia Conference on Language, Information and Computation : 20-22 December 1996, Seoul*, pages 167–176, Seoul, Korea. Kyung Hee University.

François Chollet et al. 2015. Keras. https://keras.io.

Ronan Collobert and Jason Weston. 2008. A unified architecture for natural language processing: Deep neural networks with multitask learning. In *Proceedings of the 25th international conference on Machine learning*, pages 160–167. ACM.

Jacob Devlin, Ming-Wei Chang, Kenton Lee, and Kristina Toutanova. 2018. Bert: Pre-training of deep bidirectional transformers for language understanding. *arXiv preprint arXiv:1810.04805*.

Michael Gamon. 2004. Linguistic correlates of style: authorship classification with deep linguistic analysis features. In *Proceedings of the 20th international conference on Computational Linguistics*, page 611. Association for Computational Linguistics.

Sepp Hochreiter and Jürgen Schmidhuber. 1997. Long short-term memory. *Neural computation*, 9(8):1735–1780.

Hai Hu, Wen Li, and Sandra Kübler. 2018. Detecting syntactic features of translated chinese. In *Proceedings of the Second Workshop on Stylistic Variation*, pages 20–28.

Chu-Ren Huang. 2009. Tagged chinese gigaword version 2.0, ldc2009t14. *Linguistic Data Consortium*.

Chu-Ren Huang and Lung-Hao Lee. 2008. Contrastive approach towards text source classification based on top-bag-of-word similarity. In *Proceedings of the 22nd Pacific Asia Conference on Language, Information and Computation*.

Tommi Jauhiainen, Marco Lui, Marcos Zampieri, Timothy Baldwin, and Krister Lindén. 2018. Automatic language identification in texts: A survey. *arXiv preprint arXiv:1804.08186*.

Dan Jurafsky and James H Martin. 2014. *Speech and language processing*, volume 3. Pearson London.

Sang-Bum Kim, Kyoung-Soo Han, Hae-Chang Rim, and Sung Hyon Myaeng. 2006. Some effective techniques for naive bayes text classification. *IEEE transactions on knowledge and data engineering*, 18(11):1457–1466.

Shen Li, Zhe Zhao, Renfen Hu, Wensi Li, Tao Liu, and Xiaoyong Du. 2018. Analogical reasoning on chinese morphological and semantic relations. In *Proceedings of the 56th Annual Meeting of the Association for Computational Linguistics (Volume 2: Short Papers)*, pages 138–143. Association for Computational Linguistics.

Wen Li and Liang Zou. 2017. Classifier stacking for native language identification. In *Proceedings of the 12th Workshop on Innovative Use of NLP for Building Educational Applications*, pages 390–397.

Can Liu, Wen Li, Bradford Demarest, Yue Chen, Sara Couture, Daniel Dakota, Nikita Haduong, Noah Kaufman, Andrew Lamont, Manan Pancholi, et al. 2016. Iucl at semeval-2016 task 6: An ensemble model for stance detection in twitter. In *Proceedings of the 10th International Workshop on Semantic Evaluation (SemEval-2016)*, pages 394–400.

Shervin Malmasi, Marcos Zampieri, Nikola Ljubešić, Preslav Nakov, Ahmed Ali, and Jörg Tiedemann. 2016. Discriminating between similar languages and arabic dialect identification: A report on the third dsl shared task. In *Proceedings of the 3rd Workshop on Language Technology for Closely Related Languages, Varieties and Dialects (VarDial)*, Osaka, Japan.

Christopher Manning, Mihai Surdeanu, John Bauer, Jenny Finkel, Steven Bethard, and David McClosky. 2014. The stanford corenlp natural language processing toolkit. In *Proceedings of 52nd annual meeting of the association for computational linguistics: system demonstrations*, pages 55–60.

A. M. McEnery and R. Z. Xiao. 2003. The lancaster corpus of mandarin chinese.

Tomas Mikolov, Ilya Sutskever, Kai Chen, Greg S Corrado, and Jeff Dean. 2013. Distributed representations of words and phrases and their compositionality. In *Advances in neural information processing systems*, pages 3111–3119.

Vivek Narayanan, Ishan Arora, and Arjun Bhatia. 2013. Fast and accurate sentiment classification using an enhanced naive bayes model. In *International Conference on Intelligent Data Engineering and Automated Learning*, pages 194–201. Springer.

F. Pedregosa, G. Varoquaux, A. Gramfort, V. Michel, B. Thirion, O. Grisel, M. Blondel, P. Prettenhofer, R. Weiss, V. Dubourg, J. Vanderplas, A. Passos, D. Cournapeau, M. Brucher, M. Perrot, and E. Duchesnay. 2011. Scikit-learn: Machine learning in Python. *Journal of Machine Learning Research*, 12:2825–2830.

DIAO Yan-bin. 2012. The situation and thinking about the comparative study of language in the four places across the taiwan strait [j]. *Chinese Language Learning*, 3.

Marcos Zampieri, Shervin Malmasi, Nikola Ljubešić, Preslav Nakov, Ahmed Ali, Jörg Tiedemann, Yves Scherrer, and Noëmi Aepli. 2017. Findings of the VarDial Evaluation Campaign 2017. In *Proceedings of the Fourth Workshop on NLP for Similar Languages, Varieties and Dialects (VarDial)*, Valencia, Spain.

Marcos Zampieri, Shervin Malmasi, Preslav Nakov, Ahmed Ali, Suwon Shuon, James Glass, Yves Scherrer, Tanja Samardžić, Nikola Ljubešić, Jörg Tiedemann, Chris van der Lee, Stefan Grondelaers, Nelleke Oostdijk, Antal van den Bosch, Ritesh Kumar, Bornini Lahiri, and Mayank Jain. 2018. Language Identification and Morphosyntactic Tagging: The Second VarDial Evaluation Campaign. In *Proceedings of the Fifth Workshop on NLP for Similar Languages, Varieties and Dialects (VarDial)*, Santa Fe, USA.

Marcos Zampieri, Shervin Malmasi, Yves Scherrer, Tanja Samardžić, Francis Tyers, Miikka Silfverberg, Natalia Klyueva, Tung-Le Pan, Chu-Ren Huang, Radu Tudor Ionescu, Andrei Butnaru, and Tommi Jauhiainen. 2019. A Report on the Third VarDial Evaluation Campaign. In *Proceedings of the Sixth Workshop on NLP for Similar Languages, Varieties and Dialects (VarDial)*. Association for Computational Linguistics.

Marcos Zampieri, Liling Tan, Nikola Ljubešić, Jörg Tiedemann, and Preslav Nakov. 2015. Overview of the dsl shared task 2015. In *Proceedings of the Joint Workshop on Language Technology for Closely Related Languages, Varieties and Dialects (LT4VarDial)*, pages 1–9, Hissar, Bulgaria.

SC-UPB at the VarDial 2019 Evaluation Campaign: Moldavian vs. Romanian Cross-Dialect Topic Identification

Cristian Onose, Dumitru-Clementin Cercel and **Stefan Trausan-Matu**

Faculty of Automatic Control and Computers

University Politehnica of Bucharest, Romania

{onose.cristian, clementin.cercel}@gmail.com, stefan.trausan@cs.pub.ro

Abstract

This paper describes our models for the Moldavian vs. Romanian Cross-Topic Identification (MRC) evaluation campaign, part of the VarDial 2019 workshop. We focus on the three subtasks for MRC: binary classification between the Moldavian (MD) and the Romanian (RO) dialects and two cross-dialect multiclass classification between six news topics, MD to RO and RO to MD. We propose several deep learning models based on long short-term memory cells, Bidirectional Gated Recurrent Unit (BiGRU) and Hierarchical Attention Networks (HAN). We also employ three word embedding models to represent the text as a low dimensional vector. Our official submission includes two runs of the BiGRU and HAN models for each of the three subtasks. The best submitted model obtained the following macro-averaged F_1 scores: 0.708 for subtask 1, 0.481 for subtask 2 and 0.480 for the last one. Due to a read error caused by the quoting behaviour over the test file, our final submissions contained a smaller number of items than expected. More than 50% of the submission files were corrupted. Thus, we also present the results obtained with the corrected labels for which the HAN model achieves the following results: 0.930 for subtask 1, 0.590 for subtask 2 and 0.687 for the third one.

1 Introduction

The task of discriminating between two dialects or different languages is a popular research topic which has attracted a lot of interest from the research community. Specifically, the VarDial competition proposed in recent years a number of shared tasks on different languages such as dialect identification for Arabic or German, Indo-Aryan language identification, distinguish between Mainland and Taiwan Mandarin or discriminating between Dutch and Flemish (Zampieri

et al., 2017, 2018). This year (Zampieri et al., 2019), the problem of discriminating between Romanian and Moldavian dialects was introduced as a series of three subtasks. It involves the processing of the MOROCO dataset (Butnaru and Ionescu, 2019) to construct several language classification models. The dataset contains text samples from online news outlets in the Romanian (RO) language or the Moldavian (MD) dialect. All the subtasks are closed, meaning that the use of external datasets is not allowed. Additionally, internal data, available for the MRC subtasks, must not be used between tasks. Thus, the first subtask is a binary classification between the two dialects. The second subtask involves a cross-dialect multi-class classification between six topics. More precisely, the classifier is trained using Moldavian dialect in order to classify samples from the Romanian dialect. The third subtask is similar to the second one, here the use of the dialects is reversed.

Generally, such tasks are approached using traditional machine learning algorithms, which unfortunately require handcrafted features. Recently, deep learning methods, where features are learned from the data, have been proposed (Ali, 2018). To address the MRC shared task, we propose the use of three state of the art deep learning architectures for text classification: Long Short-Term Memory cells (LSTM) (Hochreiter and Schmidhuber, 1997), Bidirectional Gated Recurrent Unit (BiGRU) (Graves and Schmidhuber, 2005) and Hierarchical Attention Networks (HAN) (Yang et al., 2016). The submission results are based only on BiGRU and HAN models for each of the three subtasks. After the competition deadline an error, caused by the quoting behaviour over the test file, was discovered. As a result our final submissions contained a smaller number of labels than expected, with approximately 50% of the files being corrupted. Thus, we present both the official

Proceedings of VarDial, pages 172–177

Minneapolis, MN, June 7, 2019 ©2019 Association for Computational Linguistics

Subtask	Training	Validation	Test
1	21719	11845	5923
2	9968	5435	5923
3	11751	6410	5923

Table 1: Dataset sample distribution between training, validation and test for each of the three subtasks.

submissions as well as later work, that includes the correction of this problem.

The study of Romanian dialects was first approached by Ciobanu and Dinu (2016). They construct binary classifiers to distinguish between Romanian and three dialects (Macedo-Romanian, Megleno-Romanian and Istro-Romanian) by exploring information provided by a set of 108 word pairs. Consequently, Butnaru and Ionescu (2019) proposed a first Moldavian and Romanian Dialectal Corpus (MOROCO) assembled from multiple news websites. On top of this dataset they construct several deep learning models for dialect identification: Character level Convolutional Neural Network (CharCNN) and an improvement CNN model using squeeze and excitation blocks (Hu et al., 2018). Additionally, they also investigate shallow string kernel methods (Ionescu et al., 2016). They conclude that string kernels achieve best performance among the studied methods.

The remainder of this paper is organized as follows. In Section 2 we briefly discuss the dataset for the three tasks. Section 3 describes the methodology behind our solution, while the experimental setup and the results are presented in Section 4. Finally, Section 5 contains details regarding our conclusions.

2 Dataset

The MOROCO dataset contains Moldavian and Romanian samples collected from one of the following news categories: culture, finance, politics, science, sports and technology. It is divided between training, validation and test for each of the three tasks as described in Table 1. The test set is combined for all the subtasks such that the labels for the first task can not be inferred. This is necessary because the second and the third subtasks are based entirely on just one of the dialects.

The data samples are provided preprocessed by replacing named entities, which could act as biases for the classifiers, with a special identifier: NE. For instance, city names or important public figures from both countries, Romania or the Republic of Moldova, are anonymized.

Besides the default processing, we also took extra steps to clean up the dataset. Text usually contains expressions which carry little to no meaning, thus, we choose to remove the following: stop words, special characters and punctuation marks all except end of sentence. Additionally, we remove the named entity identifier as they interfere with the text representations. Another important aspect is given by how we deal with the diacritics. During our experiments we analyze their impact on the performance.

3 Deep learning models

In recent years, with the increasing availability of computational resources, deep neural networks became successful for classification and regression problems (LeCun et al., 2015). At first, simple feedforward networks were used. These networks lack loops or cycles and the information moves only forward, from the input to the output nodes. The switch to other types of representations, namely Recurrent Neural Networks (RNNs), was made because of the need to map input and output nodes of varying types and sizes.

Recurrent neural networks. RNNs are neural networks that form connections between nodes along a sequence. This allows the network to exhibit internal memory with respect to the inputs which in turn enables the prediction of future steps. Due to this memory, RNNs are the preferred method for processing sequential data such as time series, text or video. Unfortunately, RNNs can suffer from training instability, exploding and vanishing gradients.

Long short-term memory. Long Short-Term Memory (LSTM) units, introduced by Hochreiter and Schmidhuber (1997), are used in recurrent neural networks as a way to prevent vanishing or exploding gradients. The units allow the errors to flow backwards through endless virtual layers which are unfolded in space. Besides the usual input and output gates, LSTM units are augmented by recurrent gates called forget gates which regulate the movement of information through the cell (Gers et al., 2000).

Gated recurrent unit. Similar to LSTM, the Gated Recurrent Unit (GRU) was introduced by Cho et al. (2014) as a method to solve the van-

Name	Vector size	Min. word count	Unique tokens	Diacritics	Training algorithm
CoRoLa	300	20	250942	Yes	FastText
NLPL	100	10	2153518	No	Word2Vec Skipgram
CC	300	-	2000000	Yes	FastText

Table 2: Word embeddings: statistics regarding training methods and dataset/parameters details.

ishing gradient problem that occurs when using standard RNNs. These types of units are closely related to LSTM having similar performance and design. The GRU layers are popular due their simpler structure, which results in faster training time. A bidirectional extension for such recurrent layers was proposed by Graves and Schmidhuber (2005). It connects two hidden layers of opposite directions in a backward and forward manner to the same output. This is useful for text processing since it can encode the context present in such structures: characters and words.

Hierarchical Attention Networks. Hierarchical Attention Networks (HAN) were introduced for document classification by Yang et al. (2016). They model the hierarchical structure of documents by using two levels of attention, for words and sentences. This translates into a document representation that differentiates between the importance of the content in various parts of the text.

The model constructs a vector representation of the raw document. They follow the two-level architecture by first encoding sequences of words to embeddings using bidirectional GRU units to preserve context information. The second attention level of the model encodes sequences of vectors representing sentences received as input from the first attention mechanism. The resulting encoding, which is constructed via the two-level attention scheme, is then used for classification.

Word embeddings. Word embeddings are methods of representing text as low dimensional fixed length numerical vectors. This representation maintains semantic and syntactic relations such as synonyms, antonyms as well as context. Neural network methods for training such embeddings were first introduced by Mikolov et al. (2013).

4 Experiments and results

We aim to provide classification models for all the subtasks from the challenge. The solutions are based on word embeddings which are used as a preprocessing step to create inputs for the classi-

fiers. In order to achieve this, we rely on a number of pretrained word vector models: Romanian Language Corpus (CoRoLa) introduced by Mititelu et al. (2018), Nordic Language Processing Laboratory (NLPL) word embedding repository (Kutuzov et al., 2017) and Common Crawl (CC) word vectors (Grave et al., 2018). The relevant details for each word vector representation model can be viewed in Table 2.

LSTM and BiGRU Models. The input for the RNN flavour models is computed by taking the mean of all word embeddings present in the text. Missing words are considered zero valued vectors. The result is a representation of the whole news item as a single embedding vector.

The LSTM architecture consists of a starting LSTM layer of size 256. This is followed by a secondary LSTM layer of 512 neurons. Next, we use dropout as a regularization technique for reducing overfitting in neural networks (Srivastava et al., 2014). The method refers to dropping out individual units during training with a probability $p = 0.3$. We use a fully connected layer consisting of 512 neurons between the recurrent layers and the output one. All LSTM layers use the tanh activation function while the fully connected one uses Rectified Linear Unit (ReLU), both empirically chosen. Finally, the output consists of a softmax activation layer of variable size depending on the subtask, 2 dimensions for the first and 6 for the second and third.

The BiGRU model is similar, it uses an initial GRU layer of 256 size followed by a bidirectional GRU layer of size 512. For both layers we apply batch normalization to accelerate the training. Similarly, we use an empirically chosen tanh activation function. This connects to two fully connected layers of 1024 and 512 neurons, both with dropout mechanism with $p = 0.3$. The output layer is the same as for the LSTM architecture.

HAN Model. Due to the two-level hierarchical attention architecture, the HAN model learns the importance of the words as a weighted sum be-

Model	Embeddings	Training F_1			Evaluation F_1			Test F_1		
		Macro	Weighted	Micro	Macro	Weighted	Micro	Macro	Weighted	Micro
BiGRU	CC	-	-	-	-	-	-	0.708	0.711	0.712
HAN	CC	-	-	-	-	-	-	0.508	0.513	0.515
LSTM	CoRoLa	0.836	0.838	0.839	0.828	0.830	0.831	0.825	0.826	0.827
LSTM	NLPL	0.804	0.806	0.806	0.796	0.797	0.797	0.798	0.799	0.799
LSTM	CC	0.858	0.858	0.858	0.854	0.855	0.855	0.847	0.848	0.848
BiGRU	CoRoLa	0.913	0.914	0.914	0.870	0.872	0.872	0.868	0.870	0.871
BiGRU	NLPL	0.871	0.872	0.873	0.835	0.837	0.838	0.834	0.836	0.838
BiGRU	CC	0.946	0.946	0.946	0.908	0.909	0.909	0.903	0.904	0.904
HAN	CC	**0.978**	**0.978**	**0.978**	**0.928**	**0.928**	**0.928**	**0.930**	**0.931**	**0.931**

Model	Embeddings	Training F_1			Evaluation F_1			Test F_1		
		Macro	Weighted	Micro	Macro	Weighted	Micro	Macro	Weighted	Micro
BiGRU	CC	-	-	-	-	-	-	0.481	0.489	0.490
HAN	CC	-	-	-	-	-	-	0.157	0.196	0.211
LSTM	CoRoLa	0.877	0.892	0.892	0.877	0.902	0.902	0.689	0.687	0.692
LSTM	NLPL	0.857	0.892	0.892	0.862	0.891	0.891	0.693	0.684	0.691
LSTM	CC	0.825	0.870	0.873	0.830	0.868	0.871	0.603	0.619	0.625
BiGRU	CoRoLa	0.922	0.941	0.941	**0.882**	**0.908**	**0.908**	0.690	0.690	0.694
BiGRU	NLPL	0.925	0.943	0.943	0.879	0.906	0.906	**0.701**	**0.692**	**0.699**
BiGRU	CC	**0.934**	0.945	0.945	**0.882**	0.903	0.903	0.649	0.652	0.658
HAN	CC	0.933	**0.959**	**0.959**	0.828	0.879	0.880	0.590	0.616	0.604

Model	Embeddings	Training F_1			Evaluation F_1			Test F_1		
		Macro	Weighted	Micro	Macro	Weighted	Micro	Macro	Weighted	Micro
BiGRU	CC	-	-	-	-	-	-	0.480	0.562	0.560
HAN	CC	-	-	-	-	-	-	0.138	0.196	0.224
LSTM	CoRoLa	0.779	0.768	0.767	0.761	0.751	0.750	0.739	0.800	0.803
LSTM	NLPL	0.775	0.762	0.763	0.764	0.751	0.751	0.787	0.834	0.834
LSTM	CC	0.743	0.740	0.742	0.738	0.734	0.735	0.790	0.843	0.844
BiGRU	CoRoLa	**0.854**	**0.840**	**0.840**	0.770	0.751	0.751	0.775	0.842	0.843
BiGRU	NLPL	0.833	0.821	0.821	0.765	0.748	0.748	**0.803**	**0.850**	**0.851**
BiGRU	CC	0.847	0.833	0.833	**0.776**	**0.757**	**0.756**	0.777	0.831	0.832
HAN	CC	0.804	0.818	0.823	0.687	0.711	0.717	0.687	0.772	0.783

Table 3: Results obtained for: subtask 1 (top), subtask 2 (middle) and subtask 3 (bottom). The best results are presented in bold. The first lines represent the official results, BiGRU represents the first run and HAN the second one. All results are grouped by model type as well as the embeddings used. We include both the results for training and evaluation datasets. Since the HAN model is computationally complex, we included only the embedding which provided the best results with the previous architectures, namely, FastText Common Crawl (CC) word vectors.

tween the word embeddings. Thus, it can create its own sentence and document models. For a consistent input, not dependent on different document and sentence sizes, the model requires two hyper parameters: maximum sentence length (number of words) and maximum document length (number of sentences). We choose these parameters by inspecting the statistics of the whole dataset to create an initial estimate which was later improved via a grid search. The best performance was achieved with a maximum sentence length of 150 words and a maximum document size of 20 sentences. Besides these parameters, we also used a grid search in order to choose a size of 200 neurons for the attention layer as well as for the BiGRU. Similarly to the previous architectures, the output consists of 2 or 6 neurons depending on the subtask.

Training configuration. We train the model using the Adam optimizer (Kingma and Ba, 2014) with the default hyper parameters. For the learning rate, we use $\alpha = 0.0005$ which was chosen using a grid search as well. We work with the training-validation split recommended by the organizers. Training is done using *tensorflow* (Abadi et al., 2016) as backend and *keras* (Chollet et al., 2015) as frontend, with a batch size of 50 for 30 epochs. During training we introduce an early stopping criterion, namely, if the cost function for the validation set does not improve for two consecutive epochs we stop.

Results. We test the proposed architecture in combination with the three presented word embeddings. The results include the official submission scores as well as the data after we corrected the input file issue. For each subtask, we present the extended results, expressed through the harmonic

	RO	MD
RO	**2517**	201
MD	207	**2998**

	CUL	FIN	POL	SCI	SPO	TEC
CUL	**152**	6	15	9	4	1
FIN	33	**562**	206	20	21	59
POL	36	67	**518**	24	29	28
SCI	10	7	6	**322**	3	13
SPO	2	12	9	0	**420**	13
TEC	19	100	20	164	27	**268**

	CUL	FIN	POL	SCI	SPO	TEC
CUL	**166**	16	15	1	13	7
FIN	7	**539**	43	0	0	16
POL	11	87	**806**	1	2	3
SCI	2	10	3	**96**	0	44
SPO	3	11	7	2	**572**	12
TEC	6	38	36	7	1	**135**

Table 4: Confusion matrices for: subtask 1 (top), subtask 2 (middle) and subtask 3 (bottom) constructed using the models which obtained the best results over the test dataset. Subtask 1 represents the classification between the Moldavian (MD) and the Romanian (RO) dialects. Subtask 2 and 3 are cross-dialect multi-class classification between: culture (CUL), finance (FIN), politics (POL), science (SCI), sports (SPO) and technology (TEC).

mean of precision and recall, F_1 score, in Table 3. Overall the HAN model outperforms the others for the first subtask and BiGRU with NLPL embeddings offers the best results for the second and third subtasks.

For the official results, the best model, BiGRU with CC embeddings, obtained macro-averaged F_1 scores as follows: 0.708 for subtask 1, 0.481 for subtask 2 and 0.480 for the third one. After the correction, the HAN with CC embedding model achieved 0.930 for subtask 1 while BiGRU with NLPL obtained 0.701 for subtask 2 and 0.803 for subtask 3. Additionally, unlike the CC embeddings, for subtasks 2 and 3 the model that obtained the best results uses embeddings without diacritics.

To better visualize and understand the misclassification behaviour we present the confusion matrices for the three subtasks in Table 4. The matrices are created using the models which achieved the best results over the test dataset. For the first subtask the error is consistent across both classes, RO and MD. Next, for the second subtask we observe high misclassification between the following classes: finance (FIN) – politics (POL), technology (TEC) – FIN and TEC – science (SCI). For the last subtask we notice that the misclassification

errors from subtask 2 hold, as well as the addition of a high error between the TEC – POL classes.

5 Conclusions

In this paper we tackled the task of Moldavian vs. Romanian cross-topic identification which is part of the VarDial 2019 evaluation campaign. We proposed deep learning solutions for all three of the competition subtasks: binary classification between the two dialects and two cross-dialect six category classification from one of the dialects to the other. The proposed architectures use state of the art recurrent neural network layers as well as hierarchical attention networks. To model the languages we used the following pretrained word embeddings: Romanian Language Corpus (CoRoLa), Nordic Language Processing Laboratory (NLPL) word embedding repository and Common Crawl (CC) word vectors. We present the official competition results together with additional tests since the official submissions suffered from an input parsing issue that corrupted 50% of the results. All extra tests are evaluated with the official script. The new results confirm the superior classification performance of the HAN model with CC embeddings for subtask 1 and BiGRU with NLPL embeddings for the other subtasks.

Acknowledgments

This work was supported by the 2008-212578 LT-fLL FP7 project.

References

Martín Abadi, Paul Barham, Jianmin Chen, Zhifeng Chen, Andy Davis, Jeffrey Dean, Matthieu Devin, Sanjay Ghemawat, Geoffrey Irving, Michael Isard, et al. 2016. Tensorflow: a system for large-scale machine learning. In *OSDI*, volume 16, pages 265–283.

Mohamed Ali. 2018. Character level convolutional neural network for arabic dialect identification. In *Proceedings of the Fifth Workshop on NLP for Similar Languages, Varieties and Dialects (VarDial 2018)*, pages 122–127.

Andrei M. Butnaru and Radu Tudor Ionescu. 2019. MOROCO: The Moldavian and Romanian Dialectal Corpus. *ArXiv*.

Kyunghyun Cho, Bart Van Merriënboer, Caglar Gulcehre, Dzmitry Bahdanau, Fethi Bougares, Holger Schwenk, and Yoshua Bengio. 2014. Learning phrase representations using RNN encoder-decoder for statistical machine translation. *arXiv preprint arXiv:1406.1078*.

François Chollet et al. 2015. Keras. `https://keras.io`.

Alina Maria Ciobanu and Liviu P Dinu. 2016. A computational perspective on the romanian dialects. In *LREC*.

Felix A. Gers, Jürgen A. Schmidhuber, and Fred A. Cummins. 2000. Learning to forget: Continual prediction with LSTM. *Neural Comput.*, 12(10):2451–2471.

Edouard Grave, Piotr Bojanowski, Prakhar Gupta, Armand Joulin, and Tomas Mikolov. 2018. Learning word vectors for 157 languages. In *Proceedings of the International Conference on Language Resources and Evaluation (LREC 2018)*.

Alex Graves and Jürgen Schmidhuber. 2005. Framewise phoneme classification with bidirectional LSTM and other neural network architectures. *Neural Networks*, 18(5-6):602–610.

Sepp Hochreiter and Jürgen Schmidhuber. 1997. Long short-term memory. *Neural computation*, 9(8):1735–1780.

Jie Hu, Li Shen, and Gang Sun. 2018. Squeeze-and-excitation networks. In *Proceedings of the IEEE conference on computer vision and pattern recognition*, pages 7132–7141.

Radu Tudor Ionescu, Marius Popescu, and Aoife Cahill. 2016. String kernels for native language identification: Insights from behind the curtains. *Computational Linguistics*, 42(3):491–525.

Diederik P Kingma and Jimmy Ba. 2014. Adam: A method for stochastic optimization. *arXiv preprint arXiv:1412.6980*.

Andrei Kutuzov, Murhaf Fares, Stephan Oepen, and Erik Velldal. 2017. Word vectors, reuse, and replicability: Towards a community repository of large-text resources. In *Proceedings of the 58th Conference on Simulation and Modelling*, pages 271–276. Linköping University Electronic Press.

Yann LeCun, Yoshua Bengio, and Geoffrey Hinton. 2015. Deep learning. *nature*, 521(7553):436.

Tomas Mikolov, Kai Chen, Greg Corrado, and Jeffrey Dean. 2013. Efficient estimation of word representations in vector space. *arXiv preprint arXiv:1301.3781*.

Verginica Barbu Mititelu, Dan Tufis, and Elena Irimia. 2018. The reference corpus of the contemporary romanian language (CoRoLa). In *Proceedings of the Eleventh International Conference on Language Resources and Evaluation (LREC-2018)*.

Nitish Srivastava, Geoffrey Hinton, Alex Krizhevsky, Ilya Sutskever, and Ruslan Salakhutdinov. 2014. Dropout: a simple way to prevent neural networks from overfitting. *The Journal of Machine Learning Research*, 15(1):1929–1958.

Zichao Yang, Diyi Yang, Chris Dyer, Xiaodong He, Alex Smola, and Eduard Hovy. 2016. Hierarchical attention networks for document classification. In *Proceedings of the 2016 Conference of the North American Chapter of the Association for Computational Linguistics: Human Language Technologies*, pages 1480–1489.

Marcos Zampieri, Shervin Malmasi, Nikola Ljubešić, Preslav Nakov, Ahmed Ali, Jörg Tiedemann, Yves Scherrer, and Noëmi Aepli. 2017. Findings of the VarDial evaluation campaign 2017. In *Proceedings of the Fourth Workshop on NLP for Similar Languages, Varieties and Dialects (VarDial)*, pages 1–15, Valencia, Spain. Association for Computational Linguistics.

Marcos Zampieri, Shervin Malmasi, Preslav Nakov, Ahmed Ali, Suwon Shon, James Glass, Yves Scherrer, Tanja Samardžić, Nikola Ljubešić, Jörg Tiedemann, et al. 2018. Language identification and morphosyntactic tagging: The second VarDial evaluation campaign. In *Proceedings of the Fifth Workshop on NLP for Similar Languages, Varieties and Dialects*. Association for Computational Linguistics.

Marcos Zampieri, Shervin Malmasi, Yves Scherrer, Tanja Samardžić, Francis Tyers, Miikka Silfverberg, Natalia Klyueva, Tung-Le Pan, Chu-Ren Huang, Radu Tudor Ionescu, Andrei Butnaru, and Tommi Jauhiainen. 2019. A Report on the Third VarDial Evaluation Campaign. In *Proceedings of the Sixth Workshop on NLP for Similar Languages, Varieties and Dialects (VarDial)*. Association for Computational Linguistics.

Discriminating between Mandarin Chinese and Swiss-German varieties using adaptive language models

Tommi Jauhiainen
Department of Digital Humanities
University of Helsinki
`tommi.jauhiainen@helsinki.fi`

Heidi Jauhiainen
Department of Digital Humanities
University of Helsinki
`heidi.jauhiainen@helsinki.fi`

Krister Lindén
Department of Digital Humanities
University of Helsinki
`krister.linden@helsinki.fi`

Abstract

This paper describes the language identification systems used by the SUKI team in the Discriminating between the Mainland and Taiwan variation of Mandarin Chinese (DMT) and the German Dialect Identification (GDI) shared tasks which were held as part of the third VarDial Evaluation Campaign. The DMT shared task included two separate tracks, one for the simplified Chinese script and one for the traditional Chinese script. We submitted three runs on both tracks of the DMT task as well as on the GDI task. We won the traditional Chinese track using Naive Bayes with language model adaptation, came second on GDI with an adaptive version of the HeLI 2.0 method, and third on the simplified Chinese track using again the adaptive Naive Bayes.

1 Introduction

The third VarDial Evaluation Campaign (Zampieri et al., 2019) included three shared tasks on language, dialect, and language variety identification. The Discriminating between Mainland and Taiwan variation of Mandarin Chinese (DMT) concentrated on finding differences between the varieties of Mandarin Chinese written on mainland China and Taiwan. The task included two tracks, one for the simplified script and another for the traditional one. The German Dialect Identification (GDI) task was already the third of its kind (Zampieri et al., 2017, 2018). In GDI 2019, the task was to distinguish between four Swiss-German dialects. The third task was that of Cuneiform Language Identification (CLI), but we did not participate in that as we were partly responsible for creating its dataset (Jauhiainen et al., 2019a).

We evaluated several language identification methods using the development sets of the DMT and GDI tasks. Our best submissions were created

using a similar language model (LM) adaptation technique to the one we used in the second Var-Dial Evaluation Campaign (Zampieri et al., 2018). In that Evaluation Campaign, we used the HeLI language identification method (Jauhiainen et al., 2016) together with a new LM adaptation approach, winning the Indo-Aryan Language Identification (ILI) and the GDI 2018 shared tasks with a wide margin (Jauhiainen et al., 2018b,c). After the second Evaluation Campaign, we had developed a new version of the HeLI method and further refined the LM adaptation technique (Jauhiainen et al., 2019b). With the HeLI 2.0 method and the refined adaptation technique, we came second in the GDI 2019 shared task using only character 4-grams as features. Furthermore, we had implemented several baseline language identifiers for the CLI shared task (Jauhiainen et al., 2019a). One of them was a Naive Bayes (NB) identifier using variable length character n-grams, which fared better than the HeLI method on the CLI dataset. We modified our LM adaptation technique to be used with the NB classifier and this fared better than the adaptive HeLI 2.0 method on both of the Chinese datasets. With the adaptive NB identifier, we won the traditional Chinese track and came third on the simplified one.

In this paper, we first go through some related work in Section 2, after which we introduce the datasets and the evaluation setup used in the DMT and the GDI shared tasks (Section 3). We then use the training and the development sets to evaluate our baseline methods (Sections 4.1 and 4.2) and the HeLI 2.0 method (Section 4.3), after which we evaluate the efficiency of our LM adaptation procedure with the HeLI 2.0 and NB methods in Sections 4.4 and 4.5. Finally we introduce and discuss the results of our official submissions (Section 5) as well as give some conclusions and ideas for future work (Section 6).

178

Proceedings of VarDial, pages 178–187
Minneapolis, MN, June 7, 2019 ©2019 Association for Computational Linguistics

2   Related work

In this section, we introduce some background information on previous studies in language identification in general, language identification in the context of Chinese and German languages, as well as LM adaptation.

2.1   Language identification in texts

Language identification (LI) is the task of identifying the language of a text. The same methods which are used for LI are generally also used for dialect and language variety identification. A comprehensive survey of language identification in general has been published in arXiv by Jauhiainen et al. (2018d).

The series of shared tasks in language identification began in 2014 with the Discriminating Between Similar languages (DSL) shared task (Zampieri et al., 2014) and similar tasks have been arranged each year since (Zampieri et al., 2015; Malmasi et al., 2016; Zampieri et al., 2017, 2018).

It is notable that, so far, deep neural networks have not gained an upper hand when compared with the more linear classification methods (Çöltekin and Rama, 2017; Medvedeva et al., 2017; Ali, 2018).

2.2   Chinese dialect identification

In the DMT shared task, the text material in the dataset is UTF-8 encoded. Before the widespread use of UTF-8, different encodings for different scripts were widely used. Li and Momoi (2001) discussed methods for automatically detecting the encoding of documents for which an encoding was unknown. They present two tables showing distributional results for Chinese characters. In their research they had found that the 4096 most frequent characters in simplified Chinese encoded in GB2312 cover 99.93 percent of all text and they report that earlier results of traditional Chinese in Big5 encoding are very similar with the 4096 most frequent characters covering 99.91% of text.

Huang and Lee (2008) used a bag of words method to distinguish between Mainland, Singapore and Taiwan varieties of Chinese. They reached an accuracy of 0.929.

Brown (2012) displays a confusion matrix of four varieties of the Chinese macrolanguage as part of his LI experiments for 923 languages. The Gan and Wu Chinese were among the languages with the highest error rates of all languages.

Huang et al. (2014) show how light verbs have different distributional tendencies in Mainland and Taiwan varieties of Mandarin Chinese. Using K-Means clustering they show that the varieties can be differentiated.

Xu et al. (2016) describe an approach to distinguish between several varieties of Mandarin Chinese: Mainland, Hong Kong, Taiwan, Macao, Malaysia, and Singapore. In another study (Xu et al., 2018), they used support vector machines (SVM) to distinguish between Gan Chinese dialects.

2.3   German dialect identification

The GDI 2019 task was already the third of its kind (Zampieri et al., 2017, 2018). In 2017, we did not participate in the shared task, which was won using an SVM meta-classifier ensemble with words and character n-grams from one to six as features (Malmasi and Zampieri, 2017). We won the 2018 edition using the HeLI method with LM adaptation and character 4-grams as features (Jauhiainen et al., 2018b). We were the only ones employing LM adaptation and won with a wide margin to the second system which was an SVM ensemble using both character and word n-grams (Benites et al., 2018).

For a more complete overview of dialect identification for the German language, we refer the reader to our recent paper where we used LM adaptation with the datasets from the GDI 2017 and 2018 shared tasks (Jauhiainen et al., 2019b). Our experiments using a refined LM adaptation scheme with the HeLI 2.0 method produced the best published identification results for both of the datasets.

2.4   Language model adaptation

Language model (LM) adaptation is a technique in which the language models used by a language identifier are modified during the identification process. It is advantageous especially when there is a clear domain (topic, genre, idiolect, time period, *etc.*) difference between the texts used as training data and the text being identified (Jauhiainen et al., 2018a,b,c). If an adaptation technique is successful, the language identifier learns the peculiarities of the new text and is better able to classify it into the given language categories. In the shared tasks of the VarDial Evaluation Campaigns, we are provided with the complete test sentence collection at once. This means, that we can additionally choose in which order we learn from the test data and even process the same test sentences several times before providing the final language labels.

The LM adaptation technique and the confidence measure we use in the systems described in this article are similar to those used earlier in speech language identification by Chen and Liu (2005) and Zhong et al. (2007). The adaptation technique is an improved version of the one we used in our winning submissions at the second VarDial Evaluation Campaign (Jauhiainen et al., 2018b,c). For a more complete overview of the subject, we refer the reader to our recent article dedicated to language model adaptation for language and dialect identification of text, where we also introduce the improved LM adaptation technique used in this paper (Jauhiainen et al., 2019b).

3 Test setup

In the shared tasks 2019, the participants were provided with separate training and development sets. All the tracks were closed ones, so no external information was to be used in preparing the language identification systems. The training and development sets were released approximately a month before the test set release. When the test sets were released, the participants had two days to submit their predictions on the tracks. The texts in the development portions could be used as an additional training data when processing the test sets and we did so in each case.

The evaluation measure used in both of the shared tasks was the macro F1-score and we used it also when comparing the different methods we used with the development data.

3.1 DMT datasets

The scripts commonly used in mainland China and Taiwan are different. In Taiwan, the traditional Chinese script is commonly used whereas in mainland China, the simplified version is the official one (Chen et al., 1996; Huang et al., 2000; McEnery and Xiao, 2003). In order to be able to concentrate on the non-scriptual differences of the two varieties of Mandarin Chinese, Putonghua (Mainland China) and Guoyo (Taiwan), the texts used for the DMT task had been transformed to use the same script. In the simplified track, the Taiwanese texts originally written in the traditional script had been converted into the simpli-

fied script and in the traditional track the texts from mainland China originally in the simplified script had been converted to the traditional script. The conversion had been made using a tool called "OpenCC".[1]

The texts used as the source for the datasets were news articles from mainland China and from Taiwan. The participants were provided with training and development sets for both simplified and traditional scripts. Both datasets had been tokenized by inserting whitespace characters between individual words. Furthermore, all punctuation had been removed. The average length of words in all DMT training sets was c. 1.7 characters. The training sets contained 9,385 sentences and the development sets consisted of additional 1,000 sentences for each variety. The test sets had 1,000 sentences as well for each variety.

3.2 GDI dataset

The GDI dataset consisted of transcribed speech utterances in four Swiss German dialects. More detailed information about the source of the texts for the GDI datasets, the ArchiMob corpus, are provided by Samardžić et al. (2016). In 2018, the GDI dataset included additional unknown dialects, which were left out in 2019. The sizes of the training and the development sets can be seen in Table 1. The average length of words in the training set was 5.5 characters. The test set contained 4,743 utterances comprising 42,699 words. As of this writing, we are not aware of the distribution of the dialects in the test set.

Variety (code)	Training	Development
Bern (BE)	27,968	7,381
Basel (BS)	26,927	9,462
Lucerne (LU)	28,979	8,650
Zurich (ZH)	28,833	8,086

Table 1: List of the Swiss German varieties used in the datasets distributed for the 2019 GDI shared task. The sizes are in words.

The training, development, and test sets included two files in addition to the speech transcriptions. The first file included normalized forms for each dialectal form in the data. The second file included 400-dimensional iVectors representing the acoustic features of the original speech data, as the text data was transliterated speech. We did not use either of the two additional files in our experiments.

---

[1] https://github.com/BYVoid/OpenCC

4 Experiments using the development data

We set out to tackle the GDI and the DMT shared tasks with the system based on the HeLI 2.0 method and LM adaptation that we had used for the GDI 2017, GDI 2018 and ILI datasets between the 2018 and 2019 VarDial Evaluation Campaigns (Jauhiainen et al., 2019b).

For the CLI shared task, we had implemented three new baseline identifiers, one of which, a Naive Bayes identifier, managed to overcome the traditional HeLI method when distinguishing between Sumerian and six Akkadian dialects (Jauhiainen et al., 2019a). We were, hence, also interested to see how well these baseline identifiers would perform in the DMT and GDI tasks.

4.1 Simple scoring and the sum of relative frequencies

The first baseline method in the CLI shared task was the simple scoring method. In simple scoring, the frequency information of individual features in the training set is ignored and each time a feature from a language model $dom(O(C_g))$ is encountered in the text M, the language g is given one point. The survey article by Jauhiainen et al. (2018d) gives the following Equation 1 for simple scoring:

$$R_{simple}(g, M) = \sum_{i=1}^{l_{MF}} \begin{cases} 1 & \text{, if } f_i \in dom(O(C_g)) \\ 0 & \text{, otherwise} \end{cases}$$

(1)

where l_{MF} is the number of individual features in the line M and f_i is its ith feature. The language g gaining the highest score R is selected as the predicted language.

The second baseline implementation for the CLI used the sum of relative frequencies of character n-grams of varying length. The method is very similar to simple scoring but, instead of simply adding a global constant to the score each time the feature is found in the language model, the observed relative frequency in the respective languages training corpus is added.

In both methods, the only parameter to be decided when using the development data was the range of the character n-grams used. These character n-grams can span word boundaries and thus long n-grams can contain several words. We experimented with a range from 1 to 20 characters

and the best attained macro F1-scores on the development sets are listed in Tables 2, 3, and 4.

In the end, we did not submit any results using the two first baseline methods as the third baseline method, the product of relative frequencies, was clearly superior to them.

4.2 Product of relative frequencies (NB)

Our third baseline method in CLI was the product of relative frequencies. The method is basically the same as Naive Bayes using the observed relative frequencies of character n-grams as probabilities. As with the two previous methods, these character n-grams can span word boundaries. Similarly to the sum of relative frequencies method, we calculate the relative frequencies for different n-grams from the training corpus, but instead of adding them together, we multiply them as in Equation 2:

$$R_{prod}(g, M) = \prod_{i=1}^{l_{MF}} \frac{c(C_g, f_i)}{l_{C_g^F}}$$

(2)

The practical implementation uses the sum of logarithms instead as computers normally cannot handle the extremely small numbers produced by multiplying the observed probabilities of complete sentences. As smoothing, in case $c(C_g, f_i)$ was equal to zero, we used 1 and multiplied the resulting logarithmic value by the penalty modifier p_{mod}. The penalty modifier and the character n-gram range used were optimized using the development set. As mentioned earlier, the NB classifier bested the other baseline methods as can be seen in Tables 2, 3, and 4.

4.3 HeLI 2.0

In the HeLI method, we calculate a score for each word using relative frequencies of words or character n-grams. The length of the character n-grams to use or whether to use the word itself is decided individually for each word encountered in the text to be identified. The whole text gets the average of the scores of the individual words, thus giving equal value to long and short words. No information spanning word boundaries are used.

We have recently introduced a version of HeLI which we decided to call 2.0 as enough changes to the HeLI method had already accumulated (Jauhiainen et al., 2019b). The HeLI 2.0 differs from the HeLI method described by Jauhiainen et al. (2016) in three ways. Firstly, we now always use

Method	n-gram range	Smoothing	Splits k	Epochs	*CMmin*	F1 dev
Naive Bayes with LM adaptation	1–15	1.3	*max*	1	0.45	0.9225
Naive Bayes	1–15	1.3	-	-	-	0.9215
Simple scoring	1–15	-	-	-	-	0.8970
HeLI 2.0 with LM adaptation	1–2 + infinite	1.01	*max*	1	-	0.8909
HeLI 2.0	1–2 + infinite	1.01	-	-	-	0.8859
Sum of rel. freq.	5–15	-	-	-	-	0.8204

Table 2: Simplified Chinese. The macro F1-scores attained by different methods on the development set. A *max* in column indicating the number of splits means that k was equal to the number of lines in the evaluation data.

Method	n-gram range	Smoothing	Splits k	Epochs	*CMmin*	F1 dev
Naive Bayes with LM adaptation	1–14	1.3	4	1	0	0.9295
Naive Bayes	1–14	1.3	-	-	-	0.9285
HeLI 2.0 with LM adaptation	1–2 + infinite	1.12	*max*	1	0.42	0.9160
HeLI 2.0	1–2 + infinite	1.12	-	-	-	0.9145
Simple scoring	1–6	-	-	-	-	0.9015
Sum of rel. freq.	5–15	-	-	-	-	0.8247

Table 3: Traditional Chinese. The macro F1-scores attained by different methods on the development set. A *max* in column indicating the number of splits means that k was equal to the number of lines in the evaluation data.

Method	n-gram range	Smoothing	Splits k	Epochs	*CMmin*	F1 dev
HeLI 2.0 with LM adaptation	4	1.12	9	112	0.15	0.8657
Naive Bayes with LM adaptation	2–6	1.08	40	96	0.16	0.8442
HeLI 2.0	4	1.12	-	-	-	0.6658
Naive Bayes	2–6	1.08	-	-	-	0.6475
Simple scoring	2–7	-	-	-	-	0.5865
Sum of rel. freq.	6–15	-	-	-	-	0.5049

Table 4: GDI 2019. The macro F1-scores attained by different methods on the development set. A *max* in column indicating the number of splits means that k was equal to the number of lines in the evaluation data.

all of the possible training material and use neither rank- nor relative frequency-based cut-off. Secondly, we changed how we calculate the smoothing value. In HeLI, we used a global penalty value for all language models. In HeLI 2.0, we calculate the penalty value relative to the size of each individual language model using a global penalty modifier p_{mod}.[2] Thirdly, when selecting the range of character n-grams to use in HeLI 2.0, the minimum size for n can be higher than one.

In this description, we define a word as a character n-gram of infinite size generated from an individual word. The model sizes used are optimized using a development corpus as is the possible use of n-grams of infinite size. Variable n_{max} is the maximum length and the n_{min} the minimum length of the used character n-grams.

The corpus derived from the training data containing only the word internal[3] n-grams of the size n for the language g is called C_g^n. The values $v_{C_g^n}(f)$ for the n-gram f are calculated for each language g, as shown in Equation 3:

$$v_{C_g^n}(f) = \begin{cases} -\log_{10}\left(\frac{c(C_g^n, f)}{l_{C_g^n}}\right) & \text{, if } c(C_g^n, f) > 0 \\ -\log_{10}\left(\frac{1}{l_{C_g^n}}\right) p_{mod} & \text{, if } c(C_g^n, f) = 0 \end{cases}$$
$$(3)$$

where $c(C_g^n, f)$ is the number of n-grams f in C_g^n.

The domain $dom(O(C^n))$ is the set of all character n-grams of length n found in the models of any of the languages $g \in G$. Separately for each individual word t on the line M to be identified, we determine the length n of the character n-grams we use. The word t is divided into overlapping character n-grams of the length n. The length n is the highest where at least one of the character n-grams generated from the word t is found in $dom(O(C^n))$. However, if an individual n-gram f generated from the word t is not found in $dom(O(C^n))$, it is discarded at this point. The number of retained n-grams is l_{tF}. The score for individual words t on the line M is then calculated as in Equation 4.

---

[2]This is the same smoothing method which we used with the product of relative frequencies.

[3]The beginning and the end of a word are marked using whitespaces.

$$v_g(t) = \sum_{i=1}^{l_{t_F}} v_{C_g^n}(f) \tag{4}$$

The whole line M is then scored as in Equation 5:

$$R_g(M) = \frac{\sum_{i=1}^{l_{M^T}} v_g(t_i)}{l_{M^T}} \tag{5}$$

where l_{M^T} is the number of words in the line M. The predicted language g of the line M is the one having the lowest score. We optimized the penalty modifier p_{mod} as well as the minimum and maximum size of the n-grams, i.e. n_{min} and n_{max}, using the developments set. Whether or not to use the charcter n-grams of infinite size (words), was also decided with the development set. The best results attained by the HeLI 2.0 method on each of the development sets can be seen in Tables 2, 3, and 4.

4.4 HeLI 2.0 with adaptive language models

The fifth method we used in the experiments with the development data was the domain-adaptive version of HeLI 2.0. We used a similar LM adaptation method in the shared tasks of VarDial 2018, clearly winning the GDI and ILI tasks. For Jauhiainen et al. (2019b), we devised an improved version of the adaptation method, which is used here. In order to select the best material to be used in LM adaptation, we need a confidence measure which indicates the best identified lines. In Jauhiainen et al. (2019b), we evaluated three confidence measures and the score difference between the best and the second best scoring languages, CM_{BS}, proved to be the best performing one. The confidence measure is calculated as in Equation 6:

$$CM_{BS}(M) = R_h(M) - R_g(M) \tag{6}$$

where g is the best and h the second best scoring language.

For the shared tasks, we get a complete set of lines to be identified as one collection. We denote an individual line M, as before, and the set of lines is denoted MC. In the adaptation algorithm, we first perform a preliminary identification using the HeLI 2.0 method for each line M of the development or the test set MC. The number of lines a to process simultaneously in adaptation is

the number of lines in MC divided by the number of splits k. The number of splits is optimized using the development set. For each line, we also calculate the confidence measure CM_{BS}. We remove a most confident lines from MC and mark them as finally identified with the given language labels. Then we add the information from the finally identified lines to their respective language models. Then we use the new language models to re-identify the lines remaining in MC, again using the a most confident lines to augment the language models. This process is repeated until all the lines in MC have been removed. In the iterative version of the adaptation method, the whole adaptation process is repeated several times (epochs).

For all submissions but one,[4] we used a confidence threshold when deciding whether the information from a line was added to the language models, that is not all lines were always used for adaptation. The confidence threshold, $CMmin$, was also optimized for the development set.[5] The number of splits, k, and the number of epochs were also optimized using the development set.

The best results using HeLI 2.0 with LM adaptation on each development set can be seen in Tables 2, 3, and 4. This was the best performing method with the GDI development set but behind NB with the traditional Chinese and even behind simple scoring with the simplified Chinese.

4.5 Naive Bayes with adaptive language models

As our NB implementation seemed to outperform the HeLI 2.0 method in some experiments, we implemented a method using it together with the same LM adaptation scheme we used with HeLI 2.0 in the previous section.

The best results using the Naive Bayes with LM adaptation on each development set can be seen in Tables 2, 3, and 4.

5 Results and discussion

The participants were allowed to submit three separate runs to each of the two tracks of the DMT shared task, as well as to the one track of the GDI shared task. For each track, we submitted results using the HeLI 2.0 with LM adaptation, the Naive

---

[4] We did not use the confidence threshold with HeLI 2.0 using LM adaptation for the simplified Chinese script.

[5] The confidence threshold was used with NB and LM adaptation for the traditional Chinese script, but it got optimized to zero.

183

Bayes, and the NB with LM adaptation thus using all submissions available to us. The parameters we used with each method were the same as with the respective development sets.

A total of seven teams provided language identification results for the DMT shared task and six teams for the GDI shared task. Tables 5, 6, and 7 show the macro F1-scores of our submitted runs on the test set. Additionally, the tables show the methods and features used by the other teams together with their F1 scores. We submitted the runs using a team name "SUKI", which is the same we have used in the previous years. The results of the other participating teams were collected from the results packages provided by the organizers after the competition. The system description papers of the other teams were not available at the time of writing. The identity of other participants was also unknown. We were, however, provided with a short description of each system[6] which we used to provide these results.

The simplified Chinese track was won by a team called "hezhou" by a clear margin to the second and the third submissions. According to their system description, the "hezhou" team used a variety of features learned from outside sources, such as a pretrained BERT model for Chinese and word-embeddings trained on People's Daily News. Their results are interesting, but they cannot be directly compared with the ones provided by other teams as the track was supposed to be a closed one.

If we discount the results of the "hezhou" team, the two top places in all three tracks of the DMT and GDI shared tasks were divided between our "SUKI" team and the team "tearsofjoy". "tearsofjoy" used a two stage SVM approach in all of their top runs. After the first stage, the most confidently identified sentences were added to the training data, this step thus functioning as LM adaptation scheme similar to ours. They also submitted results using an SVM ensemble without adaptation and their respective score differences are similar to our systems with and without LM adaptation.

Interestingly, the HeLI 2.0 with adaptation is better than naive Bayes with adaptation on GDI and vice-versa in the DMT. In DMT, the optimal character n-gram range for NB was up to 15 char-

acters, which spans several words. In the experiments with the simplified Chinese development data, even the simple scoring method performed better than the HeLI 2.0 method with LM adaptation. The optimal maximum length of character n-grams was 15 characters also when using the simple scoring method. In the Chinese data, 15 characters span on average five words. From these results we could surmise, that the poor performance of the HeLI method in the DMT shared task was at least partly due to the lack of capturing features spanning several words.

There is a notable inconsistency in our test results with the simplified Chinese. The HeLI 2.0 with LM adaptation performs almost as well as the NB with LM adaptation. This might be due to the fact that we had forgotten to use the confidence threshold with the simplified Chinese development set for the HeLI method and therefore we did not use one with the test set either. It could very well be that the use of a confidence threshold was disadvantageous with both of the Chinese test sets. Our winning submission for the traditional Chinese track used the NB with LM adaptation and with a confidence threshold of 0.[7]

The fact that we did not come in the first place in the GDI 2019 shared task is undoubtedly partly due to the fact that we did not use the provided iVector-files at all in the classification task unlike the other top three teams. Using the information from the iVectors together with our language identifier implementations would not have been trivial.

At the time of writing this article, the participants do not have access to the correct language labels of the test sets, which hinders a detailed error analysis.

6 Conclusions and future work

The two varieties of Chinese used in the DMT shared task seem to be distinguishable from each other quite well. Whether it is due to more structural or more functional differences is left to be determined by experts in Chinese.

We were happy to see that some of the other teams had taken notice of the success of our LM adaptation scheme at the ILI and the GDI 2018 shared tasks. In the GDI 2019 shared task, the use of some sort of an LM adaptation procedure was of paramount importance; the macro F1 scores rose

---

[6]As part of the submissions, the participants were asked to provide a short description.txt file.

[7]Using a confidence threshold of 0 was the result of optimization with the development set.

Team/run	Method	Features	F1 dev	F1 test
hezhou	Ensemble of BERT, LSTM, SVM, ...	word-embeddings, word n-grams, ...		0.8929
tearsofjoy, run 1	SVM with LM adaptation	ch. n-grams 1–4, word n-grams 1–2		0.8738
SUKI, run 1	**Naive Bayes with LM adaptation**	**ch. n-grams 1–15**	**0.9225**	**0.8735**
SUKI, run 3	**HeLI 2.0 with LM adaptation**	**ch. n-grams 1–2, words**	**0.8909**	**0.8710**
SUKI, run 2	**Naive Bayes**	**ch. n-grams 1–15**	**0.9215**	**0.8685**
itsalexyang	Ensemble of Naive Bayes and BiLSTM	ch. n-grams 2–3, word embeddings		0.8530
tearsofjoy, run 2	SVM ensemble	ch. n-grams 2–5, words		0.8445
Adaptcenter	Ensemble of CNN and ?	? and words		0.8124
ghpaetzold	RNN	characters		0.7934
gretelliz92	NN with 4 dense layers	TF-IDF vectors		0.7496

Table 5: Simplified Chinese. The macro F1-scores attained by submitted methods on the test set. The results of our submissions are bolded.

Team/run	Method	Features	F1 dev	F1 test
SUKI, run 1	**Naive Bayes with LM adaptation**	**ch. n-grams 1–14**	**0.9295**	**0.9085**
hezhou	Ensemble of BERT, LSTM, SVM, ...	word-embeddings, word n-grams, ...		0.9009
tearsofjoy, run 1	SVM with LM adaptation	ch. n-grams 1–4, words		0.8844
SUKI, run 2	**Naive Bayes**	**ch. n-grams 1–14**	**0.9285**	**0.8815**
SUKI, run 3	**HeLI 2.0 with LM adaptation**	**ch. n-grams 1–2, words**	**0.9160**	**0.8712**
itsalexyang	Ensemble of Naive Bayes and BiLSTM	ch. n-grams 2–3, word embeddings		0.8687
tearsofjoy, run 2	SVM ensemble	ch. n-grams 2–5, words		0.8643
Adaptcenter	Ensemble of CNN and ?	? and words		0.8317
ghpaetzold	RNN	characters		0.7959
gretelliz92	NN with 4 dense layers	TF-IDF vectors		0.7484

Table 6: Traditional Chinese. The macro F1-scores attained by different methods on the test set. The results of our submissions are bolded.

Team/run	Method	Features	F1 dev	F1 test
tearsofjoy, run 2	SVM with LM adapt.	ch. n-grams 1–5, word n-grams 1–2, iVect.		0.7593
SUKI, run 1	**HeLI 2.0 with LM adapt.**	**ch. 4-grams**	**0.8657**	**0.7541**
benf	SVM ens. with LM adapt.	various ch. and word level TF-IDF, iVect.		0.7455
SUKI, run 3	**Naive Bayes with LM adapt.**	**ch. n-grams 2–6**	**0.8442**	**0.7451**
tearsofjoy, run 3	SVM ens.	ch. n-grams 2–5, words, iVect.		0.6517
SUKI, run 2	**Naive Bayes**	**ch. n-grams 2–6**	**0.6475**	**0.6460**
BAM	Ens. of CNN, LSTM, and KRR	?		0.6255
dkosmajac	Ens. of QDA and RF	textual + iVect.		0.5616
ghpaetzold	RNN	characters		0.5575

Table 7: GDI 2019. The macro F1-scores attained by different methods on the test set. The results of our submissions are bolded.

to a completely different level when this was used. The use of LM adaptation did not have such a high importance in the DMT shared task as it did with the GDI 2019, but it still always improved the results.

If we discount the "hezhou" submission, the results of both of the shared tasks once more indicate that deep neural networks do not reach the same accuracy in language identification as SVM, NB, or the HeLI methods.

We think that the poor results of the HeLI 2.0 method on the Chinese data were partly due to the shortness of the words and the importance of information spanning word boundaries. We would like to experiment with giving the HeLI method access to a larger context to verify that this indeed

is the case. We will also seek to find a way to incorporate external information, such as that provided by the iVector-files in GDI 2019, to the task of language identification of text.

Acknowledgments

This work has been partly funded by the Kone Foundation and FIN-CLARIN. We also thank the anonymous reviewer of an earlier paper for the idea to use character n-grams of infinite size in the formulaic description of the HeLI 2.0 method instead of words.

References

Mohamed Ali. 2018. Character level convolutional neural network for German dialect identification. In *Proceedings of the Fifth Workshop on NLP for Similar Languages, Varieties and Dialects (VarDial)*, pages 172–177, Santa Fe, USA.

Fernando Benites, Ralf Grubenmann, Pius von Däniken, Dirk von Grünigen, Jan Deriu, and Mark Cieliebak. 2018. Twist Bytes German dialect identification with data mining optimization. In *Proceedings of the Fifth Workshop on NLP for Similar Languages, Varieties and Dialects (VarDial)*, pages 218–227, Santa Fe, USA.

Ralf D. Brown. 2012. Finding and Identifying Text in 900+ Languages. *Digital Investigation*, 9:S34–S43.

Çağr Çöltekin and Taraka Rama. 2017. Tübingen system in vardial 2017 shared task: experiments with language identification and cross-lingual parsing. In *Proceedings of the Fourth Workshop on NLP for Similar Languages, Varieties and Dialects (VarDial)*, pages 146–155, Valencia, Spain.

Keh-Jiann Chen, Chu-Ren Huang, Li-Ping Chang, and Hui-Li Hsu. 1996. SINICA CORPUS : Design Methodology for Balanced Corpora. In *Language, Information and Computation : Selected Papers from the 11th Pacific Asia Conference on Language, Information and Computation : 20-22 December 1996, Seoul*, pages 167–176, Seoul, Korea. Kyung Hee University.

Yingna Chen and Jia Liu. 2005. Language Model Adaptation and Confidence Measure for Robust Language Identification. In *Proceedings of International Symposium on Communications and Information Technologies 2005 (ISCIT 2005)*, volume 1, pages 270–273, Beijing, China.

Chu-Ren Huang, Feng-Yi Chen, Keh-Jiann Chen, Zhao-ming Gao, and Kuang-Yu Chen. 2000. Sinica treebank: Design criteria, annotation guidelines, and on-line interface. In *Proceedings of the Second Workshop on Chinese Language Processing: Held in Conjunction with the 38th Annual Meeting of the Association for Computational Linguistics - Volume 12*, CLPW '00, pages 29–37, Stroudsburg, PA, USA. Association for Computational Linguistics.

Chu-Ren Huang and Lung-Hao Lee. 2008. Contrastive Approach towards Text Source Classification based on Top-Bag-of-Word Similarity. In *Proceedings of the 22nd Pacific Asia Conference on Language, Information and Computation*, pages 404–410, Cebu City, Philippines.

Chu-Ren Huang, Jingxia Lin, Menghan Jiang, and Hongzhi Xu. 2014. Corpus-based study and identification of mandarin chinese light verb variations. In *Proceedings of the First Workshop on Applying NLP Tools to Similar Languages, Varieties and Dialects (VarDial)*, pages 1–10, Dublin, Ireland.

Tommi Jauhiainen, Heidi Jauhiainen, Tero Alstola, and Krister Lindén. 2019a. Language and Dialect Identification of Cuneiform Texts. In *Proceedings of the Sixth Workshop on NLP for Similar Languages, Varieties and Dialects (VarDial)*, Minneapolis, Minnesota, USA.

Tommi Jauhiainen, Heidi Jauhiainen, and Krister Lindén. 2018a. HeLI-based Experiments in Discriminating Between Dutch and Flemish Subtitles. In *Proceedings of the Fifth Workshop on NLP for Similar Languages, Varieties and Dialects (VarDial)*, pages 137–144, Santa Fe, NM.

Tommi Jauhiainen, Heidi Jauhiainen, and Krister Lindén. 2018b. HeLI-based Experiments in Swiss German Dialect Identification. In *Proceedings of the Fifth Workshop on NLP for Similar Languages, Varieties and Dialects (VarDial)*, pages 254–262, Santa Fe, NM.

Tommi Jauhiainen, Heidi Jauhiainen, and Krister Lindén. 2018c. Iterative Language Model Adaptation for Indo-Aryan Language Identification. In *Proceedings of the Fifth Workshop on NLP for Similar Languages, Varieties and Dialects (VarDial)*, pages 66–75, Santa Fe, NM.

Tommi Jauhiainen, Krister Lindén, and Heidi Jauhiainen. 2016. HeLI, a Word-Based Backoff Method for Language Identification. In *Proceedings of the Third Workshop on NLP for Similar Languages, Varieties and Dialects (VarDial3)*, pages 153–162, Osaka, Japan.

Tommi Jauhiainen, Krister Lindén, and Heidi Jauhiainen. 2019b. Language Model Adaptation for Language and Dialect Identification of Text. *arXiv preprint*, arXiv:1903.10915.

Tommi Jauhiainen, Marco Lui, Marcos Zampieri, Timothy Baldwin, and Krister Lindén. 2018d. Automatic Language Identification in Texts: A Survey. *arXiv preprint arXiv:1804.08186*.

Shanjian Li and Katsuhiko Momoi. 2001. A Composite Approach to Language/Encoding Detection. In *Nineteenth International Unicode Conference (IUC19)*, San Jose, California, USA.

Shervin Malmasi and Marcos Zampieri. 2017. German dialect identification in interview transcriptions. In *Proceedings of the Fourth Workshop on NLP for Similar Languages, Varieties and Dialects (VarDial)*, pages 164–169, Valencia, Spain.

Shervin Malmasi, Marcos Zampieri, Nikola Ljubešić, Preslav Nakov, Ahmed Ali, and Jrg Tiedemann. 2016. Discriminating Between Similar Languages and Arabic Dialect Identification: A Report on the Third DSL Shared Task. In *Proceedings of the Third Workshop on NLP for Similar Languages, Varieties and Dialects*, pages 1–14, Osaka, Japan.

A. M. McEnery and R. Z. Xiao. 2003. The lancaster corpus of mandarin chinese.

Maria Medvedeva, Martin Kroon, and Barbara Plank. 2017. When sparse traditional models outperform dense neural networks: the curious case of discriminating between similar languages. In *Proceedings of the Fourth Workshop on NLP for Similar Languages, Varieties and Dialects (VarDial)*, pages 156–163, Valencia, Spain.

Tanja Samardžić, Yves Scherrer, and Elvira Glaser. 2016. ArchiMob–A corpus of spoken Swiss German. In *Proceedings of the Language Resources and Evaluation (LREC)*, pages 4061–4066, Portoroz, Slovenia).

Fan Xu, Mingwen Wang, and Maoxi Li. 2016. Sentence-level Dialects Identification in the Greater China Region. *International Journal on Natural Language Computing (IJNLC)*, 5(6).

Fan Xu, Mingwen Wang, and Maoxi Li. 2018. Building Parallel Monolingual Gan Chinese Dialect Corpus. In *Proceedings of the Eleventh International Conference on Language Resources and Evaluation (LREC 2018)*, pages 244–249, Miyazaki, Japan. European Language Resources Association (ELRA).

Marcos Zampieri, Shervin Malmasi, Nikola Ljubeic, Preslav Nakov, Ahmed Ali, Jrg Tiedemann, Yves Scherrer, and Nomi Aepli. 2017. Findings of the VarDial Evaluation Campaign 2017. In *Proceedings of the Fourth Workshop on NLP for Similar Languages, Varieties and Dialects*, pages 1–15, Valencia, Spain.

Marcos Zampieri, Shervin Malmasi, Preslav Nakov, Ahmed Ali, Suwon Shon, James Glass, Yves Scherrer, Tanja Samardžić, Nikola Ljubešić, Jörg Tiedemann, Chris van der Lee, Stefan Grondelaers, Nelleke Oostdijk, Antal van den Bosch, Ritesh Kumar, Bornini Lahiri, and Mayank Jain. 2018. Language Identification and Morphosyntactic Tagging: The Second VarDial Evaluation Campaign. In *Proceedings of the Fifth Workshop on NLP for Similar Languages, Varieties and Dialects (VarDial)*, Santa Fe, USA.

Marcos Zampieri, Shervin Malmasi, Yves Scherrer, Tanja Samardžić, Francis Tyers, Miikka Silfverberg, Natalia Klyueva, Tung-Le Pan, Chu-Ren Huang, Radu Tudor Ionescu, Andrei Butnaru, and Tommi Jauhiainen. 2019. A Report on the Third VarDial Evaluation Campaign. In *Proceedings of the Sixth Workshop on NLP for Similar Languages, Varieties and Dialects (VarDial)*. Association for Computational Linguistics.

Marcos Zampieri, Liling Tan, Nikola Ljubešić, and Jörg Tiedemann. 2014. A Report on the DSL Shared Task 2014. In *Proceedings of the First Workshop on Applying NLP Tools to Similar Languages, Varieties and Dialects*, pages 58–67, Dublin, Ireland.

Marcos Zampieri, Liling Tan, Nikola Ljubeić, Jrg Tiedemann, and Preslav Nakov. 2015. Overview of the DSL Shared Task 2015. In *Proceedings of the Joint Workshop on Language Technology for Closely Related Languages, Varieties and Dialects (LT4VarDial)*, pages 1–9, Hissar, Bulgaria.

Shan Zhong, Yingna Chen, Chunyi Zhu, and Jia Liu. 2007. Confidence measure based incremental adaptation for online language identification. In *Proceedings of International Conference on Human-Computer Interaction (HCI 2007)*, pages 535–543, Beijing, China.

Investigating Machine Learning Methods for
Language and Dialect Identification of Cuneiform Texts

Ehsan Doostmohammadi and **Minoo Nassajian**

Computational Lingusitics Group,
Sharif University of Technology, Tehran, Iran
`{e.doostm72, m.nassajian2016}@student.sharif.edu`

Abstract

Identification of the languages written using cuneiform symbols is a difficult task due to the lack of resources and the problem of tokenization. The Cuneiform Language Identification task in VarDial 2019 addresses the problem of identifying seven languages and dialects written in cuneiform; Sumerian and six dialects of Akkadian language: Old Babylonian, Middle Babylonian Peripheral, Standard Babylonian, Neo-Babylonian, Late Babylonian, and Neo-Assyrian. This paper describes the approaches taken by `SharifCL` team to this problem in VarDial 2019. The best result belongs to an ensemble of Support Vector Machines and a naive Bayes classifier, both working on character-level features, with macro-averaged F_1-score of 72.10%.

1 Introduction

A wide range of Natural Language Processing (NLP) tasks, such as Machine Translation (MT), speech recognition, information retrieval, data mining, and creating text resources for low-resource languages benefit from the upstream task of language identification. The Cuneiform Language Identification (CLI) task in VarDial 2019 (Zampieri et al., 2019) tries to address the problem of identifying languages and dialects of the texts written in cuneiform symbols.

Identifying languages and dialects of the cuneiform texts is a difficult task, since such languages lack resources and also there is the problem of tokenization. Although there are some work addressing the problem of tokenization in some of these languages or dialects, there is not any universal method or tool available for tokenization of cuneiform texts, as such a task depends on the rules of that language, simply because cuneiform writing system is a syllabic as well as a logographic one. As a result, all the en-

deavors in this paper are based on character-level features. This work investigates different machine learning methods which are proven to be effective in text classification and compares them by their obtained F_1-score, accuracy, and training time.

In this paper, we first review the literature of language identification and the work on languages written using cuneiform writing system in 2, introduce the models used to tackle the problem of identifying such languages and dialects in 3, describe the training data in 4, and discuss the results in 5.

2 Related Work

The majority of research conducted in the field of language identification has been on textual data. However, there are some studies focusing on speech samples, such as (Hategan et al., 2009; Ali et al., 2015; Malmasi and Zampieri, 2016). Language identification systems are meant to distinguish between similar languages (Goutte et al., 2016; Williams and Dagli, 2017), language varieties (Rangel et al., 2016; Castro et al., 2017), or a set of different dialects of the same language (Malmasi et al., 2016; El Haj et al., 2018). There has also been the annually held VarDial workshop since 2014, which deals with computational methods and language resources for closely related languages, language varieties, and dialects (Zampieri et al., 2017, 2018).

Various kinds of features are used to train these systems, including bytes and encodings (Singh and Gorla, 2007; Brown, 2012), characters (van der Lee and van den Bosch, 2017; Samih and Kallmeyer, 2017), morphemes (Gomez et al., 2017; Barbaresi, 2016), and words (Duvenhage et al., 2017; Clematide and Makarov, 2017).

The most recent studies use different language identification methods, such as decision trees

Proceedings of VarDial, pages 188–193
Minneapolis, MN, June 7, 2019 ©2019 Association for Computational Linguistics

(Bora and Kumar, 2018), Bayesian network classifiers (Rangel et al., 2016), similarity measures (such as the out-of-place method (Jauhiainen et al., 2017), local ranked distance (Franco-Salvador et al., 2017), and cross entropy (Hanani et al., 2017)), SVM (Alrifai et al., 2017), and neural networks (Chang and Lin, 2014; Cazamias et al., 2015; Jurgens et al., 2017; Kocmi and Bojar, 2017).

To the extent of our knowledge, there is no work addressing the problem of language and dialect identification of cuneiform texts. Such languages, Sumerian and Akkadian for instance, are considered low-resource languages, meaning that there are only a few electronic resources for cuneiform processing. Some of these datasets include (Yamauchi et al., 2018) which developed a handwritten cuneiform character imageset, and (Chiarcos et al., 2018) which is an annotated cuneiform corpus with morphological, syntactic, and semantic tags. Furthermore, there are some early studies on rule-based morphological analyzers for these languages like (Kataja and Koskenniemi, 1988; Barthélemy, 1998; Macks, 2002; Barthélemy, 2009), and (Tablan et al., 2006).

Additionally, a small number of cuneiform text processing tasks have been carried out in which the transliterations of cuneiform characters were considered as the base feature. For instance, (Luo et al., 2015) adapted an unsupervised algorithm to recognize Sumerian personal names. Having transliterated the cuneiform corpus, they utilized the pre-knowledge and applied limited tags to pre-annotate the corpus. As another study, (Homburg and Chiarcos, 2016) conducted the first research on word segmentation on Akkadian cuneiform. They used three types of word segmentations algorithms including rule-based algorithms (such as bigram and prefix/suffix), dictionary-based algorithms (like MaxMatch, MaxMatchCombined, LCUMatching, MinWCMatch), and statistical and/or machine learning algorithms (such as C4.5, CRF, HMM, k-means, k Nearest Neighbors, MaxEnt, naive Bayes, multi-layer perceptron, and Support Vector Machines (SVM)) which work based on transliterations of cuneiform characters. The paper reports that the dictionary-based approaches obtained the best results. In addition, as one of the most recent studies on languages written in cuneiform, (Chiarcos et al., 2017) worked on a machine translation task. The used data consists of unannotated raw transliterations of Sumerian texts with their English translations. They use a morphological analyzer to extract word information to be used in the machine translation task. Moreover, a distantly supervised Part of Speech tagger and a dependency parser are applied to annotate data to facilitate the machine translation task.

3 Methodology

We investigated different machine learning methods, all of them based on character-level features, to tackle the problem. The following methods take 1- to 3-gram character TFIDF and 1- to 4-gram character count as input features and were implemented using Scikit-learn (Pedregosa et al., 2011):

- **SVM**: an SVM with a learning rate of $1e{-}6$, hinge loss, and `elasticnet` penalty, trained for 5 epochs with a random state of 11.

- **Naive Bayes**: a multinomial naive Bayes classifier with alpha of 0.14 and `fit_prior` as `True`.

- **Ensemble of SVM and naive Bayes**: a soft voting classifier which predicts the class label based on the argmax of the sums of the predicted probabilities of the SVM and the naive Bayes models.

- **Random Forest**: a random forest classifier with 25 estimators of depth 300.

- **Logistic Regression**: a logistic regression classifier with `lbfgs` optimizer, trained for 100 epochs.

We also experimented with deep learning approaches. The following two methods take character embeddings of size 32 for the 256 most common characters as input, and are trained using an Adam optimizer (Kingma and Ba, 2014) with batch size of 64 and learning rate of $1e{-}4$:

- **Convolutional Neural Network**: The concatenation of the output a set of parallel Convolutional Neural Network (CNN) layers, each with 32 filters and kernel size and stride of 2, 3, 4 and 5 which is fed to a a dense layer that maps to an $\mathbb{R}^{128}$ space and another one that maps to the $\mathbb{R}^{7}$ space of the labels. We also applied dropout with 0.5 keeping rate on CNNs output and another one with the same keeping rate on the first dense layer's output.

- **Recurrent Neural Network**: A Recurrent Neural Network (RNN) with Long Short-Term Memory (LSTM) (Hochreiter and Schmidhuber, 1997) cell of size 256 and a dense layer mapping to an $\mathbb{R}^{128}$ space and another one mapping to the $\mathbb{R}^7$ space of the labels. We also applied dropout with 0.4 keeping rate on RNN's output and another one with 0.5 keeping rate on the first dense layer's output.

4 Data Description

The data of CLI shared task is described in (Jauhiainen et al., 2019). This data consists of 7 classes: Sumerian (SUX), Old Babylonian (OLB), Middle Babylonian peripheral (MPB), Standard Babylonian (STB), Neo-Babylonian (NEB), Late Babylonian (LTB), and Neo-Assyrian (NEA). Figure 1 shows the number of samples for each label in the training data. The whole training data consists of 139,421 samples. The development set comprises 668 and the test set 985 samples per label.

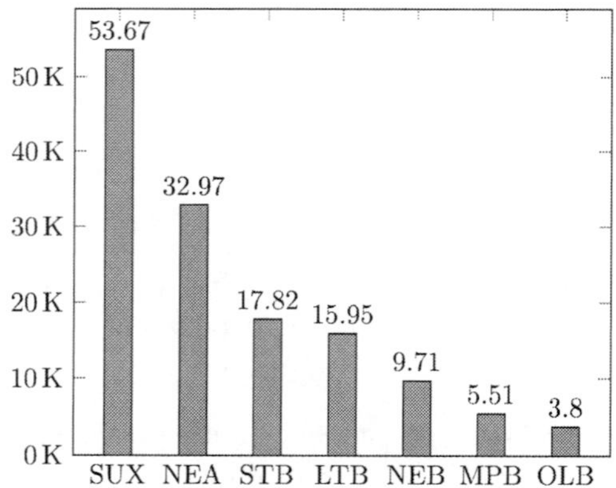

Figure 1: Number of samples for each label in the training set (in thousands).

Figure 1 shows that most of the training data belongs to SUX and NEA classes. Table 1 contains more detailed information on the data which shows that 86.35% of the data belongs to four classes of SUX, NEA, STB, LTB, whereas only 13.65% belongs to the other three.

5 Results and Discussion

Firstly, we trained the methods described in 3 and evaluated the models on development set. We

Label	# of samples	% of all
SUX	53,673	38.49%
NEA	32,966	23.64%
STB	17,817	12.78%
LTB	15,947	11.44%
NEB	9,707	6.96%
MPB	5,508	3.95%
OLB	3,803	2.72%

Table 1: Number of samples in the training set for each label and their percentage of a total of 139,421 samples ordered from the highest to the lowest.

continued with the best two methods, SVM and NB, and evaluated them on the test set. Table 2 shows the macro-averaged F_1-score, accuracy, and training time (in seconds) of the five non-deep and two deep methods on the development set. The non-deep models are trained using an `Intel(R) Core(TM) i7-7700K CPU @ 4.20GHz` CPU with 8 threads, and the deep ones using an `NVIDIA GeForce GTX 1080 Ti`.

Method	F_1-score	Accuracy	T. Time
RF	0.5201	0.5615	264.14
LR	0.6861	0.6982	40.54
NB	*0.7194*	*0.7301*	**0.15**
SVM	<u>0.7222</u>	<u>0.7309</u>	<u>1.67</u>
Ens.	**0.7268**	**0.7356**	*3.34*
CNN	0.6192	0.6249	+4K
RNN	0.6259	0.6364	+4K

Table 2: Accuracy and F_1-score on the development set, and the training time (in seconds) of the methods described in section 3: Random Forest (RF), Logistic Regression (LR), naive Bayes (NB), Support Vector Machine (SVM), Ensemble of the last two (Ens.), and Convolutional and Recurrent Neural Networks (CNN and RNN, respectively). The best result in each column is in bold, the second best underlined, and the third best in italics.

The ensemble method obtained the best F_1-score and a very short training time. On the other hand, random forest model suffers from low performance (as it is usually the case in NLP) and a relatively long training time. The CNN and RNN with embedded characters as input features performed poorly, as it is usually the case in the language identification task (Jauhiainen et al., 2018). Deep methods see benefit from large amounts of data, however when being trained with fewer data, hyperparameters play a more important role in the results, therefore further tuning them might improve the results in table 2. As of training time, the naive Bayes method was the fastest and the RNN and the CNN the slowest methods. We also experimented with one-hot encoded characters as RNN's and CNN's input features, which was not fruitful, and therefore are not included in the results.

Table 3 shows the results of the SVM and the ensemble of SVM and NB on the test set. The ensemble outperforms SVM, as on the development set.

System	F1 (macro)	Accuracy
SVM (T)	0.6660	0.6722
SVM (TD)	0.7171	0.7179
SVM + NB (TD)	**0.7210**	**0.7239**

Table 3: Results of the CLI task on the test set. T stands for training and D for development data. TD means that the model was trained on the combination of training and development data and T, only on the training data. The best result in each column is in bold.

Table 4 contains more detailed results of the best performing model on the test set, i.e. the ensemble. It shows the precision, recall, and F_1-score of the model on each class and their average. The results are ordered based on the F_1-score.

Label	Precision	Recall	F_1-score
LTB	0.8913	0.9655	0.9269
MPB	0.8109	0.8579	0.8337
OLB	0.8358	0.6924	0.7574
SUX	0.8273	0.6274	0.7136
NEA	0.5621	0.8772	0.6852
NEB	0.6775	0.5523	0.6085
STB	0.5515	0.4944	0.5214
Macro Avg.	0.7366	0.7239	0.7210

Table 4: Precision, Recall and F_1-score of all the classes and their macro average ordered from the highest to the lowest F_1-score.

Considering the results in table 4 and the confusion matrix, Late Babylonian (LTB) was the easiest class to identify with a recall of 96.55% and Middle Babylonian Peripheral (MPB) the second easiest, with a recall of 85.79% (with only 5,508 (+668) training samples). Old Babylonian (OLB) was also easy to identifiy, especially when we consider its amount training samples, 3,803 (+668). Standard Babylonian (STB) is mainly

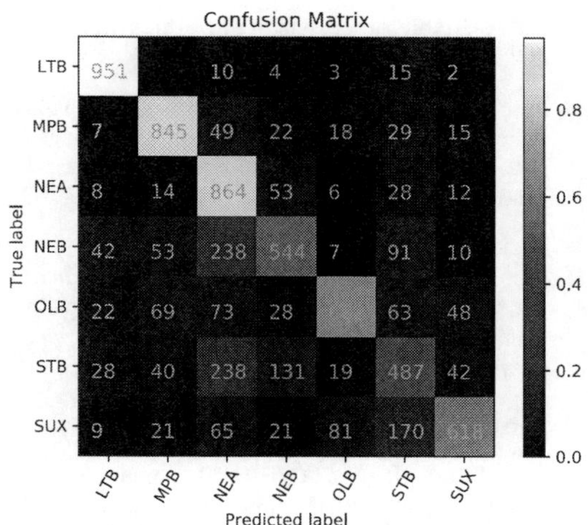

Figure 2: Confusion matrix of the ensemble model's results on the test data.

misclassified as Sumerian, and Neo-Babylonian as Standard Babylonian. Neo-Assyrian (NEA) is also among the classes with low F_1-score, but the model has achieved a very high recall, 87.72%, in this class. Neo-Assyrian (NEA) is mainly misclassified as Neo-Babylonian (NEB) and Standard Babylonian (STB).

6 Conclusion

In this paper, we investigated different machine learning methods, such as SVM and neural networks, and compared their performance in the task of language and dialect identification of cuneiform texts. The best performance was achieved by a combination of SVM and naive Bayes, using only character-level features. It was shown that characters are enough to obtain at least 72.10% F_1-score. However, the best model was not able to achieve a good result classifying some of the dialects which indicates a need for other kinds of features, such as word-level ones, and/or embedded or transferred knowledge of these languages and dialects to be used in training the deep models.

References

Ahmed Ali, Najim Dehak, Patrick Cardinal, Sameer Khurana, Sree Harsha Yella, James Glass, Peter Bell, and Steve Renals. 2015. Automatic dialect detection in arabic broadcast speech. *arXiv preprint arXiv:1509.06928*.

Khaled Alrifai, Ghaida Rebdawi, and Nada Ghneim.

2017. Arabic tweeps gender and dialect prediction. In *CLEF (Working Notes)*.

Adrien Barbaresi. 2016. An unsupervised morphological criterion for discriminating similar languages. In *3rd Workshop on NLP for Similar Languages, Varieties and Dialects (VarDial 2016)*, pages 212–220. Association for Computational Linguistics.

François Barthélemy. 1998. A morphological analyzer for akkadian verbal forms with a model of phonetic transformations. In *Proceedings of the Workshop on Computational Approaches to Semitic Languages*, pages 73–81. Association for Computational Linguistics.

François Barthélemy. 2009. The karamel system and semitic languages: structured multi-tiered morphology. In *Proceedings of the EACL 2009 Workshop on Computational Approaches to Semitic Languages*, pages 10–18. Association for Computational Linguistics.

Manas Jyoti Bora and Ritesh Kumar. 2018. Automatic word-level identification of language in assamese english hindi code-mixed data. In *4th Workshop on Indian Language Data and Resources, Proceedings of the Eleventh International Conference on Language Resources and Evaluation (LREC 2018)*, pages 7–12.

Ralf D Brown. 2012. Finding and identifying text in 900+ languages. *Digital Investigation*, 9:S34–S43.

Dayvid W Castro, Ellen Souza, Douglas Vitório, Diego Santos, and Adriano LI Oliveira. 2017. Smoothed n-gram based models for tweet language identification: A case study of the brazilian and european portuguese national varieties. *Applied Soft Computing*, 61:1160–1172.

Jordan Cazamias, Chinmayi Dixit, and Martina Marek. 2015. Large-scale language classification.

Joseph Chee Chang and Chu-Cheng Lin. 2014. Recurrent-neural-network for language detection on twitter code-switching corpus. *arXiv preprint arXiv:1412.4314*.

Christian Chiarcos, Ilya Khait, Émilie Pagé-Perron, and Maria Sukhareva. 2017. Machine translation and automated analysis of the sumerian language. In *Joint SIGHUM Workshop on Computational Linguistics for Cultural Heritage, Social Sciences, Humanities and Literature, ACL*, pages 10–16. Association for Computational Linguistics.

Christian Chiarcos, Emilie Page-Perron, Niko Schenk, Jayanth, and Lucas Reckling. 2018. Annotating sumerian: A llod-enhanced workflow for cuneiform corpora. In *Proceedings of the Language Resources and Evaluation Conference*.

Simon Clematide and Peter Makarov. 2017. Cluzh at vardial gdi 2017: Testing a variety of machine learning tools for the classification of swiss german dialects. In *Proceedings of the Fourth Workshop on NLP for Similar Languages, Varieties and Dialects (VarDial)*, pages 170–177.

Bernardt Duvenhage, Mfundo Ntini, and Phala Ramonyai. 2017. Improved text language identification for the south african languages. In *2017 Pattern Recognition Association of South Africa and Robotics and Mechatronics (PRASA-RobMech)*, pages 214–218. IEEE.

Mahmoud El Haj, Paul Edward Rayson, and Mariam Aboelezz. 2018. Arabic dialect identification in the context of bivalency and code-switching.

Marc Franco-Salvador, Greg Kondrak, and Paolo Rosso. 2017. Bridging the native language and language variety identification tasks. *Procedia computer science*, 112:1554–1561.

Helena Gomez, Ilia Markov, Jorge Baptista, Grigori Sidorov, and David Pinto. 2017. Discriminating between similar languages using a combination of typed and untyped character n-grams and words. In *Proceedings of the Fourth Workshop on NLP for Similar Languages, Varieties and Dialects (VarDial)*, pages 137–145.

Cyril Goutte, Serge Léger, Shervin Malmasi, and Marcos Zampieri. 2016. Discriminating similar languages: Evaluations and explorations. *arXiv preprint arXiv:1610.00031*.

Abualsoud Hanani, Aziz Qaroush, and Stephen Taylor. 2017. Identifying dialects with textual and acoustic cues. In *Proceedings of the Fourth Workshop on NLP for Similar Languages, Varieties and Dialects (VarDial)*, pages 93–101.

Andrea Hategan, Bogdan Barliga, and Ioan Tabus. 2009. Language identification of individualwords in a multilingual automatic speech recognition system. In *2009 IEEE International Conference on Acoustics, Speech and Signal Processing*, pages 4357–4360. IEEE.

Sepp Hochreiter and Jürgen Schmidhuber. 1997. Long short-term memory. *Neural computation*, 9(8):1735–1780.

Timo Homburg and Christian Chiarcos. 2016. Akkadian word segmentation. In *Proceedings Tenth International Conference on Language Resource Evaluation.(LREC 2016)*, pages 4067–4074.

Tommi Jauhiainen, Heidi Jauhiainen, Tero Alstola, and Krister Lindén. 2019. Language and Dialect Identification of Cuneiform Texts. In *Proceedings of the Sixth Workshop on NLP for Similar Languages, Varieties and Dialects (VarDial)*.

Tommi Jauhiainen, Krister Lindén, and Heidi Jauhiainen. 2017. Evaluation of language identification methods using 285 languages. In *Proceedings of the 21st Nordic Conference on Computational Linguistics*, pages 183–191.

Tommi Jauhiainen, Marco Lui, Marcos Zampieri, Timothy Baldwin, and Krister Lindén. 2018. Automatic language identification in texts: A survey. *arXiv preprint arXiv:1804.08186*.

David Jurgens, Yulia Tsvetkov, and Dan Jurafsky. 2017. Incorporating dialectal variability for socially equitable language identification. In *Proceedings of the 55th Annual Meeting of the Association for Computational Linguistics (Volume 2: Short Papers)*, volume 2, pages 51–57.

Laura Kataja and Kimmo Koskenniemi. 1988. Finite-state description of semitic morphology: A case study of ancient accadian. In *Coling Budapest 1988 Volume 1: International Conference on Computational Linguistics*, volume 1.

Diederik P Kingma and Jimmy Ba. 2014. Adam: A method for stochastic optimization. *arXiv preprint arXiv:1412.6980*.

Tom Kocmi and Ondřej Bojar. 2017. Lanidenn: Multilingual language identification on character window. *arXiv preprint arXiv:1701.03338*.

Chris van der Lee and Antal van den Bosch. 2017. Exploring lexical and syntactic features for language variety identification. In *Proceedings of the Fourth Workshop on NLP for Similar Languages, Varieties and Dialects (VarDial)*, pages 190–199.

Liang Luo, Yudong Liu, James Hearne, and Clinton Burkhart. 2015. Unsupervised sumerian personal name recognition. In *The Twenty-Eighth International Flairs Conference*.

Aaron Macks. 2002. Parsing akkadian verbs with prolog. In *Proceedings of the ACL-02 workshop on Computational approaches to semitic languages*.

Shervin Malmasi and Marcos Zampieri. 2016. Arabic dialect identification in speech transcripts. In *Proceedings of the Third Workshop on NLP for Similar Languages, Varieties and Dialects (VarDial3)*, pages 106–113.

Shervin Malmasi, Marcos Zampieri, Nikola Ljubešić, Preslav Nakov, Ahmed Ali, and Jörg Tiedemann. 2016. Discriminating between similar languages and arabic dialect identification: A report on the third dsl shared task. In *Proceedings of the Third Workshop on NLP for Similar Languages, Varieties and Dialects (VarDial3)*, pages 1–14.

Fabian Pedregosa, Gaël Varoquaux, Alexandre Gramfort, Vincent Michel, Bertrand Thirion, Olivier Grisel, Mathieu Blondel, Peter Prettenhofer, Ron Weiss, Vincent Dubourg, Jake Vanderplas, Alexandre Passos, David Cournapeau, Matthieu Brucher, Matthieu Perrot, and Édouard Duchesnay. 2011. Scikit-learn: Machine learning in python. *J. Mach. Learn. Res.*, 12:2825–2830.

Francisco Rangel, Marc Franco-Salvador, and Paolo Rosso. 2016. A low dimensionality representation for language variety identification. In *International Conference on Intelligent Text Processing and Computational Linguistics*, pages 156–169. Springer.

Younes Samih and Laura Kallmeyer. 2017. *Dialectal Arabic processing Using Deep Learning*. Ph.D. thesis, Ph. D. thesis, Düsseldorf, Germany.

Anil Kumar Singh and Jagadeesh Gorla. 2007. Identification of languages and encodings in a multilingual document. In *Building and Exploring Web Corpora (WAC3-2007): Proceedings of the 3rd Web as Corpus Workshop, Incorporating Cleaneval*, volume 4, page 95. Presses univ. de Louvain.

Valentin Tablan, Wim Peters, Diana Maynard, Hamish Cunningham, and K Bontcheva. 2006. Creating tools for morphological analysis of sumerian. In *LREC*, pages 1762–1765.

Jennifer Williams and Charlie Dagli. 2017. Twitter language identification of similar languages and dialects without ground truth. In *Proceedings of the Fourth Workshop on NLP for Similar Languages, Varieties and Dialects (VarDial)*, pages 73–83.

Kenji Yamauchi, Hajime Yamamoto, and Wakaha Mori. 2018. Building a handwritten cuneiform character imageset. In *Proceedings of the Eleventh International Conference on Language Resources and Evaluation (LREC-2018)*.

Marcos Zampieri, Shervin Malmasi, Nikola Ljubešić, Preslav Nakov, Ahmed Ali, Jörg Tiedemann, Yves Scherrer, and Noëmi Aepli. 2017. Findings of the VarDial Evaluation Campaign 2017. In *Proceedings of the Fourth Workshop on NLP for Similar Languages, Varieties and Dialects (VarDial)*, Valencia, Spain.

Marcos Zampieri, Shervin Malmasi, Preslav Nakov, Ahmed Ali, Suwon Shuon, James Glass, Yves Scherrer, Tanja Samardžić, Nikola Ljubešić, Jörg Tiedemann, Chris van der Lee, Stefan Grondelaers, Nelleke Oostdijk, Antal van den Bosch, Ritesh Kumar, Bornini Lahiri, and Mayank Jain. 2018. Language Identification and Morphosyntactic Tagging: The Second VarDial Evaluation Campaign. In *Proceedings of the Fifth Workshop on NLP for Similar Languages, Varieties and Dialects (VarDial)*, Santa Fe, USA.

Marcos Zampieri, Shervin Malmasi, Yves Scherrer, Tanja Samardžić, Francis Tyers, Miikka Silfverberg, Natalia Klyueva, Tung-Le Pan, Chu-Ren Huang, Radu Tudor Ionescu, Andrei Butnaru, and Tommi Jauhiainen. 2019. A Report on the Third VarDial Evaluation Campaign. In *Proceedings of the Sixth Workshop on NLP for Similar Languages, Varieties and Dialects (VarDial)*. Association for Computational Linguistics.

TwistBytes - Identification of Cuneiform Languages and German Dialects at VarDial 2019

Fernando Benites
benf@zhaw.ch

Zurich University of
Applied Sciences,
Switzerland

Pius von Däniken
vode@zhaw.ch

Zurich University of
Applied Sciences,
Switzerland

Mark Cieliebak
mc@spinningbytes.com

SpinningBytes AG,
Switzerland

Abstract

We describe our approaches for the German Dialect Identification (GDI) and the Cuneiform Language Identification (CLI) tasks at the VarDial Evaluation Campaign 2019. The goal was to identify dialects of Swiss German in GDI and Sumerian and Akkadian in CLI.

In GDI, the system should distinguish four dialects from the German speaking part of Switzerland. Our system for GDI achieved third place out of 6 teams, with a macro averaged F-1 of 74.6%. In CLI, the system should distinguish seven languages written in cuneiform script. Our system achieved third place out of 8 teams, with a macro averaged F-1 of 74.7%.

1 Introduction

The 6th Workshop on NLP for Similar Languages, Varieties and Dialects (VarDial 2019) included an evaluation campaigns with five shared tasks with the goal to find approaches which can differentiate dialects in various languages. We describe our solutions for two sub-tasks: German Dialect Identification (GDI) and Cuneiform Language Identification (CLI).

GDI The GDI task (Zampieri et al., 2019) had the goal to classify sentences into four dialects of Swiss German. Each sentence was transcribed and annotated with the dialect area of the speaker (Bern, Basel, Lucerne, and Zurich). No additional information other than the task data should be used (closed submission). The task was a continuation of similar shared tasks in previous years (Zampieri et al., 2018).

In the German speaking part of Switzerland, there exist many dialects which are quite different, and speakers of one dialect might even have difficulty understanding dialects of regions not far

away. There is no standardized writing for Swiss German.

The identification of dialect based on text is a challenging task, especially if there is no standardized written form of the dialects. First of all, transcribing audio signals to text is highly ambiguous and can be very subjective. Even with detailed transcription guidelines, the resulting text can differ significantly among annotators. This subjectivity of the annotations manifests in similar tasks such as in labelling multi-label samples (Benites, 2017). Another problem is that for short sentences there is little text which could point to a dialect. A good example can be found in the GDI dataset, which contains samples"jaja jaja" and "jaja ja ja". Both roughly translate to "yes yes" or "indeed", and both mean the same for Swiss German speakers. The first is labelled with Lucerne dialect, while the second is labeled with Zurich dialect. Therefore these samples are easily misclassified. To cope with this issue, i-Vectors were provided by the organizers this year (see Section 3.2.4).

CLI The CLI task (Jauhiainen et al., 2019) is new to VarDial and consists of classifying texts written in cuneiform script into Sumerian or one of six dialects of Akkadian: Old Babylonian, Middle Babylonian Peripheral, Standard Babylonian, Neo-Babylonian, Late Babylonian, and Neo-Assyrian. Cuneiform is one of the oldest known writing systems and has been used for 3,000 years by different cultures around Mesopotamia.

Our Solutions We describe in this paper the approaches taken by our team TwistBytes. The GDI system is an updated version of our solution for the previous year's competition (Benites et al., 2018). We improved several parameters and extended it to use semi-supervised learning and i-Vectors. For the sake of completeness, we recapitulate the base system description in Section 3.2,

Proceedings of VarDial, pages 194–201
Minneapolis, MN, June 7, 2019 ©2019 Association for Computational Linguistics

and then describe the applied modifications. This system achieved 3rd place among 6 participants at GDI, with a macro averaged F-1 of 74.6%.

For CLI, we use a linear SVM as classifier with character n-gram features and include perplexities from character n-gram language models as additional features. This system achieved 3rd place among 8 participants at CLI, with a macro averaged F-1 of 74.7%.

2 Related Work

The central focus of the evaluation campaign at VarDial is to properly identify dialect of various languages. For GDI, there have been two previous editions of the shared task, which laid the basis for dialect identification in Swiss German (Zampieri et al., 2017, 2018). Solving this problem can have a positive impact on many tasks, e.g. for POS-tagging of dialectal data (Hollenstein and Aepli, 2014), for compilation of German dialect corpora (Hollenstein and Aepli, 2015), or for automatic speech recognition of Swiss German.

Many studies tackled the problem of language and dialect identification for other languages, creating a noticeable amount of related work, described in short in the evaluation campaign reports and (Jauhiainen et al., 2018b). A typical approach uses SVMs with different feature extraction methods. The use of character language models for language identification has previously been studied by (Vatanen et al., 2010).

Our approach is most similar to MAZA, which was proposed at VarDial 2017 (Malmasi and Zampieri, 2017b). MAZA uses Term Frequency (TF) on character-n-grams and unigrams for word features to train several SVMs. Then it uses a Random Forest meta-classifier with 10-fold cross-validation on the predictions of the SVMs. We extended this approach and used Term Frequency-Inverse Document Frequency (TF-IDF) on word and on character level. We used an SVM as meta-classifier, and we did not concatenate the output of the base classifiers but summed them. Similar to (Malmasi and Zampieri, 2017a) we used a single SVM classifier for the i-Vectors. More details are given in Section 3.2.

3 Data and Methodology

3.1 Task Definition

The task of GDI is to classify a transcribed sentence from the ArchiMob data set (Samardžić

et al., 2016) into one of four classes of Swiss German dialect. Each class represents a dialect area of Swiss German: Bern (BE), Basel (BS), Lucerne (LU) and Zurich (ZH). Since the dialects are very different from Standard German, the sentences are transcribed using the guideline book by Dieth (Dieth and Schmid-Cadalbert, 1986). It is a phonetics oriented transcription method but it is orthographic and is partially adapted to standard German spelling habits and alphabet. As such it loses some of the precision and explicitness of phonetic transcription methods such as the International Phonetic Alphabet. We expected therefore that character-based and error tolerant methods will perform best, since different spellings of the same word might occur.

Table 1 shows the number of sentences in the training set, the validation set, and test set per dialect area. The training set was slightly changed in comparison to the one from last year. The validation set was the test set of 2018 GDI shared task. The sentence distribution is almost evenly balanced over all four dialect areas.

One peculiarity that occured in the data of last year was the ambiguity of labels for identical sentences, i.e. that multiple sentences with identical transcriptions had different labels. This was not the case when looking at the training and validation set in isolation[1]. Only when both were merged, the sentence "i däre ziit" was labelled as originating from Zurich in the training set and from Basel in the validation set. We expected that i-Vectors would help solving these kinds of ambiguities.

GDI dataset information					
Set	BE	BS	LU	ZH	Total
Train	3750	3268	3390	3870	14278
Validation	1053	1528	1016	932	4529
Test					4742

Table 1: Number of instances per dialect area for GDI dataset

For the Cuneiform Language Identification task, CLI (Jauhiainen et al., 2019), we have to distinguish Sumerian (SUX) and six variants of the Akkadian language: Old Babylonian (OLB), Middle Babylonian Peripheral (MPB), Standard Babylonian (STB), Neo-Babylonian (NEB), Late Baby-

---

[1] However, some sentences were on a character level very close, as pointed out in the Introduction.

CLI dataset information			
	Train	Validation	Test
LTB	15947	668	
MPB	5508	668	
NEA	32966	668	
NEB	9707	668	
OLB	3803	668	
STB	17817	668	
SUX	53673	668	
Total	139421	4676	6895

Table 2: Number of instances for CLI dataset

lonian (LTB), and Neo-Assyrian (NEA). Table 2 shows the distribution of labels per language in the dataset. The texts are all written in cuneiform script and provided as their Unicode representation. Since the different language variants are spread over multiple centuries, we assumed that the symbols in use differ across them. Table 3 shows the Jaccard Similarity (Jaccard, 1902) between the sets of unique symbols used by every language computed on the training set. Sumerian is the most dissimilar in its use of symbols compared to the other languages. This was to be expected, as it is the only language not in the Akkadian language family. We expect that dialects with lower similarity in symbol use can be easier distinguished, which was our motivation to use language modeling as part of the classification system.

3.2 System Definition TB-Meta for GDI

In this section, we describe our approach for GDI in detail. One part (meta crossvalidation) is based on the system from (Malmasi and Zampieri, 2017b) but extended in several ways. A previous version was already described in (Benites et al., 2018). The key improvements this year are the optimization of the preprocessing and and the feature extraction, a new preprocessing step between base classifier and meta-classifier, and using an SVM as meta-classifier. This year we extended our approach for GDI to also use a semi-supervised method.

We observed that much of the recognition can be performed on character level, where character bigrams can provide a key insight, while demonstrating a high efficiency. The four processing steps of the system are: a) to preprocess the sentences, b) extract features from them, c) classify with a base classifier and d) pass the predictions to a meta-classifier which, in turn, provides the final prediction. This year, we were additionally provided with i-Vectors. These represent important new features, especially given the fact that there are only few speakers per label set. That means that if we can identify the speaker and the spoken dialect at least once with high confidence, we can easily label the other sentences spoken by them. Here especially, we expect that the semi-supervised approach improves the overall performance.

3.2.1 Preprocessing

The basic preprocessing step was to split the sentences in words by using white-spaces and convert them to lower case. No stopword removal or lemmatization was performed since these steps might erase any traces of key features for differentiating between the dialects (see (Maharjan et al., 2014)). Afterwards multiple feature extraction methods were applied, as explained in the next section.

3.2.2 Feature Extraction

In this edition of the VarDial GDI task, we were provided with i-Vectors in addition to textual features. This leads to the following observation: the textual feature vectors are very sparse, as the average word occurrence is 7.4 ± 4.16 per sentence in the training set, whereas the i-Vectors are dense. This has the effect that the SVMs need to cope with multi-modal features with different density and that was the main reason why we used a separate SVM for the i-Vectors.

We use Term Frequency (TF) with n-grams for characters and words for n ranging from 1 to 7. An additional preprocessing for the classifiers employed (see Section 3.2.3) is to normalize the TF values, at least per sentence, which in some cases can improve prediction quality. Also, we calculated the TF-IDF (Manning et al., 2008), which usually gives the best single feature set for prediction quality.

For the feature extraction, we mainly used the scikit-learn[2] package with one modification: We also used a custom character bigram analyzer (referred to later as CB) in order to produce character bigrams without spaces, since the standard implementation considers all characters in the text including the spaces, especially at the beginning and

---

[2]http://scikit-learn.org

	LTB	MPB	NEA	NEB	OLB	STB	SUX
LTB	1.00	0.71	0.80	0.77	0.72	0.71	0.53
MPB	0.71	1.00	0.65	0.68	0.71	0.57	0.43
NEA	0.80	0.65	1.00	0.85	0.70	0.82	0.61
NEB	0.77	0.68	0.85	1.00	0.71	0.81	0.60
OLB	0.72	0.71	0.70	0.71	1.00	0.62	0.46
STB	0.71	0.57	0.82	0.81	0.62	1.00	0.70
SUX	0.53	0.43	0.61	0.60	0.46	0.70	1.00

Table 3: Jaccard similarities between the sets of symbols used per language in the training set of CLI

end of a word[3]. We employed TF-IDF not only on word level but also on character level.

Each of the feature extraction methods from the texts served as a separate feature set which was processed by a base classifier. The entire list is: TF word n-grams (TF-W), TF character n-grams (TF-C), TF-IDF words (TF-IDF-W), custom bigrams analyzer (CB-C), TF-C normalized to range from 0 to 1 (TF-C-N) and TF-IDF character n-grams (TF-IDF-C).

Additionally, i-Vectors were used to extract characteristics about the speaker from the audio signal. These were provided by the task organizers. They are basically a simplified variant of the joint factor analysis (Chen et al., 2014) which assured the anonymity of the speakers. As in (Suh et al., 2011), we also normalized the i-Vectors to unit length for better performance based on experiments on the validation set. We used them as input features to a separate base classifier (along with the extracted text features), that is each textual feature had their separate classifier and likewise the i-Vectors, only the output of the classifiers were merged.

3.2.3 Classifiers

Last year edition of GDI (Zampieri et al., 2018) showed that concatenating textual features for SVM produced worse prediction quality than the use of ensemble classifiers. We use the ensemble S-Classifier, which sums the predictions of the base classifiers and gives as input to a linear SVM (see Figure 1), and achieved considerably good results in GDI.

Meta Crossvalidation Classifier We used a two-tier meta-classifier bottom-up with crossvalidation (referred to as TB-Meta) to eliminate the

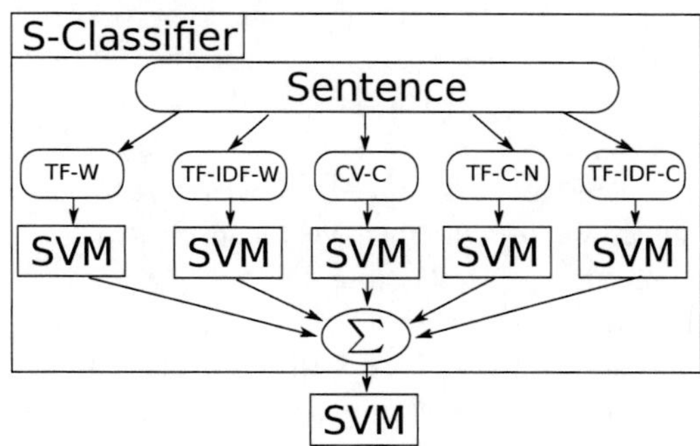

Figure 1: TB-Meta classifier workflow, with S-classifier and textual features

need for parameter/weighting search. The workflow of the system is depicted in Figure 1. First an input sentence is preprocessed, then the features are extracted and passed to the base classifiers, one classifier per feature set. The predictions of the classifiers are summed (S-Classifier output), and these intermediate predictions are passed to a last classifier (meta-classifier) that decides about the final label. The second level of the procedure also ensures that the class interdiscrimination is improved. Further, each base classifier prediction is then weighted by the meta-classifier. That means a weighting scheme and time-consuming parameter search is not needed anymore. For a detailed description please see (Benites et al., 2018).

Semi-Supervised Learning After the training, we augmented TB-Meta with a semi-supervised learning similar as in (Jauhiainen et al., 2018a). This approach consists of classifying the unlabelled test set with a model based on the training data, then selecting the predictions with the highest confidence and using them as new additional (weak) labelled training samples. The method can be very useful if there are few training samples and a test set with out-of-domain data is expected. Our approached consisted of setting a threshold for the confidence output of the SVM (fitted with regres-

---

[3]This can also be probably implemented with sklearn setting the analyzer to "char_wb" but we did not evaluate the differences in implementations.

sion) to 0.9 and in each iteration decreasing it by $\frac{i}{20}$ where i is the number of the iteration.

3.2.4 I-Vectors

There is strong indication that the i-Vectors in the context of dialect identification provide strong features for Arabic dialect classification, as described in (Bahari et al., 2014; Malmasi and Zampieri, 2017a). We used them in the context of GDI with caution, especially, because there are only few speakers in each set. On the one hand, if a speaker was identified and correctly classified, the problem would be solved. However, if there was something off with the i-Vectors of one speaker, it could throw the classifier off the right track. We integrate the i-Vectors into last year's system by training a separate base SVM classifier with the i-Vectors and the output is used as additional input for the S-classifier.

3.3 System Definition TB-LM for CLI

The TB-LM system consists of TF-IDF features, language modelling features, and a linear SVM classifier. We do not apply any preprocessing steps to the texts but work directly with the Unicode codepoints.

TF-IDF We use TF-IDF features on the symbol level for n-gram lengths from 1 to 3. Most samples in the training set are short: On average they are 7.05 symbols long, with a median length of 5 symbols. Therefore, we use only binary term frequency counts, as those tend to be more robust for classification of short texts.

Language Modelling Additionally, we train a 3-gram language model with Kneser-Ney smoothing (Kneser and Ney, 1995) for every language. We use the language model scores as additional features for every sample.

We again use scikit-learn for the TF-IDF features and the SVM, as well as nltk (*Natural Language Toolkit*[4]) for language modeling.

During experimentation, we train the system on the training set and evaluate on the validation set. For the final submission, we train on training and validation set jointly.

System	macro F-1
GDI validation set	
Random(10)	0.2468±0.0079
SVM Char-Ngram(1,7)	0.6494
TB-Meta	0.6984
TB-Meta$-iV$	0.6769
TB-Meta$-S$	0.7516
TB-Meta$-SiV$	0.9028
TB-Meta$-SiV_p$	**0.9031**
GDI test set	
TB-Meta$-iV$	0.6823
TB-Meta$-SiV$	**0.7455**
TB-Meta$-SiV_p$	0.7349

Table 4: Results for the GDI task on the validation and test set for TB approaches.

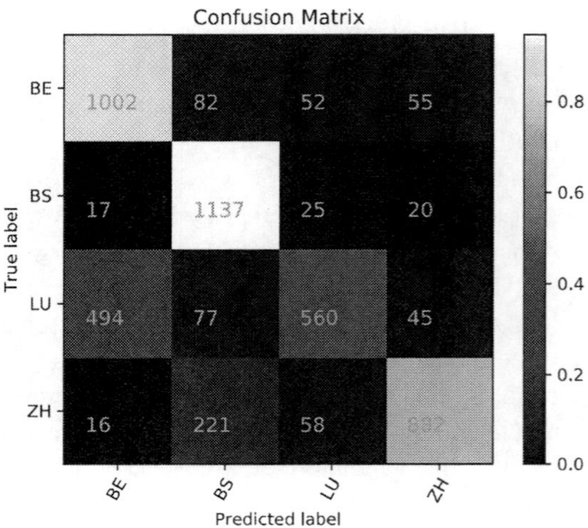

Figure 2: Confusion matrix of TB-Meta-SiV GDI

4 Results

4.1 GDI

Parameters For this year's shared task, we used a maximum of 100'000 features per subclassifier/feature set for the TB-Meta approach, based on our experimental results from last year. For the semi-supervised method we used 10 iterations.

Results Discussion We present in Table 4 the different approaches used in the GDI task and how they performed on the validation set. We also put the submitted results for comparison, which allows to see how the submitted approaches performed on the test set. TB-Meta refers to the TwistBytes Meta classifier, the $-iV$ suffix refers

---

[4]https://www.nltk.org/

Team	macro F-1	Place
tearsofjoy	0.7593	1
SUKI	0.7541	2
TwistBytes	0.7455	3
BAM	0.6255	4
dkosmajac	0.5616	5
ghpaetzold	0.5575	6

Table 5: Competition result of GDI with TwistBytes approach TB-Meta-SiV

System	F-1 (macro)	Accuracy
TB-Meta	0.6669	0.6751
TB-LM	**0.7433**	**0.7469**

Table 6: Performance of the runs submitted for the CLI task on the test set.

Team	macro F-1	Place
NRC-CNRC	0.7695	1
tearsofjoy	0.7632	2
TwistBytes	0.7433	3
PMZ	0.7387	4
ghmerti	0.7210	5
ghpaetzold	0.5562	6
ekh	0.5501	7
situx	0.1276	8

Table 7: Competition result for CLI with TwistBytes approach TB-LM

	Precision	Recall	F-1
LTB	0.93	0.95	0.94
MPB	0.87	0.84	0.85
NEA	0.60	0.84	0.70
NEB	0.73	0.49	0.58
OLB	0.89	0.43	0.58
STB	0.67	0.71	0.69
SUX	0.66	0.93	0.77
micro avg	0.74	0.74	0.74
macro avg	0.76	0.74	0.73

Table 8: Evaluation of TB-LM on the validation set of CLI

to the use of i-Vectors, the suffix $-S$ to the semi-supervised version, and $-SiV$ to i-Vectors with semi-supervised. The $_p$ index points to a different parameter set with a maximum of 90'000 features and C=1.5 for the SVM.

System TB-Meta-SiV shows a surprisingly good score of 0.90 on the validation set. As stated before, one reason could be the low numbers of speakers in the validation set. Also with a baseline composed by TF-IDF and SVM (SVM Char-Ngram(1,7), see Table 4), we achieved better results as from our approach in VarDial 2018 GDI, which was 64.6% macro F-1. This points to the fact that the data was curated, and therefore easier to classify. The assumption that the test set was similarly built like the validation set guided our approach. However, the results showed clearly that there was some difference, since the scores on the test data were significantly lower for the TB-Meta$-SiV$ systems. We intend to investigate this observation in a future study.

Figure 2 shows the confusion matrix of our system on the test data. It shows that sentences from Lucerne were often predicted as from Bern, and some of Zurich were predicted as Basel. Apart from that, error rates were mostly below 10%.

In Table 5 the results of the shared task are shown. The best three results achieved macro F-1 scores between 74.55% and 75.93%. This pushes forward by a considerable margin the results of last year. One reason might be the i-Vectors features, which were available for the first time this year. Our system achieved 74.55% macro F-1.

4.2 CLI

Table 6 shows the performance of our submitted systems on the test set of the CLI shared task. TB-Meta is the same architecture as used for GDI and described in Section 3.2.3. The TB-LM system is described in Section 3.3. Table 7 shows how our system performs compared to the other participants. We achieve third place out of 8 participants with a macro F-1 score of 0.74. Table 8 shows the performance of TB-LM on the validation set in more detail. The performance on the validation set is 0.73, which is slightly lower than on the test set.

Figure 3 shows the confusion matrix of our system on the test set, and Figure 4 shows the confusion matrix on the validation set. They are mostly similar. Overall, LTB was the easiest language to identify, with an F-1 score of 0.94. NEB and OLB were the hardest to identify, OLB having overall the lowest number of samples in the training set. Noteworthy is that the number of samples alone is not an indicator of how well a class can be distinguished. For example, MPB has the second lowest number of samples (5508) but the second high-

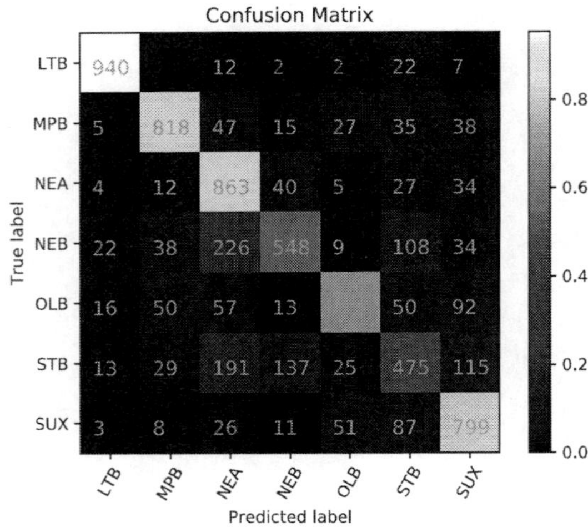

Figure 3: Confusion matrix of TB-LM for CLI on the test set

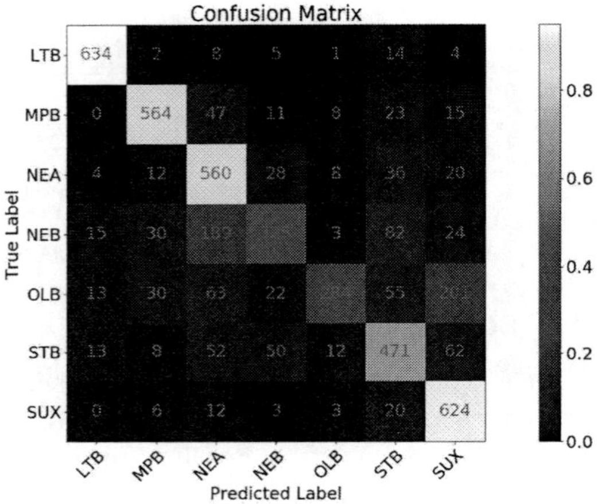

Figure 4: Confusion matrix of TB-LM for CLI on the validation set

est F-1 score (0.85), whereas SUX has by far the largest number of samples (53673), but only the third highest F-1 (0.77).

5 Conclusion

We described our dialect identification systems that were submitted to the VarDial shared tasks GDI and CLI. In GDI, we achieved 3rd place out of 6, using a linear SVM as base, semi-supervised meta crossvalidation training, multiple word and character features, and i-Vectors. In CLI, we achieved 3rd place among 8 teams, using a linear SVM with character n-gram and language model perplexity features.

Acknowledgement

We thank the task organizers for their support and the reviewers for their detailed and helpful feedback. This research has been funded by Commission for Technology and Innovation (CTI) project no. 28190.1 PFES-ES and by SpinningBytes AG, Switzerland.

References

Mohamad Hasan Bahari, Najim Dehak, Hugo Van Hamme, Lukas Burget, Ahmed M. Ali, and Jim Glass. 2014. Non-negative Factor Analysis of Gaussian Mixture Model Weight Adaptation for Language and Dialect Recognition. *IEEE/ACM Trans. Audio, Speech and Lang. Proc.*, 22(7):1117–1129.

Fernando Benites. 2017. *Multi-label Classification with Multiple Class Ontologies*. Ph.D. thesis, University of Konstanz, Konstanz.

Fernando Benites, Ralf Grubenmann, Pius von Däniken, Dirk von Grünigen, Jan Deriu, and Mark Cieliebak. 2018. Twist Bytes-German Dialect Identification with Data Mining Optimization. In *Proceedings of the Fifth Workshop on NLP for Similar Languages, Varieties and Dialects (VarDial 2018)*, pages 218–227.

Kuan-Yu Chen, Hung-Shin Lee, Hsin-Min Wang, Berlin Chen, and Hsin-Hsi Chen. 2014. I-vector based language modeling for spoken document retrieval. In *2014 IEEE International Conference on Acoustics, Speech and Signal Processing (ICASSP)*, pages 7083–7088. IEEE.

E. Dieth and C. Schmid-Cadalbert. 1986. *Schwyzertütschi Dialäktschrift: Dieth-Schreibung*. Lebendige Mundart. Sauerländer.

Nora Hollenstein and Noëmi Aepli. 2014. Compilation of a Swiss German dialect corpus and its application to PoS tagging. In *Proceedings of the First Workshop on Applying NLP Tools to Similar Languages, Varieties and Dialects*, pages 85–94.

Nora Hollenstein and Noëmi Aepli. 2015. A Resource for Natural Language Processing of Swiss German Dialects. In *GSCL*.

Paul Jaccard. 1902. Distribution comparée de la flore alpine dans quelques régions des Alpes occidentales et orientales. *Bulletin de la Murithienne*, (31):81–92.

Tommi Jauhiainen, Heidi Jauhiainen, Tero Alstola, and Krister Lindén. 2019. Language and Dialect Identification of Cuneiform Texts.

Tommi Jauhiainen, Heidi Jauhiainen, and Krister Lindén. 2018a. HeLI-based experiments in Swiss

German dialect identification. In *Proceedings of the Fifth Workshop on NLP for Similar Languages, Varieties and Dialects (VarDial 2018)*, pages 254–262.

Tommi Jauhiainen, Marco Lui, Marcos Zampieri, Timothy Baldwin, and Krister Lindén. 2018b. Automatic Language Identification in Texts: A Survey. *arXiv preprint arXiv:1804.08186*.

Reinhard Kneser and Hermann Ney. 1995. Improved backing-off for M-gram language modeling. In *ICASSP*, pages 181–184. IEEE Computer Society.

Suraj Maharjan, Prasha Shrestha, and Thamar Solorio. 2014. A Simple Approach to Author Profiling in MapReduce. In *CLEF*.

Shervin Malmasi and Marcos Zampieri. 2017a. Arabic Dialect Identification Using iVectors and ASR Transcripts. In *Proceedings of the Fourth Workshop on NLP for Similar Languages, Varieties and Dialects (VarDial)*, pages 178–183, Valencia, Spain.

Shervin Malmasi and Marcos Zampieri. 2017b. German Dialect Identification in Interview Transcriptions. In *Proceedings of the Fourth Workshop on NLP for Similar Languages, Varieties and Dialects (VarDial)*, pages 164–169, Valencia, Spain.

Christopher D. Manning, Prabhakar Raghavan, and Hinrich Schütze. 2008. *Introduction to Information Retrieval*. Cambridge University Press, New York, NY, USA.

Tanja Samardžić, Yves Scherrer, and Elvira Glaser. 2016. ArchiMob–A corpus of spoken Swiss German. In *Proceedings of the Language Resources and Evaluation (LREC)*, pages 4061–4066, Portoroz, Slovenia).

Jun-Won Suh, Seyed Omid Sadjadi, Gang Liu, Taufiq Hasan, Keith W Godin, and John HL Hansen. 2011. Exploring Hilbert envelope based acoustic features in i-vector speaker verification using HT-PLDA. In *Proc. of NIST 2011 Speaker Recognition Evaluation Workshop*.

Tommi Vatanen, Jaakko J. Väyrynen, and Sami Virpioja. 2010. Language Identification of Short Text Segments with N-gram Models. In *Proceedings of the Seventh International Conference on Language Resources and Evaluation (LREC'10)*, Valletta, Malta. European Language Resources Association (ELRA).

Marcos Zampieri, Shervin Malmasi, Nikola Ljubešić, Preslav Nakov, Ahmed Ali, Jörg Tiedemann, Yves Scherrer, and Noëmi Aepli. 2017. Findings of the VarDial Evaluation Campaign 2017. In *Proceedings of the Fourth Workshop on NLP for Similar Languages, Varieties and Dialects (VarDial)*, Valencia, Spain.

Marcos Zampieri, Shervin Malmasi, Preslav Nakov, Ahmed Ali, Suwon Shon, James Glass, Yves Scherrer, Tanja Samardžić, Nikola Ljubešić, Jörg Tiedemann, Chris van der Lee, Stefan Grondelaers,

Nelleke Oostdijk, Antal van den Bosch, Ritesh Kumar, Bornini Lahiri, and Mayank Jain. 2018. Language Identification and Morphosyntactic Tagging: The Second VarDial Evaluation Campaign. In *Proceedings of the Fifth Workshop on NLP for Similar Languages, Varieties and Dialects (VarDial)*, Santa Fe, USA.

Marcos Zampieri, Shervin Malmasi, Yves Scherrer, Tanja Samardžić, Francis Tyers, Miikka Silfverberg, Natalia Klyueva, Tung-Le Pan, Chu-Ren Huang, Radu Tudor Ionescu, Andrei Butnaru, and Tommi Jauhiainen. 2019. A Report on the Third VarDial Evaluation Campaign. In *Proceedings of the Sixth Workshop on NLP for Similar Languages, Varieties and Dialects (VarDial)*. Association for Computational Linguistics.

DTeam @ VarDial 2019: Ensemble based on skip-gram and triplet loss neural networks for Moldavian vs. Romanian cross-dialect topic identification

Diana-Elena Tudoreanu

University of Bucharest

14 Academiei, Bucharest, Romania

dianatudoreanu@gmail.com

Abstract

This paper presents the solution proposed by DTeam in the VarDial 2019 Evaluation Campaign for the Moldavian vs. Romanian cross-topic identification task. The solution proposed is a Support Vector Machines (SVM) ensemble composed of a two character-level neural networks. The first network is a skip-gram classification model formed of an embedding layer, three convolutional layers and two fully-connected layers. The second network has a similar architecture, but is trained using the triplet loss function. The results obtained on the test set show a macro-F_1 score of 0.89 for subtask 1 (binary classifications of the Moldavian and Romanian dialects), which places us on the first place among 5 teams. For subtask 2 (classifying Romanian samples into topics while training on Moldavian samples), we obtained a macro-F_1 of 0.39, which places us on the third place. For subtask 3 (classifying Moldavian samples into topics while training on Romanian samples), we obtained a macro-F_1 of 0.44, which places us once again on the third place.

1 Introduction

The VarDial 2019 Evaluation Campaign (Zampieri et al., 2019) proposes a Moldavian vs. Romanian cross-topic (MRC) identification problem, comprised of three tasks. The first task is a binary classification by dialect, meaning that a classifier would have to differentiate between Romanian and Moldavian dialects. The second and third tasks are cross-dialect multi-class categorization by topic tasks. The second tasks is classifying Romanian samples into topics while training on Moldavian samples and the third is classifying Moldavian samples into topics while training on Romanian samples. The samples for both training and testing are provided with the

MOROCO – Moldavian and Romanian Dialectal Corpus – dataset (Butnaru and Ionescu, 2019).

The MOROCO dataset contains over 33k text samples in both Romanian and Moldavian collected from news domains covering six topics: culture, finance, politics, science, sports, tech. The samples were divided into training (21k), validation (6k), and test (6k) samples. For the VarDial 2019 Evaluation Campaign, the validation and test sets were combined into a single development set. The organizers provided an additional test set of 6k samples. In each text sample, proper nouns were replaced with a token, namely "NE" in order to prevent classifiers from taking decisions based on country-specific nouns.

Our approach for the MRC shared task is to build an ensemble model that combines two character-level neural networks through an SVM (Cortes and Vapnik, 1995) classifier. The first network is a skip-gram classification model formed of an embedding layer, three convolutional layers and two fully-connected layers. The second network has a similar architecture, but is trained using the triplet loss function (Schroff et al., 2015). We participated in all three MRC subtasks and we managed to rank on the first place in the first subtask (Moldavian vs. Romanian dialect identification), with a macro-F_1 score of 0.89, surpassing the other five participants by more than 10%. Due to the lack of time, we did not manage to properly train our models for subtasks 2 and 3. Consequently, we ranked after the other two participants in subtasks 2 and 3.

The rest of this paper is organized as follows. Related art on dialect identification is presented in Section 2. Our approach is presented in Section 3. The empirical results are presented in Section 2. Conclusions and future work directions are presented in Section 5.

Proceedings of VarDial, pages 202–208

Minneapolis, MN, June 7, 2019 ©2019 Association for Computational Linguistics

2 Related Work

In recent years, there have been many approaches proposed for discriminating dialects (Ali, 2018; Ali et al., 2016; Belinkov and Glass, 2016; Butnaru and Ionescu, 2018; Çöltekin and Rama, 2016, 2017; Goutte and Léger, 2016; Ionescu and Popescu, 2016; Ionescu and Butnaru, 2017; Kumar et al., 2018; van der Lee and van den Bosch, 2017). While some of these approaches extract handcrafted features and apply linear classifiers on top (Butnaru and Ionescu, 2018; Ionescu and Popescu, 2016; Ionescu and Butnaru, 2017), other approaches are based on deep learning techniques (Ali, 2018). Although deep neural networks attain top results in many NLP tasks, e.g. machine translation (Gehring et al., 2017), language modelling (Kim et al., 2016; Dauphin et al., 2017), part-of-speech tagging (Santos and Zadrozny, 2014), it appears that shallow approaches attain superior results in dialect identification, at least according to the previous VarDial evaluation campaigns (Malmasi et al., 2016; Zampieri et al., 2017, 2018). Although the evidence points in this direction, our method is based on testing new deep learning models for dialect identification, that have the potential to improve the results. Our interest is focused on neural networks trained using triplet loss, which has not been applied before in dialect identification, to our knowledge.

Closer to our work, Butnaru and Ionescu (2019) proposed a dataset and several models to discriminate between Moldavian and Romanian dialects. The authors proposed two approaches that use character-level features, inspired by previous VarDial evaluation campaigns (Malmasi et al., 2016; Zampieri et al., 2017, 2018), in which dialect identification methods (Ali, 2018; Belinkov and Glass, 2016; Butnaru and Ionescu, 2018) based on character n-grams attained top ranks. Their first approach is a shallow model based on string kernels (Butnaru and Ionescu, 2018; Cozma et al., 2018; Ionescu and Popescu, 2016; Ionescu and Butnaru, 2017; Ionescu et al., 2016) and Kernel Ridge Regression. Their second approach is based on convolutional neural networks with squeeze-and-excitation blocks. Different from Butnaru and Ionescu (2019), we explore only deep learning approaches, by combining two neural networks trained using different loss functions. Similar to Butnaru and Ionescu (2019), our networks take as input character encodings.

3 Methodology

3.1 Preprocessing

Each sample in the MOROCO dataset is preprocessed using the same method regardless of the subtask or the algorithm used. We have reduced the alphabet size down to 85 characters consisting of uppercase and lowercase Romanian letters, digits and commonly used symbols. Each unused character is replaced with a blank character and the named entity token NE is replaced with a single character.

3.2 Feature Extraction

For the competition results, we added an embedding layer consisting of a $85 * 128$ matrix, where 85 is the alphabet size and 128 the embedding size. We apply a one-hot transformation to the input, then multiply the one-hot vector with the embedding layer. This layer is trained at the same time with the neural networks.

For the post-competition results, we built a skip-gram model (Mikolov et al., 2013) based on character n-grams. The model is trained on the top 40k 5-grams from the corpus, in order to learn the n-gram embeddings of the most common n-grams. The embedding size of each n-gram is set to 150. We pre-train the skip-gram model using sub-sampling and negative sampling techniques, which are shown to improve accuracy and convergence speed.

During pre-training, each text sample is divided into contiguous substrings of 5000 characters. When a text sample has less than 5000 characters, we apply 0-padding at the right. During inference, we keep the first 5000 characters of each text sample, also 0-padding the shorter strings.

In order to build our representation, we apply the skip-gram model to each text sample, by replacing every 5-gram with its corresponding embedding learned by the skip-gram model. If the 5-gram is not in the top 40k, it is replaced by a zero vector of size 150. After generating the representation corresponding to each text sample, we provide it as input for training our two neural networks.

3.3 Ensemble of Neural Networks

The method used for predicting the labels on the test is based on an SVM ensemble that combines the predictions of two deep neural networks, a triplet loss network and a skip-gram convolutional

Subtask	macro-F1	weighted-F1	accuracy
1	0.9296	0.9301	0.9302
2	0.6594	0.6596	0.6672
3	0.7621	0.8094	0.8114

Table 1: Results of our ensemble method on the development set of the MRC shared task comprised of three subtasks.

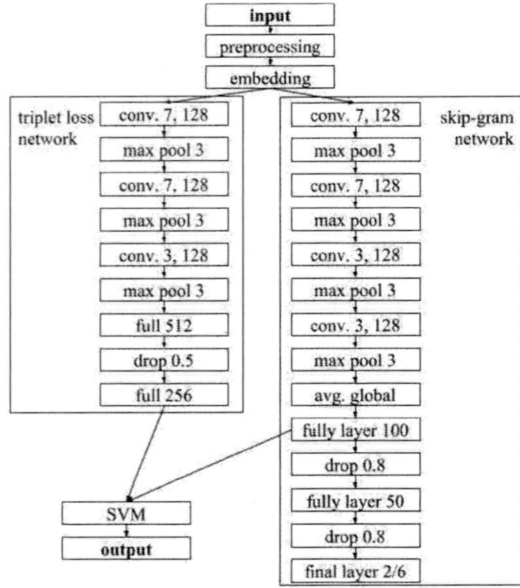

Figure 1: Our processing pipeline.

network. The ensemble schema is pictured in Figure 1.

The triplet loss neural network learns an embedding of size 256 for each sentence. The network is trained using the triplet loss (Schroff et al., 2015). The goal of a triplet loss network is to minimize the distance in the embedding space between two samples of the same class and maximize the distance between two samples of different classes. In other words, we want the distance between the differently labeled samples to be larger than the distance between same labeled samples by a margin α.

Given a triplet composed of an anchor sample, a positive sample, and a negative one, the triplet loss tries to minimize the distance between the anchor and the positive sample, while maximizing at the same time the distance between the anchor and the negative sample. Formally, the loss that we are trying to minimize is:

$$\mathcal{L}(\theta, a, p, n) = \max(d(a, p) - d(a, n) + \alpha, 0), \tag{1}$$

where θ represents the weights learned by the neural network, a is the anchor sample, p is the positive sample, n is the negative sample and α is the margin. In our experiments, we set the margin hyper-parameter to $\alpha = 1$. As distance metric, we use the Euclidean distance:

$$d(x, y) = \sqrt{(x_1 - y_1)^2 + ... + (x_m - y_m)^2}, \tag{2}$$

where m is the number of features in vectors x and y. Each iteration consists of a mini-batch of 30 triplets (a, p, n) from the training samples. The number of iterations is 9000 on all sub-tasks and was chosen based on the loss obtained on the development samples. After every epochs, the training data is shuffled.

The triplet loss network has 3 convolutional layers, each one of 128 unidimensional filters. The filter support on each convolutional layer is 7, 7, and 3 respectively. Each convolutional layer is followed by an unidimensional max pooling layer of size 3. The last max pooling layer is followed by a fully connected layer of size 512, having a dropout rate of 0.5. The network ends with a fully connected layer of 256 neurons, which represent the final embedding of the input text sample. Both the fully and the convolutional layers have a leaky Rectified Linear Unit (ReLU) activation function. The learning algorithm is the Adam optimizer and the learning rate is set to 0.00005.

The skip-gram convolutional network has a similar architecture, with a extra convolutional layer. There are 4 convolutional layers with unidimensional filters of sizes 7, 7, 3, and 3, respectively. Each convolutional layer is followed by a unidimensional max pooling of size 3. This is followed by an average global pooling layer, which reduces the size of the representation. Two fully-connected layers with 100 and 50 neurons, respectively, come after the global pooling layer. Each fully-connected layer has a dropout rate of 0.8. Finally, the last layer is composed of 2 neurons for the first MRC subtask, each corresponding to one dialect (Moldavian or Romanian). For the second and the third MRC substaks, the last layer is composed of 6 neurons, each corresponding to one of the six topics. The last layer is based on softmax loss. Similarly to the triplet loss network, the layers have leaky ReLU activation functions and the optimization algorithm is Adam. In this case, the learning rate is 0.0001 and the mini-batch size is 120 samples. The number of iterations is 9000 for the first sub-task, 10000 for the second and 12000 for the third, with the data being reshuffled every epoch.

The input of the ensemble is composed of the last layer of the triplet loss network concatenated with the intermediate fully-connected layer of size 100 of the classification network. The final model is represented by an SVM classifier. The hyper-parameters of the SVM (kernel type and C) are selected through grid search on the development set.

4   Experiments

4.1   Dataset

The MOROCO dataset used in the MRC shared task contains over 39k text samples in both Romanian and Moldavian collected from news domains covering six topics: culture, finance, politics, science, sports, tech. The samples were divided into training (21k), development (12k), and test (6k) samples. In each text sample, proper nouns were replaced with a token, namely "NE" in order to prevent classifiers from taking decisions based on country-specific nouns.

4.2   Parameter Tuning

We apply grid search on the development set to tune the hyper-parameters of the final SVM ensemble. The parameters considered are $0.1, 0.5, 1$, and 5 for the regularization parameter C, and *RBF* or *linear* for the kernel. We use the implementation available in LibSVM (Chang and Lin, 2011). Upon applying grid search, we found the following optimal parameters: the regularization parameter C is equal to 0.5, the kernel type is RBF. The corresponding parameter of the RBF kernel, γ, is set to 0.001.

The accuracy of the classification model were better than the triplet loss network in all tasks and in some cases the ensemble did not achieve better accuracy than the classifier, as shown in Table 1.

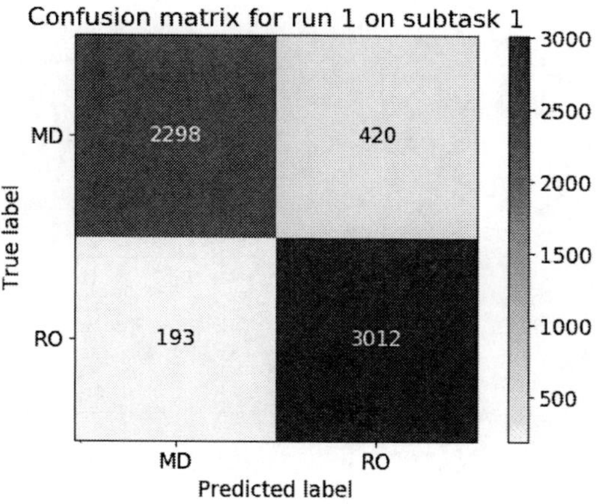

Figure 2: Confusion matrix of our ensemble model on the first MRC subtask.

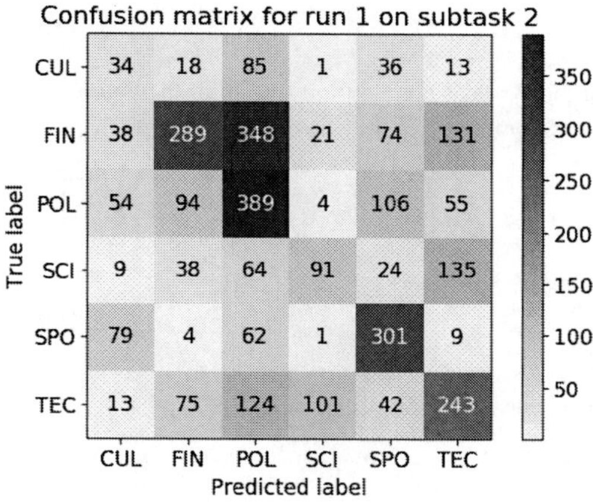

Figure 3: Confusion matrix of our ensemble model on the second MRC subtask.

4.3   Results

Our results on the test set of the MRC shared task are presented in Table 2. The results obtained on the test set show a macro-F_1 score of 0.89 for subtask 1 (binary classification of the Moldavian and Romanian dialects), which places us on the first place among 5 teams. Compared to the second team, our performance is 0.09 higher. The corresponding confusion matrix is illustrated in Figure 2. We notice that the number of misclassified Moldavian samples is twice the number of misclassified Romanian samples. This suggests that the algorithm is slightly biased in favor of Romanian.

For subtask 2 (classifying Romanian samples into topics while training on Moldavian samples), we obtained a macro-F_1 of 0.39, which places us on the third place. Compared to the first team,

Subtask	macro-F1	weighted-F1	accuracy
1	0.8949	0.8960	0.8965
2	0.3856	0.4145	0.4202
3	0.4472	0.5440	0.5367

Table 2: Results of our ensemble method on the test set of the MRC shared task comprised of three subtasks.

Subtask	macro-F1	weighted-F1	accuracy
1	0.9340	0.9345	0.9346
2	0.6509	0.6531	0.6620
3	0.7521	0.8004	0.8027

Table 3: Post-competition results of our ensemble method on the test set of the MRC shared task comprised of three subtasks.

Subtask	macro-F1	weighted-F1	accuracy
1	0.9334	0.9340	0.9341
2	0.6306	0.6321	0.6383
3	0.7360	0.7893	0.7895

Table 4: Post-competition results of the neural network based on softmax loss on the test set of the MRC shared task comprised of three subtasks.

Subtask	macro-F1	weighted-F1	accuracy
1	0.8690	0.8701	0.8705
2	0.6350	0.6368	0.6468
3	0.7308	0.7816	0.7855

Table 5: Post-competition results of the neural network based on triplet loss on the test set of the MRC shared task comprised of three subtasks.

Subtask	Method	macro-F1	weighted-F1	accuracy
1	CNN	0.9275	0.9276	0.9271
	Ensemble	0.9340	0.9345	0.9346
2	CNN	0.5504	0.5627	0.5367
	Ensemble	0.6509	0.6531	0.6620
3	CNN	0.7249	0.7160	0.6270
	Ensemble	0.7521	0.8004	0.8028

Table 6: Comparison between post-competition results of the ensemble and our reimplementation of the character-level CNN of Butnaru and Ionescu (2019) on the test set of the MRC shared task.

our performance is 0.2 lower. The corresponding confusion matrix is illustrated in Figure 3. The confusion matrix suggests a bias towards the *politics* label, one of the reasons being that the number of Moldavian politics samples is six times higher than the Romanian ones. We also notice a strong confusion between *finance* and *politics*. The classes best classified are *politics* and *sports* while the worse classified are *science* and *culture*. It seems that *science* is often confused for *technology*.

For subtask 3 (classifying Moldavian samples into topics while training on Romanian samples), we obtained a macro-F_1 of 0.44, which places us once again on the third place. Compared to the first team, our performance is 0.08 lower. The corresponding confusion matrix is illustrated in Figure 4. Similarly to the second subtask, our model provides better precision in classifying *politics* and *sports*, followed closely by *finance*. This time, *politics* is being labeled as *finance* more frequently, as opposed to what we notice in Figure

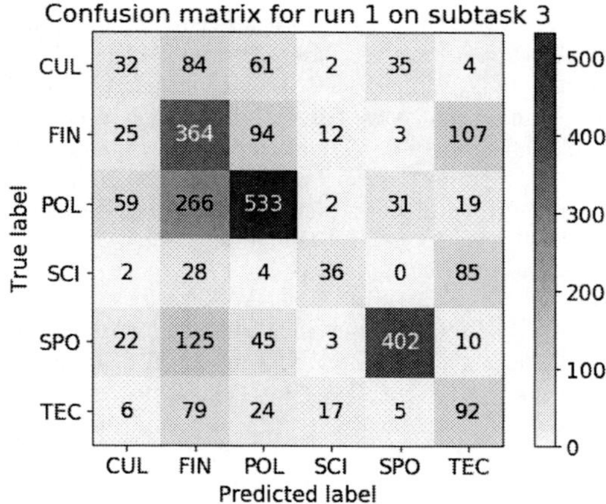

Figure 4: Confusion matrix of our ensemble model on the third MRC subtask.

3. Again, *culture* and *science* are misclassified the most, with *science* being labeled as *technology* and *culture* as either *finance* or *politics*.

Given the overall results, we can conclude that the models were better in discriminating between dialects than in distinguishing the topics in cross-dialect settings. A possible reason for this is the fact that the embedding layer is trained at the same time as the networks and it might require more training for cross-dialect multi-class classifiers. We notice that when we pre-train the skip-gram (in post-competition) we obtain less discrepancy between results.

4.4 Post-competition Results

We report post-competition results in Table 3. The ensemble model shows a macro-F_1 score of 0.93 for subtask 1, a 0.66 score for subtask 2 and a 0.80 score for subtask 3. The increased results are due to the pre-trained skip-gram applied to the data as opposed to the embedding layer. Results of individual models are presented in Tables 4 and 5. Although the individual triplet loss network does not attain good results by itself, it provides useful information to the ensemble.

We also offer a comparison to the results of the character-level CNN method in Butnaru and Ionescu (2019), since it is closer to our work, in Table 6.

5 Conclusion

We conclude that our ensemble model does a good job for binary classification, while the results for the last two subtasks can be further improved. Some future work could be testing other classification algorithms for the final ensemble, such as Logistic Regression.

Acknowledgments

We thank reviewers for their useful comments.

References

Ahmed Ali, Najim Dehak, Patrick Cardinal, Sameer Khurana, Sree Harsha Yella, James Glass, Peter Bell, and Steve Renals. 2016. Automatic Dialect Detection in Arabic Broadcast Speech. In *Proceedings of INTERSPEECH*, pages 2934–2938.

Mohamed Ali. 2018. Character level convolutional neural network for arabic dialect identification. In *Proceedings of VarDial*, pages 122–127.

Yonatan Belinkov and James Glass. 2016. A Character-level Convolutional Neural Network for Distinguishing Similar Languages and Dialects. In *Proceedings of VarDial*, pages 145–152.

Andrei Butnaru and Radu Tudor Ionescu. 2019. MOROCO: The Moldavian and Romanian Dialectal Corpus. *arXiv preprint arXiv:1901.06543*.

Andrei M. Butnaru and Radu Tudor Ionescu. 2018. UnibucKernel Reloaded: First Place in Arabic Dialect Identification for the Second Year in a Row. In *Proceedings of VarDial*, pages 77–87.

Çağri Çöltekin and Taraka Rama. 2016. Discriminating Similar Languages with Linear SVMs and Neural Networks. In *Proceedings of VarDial*, pages 15–24, Osaka, Japan.

Çağr Çöltekin and Taraka Rama. 2017. Tübingen system in vardial 2017 shared task: experiments with language identification and cross-lingual parsing. In *Proceedings of VarDial*, pages 146–155, Valencia, Spain.

Chih-Chung Chang and Chih-Jen Lin. 2011. LibSVM: A Library for Support Vector Machines. *ACM Transactions on Intelligent Systems and Technology*, 2:27:1–27:27. Software available at http://www.csie.ntu.edu.tw/~cjlin/libsvm.

Corinna Cortes and Vladimir Vapnik. 1995. Support Vector Networks. *Machine Learning*, 20(3):273–297.

Mădălina Cozma, Andrei M. Butnaru, and Radu Tudor Ionescu. 2018. Automated essay scoring with string kernels and word embeddings. In *Proceedings of ACL*, pages 503–509.

Yann Dauphin, Angela Fan, Michael Auli, and David Grangier. 2017. Language Modeling with Gated Convolutional Networks. In *Proceedings of ICML*, pages 933–941.

Jonas Gehring, Michael Auli, David Grangier, and Yann Dauphin. 2017. A Convolutional Encoder Model for Neural Machine Translation. In *Proceedings of ACL*, pages 123–135.

Cyril Goutte and Serge Léger. 2016. Advances in Ngram-based Discrimination of Similar Languages. In *Proceedings of VarDial*, pages 178–184, Osaka, Japan.

Radu Tudor Ionescu and Andrei M. Butnaru. 2017. Learning to Identify Arabic and German Dialects using Multiple Kernels. In *Proceedings of VarDial*, pages 200–209.

Radu Tudor Ionescu and Marius Popescu. 2016. UnibucKernel: An Approach for Arabic Dialect Identification based on Multiple String Kernels. In *Proceedings of VarDial*, pages 135–144.

Radu Tudor Ionescu, Marius Popescu, and Aoife Cahill. 2016. String kernels for native language identification: Insights from behind the curtains. *Computational Linguistics*, 42(3):491–525.

Yoon Kim, Yacine Jernite, David Sontag, and Alexander M. Rush. 2016. Character-Aware Neural Language Models. In *Proceedings of AAAI*, pages 2741–2749.

Ritesh Kumar, Bornini Lahiri, Deepak Alok, Atul Kr. Ojha, Mayank Jain, Abdul Basit, and Yogesh Dawar. 2018. Automatic Identification of Closely-related Indian Languages: Resources and Experiments. In *Proceedings of LREC*.

Shervin Malmasi, Marcos Zampieri, Nikola Ljubešić, Preslav Nakov, Ahmed Ali, and Jörg Tiedemann. 2016. Discriminating between Similar Languages and Arabic Dialect Identification: A Report on the Third DSL Shared Task. In *Proceedings of VarDial*, pages 1–14.

Tomas Mikolov, Kai Chen, Greg Corrado, and Jeffrey Dean. 2013. Efficient Estimation of Word Representations in Vector Space. In *Proceedings of ICLR*.

Cicero D. Santos and Bianca Zadrozny. 2014. Learning character-level representations for part-of-speech tagging. In *Proceedings of ICML*, pages 1818–1826.

Florian Schroff, Dmitry Kalenichenko, and James Philbin. 2015. FaceNet: A unified embedding for face recognition and clustering. In *Proceedings of the IEEE Conference on Computer Vision and Pattern Recognition*, pages 815–823.

Chris van der Lee and Antal van den Bosch. 2017. Exploring Lexical and Syntactic Features for Language Variety Identification. In *Proceedings of VarDial*, pages 190–199, Valencia, Spain.

Marcos Zampieri, Shervin Malmasi, Nikola Ljubešić, Preslav Nakov, Ahmed Ali, Jörg Tiedemann, Yves Scherrer, and Noëmi Aepli. 2017. Findings of the VarDial Evaluation Campaign 2017. In *Proceedings of VarDial*, pages 1–15.

Marcos Zampieri, Shervin Malmasi, Preslav Nakov, Ahmed Ali, Suwon Shon, James Glass, Yves Scherrer, Tanja Samardžić, Nikola Ljubešić, Jörg Tiedemann, Chris van der Lee, Stefan Grondelaers, Nelleke Oostdijk, Antal van den Bosch, Ritesh Kumar, Bornini Lahiri, and Mayank Jain. 2018. Language Identification and Morphosyntactic Tagging: The Second VarDial Evaluation Campaign. In *Proceedings of VarDial*, pages 1–17.

Marcos Zampieri, Shervin Malmasi, Yves Scherrer, Tanja Samardžić, Francis Tyers, Miikka Silfverberg, Natalia Klyueva, Tung-Le Pan, Chu-Ren Huang, Radu Tudor Ionescu, Andrei Butnaru, and Tommi Jauhiainen. 2019. A Report on the Third VarDial Evaluation Campaign. In *Proceedings of VarDial*.

Experiments in Cuneiform Language Identification

Gustavo Henrique Paetzold[1], Marcos Zampieri[2]
[1]Universidade Tecnológica Federal do Paraná, Toledo-PR, Brazil
[2]University of Wolverhampton, Wolverhampton, United Kingdom
ghpaetzold@utfpr.edu.br

Abstract

This paper presents methods to discriminate between languages and dialects written in Cuneiform script, one of the first writing systems in the world. We report the results obtained by the *PZ* team in the Cuneiform Language Identification (CLI) shared task organized within the scope of the VarDial Evaluation Campaign 2019. The task included two languages, Sumerian and Akkadian. The latter is divided into six dialects: Old Babylonian, Middle Babylonian peripheral, Standard Babylonian, Neo Babylonian, Late Babylonian, and Neo Assyrian. We approach the task using a meta-classifier trained on various SVM models and we show the effectiveness of the system for this task. Our submission achieved 0.738 F1 score in discriminating between the seven languages and dialects and it was ranked fourth in the competition among eight teams.

1 Introduction

As discussed in a recent survey (Jauhiainen et al., 2018), discriminating between similar languages, national language varieties, and dialects is an important challenge faced by state-of-the-art language identification systems. The topic has attracted more and more attention from the CL/NLP community in recent years with publications on similar languages of the Iberian peninsula (Zubiaga et al., 2016), and varieties and dialects of several languages such as Greek (Sababa and Stassopoulou, 2018) and Romanian (Ciobanu and Dinu, 2016) to name a few.

As evidenced in Section 2, the focus of most of these studies is the identification of languages and dialects using contemporary data. A few exceptions include the work by Trieschnigg et al. (2012) who applied language identification methods to historical varieties of Dutch and the work by Jauhiainen et al. (2019) on languages written in cuneiform script: Sumerian and Akkadian.

Cuneiform is an ancient writing system invented by the Sumerians for more than three millennia.

In this paper we describe computational approaches to language identification on texts written in cuneiform script. For this purpose we use the dataset made available by Jauhiainen et al. (2019) to participants of the Cuneiform Language Identification (CLI) shared task organized at VarDial 2019 (Zampieri et al., 2019). Our submission, under the team name *PZ*, is an adaptation of an n-gram-based meta-classifier system which showed very good performance in previous language identification shared tasks (Malmasi and Zampieri, 2017b,a). Furthermore, we compare the performance of the meta-classifier to the submissions to the CLI shared task and, in particular, to a deep learning approach submitted by the team *ghpaetzold*. It has been shown in previous language identification studies (Medvedeva et al., 2017; Kroon et al., 2018) that deep learning approaches do not outperform n-gram-based methods and we were interested in investigating whether this is also true for the languages and dialects included in CLI.

2 Related Work

Since its first edition in 2014, shared tasks on similar language and dialect identification have been organized together with the VarDial workshop co-located with international conferences such as COLING, EACL, and NAACL. The first and most well-attended of these competitions was the Discrminating between Similar Languages (DSL) shared task which has been organized between 2014 and 2017 (Malmasi et al., 2016b; Zampieri et al., 2014, 2015, 2017). The DSL provided the first benchmark for evaluation of language identification systems developed for similar languages and language varieties using the DSL Corpus Col-

Proceedings of VarDial, pages 209–213
Minneapolis, MN, June 7, 2019 ©2019 Association for Computational Linguistics

Language or Dialect	Code	Texts	Lines	Signs
Late Babylonian	LTB	671	31,893	ca. 260,000
Middle Babylonian peripheral	MPB	365	11,015	ca. 95,000
Neo-Assyrian	NE	3,570	65,932	ca. 490,000
Neo-Babylonian	NEB	1,212	19,414	ca. 200,000
Old Babylonian	OLB	527	7,605	ca. 65,000
Standard Babylonian	STB	1,661	35,633	ca. 390,000
Sumerian	SUX	5,000	107,345	ca. 400,000
Total		13,006	278,837	ca. 1,900,000

Table 1: Number of texts, lines, and signs in each of the seven languages and dialects in the dataset of Jauhiainen et al. (2019), from which the instances of the CLI datasets were taken.

lection (DSLCC) (Tan et al., 2014), a multilingual benchmarked dataset compiled for this purpose. In 2017 and 2018, VarDial featured evaluation campaigns with multiple shared tasks not only on language and dialect identification but also on other NLP tasks related to language and dialect variation (e.g. morphosyntactic tagging, and cross-lingual dependency parsing). With the exception of the DSL, the language and dialect identification competitions organized at VarDial focused on groups of dialects from the same language such as Arabic (ADI shared task) and German (GDI shared task).

The focus of the aforementioned language and dialect identification competitions was diatopic variation and thus the data made available in these competitions was synchronic contemporary corpora. In the 2019 edition of the workshop, for the first time, a task including historical languages was organized. The CLI shared task provided participants with a dataset containing languages and dialects written in cuneiform script: Sumerian and Akkadian. Akkadian is divided into six dialects in the dataset: Old Babylonian, Middle Babylonian peripheral, Standard Babylonian, Neo Babylonian, Late Babylonian, and Neo Assyrian (Jauhiainen et al., 2019).

The CLI shared task is an innovative initiative that opens new perspectives in the computational processing of languages written in cuneiform script. There have been a number of studies applying computational methods to process these languages (e.g. Sumerian (Chiarcos et al., 2018)), but with the exception of Jauhiainen et al. (2019), to the best of our knowledge, no language identification studies have been published. CLI is the first competition organized on cuneiform script texts in particular and in historical language identification in general.

3 Methodology and Data

The dataset used in the CLI shared task is described in detail in Jauhiainen et al. (2019). All of the data included in the dataset was collected from the Open Richly Annotated Cuneiform Corpus (Oracc)[1] which contains transliterated texts. Jauhiainen et al. (2019) created a tool to transform the texts back to the cuneiform script. The dataset features texts from seven languages and dialects amounting to a little over 13,000 texts. The list of languages and dialects is presented in Table 1.

3.1 System Description

Our submission to the CLI shared task is a system based on a meta-classifier trained on several SVM models. Meta-classifiers (Giraud-Carrier et al., 2004) and ensemble learning methods have proved to deliver competitive performance not only in language identification (Malmasi and Zampieri, 2017b,a) but also in many other text classification tasks (Malmasi et al., 2016a; Sulea et al., 2017).

The meta-classifier is an adaptation of previous submissions to VarDial shared tasks described in (Malmasi and Zampieri, 2017a). It is essentially a bagging ensemble trained on the outputs of linear SVM classifiers. As features, the system uses the following character n-gram and character skip-gram features:

- character n-grams of order 1–5;

- 1-skip character bigrams and trigrams;

- 2-skip character bigrams and trigrams;

- 3-skip character bigrams and trigrams.

Each feature class is used to train a single linear SVM classifier using LIBLINEAR (Fan et al.,

---

[1]http://oracc.museum.upenn.edu/

2008). The outputs of these SVM classifiers on the training data are then used to train the meta-classifier.

4 Results

Table 2 showcases the results obtained by our team (*PZ* in bold) and the best submission by each of the eight teams which participating in the CLI shared task. Even though the competition allowed the use of other datasets (open submission), we have used only the dataset provided by the shared task organizers to train our model.

Our submission was ranked 4th in the shared task, only a few percentage points below the top-3 systems: *NRC-CNRC*, *tearsofjoy*, and *Twist Bytes*. The meta-classifier achieved much higher performance at distinguishing between these Mesopotamian languages and dialects than the neural model by *ghpaetzold*, which ranked 6th in the competition. We present this neural model in more detail comparing its performance to our meta-classifier in Section 4.1.

System	F1 (macro)
NRC-CNRC	0.769
tearsofjoy	0.763
Twist Bytes	0.743
PZ	**0.738**
ghmerti	0.721
ghpaetzold	0.556
ekh	0.550
situx	0.128

Table 2: Results for the CLI task obtained by the team *PZ* (in bold) in comparison to the the best entries of each of the eight teams in the shared task. Results reported in terms of F1 (macro).

4.1 Comparison to a Neural Model

We take the opportunity to compare the performance of our system with an entirely different type of model submitted by team *ghpaetzold*. This comparison was motivated by the lower performance obtained by the neural models in comparison to traditional machine learning models in previous VarDial shared tasks (Zampieri et al., 2018). It was made possible due to the collaboration between the *ghpaetzold* team and ours.[2]

As demonstrated by Ling et al. (2015), compositional recurrent neural networks can offer very reliable performance on a variety of NLP tasks. Previous language identification and dialect studies (Medvedeva et al., 2017; Kroon et al., 2018; Butnaru and Ionescu, 2019) and the results of the previous shared tasks organized at VarDial (Zampieri et al., 2017, 2018), however, showed that deep learning approaches do not outperform more linear n-gram-based methods so we were interested in comparing the performance of a neural model to the meta-classifier for this dataset.

A compositional network is commonly described as a model that builds numerical representations of words based on the sequence of characters that compose them. They are inherently more time-consuming to train than typical neural models that use traditional word vectors because of the added parameters, but they compensate by being able to handle any conceivable word passed as input with very impressive robustness (Paetzold, 2018, 2019).

The model takes as input a sentence and produces a corresponding label as output. First, the model vectorizes each character of each word in the sentence using a typical character embedding layer. It then passes the sequence of vectors through a set of 2 layers of Gated Recurrent Units (GRUs) and produces a numerical representation for each word as a whole. This set of representations is then passed through another 2-layer set of GRUs to produce a final vector for the sentence as a whole, and then a dense layer is used to produce a softmax distribution over the label set. The model uses 25 dimensions for character embeddings, 30 nodes for each GRU layer and 50% dropout. A version of each model was saved after each epoch so that the team could choose the one with the lowest error on the development set as their submission.

Inspecting the two confusion matrices depicted in Figures 1 and 2, we found that the neural model did not do very well at differentiating between Standard Babylonian and Neo Assyrian, as well as between Neo Babylonian and Neo Assyrian, leading to many misclassifications. These two language pairs were also the most challenging for the meta-classifier, however, the number of missclassified instances by the meta-classifier was much lower.

---

[2]One of the *ghpaetzold* team members was also a member of the *PZ* team.

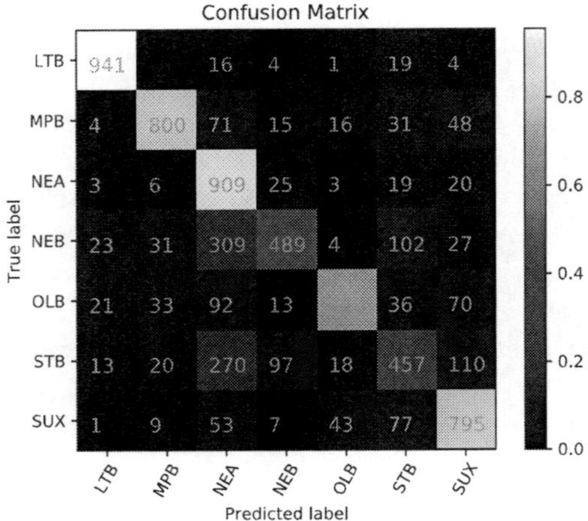

Figure 1: Confusion matrix for the meta-classifier.

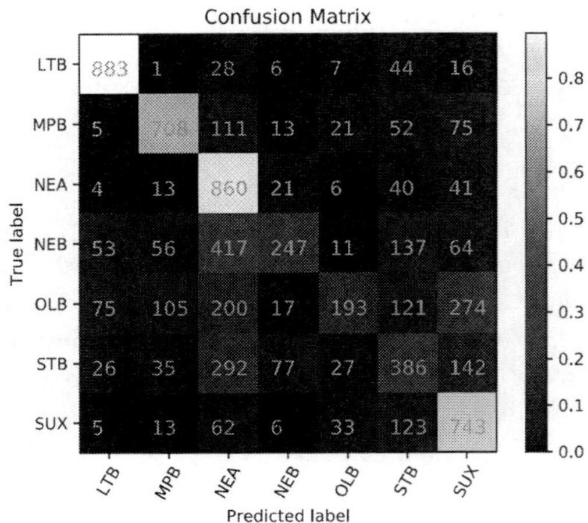

Figure 2: Confusion matrix for the neural model.

5   Conclusion and Future Work

In this paper we presented a meta-classifier system submitted by the team *PZ* to the Cuneiform Language Identification shared task organized at VarDial 2019. Our submission is an adaptation of a sophisticated meta-classifier which achieved high performance in previous language and dialect identification shared tasks at VarDial (Malmasi and Zampieri, 2017a). The meta-classifier combines the output of multiple SVM classifers trained on character-based features. The meta-classifier ranked 4th in the competition among eight teams only a few percentage points below the top-3 systems in the competition.

Finally, we compared the performance of the meta-classifier with a compositional RNN model that uses only the text from the instance as input trained on the same dataset. The comparison shows that, while the neural model does offer competitive performance against some of the systems submitted to the shared task, the more elaborate features used by the meta-classifier allows it to much more proficiently distinguish between very similar language pairs, such as Neo Babylonian and Neo Assyrian, leading to a performance gain of 18.2% F-score and 2 positions in the shared task rankings. The results obtained by the meta-classifier in comparison to the neural model corroborate the findings of previous studies (Medvedeva et al., 2017) in the last two VarDial evaluation campaigns (Zampieri et al., 2017, 2018).

In the future we would like to analyze the results obtained by the highest performing teams in the CLI shared task. The top team achieved the best performance in the competition using a neural-based method. This is, to the best of our knowledge, the first time in which a deep learning approach outperforms traditional machine learning methods in one of the VarDial shared tasks. The great performance obtained by the NRC-CNRC team might be explained by the use of more suitable deep learning methods such as BERT (Devlin et al., 2018).

Acknowledgements

We would like to thank Shervin Malmasi for his valuable suggestions and feedback. We further thank the CLI shared task organizer, Tommi Jauhiainen, for organizing this interesting shared task.

We gratefully acknowledge the support of NVIDIA Corporation with the donation of the Titan V GPU used for this research.

References

Andrei Butnaru and Radu Tudor Ionescu. 2019. MO-ROCO: The Moldavian and Romanian Dialectal Corpus. *arXiv preprint arXiv:1901.06543*.

Christian Chiarcos, Émilie Pagé-Perron, Ilya Khait, Niko Schenk, and Lucas Reckling. 2018. Towards a Linked Open Data Edition of Sumerian Corpora. In *Proceedings of LREC*.

Alina Maria Ciobanu and Liviu P Dinu. 2016. A computational perspective on the romanian dialects. In *Proceedings of LREC*.

Jacob Devlin, Ming-Wei Chang, Kenton Lee, and Kristina Toutanova. 2018. BERT: Pre-training of

Deep Bidirectional Transformers for Language Understanding. *arXiv preprint arXiv:1810.04805*.

Rong-En Fan, Kai-Wei Chang, Cho-Jui Hsieh, Xiang-Rui Wang, and Chih-Jen Lin. 2008. LIBLINEAR: A Library for Large Linear Classification. *Journal of Machine Learning Research*, 9(Aug):1871–1874.

Christophe Giraud-Carrier, Ricardo Vilalta, and Pavel Brazdil. 2004. Introduction to the Special Issue on Meta-learning. *Machine learning*, 54(3):187–193.

Tommi Jauhiainen, Heidi Jauhiainen, Tero Alstola, and Krister Lindén. 2019. Language and Dialect Identification of Cuneiform Texts. In *Proceedings of VarDial*.

Tommi Jauhiainen, Marco Lui, Marcos Zampieri, Timothy Baldwin, and Krister Lindén. 2018. Automatic language identification in texts: A survey. *arXiv preprint arXiv:1804.08186*.

Martin Kroon, Masha Medvedeva, and Barbara Plank. 2018. When Simple N-gram Models Outperform Syntactic Approaches: Discriminating between Dutch and Flemish. In *Proceedings of VarDial*.

Wang Ling, Tiago Luís, Luís Marujo, Ramón Fernandez Astudillo, Silvio Amir, Chris Dyer, Alan W Black, and Isabel Trancoso. 2015. Finding function in form: Compositional character models for open vocabulary word representation. *arXiv preprint arXiv:1508.02096*.

Shervin Malmasi and Marcos Zampieri. 2017a. Arabic Dialect Identification Using iVectors and ASR Transcripts. In *Proceedings of VarDial*.

Shervin Malmasi and Marcos Zampieri. 2017b. German Dialect Identification in Interview Transcriptions. In *Proceedings of VarDial*.

Shervin Malmasi, Marcos Zampieri, and Mark Dras. 2016a. Predicting Post Severity in Mental Health Forums. In *Proceedings of CLPsych*.

Shervin Malmasi, Marcos Zampieri, Nikola Ljubešić, Preslav Nakov, Ahmed Ali, and Jörg Tiedemann. 2016b. Discriminating between Similar Languages and Arabic Dialect Identification: A Report on the Third DSL Shared Task. In *Proceedings of VarDial*.

Maria Medvedeva, Martin Kroon, and Barbara Plank. 2017. When Sparse Traditional Models Outperform Dense Neural Networks: The Curious Case of Discriminating between Similar Languages. In *Proceedings of VarDial*.

Gustavo Paetzold. 2018. UTFPR at IEST 2018: Exploring Character-to-Word Composition for Emotion Analysis. In *Proceedings of WASSA*.

Gustavo Paetzold. 2019. UTFPR at SemEval-2019 Task 6: Relying on Compositionality to Find Offense. In *Proceedings of SemEval*.

Hanna Sababa and Athena Stassopoulou. 2018. A Classifier to Distinguish Between Cypriot Greek and Standard Modern Greek. In *Proceedings of SNAMS*.

Octavia-Maria Sulea, Marcos Zampieri, Shervin Malmasi, Mihaela Vela, Liviu P Dinu, and Josef van Genabith. 2017. Exploring the use of Text Classification in the Legal Domain. *Proceedings of ASAIL*.

Liling Tan, Marcos Zampieri, Nikola Ljubešić, and Jörg Tiedemann. 2014. Merging Comparable Data Sources for the Discrimination of Similar Languages: The DSL Corpus Collection. In *Proceedings BUCC*.

Dolf Trieschnigg, Djoerd Hiemstra, Mariët Theune, Franciska Jong, and Theo Meder. 2012. An Exploration of Language Identification Techniques in the Dutch Folktale Database. In *Proceedings of the Workshop on Adaptation of Language Resources and Tools for Processing Cultural Heritage*.

Marcos Zampieri, Shervin Malmasi, Nikola Ljubešić, Preslav Nakov, Ahmed Ali, Jörg Tiedemann, Yves Scherrer, and Noëmi Aepli. 2017. Findings of the VarDial Evaluation Campaign 2017. In *Proceedings of VarDial*.

Marcos Zampieri, Shervin Malmasi, Preslav Nakov, Ahmed Ali, Suwon Shuon, James Glass, Yves Scherrer, Tanja Samardžić, Nikola Ljubešić, Jörg Tiedemann, Chris van der Lee, Stefan Grondelaers, Nelleke Oostdijk, Antal van den Bosch, Ritesh Kumar, Bornini Lahiri, and Mayank Jain. 2018. Language Identification and Morphosyntactic Tagging: The Second VarDial Evaluation Campaign. In *Proceedings of VarDial*.

Marcos Zampieri, Shervin Malmasi, Yves Scherrer, Tanja Samardžić, Francis Tyers, Miikka Silfverberg, Natalia Klyueva, Tung-Le Pan, Chu-Ren Huang, Radu Tudor Ionescu, Andrei Butnaru, and Tommi Jauhiainen. 2019. A Report on the Third VarDial Evaluation Campaign. In *Proceedings of VarDial*.

Marcos Zampieri, Liling Tan, Nikola Ljubešić, and Jörg Tiedemann. 2014. A report on the DSL shared task 2014. In *Proceedings of VarDial*.

Marcos Zampieri, Liling Tan, Nikola Ljubešić, Jörg Tiedemann, and Preslav Nakov. 2015. Overview of the dsl shared task 2015. In *Proceedings of LT4VarDial*.

Arkaitz Zubiaga, Inaki San Vicente, Pablo Gamallo, José Ramom Pichel, Inaki Alegria, Nora Aranberri, Aitzol Ezeiza, and Víctor Fresno. 2016. Tweetlid: A Benchmark for Tweet Language Identification. *Language Resources and Evaluation*, 50(4):729–766.

Comparing Pipelined and Integrated Approaches to Dialectal Arabic Neural Machine Translation

Pamela Shapiro
Johns Hopkins University
pshapiro@jhu.edu

Kevin Duh
Johns Hopkins University
kevinduh@cs.jhu.edu

Abstract

When translating diglossic languages such as Arabic, situations may arise where we would like to translate a text but do not know which dialect it is. A traditional approach to this problem is to design dialect identification systems and dialect-specific machine translation systems. However, under the recent paradigm of neural machine translation, shared multi-dialectal systems have become a natural alternative. Here we explore under which conditions it is beneficial to perform dialect identification for Arabic neural machine translation versus using a general system for all dialects.

1 Introduction

Arabic exhibits a linguistic phenomenon called diglossia—speakers use Modern Standard Arabic (MSA) for formal settings and local dialects for informal settings. There are broad categories of dialects by region, such as Levantine or Maghrebi. However, dialects also vary at a finer-grained level, even within individual countries. An additional complication is that code-switching, i.e. mixing MSA and dialect, is a common occurrence (Elfardy et al., 2014). To put the importance of handling Arabic dialects in perspective, Ethnologue lists Arabic as having the 5th highest number of L1 speakers, spread over 21 regional dialects.[1]

The bulk of work on translating Arabic dialects uses rule-based and statistical machine translation, and much of it is translating between dialects and MSA. Generally, this work builds systems for specific dialects, with substantial amounts of information about the dialects themselves built in (Harrat et al., 2017).

In the meantime, neural machine translation has become the dominant paradigm, and with it multi-lingual systems have become a more natural possibility (Firat et al., 2016). These systems know nothing about the specific languages involved, but use shared embedding spaces and parameters to yield benefits especially with lower-resource languages. It is a natural extension to apply this to the space of Arabic dialects (Hassan et al., 2017).

There are many possibilities of what exactly a multilingual system might look like, but we focus on one particular decision: Suppose we want to be able to translate a test sentence from an unknown dialect. Is it better to perform dialect identification and then translate with a finely tuned system for that dialect (i.e. a pipelined approach)? Or is it better to throw everything into one integrated, multilingual system[2] which we use for all input regardless of dialect? And how accurate does our dialect identification have to be for the pipeline approach to be useful?

We perform a set of exploratory experiments quantifying this trade-off on LDC data consisting of MSA, Levantine, and Egyptian bitexts, using a standard Transformer architecture (Vaswani et al., 2017). The experimental setup is illustrated in Figure 1 and described in detail in Section 4. To explore the effect of quality of dialect identification, we perform a set of artificial experiments where we add increasing amounts of random noise to reduce language identification accuracy.

Our results show that in some scenarios, depending on the language identification accuracy, there is a cross-over point where the pipelined approach outperforms the integrated, multilingual approach in terms of BLEU scores, and vice versa. We then propose avenues for future work in this direction, based on our initial observations.

---

[1]https://www.ethnologue.com/statistics/size

[2]In the case of this paper, "multilingual" system refers to a single multi-dialectal system trained on multiple Arabic dialects.

Proceedings of VarDial, pages 214–222
Minneapolis, MN, June 7, 2019 ©2019 Association for Computational Linguistics

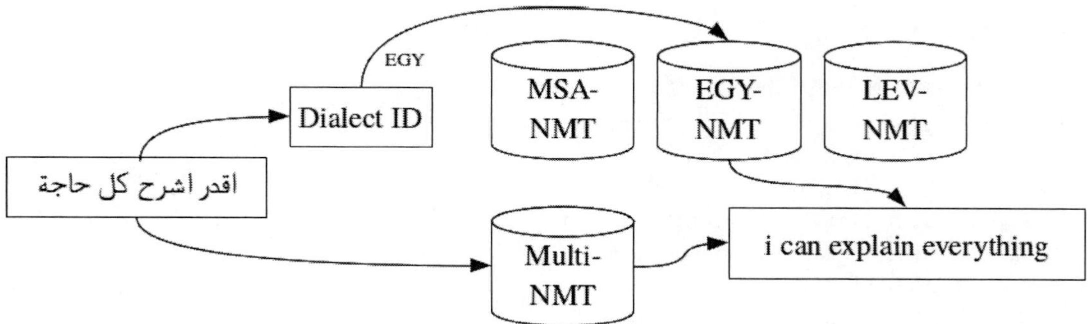

Figure 1: Illustration of our setup. Here, a test sentence of unknown dialect either gets run through a pipeline, where it is classified as Egyptian and then run through an Egyptian-tuned system, or is run through an integrated, multidialectal system.

2 Arabic Dialects

We provide here some background on Arabic dialectal variation for context. Modern Standard Arabic is the formal variety of Arabic, learned in schools and used for formal texts and newscasts. MSA is rooted in the Classical Arabic of the Qur'an, though there have been changes in vocabulary and certain aspects of grammar over time.

However, for most speakers their native language is a regional dialect of Arabic which diverges substantially. One theme among the dialects is the disappearance of certain grammatical attributes of MSA, such as case and the dual form. The dialects also display lexical and phonetic divergences, with some modification of grammatical structures such as tense markers. (Versteegh, 2014; Watson, 2007)

One major challenge of working with dialects in an NLP setting is that they have not been historically written down. However, with the rise of informal texts on the internet and social media, it is more common for dialectal Arabic to appear on the internet, but without having formalized orthography. In fact, it is common on social media to use Latin script including numerals to represent Arabic sounds, dubbed Arabizi (Bies et al., 2014). We work with data which is in the Arabic script only, but Arabizi is an important phenomenon to keep in mind for future work.

The exact regional groupings of regional dialects are not entirely consistent, but here are a few major groupings (including the two which we work with in this paper):

1. **Maghrebi**: spoken in Morocco, Algeria, Tunisia, Libya, Western Sahara, and Mauritania. Maghrebi has French and Berber influences, and not generally mutually intelligible with Eastern dialect groups. (Turki et al., 2016)

2. **Egyptian**: unusual in the amount of media available for NLP, such as Egyptian Arabic Wikipedia. Egypt has produced cinema in Egyptian Arabic that is distributed across the Arab world, increasing the reach of the dialect.

3. **Levantine**: spoken in parts of Lebanon, Jordan, Syria, Palestine, Israel, and Turkey.

4. **Arabian Peninsula**: includes subcategories such as Gulf (spoken along the Persian Gulf) and Hejazi (spoken in parts of Saudi Arabia including Mecca).

5. **Iraqi**: spoken in Iraq and parts of neighboring countries, also called Mesopotamian Arabic.

Zaidan and Callison-Burch (2014) detail in particular the ways in which dialectal varieties might manifest in their written form, from an NLP perspective. For instance, with respect to morphology, they note that the disappearance of grammatical case in dialects mostly only appears in the accusative when a suffix is added, because case in MSA generally are denoted by short vowels which are usually omitted from text. The disappearance of duals and feminine plurals is also noticeable, as well as the addition of more complex cliticization (such as circumfix negation). With respect to syntax, they note that VSO word order is more prevalent in MSA than dialects. Finally, lexical differences are noticeable in text as well.

215

3 Related Work

3.1 Translating Arabic Dialects

Harrat et al. (2017) provide a survey of machine translation for Arabic dialects. There has been a lot of work translating between dialects and MSA, primarily rule-based (Salloum and Habash, 2012), with some statistical machine translation approaches (Meftouh et al., 2015), which also translates between different dialects. More recently, Erdmann et al. (2017) translate between dialects with statistical MT, additionally modeling morphology and syntax.

Translating between Arabic dialects and other languages has dealt primarily with English as the other language, as we do here. Most work on this has been done with statistical machine translation systems, and generally involves pivoting through MSA or rule-based conversions to MSA. Sawaf (2010) use a hybrid rule-based, SMT system to translate dialectal Arabic. Zbib et al. (2012) explore the effects of different amounts of dialectal bitext versus MSA for SMT and try pivoting through MSA. Sajjad et al. (2013) adapts Egyptian Arabic to look like MSA with character-level transformations and uses SMT with phrase table merging to incorporate MSA-to-English data. We model our data setup after this paper, additionally using the Levantine data from the LDC corpus they use for Egyptian data (LDC2012T09). Meanwhile, Salloum et al. (2014) develop several variants of MSA and DA using SMT, and learn a Naive Bayes Classifier to determine which system would be best suited to translate data of unknown dialect. This is similar to our work in considering the possibility of the dialect being unknown, though we consider Neural Machine Translation (NMT) approaches.

As for using NMT on dialectal Arabic, Guellil et al. (2017) try using NMT on transliterated Algerian data and find that SMT outperforms it. Meanwhile, Hassan et al. (2017) generate synthetic Levantine data using monolingual word embeddings and add that to MSA-English data, briefly considering both multilingual and fine-tuning approaches as we do. While their main focus is the generation of synthetic data with monolingual data, we instead focus on investigating multilingual and fine-tuning approaches and how they interact with dialect identification when the dialect is unknown, additionally exploring the effect of Byte-Pair Encoding (BPE).

3.2 Neural Machine Translation for Dialects and Varieties

While NMT for Arabic dialects has not been extensively explored, there has been some work translating dialects and varieties with NMT recently. Costa-jussà et al. (2018) find that NMT improves over SMT for translating between Brazilian and European Portuguese, though that is a higher resource setting. Lakew et al. (2018b) use a multilingual Transformer for language varieties, as we do. However, their focus is translating into the different varieties rather than from an unknown variety, and they do not work with Arabic.

3.3 Arabic Dialect Identification

There has been a lot of work on Arabic dialect identification. Notably, Zaidan and Callison-Burch (2014) collect crowd-sourced dialect identification annotations and train classifiers to distinguish between MSA, Gulf, Levantine, and Egyptian varieties of Arabic, achieving accuracies ranging from 69.1% to 86.5%. More recently, Salameh and Bouamor (2018) have begun to focus on finer-grained classification, classifying dialects across 25 different cities. They develop a system with fine-grained accuracy of 67.9% for sentences with an average length of 7 words, and more than 90% with 16 words. Here we analyze how NMT is affected by dialect identification only between MSA, Egyptian, and Levantine. However, with the upcoming release of the MADAR corpus (Bouamor et al., 2018), we hope to extend this analysis to the finer-grained case in future work.

3.4 Multilingual NMT

One of the benefits of neural machine translation is the ease of sharing parameters across models, lending itself well to multilingual machine translation (Firat et al., 2016; Johnson et al., 2017; Lee et al., 2017). A multilingual approach uses all of the training data together (possibly up-sampling low-resource languages) to build one model with a single set of parameters.

On the other hand, people have also found transfer learning by simple fine-tuning to work well, especially between related high-resource and low-resource languages (Zoph et al., 2016). The multilingual approach has the benefit of not requiring us to know which dialect we are translating. Meanwhile, with enough training data in the correct dialect, we may be able to do better than that with the fine-tuning approach. This is the trade-off we explore here. We use a Transformer model (Vaswani et al., 2017), as it has seen to do perform better in general as well as in the multilingual setting (Lakew et al., 2018a).

4 Models

We use a Transformer model for all of our experiments (Vaswani et al., 2017). The Transformer is a recent alternative to recurrent neural sequence-to-sequence models. Instead of just using attention to connect encoder recurrent states to decoder recurrent states, the Transformer expands the function of attention to encompass the main task. It uses self-attention, which is attention applied to two states within the same sequence, as the foundation for sequence representations, rather than an RNN. The Transformer also increases the power of attention with multi-head attention, which performs an attention function several times in parallel, concatenates, and then projects the representation.

In the Transformer, the encoder consists of several layers of multi-head self-attention paired with a feedforward network. The decoder is similar but also has multi-head attention over the encoder output and masks future decoder output tokens. This model has been shown to achieve state-of-the-art in neural machine translation, and we can use it for multilingual or fine-tuning setups the same way we would a sequence-to-sequence model as in Sutskever et al. (2014).

With regards to the different ways we train the Transformer, we describe our setup, illustrated in Figure 1.

4.1 Multidialectal Model

One approach to being able to translate sentences of unknown dialect is to train a system in a "multilingual," or here multidialectal fashion. The simplest variant, introduced in Johnson et al. (2017), uses a shared wordpiece vocabulary and trains with data from several languages, adding a tag indicating the language at the beginning of each sentence. We follow this approach, but removing the tag, as in (Lee et al., 2017), and using a Transformer. We use a shared subword vocabulary by applying Byte-Pair Encoding (BPE) to the data for all variants concatenated (Sennrich et al., 2016). However, here we are not dealing with completely different languages, but rather variants of a language.

4.2 Dialect ID and Dialect-Tuned Models

On the other hand, dialect identification is an active area of research, and an alternative approach is to design a dialect-specific model for each dialect. One could simply train a system on dialect data alone. However, since dialects of Arabic are generally far lower-resource than MSA, this is difficult for NMT. To leverage the MSA to benefit the dialect-specific system, we follow the approach of Zoph et al. (2016), simply continuing to train on the low-resource dialects from the model trained on high-resource MSA. Again, we use a shared subword vocabulary trained on all of our training data of all variants, to avoid problems with out-of-vocabulary words.

5 Experiments

We perform experiments comparing multidialectal and dialect-tuned approaches, and then focus on the effect of misclassified dialects with a set of experiments adding synthetic noise to our language classification.

5.1 Data

For MSA training data, we use 5 million sentences of UN Data (Ziemski et al., 2016), in addition to GALE data, LDC2004T17, and LDC2004T18. For MSA dev data, we used NIST OpenMT '08, and for MSA test data, we used NIST OpenMT '09. For Egyptian and Levantine data, we used LDC2012T09, reserving the last 6k sentences of each for dev, test1, and test2 respectively. We only show results for test1 here, and reserve test2 for future use. We normalized the Arabic orthography, tokenized, cleaned, and deduplicated.[3] We applied BPE with 10k, 30k, and 50k merge operations, training on the concatenation of all of the training data. The final counts of sentences for our data are shown in Table 2.

5.2 Implementation

We use the Sockeye (Hieber et al., 2017) implementation of a Transformer (Vaswani et al., 2017) for all of our experiments. We used 6 layers, 512-dimensional embeddings, 8 attention heads, and

---

[3] By normalize the orthography, we mean that we removed diacritics and tatweels and normalized alefs and yas. For tokenization, we used the Moses tokenizer for English, since it does not have one for Arabic. We did not apply Arabic-specific tokenization that segments clitics as well.

	Multidialectal			Dialect-Tuned		
	10k BPE	30k BPE	50k BPE	10k BPE	30k BPE	50k BPE
MSA	38.23	**38.49**	38.22	36.42	38.04	36.79
EGY	22.44	21.93	21.12	**22.79**	21.64	20.86
LEV	22.31	21.89	21.47	**23.78**	22.68	22.35

Table 1: Multidialectal and dialect-tuned approaches for different BPE sizes. In this experiment, we assume the dialect of the test sentences are known so that the correct Dialect-Tuned models can be applied.

	train	dev	test1	test2
MSA	4,266k	1.4k	1.3k	N/A
EGY	32k	2k	2k	2k
LEV	129k	2k	2k	2k

Table 2: Number of sentences in dataset splits.

2048 hidden units in feed forward layers. We optimize with Adam (Kingma and Ba, 2014), with an initial learning rate of 0.0002, and a learning rate reduce factor of 0.9, applying label smoothing with a smoothing parameter of 0.1. We select the model based on dev BLEU. This is from the sockeye-recipes default medium transformer model[4], which closely but not exactly follows the official AWS sockeye autopilot Transformer model[5]

For our multidialectal experiments, we do not do any up-sampling of the lower-resource data, though this would be another axis to explore in future work.

5.3 Artificially Noised Dialect Identification

With the goal of exploring the importance of dialect identification in this context, we examine how the fine tuning approach suffers as we add artificial noise to to dialect identification. We do this by some percentage of the time randomly choosing one of the other models to decode with. We do this at intervals of 10%. To be precise, we provide pseudocode of the approach below.

$\mathcal{D} = \{MSA, LEV, EGY\}$

for test sentence s with true dialect $d \in \mathcal{D}$ **do**

    With probability p, switch model dialect $\hat{d}$

    if Switching **then**

        Sample $\hat{d}$ uniformly from $\mathcal{D} \setminus d$

    else

$$\hat{d} = d$$

Translation $t =$ decode($model_{\hat{d}}, s$)

6 Results

As an initial experiment, we compare the two approaches in the case where the dialect of the test sentence is known. The test1 BLEU scores of the multidialectal and dialect-tuned approaches for different BPE sizes are in Table 1. We can see that scores are pretty consistent across BPE sizes, with 10k being best for EGY and LEV while 30k is best for MSA. As we'd expect, with complete information about dialects, the fine tuning approach for EGY and LEV achieves the highest scores. With LEV, which has more available training data, this trend is clearer across BPE sizes. With EGY, which has a much smaller amount of training data, this gain is only achieved in the best BPE size for EGY of 10k. Interestingly, the multidialectal model does best for MSA, rather than the model trained only on MSA. It is possible that the comparatively small amount of dialectal data provides useful regularization for the MSA model, or that it is benefiting from the shared aspects of the dialects.

Our main results are shown in Figure 2. Here, we plot the BLEU score of each test set, MSA, EGY, and LEV, as the amount of noise we've added to dialect identification increases. It is interesting to see that in all cases, it consistently degrades as more noise is added, but ultimately doesn't reach a terribly low score even at 100% noise. We include the multidialectal system's performance as a horizontal dotted line. Where the lines intersect in the EGY and LEV case represents at what level of noise we have lost the benefit of dialect identification. So, by 20% error in both cases, we might as well be using the multidialectal system.

We note that this result (crossover at 20%) should be interpreted in light of the training data and the models we used. The cross-over point in

---

[4] https://github.com/kevinduh/sockeye-recipes/blob/master/hpm/tm1.hpm-template

[5] https://github.com/awslabs/sockeye/blob/master/sockeye_contrib/autopilot/models.py

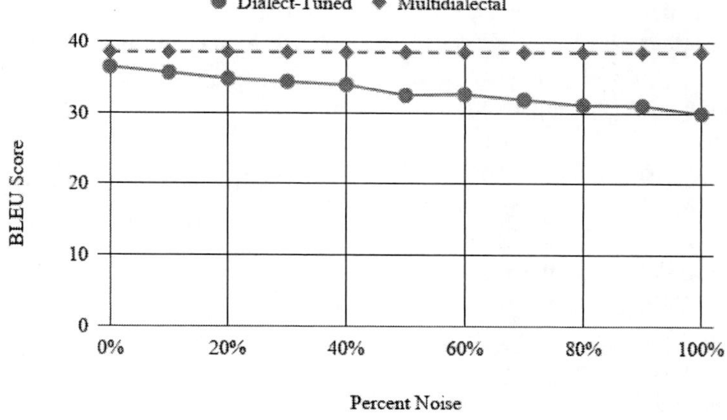

(a) Modern Standard Arabic Base Model

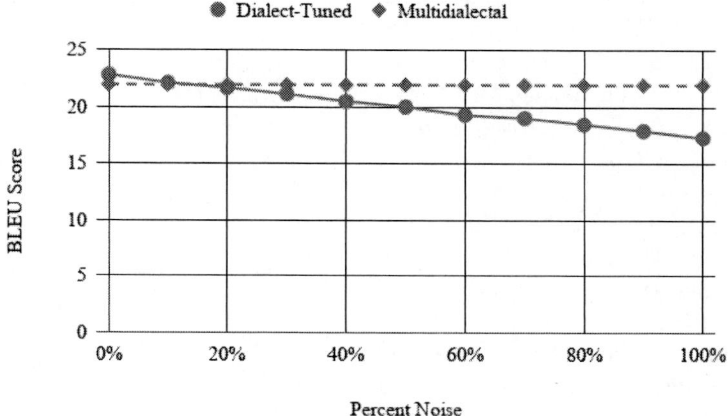

(b) Egyptian-Tuned Model

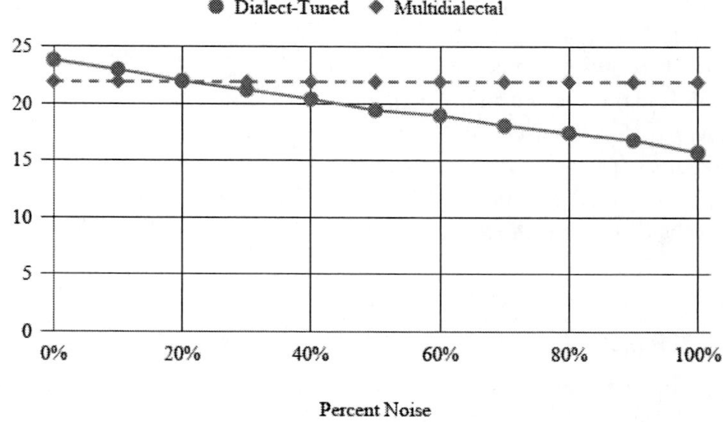

(c) Levantine-Tuned Model

Figure 2: Effect of noise on fine tuning models with 10k BPE. The dialect-tuned models are models fined-tuned on specific dialects, applied with noisy dialect identification. We provide the multidialectal model performances for comparison.

BLEU score between multidialectal and dialect-tuned models will depend on the relative strengths of each model. Further, dialect identification errors may be correlated (e.g. higher confusion between two close-by dialects, compared to two faraway ones). In other words, we imagine for different datasets and models, it will be important to rerun this analysis. We also hypothesize the the results may vary by sentence length, as well, which influences language identification accuracy.

To understand which combinations of test sentences and models are least and most compatible, we also present a matrix of all combinations of model and test set in 3. We can see that EGY and LEV test sets are much more harmed by the MSA model than the LEV- and EGY- tuned models respectively. It is possible that there is some shared vocabulary between EGY and LEV that it is learning, or that the EGY and LEV training sets are just a closer domain to each other than to MSA.

Finally, we use a very simple baseline for dialect ID to see how it performs. We train a model for language ID with `langid.py` (Lui and Baldwin, 2012), which uses naive Bayes classifier with a multinomial event model. Training `langid.py` on our data does not work well for dialect ID—in particular, the system is very sensitive to data size. It would probably be better to provide larger quantities of monolingual data for this if avaiable. However, we report results here to give a sense of how a very basic language ID system might perform. We try training it in two ways: (1) with the data proportions left as-is and (2) upsampling the EGY and LEV data sizes to match the MSA data size. (1) results in predicting almost all sentences as MSA, and (2) results in predicting almost all sentences as EGY. As you can see in Table 4, this results in (1) performing well only on MSA and (2) performing well only on EGY, with the other results being heavily degraded.

7   Discussion

While adding random noise is not necessarily reflective of the cases in which dialect identification systems would be likely to make errors, it does help us get an idea of how useful it is to tune an NMT model to a specific Arabic dialect, in light of faulty knowledge about which dialect it is.

Our mutidialectal approach performs competitively with the tuned approaches, but at a well-chosen BPE size and with less than 20% error, it

does seem beneficial to tune to the dialect. A couple factors seem to contribute to whether it is useful, beyond error rate of dialect system:

1. **BPE Merge Hyperparameter**: The dialects seem to perform best at the lowest BPE merge hyperparameter that we tried. This is the lower range of BPE settings usually used, but it would be worthwhile to explore this with even lower settings. As the merge hyperparameter decreases, we are getting closer to character-level, which may be able to handle the shared subwords across dialects better in light of varied morphological inflections.

2. **Amount of Training Data**: There does seem to be a difference in performance of tuned models between EGY and LEV which lines up with data size. There is much less EGY training data, and the fine-tuning process converges very quickly on the data. On the other hand, LEV has a decent amount of training data and shows more consistent improvements over the multidialectal model.

One trend we observed that is worth noting, is that the average sentence length differs substantially from MSA to EGY and LEV in our test sets, which may make sense given the more formal content of MSA. This might have some implications for NMT and dialect identification. Dialect identification is known to be harder on shorter sentences. Meanwhile, NMT can sometimes be hard on very long sentences. It is worth looking into these subtleties for future work understanding how to optimize NMT translation of unknown dialects of Arabic.

8   Future Work

One area for future work would be further exploring how this setup interacts with existing dialect identification systems to determine their usefulness for Arabic NMT of unknown dialects.

Additionally, the role of morphology in this setup with BPE would be useful to explore. It is possible that models that incorporate characters would be more useful at capturing shared information between MSA and dialects.

Finally, it would be great to test this on more dialects. We hope to do experimentation on larger dialectal corpora in the future, such as the soon-to-be-released MADAR corpus (Bouamor et al., 2018).

		Test Set		
		MSA	EGY	LEV
	MSA	**36.42**	27.38	25.39
Model	EGY	10.33	**22.79**	19.81
	LEV	8.24	15.70	**23.78**

Table 3: How each model performs on each test set.

	Test Set		
	MSA	EGY	LEV
No up-sampling	36.24	10.35	8.25
Up-sampling	27.56	22.79	15.71

Table 4: How well the pipelined approach does with `langid.py` as dialect ID.

9 Conclusion

We have done a set of preliminary experiments exploring a couple different approaches to translating Arabic of unknown dialect. An integrated, multi-dialectal model proved to be beneficial for MSA. Meanwhile, with a dialect identification error rate less than 20% and with a small enough BPE size and large enough training data, using a pipelined approach with a dialect-tuned model proves to be beneficial. We hope that this can be beneficial for determining future directions translating Arabic dialects.

10 Acknowledgments

This work is supported in part by the Office of the Director of National Intelligence (ODNI), Intelligence Advanced Research Projects Activity (IARPA), via contract FA8650-17-C-9115. The views and conclusions contained herein are those of the authors and should not be interpreted as necessarily representing the official policies, either expressed or implied, of ODNI, IARPA, or the U.S. Government. The U.S. Government is authorized to reproduce and distribute reprints for governmental purposes notwithstanding any copyright annotation therein.

References

Ann Bies, Zhiyi Song, Mohamed Maamouri, Stephen Grimes, Haejoong Lee, Jonathan Wright, Stephanie Strassel, Nizar Habash, Ramy Eskander, and Owen Rambow. 2014. Transliteration of arabizi into arabic orthography: Developing a parallel annotated arabizi-arabic script sms/chat corpus. In *Proceedings of the EMNLP 2014 Workshop on Arabic Natural Language Processing (ANLP)*, pages 93–103.

Houda Bouamor, Nizar Habash, Mohammad Salameh, Wajdi Zaghouani, Owen Rambow, Dana Abdulrahim, Ossama Obeid, Salam Khalifa, Fadhl Eryani, Alexander Erdmann, et al. 2018. The madar arabic dialect corpus and lexicon. In *Proceedings of the Eleventh International Conference on Language Resources and Evaluation (LREC-2018)*.

Marta R Costa-jussà, Marcos Zampieri, and Santanu Pal. 2018. A neural approach to language variety translation. In *Proceedings of the Fifth Workshop on NLP for Similar Languages, Varieties and Dialects (VarDial 2018)*, pages 275–282.

Heba Elfardy, Mohamed Al-Badrashiny, and Mona Diab. 2014. Aida: Identifying code switching in informal arabic text. In *Proceedings of The First Workshop on Computational Approaches to Code Switching*, pages 94–101.

Alexander Erdmann, Nizar Habash, Dima Taji, and Houda Bouamor. 2017. Low resourced machine translation via morpho-syntactic modeling: the case of dialectal arabic. *arXiv preprint arXiv:1712.06273*.

Orhan Firat, Kyunghyun Cho, and Yoshua Bengio. 2016. Multi-way, multilingual neural machine translation with a shared attention mechanism. In *Proceedings of NAACL-HLT*, pages 866–875.

Imane Guellil, Faiçal Azouaou, and Mourad Abbas. 2017. Comparison between neural and statistical translation after transliteration of algerian arabic dialect. *WiNLP: Women & Underrepresented Minorities in Natural Language Processing (co-located with ACL 2017)*, pages 1–5.

Salima Harrat, Karima Meftouh, and Kamel Smaili. 2017. Machine translation for arabic dialects (survey). *Information Processing & Management*.

Hany Hassan, Mostafa Elaraby, and Ahmed Tawfik. 2017. Synthetic data for neural machine translation of spoken-dialects. *arXiv preprint arXiv:1707.00079*.

Felix Hieber, Tobias Domhan, Michael Denkowski, David Vilar, Artem Sokolov, Ann Clifton, and Matt Post. 2017. Sockeye: A toolkit for neural machine translation. *arXiv preprint arXiv:1712.05690*.

Melvin Johnson, Mike Schuster, Quoc V Le, Maxim Krikun, Yonghui Wu, Zhifeng Chen, Nikhil Thorat, Fernanda Viégas, Martin Wattenberg, Greg Corrado, et al. 2017. Googles multilingual neural machine translation system: Enabling zero-shot translation. *Transactions of the Association for Computational Linguistics*, 5:339–351.

Diederik P Kingma and Jimmy Ba. 2014. Adam: A method for stochastic optimization. *arXiv preprint arXiv:1412.6980*.

Surafel Melaku Lakew, Mauro Cettolo, and Marcello Federico. 2018a. A comparison of transformer and recurrent neural networks on multilingual neural machine translation. In *Proceedings of the 27th International Conference on Computational Linguistics*, pages 641–652.

Surafel Melaku Lakew, Aliia Erofeeva, and Marcello Federico. 2018b. Neural machine translation into language varieties. In *Proceedings of the Third Conference on Machine Translation: Research Papers*, pages 156–164.

Jason Lee, Kyunghyun Cho, and Thomas Hofmann. 2017. Fully character-level neural machine translation without explicit segmentation. *Transactions of the Association for Computational Linguistics*, 5:365–378.

Marco Lui and Timothy Baldwin. 2012. langid. py: An off-the-shelf language identification tool. In *Proceedings of the ACL 2012 system demonstrations*, pages 25–30. Association for Computational Linguistics.

Karima Meftouh, Salima Harrat, Salma Jamoussi, Mourad Abbas, and Kamel Smaili. 2015. Machine translation experiments on padic: A parallel arabic dialect corpus. In *Proceedings of the 29th Pacific Asia Conference on Language, Information and Computation*, pages 26–34.

Hassan Sajjad, Kareem Darwish, and Yonatan Belinkov. 2013. Translating dialectal arabic to english. In *Proceedings of the 51st Annual Meeting of the Association for Computational Linguistics (Volume 2: Short Papers)*, volume 2, pages 1–6.

Mohammad Salameh and Houda Bouamor. 2018. Fine-grained arabic dialect identification. In *Proceedings of the 27th International Conference on Computational Linguistics*, pages 1332–1344.

Wael Salloum, Heba Elfardy, Linda Alamir-Salloum, Nizar Habash, and Mona Diab. 2014. Sentence level dialect identification for machine translation system selection. In *Proceedings of the 52nd Annual Meeting of the Association for Computational Linguistics (Volume 2: Short Papers)*, volume 2, pages 772–778.

Wael Salloum and Nizar Habash. 2012. Elissa: A dialectal to standard arabic machine translation system. *Proceedings of COLING 2012: Demonstration Papers*, pages 385–392.

Hassan Sawaf. 2010. Arabic dialect handling in hybrid machine translation. In *Proceedings of the conference of the association for machine translation in the americas (amta), denver, colorado.*

Rico Sennrich, Barry Haddow, and Alexandra Birch. 2016. Neural machine translation of rare words with subword units. In *Proceedings of the 54th Annual Meeting of the Association for Computational Linguistics (Volume 1: Long Papers)*, volume 1, pages 1715–1725.

Ilya Sutskever, Oriol Vinyals, and Quoc V Le. 2014. Sequence to sequence learning with neural networks. In *Advances in neural information processing systems*, pages 3104–3112.

Houcemeddine Turki, Emad Adel, Tariq Daouda, and Nassim Regragui. 2016. A conventional orthography for maghrebi arabic. In *Proceedings of the International Conference on Language Resources and Evaluation (LREC)*.

Ashish Vaswani, Noam Shazeer, Niki Parmar, Jakob Uszkoreit, Llion Jones, Aidan N Gomez, Łukasz Kaiser, and Illia Polosukhin. 2017. Attention is all you need. In *Advances in Neural Information Processing Systems*, pages 5998–6008.

Kees Versteegh. 2014. *Arabic Language*. Edinburgh University Press.

Janet CE Watson. 2007. *The Phonology and Morphology of Arabic*. OUP Oxford.

Omar F Zaidan and Chris Callison-Burch. 2014. Arabic dialect identification. *Computational Linguistics*, 40(1):171–202.

Rabih Zbib, Erika Malchiodi, Jacob Devlin, David Stallard, Spyros Matsoukas, Richard Schwartz, John Makhoul, Omar F Zaidan, and Chris Callison-Burch. 2012. Machine translation of arabic dialects. In *Proceedings of the 2012 conference of the north american chapter of the association for computational linguistics: Human language technologies*, pages 49–59. Association for Computational Linguistics.

Michal Ziemski, Marcin Junczys-Dowmunt, and Bruno Pouliquen. 2016. The united nations parallel corpus v1. 0. In *Lrec*.

Barret Zoph, Deniz Yuret, Jonathan May, and Kevin Knight. 2016. Transfer learning for low-resource neural machine translation. *arXiv preprint arXiv:1604.02201*.

Cross-lingual Annotation Projection Is Effective for Neural Part-of-Speech Tagging

Matthias Huck and **Diana Dutka** and **Alexander Fraser**

Center for Information and Language Processing

LMU Munich

Munich, Germany

{mhuck, fraser}@cis.lmu.de   diana.dutka@gmail.com

Abstract

We tackle the important task of part-of-speech tagging using a neural model in the zero-resource scenario, where we have no access to gold-standard POS training data. We compare this scenario with the low-resource scenario, where we have access to a small amount of gold-standard POS training data. Our experiments focus on Ukrainian as a representative of under-resourced languages. Russian is highly related to Ukrainian, so we exploit gold-standard Russian POS tags. We consider four techniques to perform Ukrainian POS tagging: zero-shot tagging and cross-lingual annotation projection (for the zero-resource scenario), and compare these with self-training and multilingual learning (for the low-resource scenario). We find that cross-lingual annotation projection works particularly well in the zero-resource scenario.

1   Introduction

Little or no hand-annotated part-of-speech training data exists for the vast majority of languages in the world. This work investigates POS-tagging for under-resourced languages with a state-of-the-art neural network model. We consider how best to deal with the zero-resource scenario (i.e., no availability of any POS-labeled training data for the targeted language). To better understand this scenario, we compare it with the low-resource scenario (i.e., availability of a small POS-labeled training corpus). We thoroughly compare four techniques, including: *zero-shot tagging* and *cross-lingual annotation projection* from a linguistically related higher-resource language (for the zero-resource scenario), as well as *self-training* and *multilingual learning* (for the low-resource scenario).

A controlled experimental design is established for our study. We aim for immediate comparability of all tested tagging strategies of both scenarios, zero-resource and low-resource. We therefore opt to carry out both the zero-resource and the low-resource experiments on the same language, Ukrainian, and measure tagging accuracy on one common test set. A small amount of manually POS-annotated Ukrainian training data is available, which we use for supervised low-resource training. We simulate the zero-resource scenario by not using any POS-annotated Ukrainian training data. Russian is a higher-resource language which is linguistically closely related to Ukrainian. We use a larger POS-annotated Russian corpus for multilingual learning and zero-shot tagging experiments, and an unlabeled Russian–Ukrainian parallel corpus for the cross-lingual projection annotation experiment. To strengthen the upper-bound result for low-resource tagging, we consider the improvements possible through self-training, for which we use the Ukrainian side of the Russian–Ukrainian parallel corpus in order to maintain comparability. Our experimental design allows us to directly assess whether the tagging quality of any zero-resource strategy is approaching the accuracies of supervised low-resource strategies. We find that zero-shot tagging does not yield satisfactory quality, even if we operate on a higher linguistic abstraction level with word stems, which are often very similar in Ukrainian and Russian. But the empirical results show that annotation projection from a closely-related language is a very effective strategy for training neural POS taggers.

2   Related Work

Annotation projection for POS-tagging was first explored by Yarowsky and Ngai (2001) for cross-lingual transfer from English to French. Our basic approach shares much of Yarowsky and Ngai's

Proceedings of VarDial, pages 223–233

Minneapolis, MN, June 7, 2019 ©2019 Association for Computational Linguistics

original idea and reaffirms the efficacy of annotation projection also with a state-of-the-art neural sequence tagging model (Wang et al., 2015) and on the modern universal POS-annotation scheme (Petrov et al., 2012).

Since 2001, in addition to POS-tagging, annotation projection has been successfully applied to other tasks such as named entity recognition (Yarowsky et al., 2001; Enghoff et al., 2018), word sense tagging (Bentivogli et al., 2004), semantic role labeling (Pado and Lapata, 2005, 2009; van der Plas et al., 2011; Aminian et al., 2017), or dependency parsing (Hwa et al., 2005; Tiedemann, 2014; Rasooli and Collins, 2015; Agić et al., 2016; Aufrant et al., 2016). Kim et al. (2011) presented an integration into a full pipeline for information extraction. Open-source software tools for annotation projection are now available online (Akbik and Vollgraf, 2018, 2017).

To avoid unnecessarily noisy data, unlike previous authors, Lacroix et al. (2016) did not apply heuristics to fix certain word alignment links that pose difficulties to annotation projection. They demonstrated that it is simpler and more effective to ignore unaligned words as well as many-to-many alignments. In our work, we likewise settle on a simple technique based on a one-directional word alignment.

Xi and Hwa (2005) have combined projected POS-annotation with a small manually annotated corpus in a low-resource scenario. Newer research on annotation projection for POS-tagging has looked at historical languages (Meyer, 2011; Sukhareva et al., 2017) and sign language (Östling et al., 2015). Notable exceptions are the works of Wisniewski et al. (2014), examining annotation projection for a CRF tagging model (Lavergne et al., 2010) on living spoken languages, and of Agić et al. (2015). Meyer (2011) tags Old Russian via annotation projection from modern Russian translations. Sukhareva et al. (2017) POS-tag the extinct Hittite language through projection from German. Recent related work on neural POS-tagging has mostly focused on robustness through character-level modeling (Heigold et al., 2016, 2018; dos Santos and Zadrozny, 2014; Labeau et al., 2015) or on architectural improvements (Huang et al., 2015; Ma and Hovy, 2016; Yasunaga et al., 2018). Kim et al. (2017) have proposed an interesting neural tagging architecture that allows for multilingual learning with a language-specific component integrated with another cross-lingually shared component. We are however not aware of many prior studies that systematically explore annotation projection for cross-lingual transfer in neural POS-tagging of living spoken languages. Steps in this direction have been taken only lately by Fang and Cohn (2016), Plank and Agić (2018) and Anastasopoulos et al. (2018). We follow up on this line of research with our work.

3 Methods

Research questions. We ask two central research questions in this work, one for each of the considered scenarios:

Low-resource scenario: When the amount of hand-labeled training data is small for the targeted language, how effectively can we further improve the tagger by employing auxiliary resources? Specifically, how helpful is the use of additional unlabeled corpora (*self-training*) and corpora in a different language (*multilingual learning*)?

Zero-resource scenario: When there isn't any hand-labeled training data available for the targeted language, how effectively can we harness knowledge from annotated corpora in a different, but related language? Specifically, is tagging quality close to supervised low-resource conditions attainable with either a plain foreign-language tagging model (*zero-shot tagging*) or via annotation projection from a foreign language (*cross-lingual transfer*)?

Neural tagging model. Depending on the context, the part-of-speech of a word may vary. E.g., the English word "green" takes a different POS (adjective, noun, verb) in each of the following three sentences:

```
The recipe requires green mangoes.
She took 63 shots to reach the green.
How can we green our campus?
```

The need to resolve such ambiguities is one of the challenges in POS-tagging, and is the reason why the task requires sequence labeling instead of just a simple dictionary lookup. Another challenge is imposed by words that are out-of-vocabulary (OOV) to the tagger—a pressing issue especially under low-resource conditions, where many valid word forms of the language are not observed in training data.

We utilize a Bidirectional Long Short-Term Memory (BLSTM) neural network model (Hochreiter and Schmidhuber, 1997) to build our sequence taggers. BLSTMs are recurrent neural networks (RNNs) that are capable of learning long-term dependencies, taking into account both the previous and the following context. RNNs generally show great results at processing sequential data. They are widely adopted in natural language processing, including the POS-tagging task (Wang et al., 2015). Other statistical sequence labeling methods, such as maximum entropy tagging models (Ratnaparkhi, 1996) or conditional random fields (Lafferty et al., 2001; Lavergne et al., 2010), are nowadays often outperformed by neural network methods (Collobert et al., 2011).

3.1 Self-Training

Given sufficient amount of labeled data, it is possible to build high-performance tools with direct supervision, but since there are languages that do not have enough suitable data to train a model, it is reasonable to employ semi-supervised methods. Those include self-training, which was previously discussed by McClosky et al. (2006), inter alia. Self-training requires labeled and unlabeled data and can be applied to low-resource languages. "Semi-supervised and unsupervised methods are important because good labeled data is expensive, whereas there is no shortage of unlabeled data" (McClosky et al., 2006).

3.2 Multilingual Learning

The multilingual learning method is suitable for under-resourced languages with little annotated data. The training set is enlarged through the texts of a related language. The idea is to shuffle original Ukrainian training sentences with the Russian labeled data to get more annotated texts.

3.3 Zero-shot Tagging

A zero-shot strategy can be pursued in case no annotated text exists for the resource-poor language. The zero-shot approach applies a tagging model trained for a closely related language.

There is quite some vocabulary intersection between Ukrainian and Russian (cf. Section 4.3), and the grammatical structure and word order of sentences are expected to be similar in the two related languages. We will however determine in the experimental section that these similarities

Open class words	Closed class words
ADJ: adjective	ADP: adposition
ADV: adverb	AUX: auxiliary
INTJ: interjection	CCONJ: coordinating conjunction
NOUN: noun	DET: determiner
PROPN: proper noun	NUM: numeral
VERB: verb	PART: particle
	PRON: pronoun
	SCONJ: subordinating conjunction
Other	
PUNCT: punctuation SYM: symbol X: other	

Table 1: Universal Dependencies tags.

are not strong enough to be able to use a model trained for Russian to tag Ukrainian sentences (Section 5.2.4).

3.4 Cross-lingual Transfer

The cross-lingual transfer approach relies on the availability of cross-lingual supervision and is suitable for languages that do not have any annotated data, but for which there is an available parallel corpus with a high-resource language. A POS-tagger for the high-resource language can be applied to automatically annotate the source side (here: Russian) of the parallel corpus. The source annotation is then projected to the target side (here: Ukrainian) (Yarowsky and Ngai, 2001). After that, a tagger for the resource-poor language can be trained on the target side of the parallel corpus with its associated projected automatic source-side annotation. This provides another solution in the case of a complete lack of gold-standard training data, the zero-resource scenario.

4 Corpus-linguistic Analysis

Ukrainian, as an under-resourced language, has a relatively small amount of suitable data that can be freely obtained from the web. There are two main data sources that are used throughout this work: annotated Ukrainian and Russian texts from the Universal Dependencies project and a Russian–Ukrainian parallel corpus of news texts. This section provides a description of the data as well as a quantitative comparison of the Russian and Ukrainian data sets.

4.1 Data

Universal Dependencies. The annotated data used to train taggers is taken from the Universal Dependencies corpora for Russian and

Ukrainian.[1] Universal Dependencies (UD) is a project based on open collaboration that is developing cross-linguistically consistent treebank annotation for many languages. The annotation scheme is based on an evolution of Stanford dependencies (de Marneffe et al., 2006; de Marneffe and Manning, 2008; de Marneffe et al., 2014) and Google universal part-of-speech tags (Petrov et al., 2012). The 17 UD core part-of-speech categories are listed in Table 1. Additional lexical and grammatical properties of words are distinguished by extra features that are not part of the tag set.

Russian–Ukrainian parallel corpus. The Russian–Ukrainian parallel corpus was created by ElVisti Information Center.[2] A fragment of 100,000 sentences is freely available for scientific and educational purposes.[3] The corpus consists of web publications of news articles and was created as a resource for building machine translation systems (Lande and Zhygalo, 2008).

4.2 Relatedness of Ukrainian and Russian

Slavic languages descend from a common predecessor, called Proto-Slavonic. Russian and Ukrainian belong to East Slavic, one of three regional subgroups of Slavic languages, which is also the largest group as for the number of speakers (Carlton, 1991).

Alphabet. Both Russian and Ukrainian use the Cyrillic script and have 33 letters each. However, there are differences in their alphabets. Unlike Russian, the letters Ёё, ъ, Ыы, Ээ are not used in Ukrainian, and Ukrainian has extra letters Ґґ, Єє, Іі, Її, which are not found in Russian. The apostrophe occurs in words of both languages, but in Russian it is not very common and mainly used in foreign proper nouns.

Vocabulary. Despite the fact that the languages share some of their vocabularies with similar pronunciation and spelling, they often have different semantic shades. Having a common predecessor language, Russian and Ukrainian have retained many identical word stems. Stemming techniques will be explored in this work in order to capitalize on such similarities between the two related languages and improve Ukrainian POS-tagging.

[1] http://universaldependencies.org
[2] http://visti.net
[3] http://ling.infostream.ua

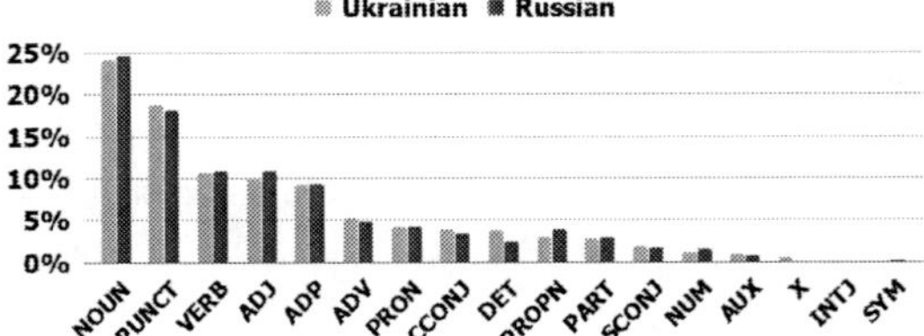

Figure 1: Tag distribution in training sets.

Ambiguity	Ukrainian		Russian	
	Types	Tokens	Types	Tokens
1	25940	65780	128082	812855
2	374	13111	2682	143338
3	46	2727	152	57793
4	13	2245	24	55035
5	3	1606	7	11489
6	–	–	2	6750

Table 2: Tag ambiguity.

Morphosyntax. Russian and Ukrainian also have similarities in their morphosyntactic features. For example, in both languages, the adjective, participle and possessive pronoun agree with the noun in case, gender and number. The verb has separate forms for different genders in the past but does not have gender variations in other tenses. There are three persons and two numbers.

4.3 Quantitative Comparison

Amount of data. The annotated UD data set for the Russian language is an order of magnitude bigger than the Ukrainian. The Ukrainian training corpus contains 85K annotated tokens in 5K sentences, the Russian corpus 1M tokens in 61K sentences.

Tag statistics. The distribution of tags in the Ukrainian and in the Russian UD training sets is quite similar, as can be seen in Figure 1. The most frequent tags in both corpora are *NOUN* and *PUNCT*, which account for nearly 25% and 20% of the tokens, respectively. Together with *VERB*, *ADJ* and *ADP*, they cover over 70% of the texts. The rank-frequency distribution of POS-tags approximately complies with Zipf's law (Zipf, 1932).

The words in both Russian and Ukrainian are mostly unambiguous. The bigger part of the training data vocabulary is always annotated with the same tag (Table 2). Some words occur with up to five different tags in Ukrainian and up to six in Russian, but those are quite rare cases.

Shared voc.		Words	Stems
Ukr	Types	2998 / 26376 11.4 %	3442 / 15821 21.8 %
	Tokens	35395 / 85469 41.4 %	47789 / 85469 55.9 %
Rus	Types	2998 / 130949 2.3 %	3442 / 48652 7.1 %
	Tokens	392319 / 1087260 36.1 %	550297 / 1087260 50.6 %

Table 3: Shared vocabulary before and after stemming.

Shared vocabulary. Taking into account that Ukrainian and Russian are related, it makes sense to examine their lexicons for common words. An overview of the shared vocabulary is given in Table 3 (left-hand column). There are only 2998 words appearing in lexicons of both languages. However, when counting their actual occurrences in the text we can see that common words are frequent throughout the texts. In Ukrainian, for example, 41% of the training texts consist of words that can be found in both languages.

These words are also mainly tagged in the same way. About 79% (2358 out of 2998) are tagged in both languages with the same tag (or tags). Another 13% (388 out of 2998) are tagged with the partially same tags.[4] The rest of the words of the shared vocabulary (about 8%) are annotated with completely different tags in each language.

Stemming. Since both Russian and Ukrainian are richly inflected languages, but closely related to each other, many differences in their word surface form vocabularies might be caused by inflection diversities. Table 3 (right-hand column) provides statistics of the stemmed Russian and Ukrainian training sets to examine whether the amount of shared vocabulary is higher after the words are reduced to their stem forms. Russian text is stemmed with the Snowball stemmer (Porter, 1980) from the NLTK package.[5] The stemmer for Ukrainian is an implementation found on GitHub posted by Kyrylo Zakharov.[6]

The size of the shared vocabulary rises from 2998 to 3442 types after stemming. Although this increase in vocabulary overlap seems marginal, in terms of the occurrences there is a more significant

change. After the stemming, the shared vocabulary tokens in the training sets of both languages amount to over 50%.

5 Experiments

5.1 Experimental Setup

5.1.1 BLSTM Tagger

An open-source re-implementation of Wang et al.'s BLSTM tagging architecture is used for our experiments.[7] We configure a hidden layer size of 100, embedding dimensions of 300, a maximum training sequence length of 100, and a batch size of 32. We optimize with RMSprop, a variation of RProp (Riedmiller and Braun, 1993), at a learning rate of 0.001. A sample sized 20% of the training data is removed and used for validation. To counteract overfitting, we store model checkpoints and do early stopping.

Word embeddings. Word embeddings help render more information regarding the word since they carry semantic and syntactic information and capture the meaning of words, the relationship between words, and the context of different words. This is useful for tagging and many other tasks in natural language processing (Plank et al., 2016; Wiegandt et al., 2017).

Pre-trained embeddings used in this work were downloaded from an open repository provided by Facebook Research.[8] These embeddings were trained with `fastText`[9] on Wikipedia using the skip-gram model with default parameters (Bojanowski et al., 2017).

5.1.2 Frequency Tagger

We additionally built a simple Frequency tagger that annotates each word in isolation with its most frequent tag. The only calculations that are required are tag counts per word in the training data. As soon as the occurrences are counted, the Frequency tagger is ready to annotate sentences.

OOVs are tagged with the majority class, which in both languages is *NOUN*. There are 3771 words in the Ukrainian test set that are new to the Frequency tagger, which means that 25.8% of the text cannot be tagged based on evidence. In Russian,

---

[4]For example: the word вести can be tagged in Russian as *VERB* or *NOUN*, in Ukrainian only as *NOUN*.

[5]`http://www.nltk.org/_modules/nltk/stem/snowball.html`

[6]`https://github.com/Amicel3/ukr_stemmer`

[7]`https://github.com/aneesh-joshi/LSTM_POS_Tagger`

[8]`https://github.com/facebookresearch/fastText/blob/master/docs/pretrained-vectors.md`

[9]`https://fasttext.cc`

Russian Test	
Model	**Accuracy**
Frequency Tagger	90.7 %
BLSTM + RE	91.3 %
BLSTM + PE	94.4 %
Stem BLSTM + RE	92.3 %

Table 4: Overview of the conducted tagging experiments on Russian test data (and trained on Russian data): PE - pre-trained embeddings; RE - randomly initialized embeddings; Stem - stemming.

Ukrainian Test	
Model	**Accuracy**
trained on Ukrainian data	
Frequency Tagger	81.6 %
BLSTM + RE	80.0 %
BLSTM + PE	85.4 %
Self-trained BLSTM + PE	86.2 %
Stem BLSTM + RE	84.1 %
trained on Russian data	
Zero-shot BLSTM + PE	51.5 %
Zero-shot Stem BLSTM + RE	56.1 %
trained on projected annotation	
Cross-lingual Transfer	84.4 %
trained on both languages	
Multilingual BLSTM + PE	86.4 %
Multilingual Stem BLSTM + RE	87.3 %

Table 5: Overview of the conducted tagging experiments on Ukrainian test data.

the fraction of unknown words is smaller (9.4%). This can be explained by the much bigger size of the training set that covers more of the Russian vocabulary.

5.2 Experimental Results

We now present the results for all the investigated techniques. The tagging accuracies for all experiments on the Ukrainian test set are collectively shown in Table 5. Some further empirical observations, e.g. on the taggers' ability to correctly handle OOV words, will also be discussed below. Supplementary tagging accuracies of Russian POS-taggers measured on a Russian test set are reported in Table 4.

5.2.1 Low-resource Supervision Results

The baseline taggers (Frequency and BLSTM) for Russian and for Ukrainian are trained on annotated UD data for the respective language. For the BLSTM models, there are two flavors: one with randomly initialized embeddings (BLSTM + RE) and one with pre-trained

Accuracy	**Tags**
~99%	NOUN, PUNCT
91-99%	PRON, CCONJ, SCONJ, AUX, ADP
71-90%	PART, ADV, NUM, DET
51-70%	–
41-50%	VERB, PROPN, SYM
31-40%	ADJ, INTJ
11-30%	–
<10%	X

Table 6: Prediction quality per part-of-speech (of the Ukrainian BLSTM + PE tagging model).

word embeddings (BLSTM + PE). The Russian BLSTM taggers are built with the exact same hyperparameters as the Ukrainian BLSTM taggers but show better results in the evaluation. This is because the Russian model is trained on more data.

On Ukrainian, the BLSTM with randomly initialized embeddings (RE) achieves better results on tag prediction for OOVs than the Frequency tagger (53% vs. 40% correct), but surprisingly does not outperform the Frequency tagger in overall accuracy (BLSTM + RE: 80.0%, Frequency: 81.6%; Table 5). However, the use of pre-trained embeddings in the BLSTM model increases the overall accuracy by about +5% absolute (BLSTM + PE: 85.4%). OOV tag prediction is boosted further to 58% of unknowns correctly labeled.

Table 6 shows the prediction quality per individual POS of the Ukrainian BLSTM + PE model. 11 out of 17 tags are predicted with accuracies above 70%. The most inaccurate predictions are made for the X tag which is used for cases of code-switching. Since the tag is used when it is not possible (or meaningful) to analyze the word, it is difficult for a neural network to learn to recognize it without additional features.

5.2.2 Self-Training Results

In self-training, the existing model first labels unlabeled data. We apply our BLSTM + PE model to automatically tag the Ukrainian side of the Russian–Ukrainian parallel corpus. This step provides us with new synthetically annotated data, which is then treated as truth and appended to the original training corpus to re-train the tagger.

The tagger trained with additional synthetically annotated data improves just moderately over the tagger trained on only the hand-labeled UD corpus (86.2% vs. 85.4% overall accuracy; Table 5). Self-training is thus barely effective despite the 20-fold augmentation of training instances through

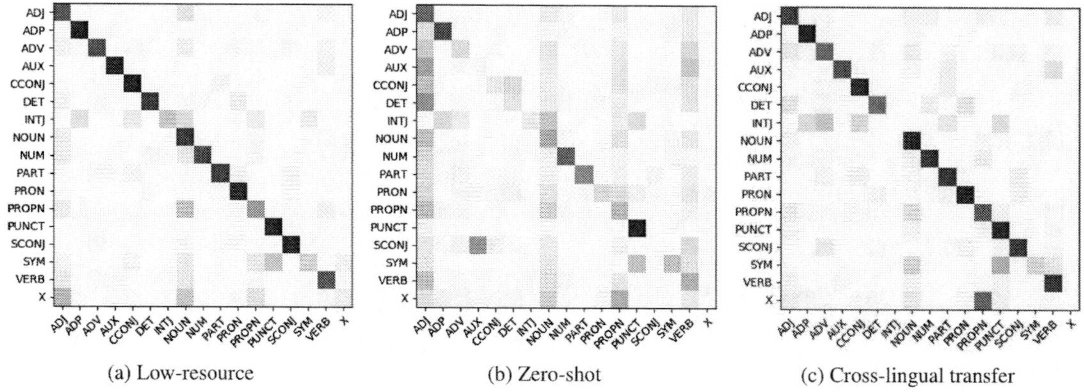

(a) Low-resource   (b) Zero-shot   (c) Cross-lingual transfer

Figure 2: Confusion matrix heatmaps.

the synthetic corpus. Clark et al. (2003) have previously reported similar findings. In the literature, inefficacy of self-training is occasionally attributed to a domain mismatch of the synthetically annotated data. In our case, all corpora are from the same domain (news text), though. The main benefit of self-training that we observe is an increase of correctly tagged OOVs (of around +5% absolute, from 58% to 63%).

5.2.3 Multilingual Learning Results

The multilingual learning approach yields an improvement of one percentage point (86.4% accuracy) compared to the low-resource BLSTM + PE tagger trained on only the Ukrainian data.

We oversampled the Ukrainian corpus to balance out the fraction of data from each language and avoid a bias towards Russian. The Ukrainian data was copied and added to the mixed training set until it reached the size of the Russian data. We also tried undersampling of Russian data and plain concatenation. The differences in tagging accuracy were minor (undersampling: 86.0%, concatenation: 86.2%), but oversampling of Ukrainian worked best.

5.2.4 Zero-shot Tagging Results

In the zero-shot tagging experiment, the BLSTM model trained on the Russian UD corpus (with pre-trained word embeddings) is applied to the Ukrainian test set. The Russian model's accuracy on the Russian test set had reached 94.4% (Table 4). Yet, when being run on the related Ukrainian language, just over 50% of Ukrainian words are correctly annotated by the Russian tagger (Table 5). This cannot be considered a satisfactory outcome.

5.2.5 Cross-lingual Transfer Results

The idea of the cross-lingual transfer is to project tags from the annotated part of the parallel corpus to its unlabeled translation to produce training data for the under-resourced language. The success of cross-lingual transfer depends not only on the quality of the source language annotation, but also on the reliability of the annotation projection.

We rely on standard statistical word alignment algorithms (Brown et al., 1993) as the basis of POS annotation projection from Russian to Ukrainian. The parallel corpus is aligned with `fast_align`,[10] an unsupervised word aligner introduced by Dyer et al. (2013). For phrase-based machine translation, the two alignment directions (*forward* and *reverse*) are typically combined to a symmetrized alignment. But for annotation projection, it is more convenient to use one-directional alignment with one Ukrainian token never being aligned to multiple tokens on the Russian side. The annotation projection across the alignment then becomes straightforward.[11] No disambiguation heuristics are necessary, which could be a source of additional errors.[12]

The BLSTM tagger supervised with gold-standard Ukrainian annotation (Section 5.2.1) outperforms the cross-lingual transfer tagger by only one percentage point (Table 5), despite the latter not requiring and not using any manually annotated Ukrainian training data. The confusion matrix heatmaps in Figure 2 visually illustrate the su-

---

[10] https://github.com/clab/fast_align

[11] The projected label of each Ukrainian token is taken from the single Russian-side token that it's aligned with. Vice versa, note that we permit 1-to-many projection from one Russian token to multiple Ukrainian tokens in this setting.

[12] We experimented with other word alignment variants but could not improve over the reported result.

229

periority of cross-lingual transfer over zero-shot tagging, and how the two compare to the low-resource supervision baseline BLSTM. The result highlights that a competitive neural tagger can be trained even under zero-resource conditions. A parallel corpus with a related language and the existence of a tagger for that related language enable effective cross-lingual transfer. A BLSTM model trained on projected annotation seems to cope very well with the language transfer.

5.2.6 Stemming Results

In Section 4.3 it was demonstrated that the number of common words grew after stemming was applied. We now test whether stemming has a positive impact on tagging quality. Since the pre-trained word embeddings were trained on full word surface forms, the embeddings for these experiments are randomly initialized.

The Stem BLSTM + RE result in Table 4 shows that compared to the previous taggers trained on random embeddings, the accuracy for Russian grows by about one percentage point. There are even bigger improvement for the Ukrainian tagger, which reaches 84.1% accuracy (Table 5).

Stemming benefits the performance of the POS-tagger, since the number of unknown tokens in the test data is reduced. The number of OOVs that are tagged correctly in Ukrainian increases to 61% from the initial 53%. The error rate among the known vocabulary is reduced by 2% absolute compared to the non-stemmed model.

Applying the Russian stem POS-tagger to the Ukrainian stemmed test set results in a nice accuracy improvement (about +4%) over the previous zero-shot attempt on full word forms. The zero-shot tagging quality remains weak, though, even with stemming.

In order to also examine the multilingual learning strategy over stem forms, the last model in this series of experiments is trained on concatenated stemmed Ukrainian and stemmed Russian data. The model achieves about +1% absolute improvement compared to the previous best result for Ukrainian. Tagging accuracy is reaching 87.3%, beating the result with the model trained on full forms of the same concatenation of corpora. We found that the stem system version is actually slightly worse at predicting tags of known Ukrainian words, but OOVs are handled much better (69% vs. 57% correct tags for unseen Ukrainian words).

6 Summary of Findings

The observations that have been made in the course of this work can be briefly summarized as follows: 1) Pre-trained word embeddings are important for better tagging quality since they represent contextual similarities between words. 2) A semi-supervised approach (*self-training*) showed only moderate gains despite a notable increase of the training corpus with synthetically labeled data. 3) Mixing larger related-language annotated data into the training corpus (*multilingual learning*) slightly improved the tagging accuracy for the low-resource language. 4) Applying a Russian tagger on Ukrainian (*zero-shot*) did not show satisfactory results, which could be due to the relatively small amount of shared vocabulary and certain differences in grammar. 5) Given a parallel corpus, a competitive neural POS-tagger can be trained without any initial annotated data (using *cross-lingual transfer* via annotation projection), which can be viewed as a good solution in the zero-resource scenario. 6) Bridging words by reducing them to their stems has a positive influence since both languages are highly inflected. The number of types is lowered and the tagger can abstract from the sparsity of inflected surface forms.

The best accuracy for Ukrainian (87.3%) was achieved when a multilingual model was trained on both Russian and Ukrainian stemmed training corpora. Potentially, through a combination of stemmed words and pre-trained stem embeddings, further improvements could be attained. For the important zero-resource scenario, cross-lingual projection worked best, and we achieved an accuracy rate of 84.4%. Here there is likely to be room for further improvement by tailoring the word alignment more to the task.

7 Conclusion

We carried out an evaluation on Ukrainian neural POS-tagging for both low-resource and zero-resource scenarios. For low-resource, multilingual learning works best, suggesting that even for languages which do have some gold-standard POS training data, multilingual learning through combining the training data with data from closely related languages is of strong interest. For zero-resource, cross-lingual annotation projection works best, suggesting that where parallel corpora with a related language are available, cross-lingual projection should be strongly considered.

Acknowledgment

This project has received funding from the European Research Council (ERC) under the European Union's Horizon 2020 research and innovation programme (grant agreement № 640550).

References

Željko Agić, Dirk Hovy, and Anders Søgaard. 2015. If all you have is a bit of the Bible: Learning POS taggers for truly low-resource languages. In *Proceedings of the 53rd Annual Meeting of the Association for Computational Linguistics and the 7th International Joint Conference on Natural Language Processing (Volume 2: Short Papers)*, pages 268–272, Beijing, China. Association for Computational Linguistics.

Željko Agić, Anders Johannsen, Barbara Plank, Héctor Martínez Alonso, Natalie Schluter, and Anders Søgaard. 2016. Multilingual Projection for Parsing Truly Low-Resource Languages. *Transactions of the Association for Computational Linguistics*, 4(1):301–312.

Alan Akbik and Roland Vollgraf. 2017. The Projector: An Interactive Annotation Projection Visualization Tool. In *Proceedings of the 2017 Conference on Empirical Methods in Natural Language Processing: System Demonstrations*, pages 43–48. Association for Computational Linguistics.

Alan Akbik and Roland Vollgraf. 2018. ZAP: An Open-Source Multilingual Annotation Projection Framework. In *Proceedings of the Eleventh International Conference on Language Resources and Evaluation (LREC-2018)*. European Language Resource Association.

Maryam Aminian, Mohammad Sadegh Rasooli, and Mona Diab. 2017. Transferring Semantic Roles Using Translation and Syntactic Information. In *Proceedings of the Eighth International Joint Conference on Natural Language Processing (Volume 2: Short Papers)*, pages 13–19, Taipei, Taiwan. Asian Federation of Natural Language Processing.

Antonios Anastasopoulos, Marika Lekakou, Josep Quer, Eleni Zimianiti, Justin DeBenedetto, and David Chiang. 2018. Part-of-Speech Tagging on an Endangered Language: a Parallel Griko-Italian Resource. In *Proceedings of the 27th International Conference on Computational Linguistics*, pages 2529–2539. Association for Computational Linguistics.

Lauriane Aufrant, Guillaume Wisniewski, and François Yvon. 2016. Zero-resource Dependency Parsing: Boosting Delexicalized Cross-lingual Transfer with Linguistic Knowledge. In *Proceedings of COLING 2016, the 26th International Conference on Computational Linguistics: Technical Papers*, pages 119–130. The COLING 2016 Organizing Committee.

Luisa Bentivogli, Pamela Forner, and Emanuele Pianta. 2004. Evaluating Cross-Language Annotation Transfer in the MultiSemCor Corpus. In *COLING 2004: Proceedings of the 20th International Conference on Computational Linguistics*.

Piotr Bojanowski, Edouard Grave, Armand Joulin, and Tomas Mikolov. 2017. Enriching Word Vectors with Subword Information. *Transactions of the Association for Computational Linguistics*, 5:135–146.

Peter F. Brown, Stephen A. Della Pietra, Vincent J. Della Pietra, and Robert L. Mercer. 1993. The Mathematics of Statistical Machine Translation: Parameter Estimation. *Computational Linguistics*, 19(2):263–311.

Terence R Carlton. 1991. *Introduction to the phonological history of the Slavic languages*. Slavica Publishers Columbus, Ohio.

Stephen Clark, James Curran, and Miles Osborne. 2003. Bootstrapping POS-taggers using unlabelled data. In *Proceedings of the Seventh Conference on Natural Language Learning at HLT-NAACL 2003*.

Ronan Collobert, Jason Weston, Leon Bottou, Michael Karlen, Koray Kavukcuoglu, and Pavel Kuksa. 2011. Natural language processing (almost) from scratch. *Journal of Machine Learning Research*, 12(Aug):2493–2537.

Chris Dyer, Victor Chahuneau, and Noah A. Smith. 2013. A Simple, Fast, and Effective Reparameterization of IBM Model 2. In *Proceedings of the 2013 Conference of the North American Chapter of the Association for Computational Linguistics: Human Language Technologies*, pages 644–648. Association for Computational Linguistics.

Jan Vium Enghoff, Søren Harrison, and Željko Agić. 2018. Low-resource named entity recognition via multi-source projection: Not quite there yet? In *Proceedings of the 2018 EMNLP Workshop W-NUT: The 4th Workshop on Noisy User-generated Text*, pages 195–201, Brussels, Belgium. Association for Computational Linguistics.

Meng Fang and Trevor Cohn. 2016. Learning when to trust distant supervision: An application to low-resource POS tagging using cross-lingual projection. In *Proceedings of The 20th SIGNLL Conference on Computational Natural Language Learning*, pages 178–186, Berlin, Germany. Association for Computational Linguistics.

Georg Heigold, Josef van Genabith, and Günter Neumann. 2016. Scaling character-based morphological tagging to fourteen languages. In *Big Data (Big Data), 2016 IEEE International Conference on*, pages 3895–3902. IEEE.

Georg Heigold, Stalin Varanasi, Günter Neumann, and Josef Genabith. 2018. How Robust Are Character-Based Word Embeddings in Tagging and

MT Against Wrod Scramlbing or Randdm Nouse? In *Proceedings of the 13th Conference of the Association for Machine Translation in the Americas (Volume 1: Research Papers)*, pages 68–80. Association for Machine Translation in the Americas.

Sepp Hochreiter and Jürgen Schmidhuber. 1997. Long Short-Term Memory. *Neural Comput.*, 9(8):1735–1780.

Zhiheng Huang, Wei Xu, and Kai Yu. 2015. Bidirectional LSTM-CRF Models for Sequence Tagging. *CoRR*, abs/1508.01991.

Rebecca Hwa, Philip Resnik, Amy Weinberg, Clara Cabezas, and Okan Kolak. 2005. Bootstrapping parsers via syntactic projection across parallel texts. *Natural Language Engineering*, 11(3):311–325.

Joo-Kyung Kim, Young-Bum Kim, Ruhi Sarikaya, and Eric Fosler-Lussier. 2017. Cross-Lingual Transfer Learning for POS Tagging without Cross-Lingual Resources. In *Proceedings of the 2017 Conference on Empirical Methods in Natural Language Processing*, pages 2832–2838. Association for Computational Linguistics.

Seokhwan Kim, Minwoo Jeong, Jonghoon Lee, and Gary Geunbae Lee. 2011. A Cross-lingual Annotation Projection-based Self-supervision Approach for Open Information Extraction. In *Proceedings of 5th International Joint Conference on Natural Language Processing*, pages 741–748. Asian Federation of Natural Language Processing.

Matthieu Labeau, Kevin Löser, and Alexandre Allauzen. 2015. Non-lexical neural architecture for fine-grained POS Tagging. In *Proceedings of the 2015 Conference on Empirical Methods in Natural Language Processing*, pages 232–237. Association for Computational Linguistics.

Ophélie Lacroix, Lauriane Aufrant, Guillaume Wisniewski, and François Yvon. 2016. Frustratingly Easy Cross-Lingual Transfer for Transition-Based Dependency Parsing. In *Proceedings of the 2016 Conference of the North American Chapter of the Association for Computational Linguistics: Human Language Technologies*, pages 1058–1063, San Diego, California. Association for Computational Linguistics.

John Lafferty, Andrew McCallum, Fernando Pereira, et al. 2001. Conditional random fields: Probabilistic models for segmenting and labeling sequence data. In *Proceedings of the eighteenth international conference on machine learning, ICML*, volume 1, pages 282–289.

Dmitry V. Lande and V. V. Zhygalo. 2008. About the creation of a parallel bilingual corpora of web-publications. *CoRR*, abs/0807.0311.

Thomas Lavergne, Olivier Cappé, and François Yvon. 2010. Practical Very Large Scale CRFs. In *Proceedings of the 48th Annual Meeting of the Association for Computational Linguistics*, pages 504–513. Association for Computational Linguistics.

Xuezhe Ma and Eduard Hovy. 2016. End-to-end Sequence Labeling via Bi-directional LSTM-CNNs-CRF. In *Proceedings of the 54th Annual Meeting of the Association for Computational Linguistics (Volume 1: Long Papers)*, pages 1064–1074. Association for Computational Linguistics.

Marie-Catherine de Marneffe, Timothy Dozat, Natalia Silveira, Katri Haverinen, Filip Ginter, Joakim Nivre, and Christopher D. Manning. 2014. Universal Stanford dependencies: A cross-linguistic typology. In *Proceedings of the Ninth International Conference on Language Resources and Evaluation (LREC-2014)*. European Language Resources Association (ELRA).

Marie-Catherine de Marneffe, Bill MacCartney, and Christopher D. Manning. 2006. Generating Typed Dependency Parses from Phrase Structure Parses. In *Proceedings of the Fifth International Conference on Language Resources and Evaluation (LREC'06)*. European Language Resources Association (ELRA).

Marie-Catherine de Marneffe and Christopher D. Manning. 2008. The Stanford typed dependencies representation. In *Coling 2008: Proceedings of the Workshop on Cross-Framework and Cross-Domain Parser Evaluation*, CrossParser '08, pages 1–8, Stroudsburg, PA, USA. Association for Computational Linguistics.

David McClosky, Eugene Charniak, and Mark Johnson. 2006. Effective Self-Training for Parsing. In *Proceedings of the Human Language Technology Conference of the NAACL, Main Conference*.

Roland Meyer. 2011. New wine in old wineskins?—Tagging Old Russian via annotation projection from modern translations. *Russian Linguistics*, 35(2):267–281.

Robert Östling, Carl Börstell, and Lars Wallin. 2015. Enriching the Swedish Sign Language Corpus with Part of Speech Tags Using Joint Bayesian Word Alignment and Annotation Transfer. In *Proceedings of the 20th Nordic Conference of Computational Linguistics (NODALIDA 2015)*, pages 263–268. Linköping University Electronic Press, Sweden.

Sebastian Pado and Mirella Lapata. 2005. Cross-linguistic Projection of Role-Semantic Information. In *Proceedings of Human Language Technology Conference and Conference on Empirical Methods in Natural Language Processing*.

Sebastian Pado and Mirella Lapata. 2009. Cross-lingual Annotation Projection of Role-semantic Information. *Artificial Intelligence Research*, 36:307–340.

Slav Petrov, Dipanjan Das, and Ryan McDonald. 2012. A universal part-of-speech tagset. In *Proceedings of the Eight International Conference on Language Resources and Evaluation (LREC'12)*, Istanbul, Turkey. European Language Resources Association (ELRA).

Barbara Plank and Željko Agić. 2018. Distant Supervision from Disparate Sources for Low-Resource Part-of-Speech Tagging. In *Proceedings of the 2018 Conference on Empirical Methods in Natural Language Processing*, pages 614–620, Brussels, Belgium. Association for Computational Linguistics.

Barbara Plank, Anders Søgaard, and Yoav Goldberg. 2016. Multilingual Part-of-Speech Tagging with Bidirectional Long Short-Term Memory Models and Auxiliary Loss. In *Proceedings of the 54th Annual Meeting of the Association for Computational Linguistics*, pages 412–418, Berlin, Germany. Association for Computational Linguistics.

Lonneke van der Plas, Paola Merlo, and James Henderson. 2011. Scaling up Automatic Cross-Lingual Semantic Role Annotation. In *Proceedings of the 49th Annual Meeting of the Association for Computational Linguistics: Human Language Technologies*, pages 299–304. Association for Computational Linguistics.

Martin Porter. 1980. An algorithm for suffix stripping. *Program: electronic library and information systems*, 14(3):130–137.

Mohammad Sadegh Rasooli and Michael Collins. 2015. Density-Driven Cross-Lingual Transfer of Dependency Parsers. In *Proceedings of the 2015 Conference on Empirical Methods in Natural Language Processing*, pages 328–338, Lisbon, Portugal. Association for Computational Linguistics.

Adwait Ratnaparkhi. 1996. A Maximum Entropy Model for Part-Of-Speech Tagging. In *Conference on Empirical Methods in Natural Language Processing*.

Martin Riedmiller and Heinrich Braun. 1993. A direct adaptive method for faster backpropagation learning: the RPROP algorithm. In *IEEE International Conference on Neural Networks*, pages 586–591 vol.1.

Cicero dos Santos and Bianca Zadrozny. 2014. Learning Character-level Representations for Part-of-Speech Tagging. In *Proc. of ICML*, pages 1818–1826, Bejing, China.

Maria Sukhareva, Francesco Fuscagni, Johannes Daxenberger, Susanne Görke, Doris Prechel, and Iryna Gurevych. 2017. Distantly Supervised POS Tagging of Low-Resource Languages under Extreme Data Sparsity: The Case of Hittite. In *Proceedings of the Joint SIGHUM Workshop on Computational Linguistics for Cultural Heritage, Social Sciences, Humanities and Literature*, pages 95–104. Association for Computational Linguistics.

Jörg Tiedemann. 2014. Rediscovering Annotation Projection for Cross-Lingual Parser Induction. In *Proceedings of COLING 2014, the 25th International Conference on Computational Linguistics: Technical Papers*, pages 1854–1864, Dublin, Ireland. Dublin City University and Association for Computational Linguistics.

Peilu Wang, Yao Qian, Frank K. Soong, Lei He, and Hai Zhao. 2015. Part-of-speech tagging with bidirectional long short-term memory recurrent neural network. *CoRR*, abs/1510.06168.

David Luis Wiegandt, Leon Weber, Ulf Leser, Maryam Habibi, and Mariana Neves. 2017. Deep learning with word embeddings improves biomedical named entity recognition. *Bioinformatics*, 33(14):i37–i48.

Guillaume Wisniewski, Nicolas Pécheux, Souhir Gahbiche-Braham, and François Yvon. 2014. Cross-Lingual Part-of-Speech Tagging through Ambiguous Learning. In *Proceedings of the 2014 Conference on Empirical Methods in Natural Language Processing (EMNLP)*, pages 1779–1785. Association for Computational Linguistics.

Chenhai Xi and Rebecca Hwa. 2005. A Backoff Model for Bootstrapping Resources for Non-English Languages. In *Proceedings of Human Language Technology Conference and Conference on Empirical Methods in Natural Language Processing*.

David Yarowsky and Grace Ngai. 2001. Inducing Multilingual POS Taggers and NP Bracketers via Robust Projection Across Aligned Corpora. In *Second Meeting of the North American Chapter of the Association for Computational Linguistics*.

David Yarowsky, Grace Ngai, and Richard Wicentowski. 2001. Inducing Multilingual Text Analysis Tools via Robust Projection across Aligned Corpora. In *Proceedings of the First International Conference on Human Language Technology Research*.

Michihiro Yasunaga, Jungo Kasai, and Dragomir Radev. 2018. Robust Multilingual Part-of-Speech Tagging via Adversarial Training. In *Proceedings of the 2018 Conference of the North American Chapter of the Association for Computational Linguistics: Human Language Technologies, Volume 1 (Long Papers)*, pages 976–986. Association for Computational Linguistics.

George Kingsley Zipf. 1932. *Selected Studies of the Principle of Relative Frequency in Language*. Harvard University Press.

Author Index